THE SORCERY OF COLOR

ELISA LARKIN NASCIMENTO

THE SORCERY

OF COLOR

*Identity, Race, and
Gender in Brazil*

TEMPLE UNIVERSITY PRESS
Philadelphia

TEMPLE UNIVERSITY PRESS
1601 North Broad Street
Philadelphia PA 19122
www.temple.edu/tempress

Originally published in Portuguese by Selo Negro as *O Sortilégio da Cor: Identidade , Raça e Gênero no Brasil*
Copyright © 2003 by Elisa Larkin Nascimento

Title page illustration:
Abdias Nascimento, *Opachorô de Oxalá*. Nankin ink on paper, 15 x 20 cm. Buffalo, 1979.

♾ The paper used in this publication meets the requirements of the American National Standard for Information Sciences—Permanence of Paper for Printed Library Materials, ANSI Z39.48-1992

Library of Congress Cataloging-in-Publication Data

Nascimento, Elisa Larkin.
[O sortilegio da cor. English]
The sorcery of color : identity, race, and gender in Brazil / Elisa Larkin Nascimento.
    p. cm.
Includes bibliographical references and index.
    ISBN 10: 1–59213–350–9 (cloth : alk. paper)
    ISBN 13: 978–1–59213–350–5 (cloth : alk. paper)
    1. Blacks—Brazil—Social conditions. 2. Blacks—Brazil—Politics and government. 3. Racism—Brazil. 4. Sexism—Brazil. 5. Brazil—Race relations. I. Title.
F2659.N4N38513 2006
305.800981—dc22

121207P

I dedicate this book to my parents

Margaret Joseph Larkin
Daniel Irving Larkin (in memoriam)
Joanne Kryder Larkin (in memoriam)

And to my son
Osiris Kwesi

Graciliano Ramos ... formulated a basic postulate of contemporary philosophy according to which, when we voluntarily identify with what conditions us, we turn narrowness into depth.

—GUERREIRO RAMOS[1]

CONTENTS

ACKNOWLEDGMENTS

MANY PEOPLE supported and encouraged the making of this book. In the first place, I thank Ronilda Ribeiro, my PhD advisor at the University of São Paulo Institute of Psychology, and José Flávio Pessoa de Barros, founder of the African and Afro-American Studies Program at Rio de Janeiro State University, as well as Professors Anani Dzidzienyo of Brown University, J. Michael Turner of Hunter College, CUNY, Angela Gilliam, Carlos Moore, Edith Piza, Miriam Expedita Caetano, and Vilma do Couto e Silva.

Special thanks to Cláudia Moraes Rego for the rich dialogue that contributed enormously to the making of this text; to Carlos Alberto Medeiros for revising part of the Portuguese original; and to Osiris Kwesi Larkin Nascimento for support with editing and orthography. Thanks to Carlos Henrique Bemfica for his assistance with bibliographical data.

Thanks also to Vanda Maria de Souza Ferreira, Dulce Vasconcellos, Dandara, Conceição Evaristo, Jurema Agostinho Nunes, Néia Daniel de Alcântara, Carmen Luz, Cida Bento, Maria Lúcia da Silva, and Marilza de Souza Martins for their time and the interviews they generously gave me.

For their competence and spirit of collaboration, I am grateful to Helena Rodrigues de Souza and Rosinê Cruz.

To Sebastião Lúcio da Silva (in memoriam), my thanks for his eternal good nature and infallible willingness to help.

A special tribute to Afonnso Drumond, an extraordinary human being and man of culture, for the talent and axé his partnership has brought to IPEAFRO's projects and destiny.

Dreams and disappointments, joys and frustrations woven in the time I have shared with Abdias led, directly or indirectly, to the making of this book. The responsibility for its content, of course, is solely mine.

FOREWORD BY
KABENGELE MUNANGA

ELISA LARKIN NASCIMENTO'S most recent work delves deeply into past, present, and future concerns that have, do, and will continue to torment the life of Brazilian descendants of Africans. I believe these concerns converge in the process of building identity. It is a multifaceted identity which—from the point of view of populations that have been made subservient, as in the case of black men and women—constrains the exercise of their freedom and denies them full citizenship as well as generic and specific human rights.

As an object of ideological manipulation in the discourse of the elite in power, as well as in prevailing academic notions forged by intellectuals at the service of the ruling class, identity constitutes a tool of political domination and cultural subjection. The idea of "national identity" is used in Brazil to deny recognition of specificity to the Afro-Brazilian population, for example. In this way it becomes an obstacle to the implementation of compensatory policies benefiting those who have been the targets of racism and racial discrimination over centuries.

In the thought and rhetoric of the Brazilian elite, national identity is said to be forged out of racial and cultural unity based on miscegenation and cultural mixture. These last two have been translated into language about the Brazilian "race of mestizos" and "mestizo culture and identity."

This discourse is most certainly the vehicle of a "whitening" ideology that preaches annihilation of the building blocks of black identity. The question then becomes: what could be a national "mestizo" identity in a country where whiteness is the basic reference for everything? Elisa Larkin Nascimento's reflections bring out the very interesting concept of virtual whiteness, which conveys the rejection of blackness concomitant with the preference for whiteness that results from a mainstream discourse that is centered on the concept of national identity.

The author considers and refutes certain leftist critiques of black antiracist social movements. Afrocentricity, as understood by African American scholar Molefi K. Asante, serves as a basis of resistance against Western ethnocentrism and the hegemony of whiteness. But it does not oppose cultural dynamics and intercultural exchange, as hasty critics have alleged without referencing the texts. Using categories of identity proposed by sociologist Manuel Castells, the author sees Asante's Afrocentricity as the starting point for a black identity of resistance that can serve as a mobilizing platform for building a political project identity while seeking profound transformation of society. Or, as Professor Milton Santos has said, to be a citizen of the world it is necessary, first, to be a citizen of the place from which one speaks. In other words, intercultural dialogue is only possible when the subjects' original identity and historical-cultural community have been accepted by the participants in that dialogue. As with Afrocentricity, the author critically analyzes early and mid-twentieth century Brazilian black social movements, including the Brazilian Black Front and the Black Experimental Theater (TEN). She looks at contemporary black movements and their contributions to current perspectives on gender relations. She seeks to restore to these movements their true historical contribution in the fight against racial oppression, independent of the ideological position they assumed throughout Brazil's political history. For example, though a few of the members of these movements have defended monarchy due to political circumstance, this does not negate the merits of their work in denouncing Brazilian racism, unmasking the myth of racial democracy, and organizing a movement for the integration and effective political participation of the black population. Through detailed research, the author restores TEN's true contribution to black identity and the fight against racism. She critiques leftist intellectual positions that classified TEN as "petit bourgeois." For decades, such allegations effectively held back the debate on affirmative action policies by diluting black specificity into an abstract, general social issue devoid of race, sex, religion, and history. The proponents of this dilution moved against the current of building specific identities, an ideal that constitutes the cornerstone of any democratic society.

Thus, Nascimento's position is close to those of Canadian philosopher Charles Taylor and African-Caribbean psychiatrist and philosopher Frantz Fanon. Taylor and Fanon both asserted the need not only to articulate new, positive images of those victimized by domination, but also to publicly recognize their identities as a preliminary condition to the implementation of affirmative action policies.

This book's critical eye does not spare those who seek to deny the similarities and cultural affinities among sub-Saharan African peoples and see so-called black Africa as a mosaic of culturally diverse peoples who have nothing in common except the abundance of melanin and Negroid features. In her assertion that unity is contained in diversity and vice versa, the author reminds us of the renowned African thinkers and Senegalese writers, Cheikh Anta Diop and Alioune Diop (founder of the journal *Présence Africaine*), who—along with others including the German researchers Leo Frobenius and Diedrich Westermann, and the French scholars, J. Jacques Maquet and Denise Paulme—coined the concept of "Africanity" and asserted the existence of an African civilization in the singular. Nor does Nascimento's incisive analysis spare certain reformulations by young Brazilian intellectuals who mechanically have separated the concepts of racialism and racism, as if they were distinct ideologies, identifying a brand of racialism in Negritude. Through a dense thought process, Nascimento first explores the complexity of concepts involving the theme of black identity before moving on to consider the most current perspectives of black struggle in Brazilian society. Her work is instigating and opens new horizons in intellectual debate on the Brazilian black population's dilemmas and future.

Kabengele Munanga
Full Professor, Department of Anthropology
Vice-Director of the Center of African Studies
Vice-Director of the Contemporary Art Museum
University of São Paulo (USP)

INTRODUCTION

H UMAN EXPERIENCE carries with it the challenge of understanding life as we are living it. Changes and social dynamics displace set ideas, underlying aspects of phenomena become evident and modify concepts about those phenomena; widely known facts are obscured only to reemerge with new implications. Reality as we know it can be reconfigured by the intervention of factors that were in existence before but went unperceived or were hidden from view.

This process has a political dimension: the possibility of manipulating knowledge to change reality. The dynamics of seeking, constructing, and suppressing information and the intervention of those who propose to use this reconfiguration to operate changes are the ethical grounds on which human knowledge is developed. Like everything human, there is a dimension of power to this dynamic, which generates tension between those who control knowledge and those who seek it in order to intervene and transform themselves and the world around them.

The building of knowledge in Western civilization was largely the search for power over nature and over other human beings who were considered part of nature and therefore to be submitted to the control of knowledge. Western science was developed at a time when peoples formerly unknown to Europeans were "discovered," and scientific method was put to the task of helping Europeans dominate those peoples. The conquest and occupation of new lands by the "natural" right of those who considered themselves superior to the natives led to the genocide, subjugation, and enslavement of these "others" in order to build the modern world. Within this process, scientific theories were fabricated to justify genocide and subjugation. These theories would later contribute to the rationalization of further genocide against a minority of Western people targeted by discrimination. It was not until this point that the West perceived the barbarity of justifying genocide and science made a turnaround to deny its earlier justifications. However, the effects of centuries of domination could hardly be erased by a new manifesto of scientific rhetoric. Peoples who had formerly been the objects of scientific method began to unveil their own realities, which had been kept obscured. In this way, formerly oppressed peoples not only came to intervene in the constitution of knowledge but also challenged its very foundation.

In the Western world itself, scientific method was concerned with "progress" defined in relation to the production of material goods, and soon proved limited in elucidating the human existential dilemma. Also, the traditional goal of neutral and objective observation refused to materialize, even in the exact sciences, in which it has been recognized that the researcher's intervention and outlook can influence outcomes. As scientific method came under question, the challenge arose to look for alternative ways to understand reality.

A researcher joining this march of knowledge can contribute to the dynamics of culture and social environment, a fact that raises ethical and political questions about the researcher's place and procedure. Research can only begin with living experience, which makes it important to say a few words about my own life and the paths that brought me to the present work.

This book emerged from my participation in a larger search for ways to contribute to the articulation of public policies that can adequately deal with the operation of Brazilian racism in the education system. In 1981, when Abdias Nascimento and I created the Afro-Brazilian Studies and Research Institute (IPEAFRO), this reality was being discussed by the Afro-Brazilian social movement, which would grow and make its demands echo ever stronger. These demands were etched into the legislative process that created the 1988 Constitution, and have been present in the articulation of recent education policy. Yet now, as in 1981, the black movement in Brazil is still working to unveil a reality of racial inequality that has been hidden for generations by those dedicated to maintaining a rosy image of race relations in Brazilian society. I maintain that the construction of this image of "racial democracy" was made possible by what I will call the sorcery of color, a founding and defining characteristic of race relations in this country.

This research project had its beginnings in a much earlier engagement in the study and experience of efforts to build a pluralist democratic society. As a high school exchange student, I had lived in Brazil and was fascinated by issues of cultural plurality, which the country revealed to me. Later I worked in the United States antiwar, civil rights, antiapartheid, and women's movements, as well as the Attica Brothers' Legal Defense and a Neighborhood Legal Services office in Buffalo's Latino community. At the time, the almost obsessive fascination of many leftist intellectuals with classic European authors contrasted starkly against personal experiences that highlighted gender, ethnic, and race relations as crucial political issues and against the specific experiences of what was then called the Third World. It seemed clear to me that these issues, which profoundly affected people's lives, were derived as much from the colonialist legacy of racism as from class relations in capitalist society. Yet that legacy was obscured by the conventional wisdom of class analysis.

At a time when these were pressing matters in my life, I met Afro-Brazilian artist, activist, and intellectual Abdias Nascimento. It was as if a set of theoretical considerations had jumped off a history page and come to life. My experience in Brazil had left me with the unforgettable image of a pluralistic society marked by severe inequalities; this man's biography was a living portrait of Afro-Brazilian resistance against those inequalities. At the same time that I worked with him to take that message of resistance to world audiences, I also pursued my own research on Pan-Africanism. As we were in the midst of sealing a partnership for life, I also had the opportunity of participating in some important watersheds of the Pan-African movement with Abdias. These moments included the first meetings of the African Writers' Union, the Second World Festival of Black and African Arts and Culture (Lagos, 1977) and the First Congress of Black Culture in the Americas, as well as the creation of the Zumbi Memorial and the Unified Black Movement (MNU) in Brazil in 1978.

Later, Abdias and I moved to Brazil and began to engage in the rebuilding of the state of law as the 1964 military regime was giving way to a gradual political liberalization. With the support of São Paulo's Archbishop Dom Paulo Evaristo Arns, we created the Afro-Brazilian Studies and Research Institute (IPEAFRO), which was initially housed at the Pontifical Catholic University of São Paulo. The first congressional elections were held in 1982, the same year that IPEAFRO organized the Third Congress of Black Culture in the Americas. In 1983, Abdias Nascimento took office as the first Afro-Brazilian congressman whose political platform was built on the issues of antidiscrimination and public policies to build racial equality. I had the opportunity to take part in the drafting of his bills of law, including the first affirmative action proposal (P.L. 1.331/1983) and a major antidiscrimination measure (P.L. 1.661/1983), as well as the drafting of constitutional provisions dealing with policies for building racial equality.

One of our major goals with IPEAFRO was to contribute to the inclusion of African world culture and history in Brazilian education and to help prepare teachers to deal not only with curriculum content but also with the dynamics of race relations in the classroom. To this end, we organized seminars and events as well as teacher training courses—including one entitled *Sankofa*, held at the State University of Rio de Janeiro from 1985 to 1995— and published several books.[1] These actions involve issues of identity, since they have to do with social dynamics built on an image of African descendants created by racist ideology, which has been reflected in educational institutions and curricula.

As the Afro-Brazilian social movement grew in activity and political weight, the proposal to modify school curricula gradually gained acceptance. This goal was inscribed in the principle of cultural plurality that had been expressed in the 1988 Constitution and in the passing of myriad municipal and state legislative measures mandating the incorporation of Afro-Brazilian history and culture in school curricula. These developments later culminated in the passage of federal law 10.639/2003, which made the same provision for the country as a whole. But there was a large gap between legislative recognition of the need for change and daily practice in the schools. This fact led IPEAFRO to organize events for teachers and policy makers, and to offer teacher training on African and African Diaspora history and culture. For these activities, we adopted the name *Sankofa* from the West African *Adinkra* system of ideographic writing and proverbial wisdom, which denotes the need to know the past in order to build the present and the future. At the same time, a significant grassroots community movement, the College Entrance Preparation Courses for Blacks and the Poor, was raising the issue of Afro-Brazilian access to university education. Fewer than one percent of university students in Brazil are black, though the general population is officially 45 percent black. The grassroots community-based College Entrance Preparation courses offered free preparation for the *vestibular*, standardized college entrance exams that were the only criterion of admission to university. Certain universities offered scholarships to students admitted from these courses. This development highlighted the need to provide theoretical and informational bases for a new approach to education, one that could accommodate this new student population, which was interested in elucidating its own history, culture, and experience. In this context and in this spirit I embarked on the present research project with the objective of contributing to this end.

While my life partnership with Abdias Nascimento cannot help but have an impact on my understanding of certain issues, it is also true that I already possessed a basic outlook, which I brought into the relationship. I do not believe it has been significantly altered, but certainly its development has been enriched by the opportunity to share the experiences, observations, and reflections of a longtime veteran of the Afro-Brazilian movement. In any case, neutral objectivity remains an illusionary goal for the researcher in the social sciences. I believe that the information and observations recorded here can be useful and elucidating—indeed, particularly those aspects gleaned partly from access to my husband's life work and archives. For example, existing literature in English and in Portuguese does not include much beyond a passing mention of the Black Experimental Theater and its offshoots and legacy. Often the only references are facile dismissals of the organization as elitist, self-contradictory, and tinged with reverse racism. In my view, the issues involved both in this characterization and in a more detailed consideration of the organization's trajectory are essential to the understanding of Brazilian race relations and the African Diaspora experience.

Initially, two obstacles to the discussion of these issues must be overcome. In Brazil, any mention of racism unfailingly elicits a warning against the danger of what is considered to be even more pernicious: the possibility of reverse racism by the target population against the mainstream one—blacks' racism against whites. This specter is raised particularly with respect to Afro-Brazilian organizations. Such a dynamic in the debate generally halts communication before it can begin. It is part of what singularly characterizes racism in Brazil: silence and ideological repression. As it is commonly understood, a racist is someone who speaks of racism or mentions that someone else is black; silence is considered the nonracist attitude. A pillar of domination, silence is one of racism's most effective devices in Brazil.

Complementing silence, the process of making African descendants invisible as actors and creators in national history and culture is another form and symptom of racism. This tendency permeates Brazilian life, and is reinforced by the appropriation of Afro-Brazilian culture and history as part of a "Brazilian" identity defined apart from, and exclusive of, the African matrix. The absence of African descendants from school curricula and textbooks is a result of this process, which is another characteristic of the sorcery of color. By recording some aspects of this suppressed history, I hope to contribute to the efforts to overcome this constructed invisibility of African descendants.

The second obstacle to the discussion of race in Brazil is resistance to the idea that African populations in different parts of the world share a common experience. The presumption is that blacks in Brazil are in a unique situation determined solely by the circumstances of their society and have little or nothing in common with black populations in other parts of the world. Critics have frequently accused the black social movement in Brazil of attempting to import foreign standards and raising a problem that has never existed before. On the other hand, the concerns of the black movement often revolve around issues specific to Brazil rather than racism as a world phenomenon.

But racist domination is worldwide in scope. It derives from the historical imposition of Western hegemony over non-Western peoples and its essence is expressed in the ideology of white supremacy. The standard of whiteness affects the identity constructs of all dominated peoples, making the issue of identity crucial, but oftentimes, it is expressed in specific local terms. In Brazil, the sorcery of color transforms mixed-race identity into a permanent search for the simulation of whiteness.

Thus, I set out to seek a theoretical foundation to deal with racism and identity in the global context and shed new light on what has been considered, I believe erroneously, a series of characteristics unique to Brazil. While the sorcery of color creates situations and produces effects peculiar to Brazil, it is grounded in the global phenomena of white supremacy and Western hegemony, which in turn share a broad common ground with patriarchy and gender oppression. I suggest that these two areas of social change have recently become inseparable. Therefore, the present work seeks to approach race and gender simultaneously, with a theoretical grounding articulated in terms of resisting and breaking down barriers, which will eventually lead to the building of new identities. Some choices I made regarding terminology should be clarified from the start. I use the word "American" in the broad continental sense, including North, South, and Central America and the Caribbean. Thus, the term "African American" refers not only to blacks in the United States but to those in all the Americas. I also use the terms "indigenous," "First Nation," or "Native American" in the same sense, and I adopt the practice of the Afro-Brazilian social movement by using the term, "African descendant," and its counterpart, "African Brazilian," to emphasize the historical and cultural references to African origin. I use the phrase, "African descendant," because it retains the reference to identity links among Africans wherever they are in the world. I use the term "Diaspora" in the sense of geographic dispersion of a people who, while spread over the world in new social and historical conditions, maintain their reference to origin and identity. In the case of African peoples, this does not refer only to the process of enslavement but also to previous moments in which dispersion took place in a context of freedom and sovereignty.

This book conceives ideology as an ordered system of ideas, norms, rules, and representations that operate socially and are perceived, or often remain unperceived, as if they have existed by or for themselves, separately and independently of social, material, and historical conditions. The essence of ideology is that it obscures the process of forming these ideas, representations, norms, and rules in the context of power relations. Ideology's function is to prevent those who are being dominated from perceiving the mechanism of domination.

In this book, I hope to unveil facts and considerations that have been kept hidden and reveal new ones that have been emerging from recent efforts to transform power relations in Brazil. This effort is worthwhile not only for the intrinsic value of such facts and considerations, but also for their utility in effecting social change. I hope to contribute to the effective implementation of recent federal legislation mandating inclusion of African and Afro-Brazilian culture and history in school curricula. In this way, I hope to participate in the creation of new spaces and possibilities for the effective exercise of African Brazilians' human and civil rights.

Very few works in Portuguese, and none in English to date, have examined the meaning, import, and history of psychology in regard to the ideology of race and its social impact in Brazil. In Chapter 3 of this work I seek to do this and also to treat the implications of the consideration of race in the practice of psychology by looking at evidence of a new way of therapeutic listening, which I call an "Afro-Brazilian ear."

At the end of the text I have included a bibliographical note on English-language sources on issues discussed in this book. A few of these works in English make brief reference to the Black Experimental Theater (TEN), an important civil and cultural rights movement in Rio de Janeiro between 1944 and 1968. None of them, however, involve an in-depth study of that organization and its critics, which is a task I take on in *The Sorcery of Color*. I also look at the Afro-Brazilian activism of São Paulo in the first part of the twentieth century from a perspective that emphasizes continuity and coherence with the demands and ideas of later movements. In the process, I engage in some critical reflection on certain analyses that have been proposed heretofore. I examine the Afro-Brazilian relationship to the Negritude movement and the significance of that movement in historical perspective. To this end, I look closely at TEN—its actors, activities, texts, and intentions—and I place it in the context of African world theater and dramatic literature. In this process, I articulate some critical observations on existing work around this theme.

The research for this book was greatly facilitated by my access to the records and archives of TEN, which have been collected by its creator, Abdias Nascimento. They are now in the custody of the Afro-Brazilian Studies and Research Institute (IPEAFRO), which we founded in 1981. IPEAFRO is currently organizing these papers for preservation, a project that began in 2003 with an initial grant from the Ford Foundation. IPEAFRO is working with Brazil's National Library, the Library of Congress Rio de Janeiro Office, the Center for Research Libraries, and the Catholic University of Rio de Janeiro (PUC-Rio), to convert these materials to microfilm and ultimately to digitize them for online consultation.

Clearly, the story I tell in this book is documented by these papers and has been shaped by the testimony of the protagonists of the events they record. I believe that the facts and viewpoints of this history, along with other information and considerations brought to this work, will help English-speaking readers to understand the Brazilian panorama of race relations with its sorcery of color and its penchant for virtual whiteness.

1

IDENTITY, RACE, AND GENDER

I N THE CONTEMPORARY WORLD of globalization, a unitary market culture is accompanied by severe economic inequalities. Transmitted by information technology and the mass communications media, this one-dimensional culture wields enormous power. But the assertion of specific identities by groups within larger societies or cultures has staked out areas of resistance to globalization. These days, more and more emphasis is placed on identity as a category of analysis in the social sciences. The reasons for this trend are not hard to identify.

The twentieth century saw three phenomena that deeply changed the world social and political order: Colonized peoples challenged Western hegemony, winning independence at considerable cost. Feminists challenged patriarchy and environmentalists confronted the thoughtless exploitation of natural resources. The civil rights and Black Power movements shook the United States. At the same time, Native American, Hispanic, and Caribbean people were also seeking to build freedom under the rule of law. Immigrants from former colonies settled in what had been the European seats of colonial power, seeking to exercise rights of "citizenship" inherited from the colonial system. The disintegration of the Soviet Union and the collapse of Eastern European states brought latent ethnic, cultural, and nationalist conflicts to the fore, unleashing a fratricidal scenario of war and violence. In sum, the coexistence of diverse communities within pluralistic societies has raised urgent issues. The issues have been intensified by the complexities of U.S. hegemony in relation to Israel, Palestine, and the Islamic world, which has become more frightening since September 2001. These events and trends highlight the importance of identity in today's world.

This chapter begins by considering identity as the result of the individual's relationship to society and goes on to look at race and gender within the dynamics of domination. I contend that these issues cannot be understood adequately without reference to the social movements that initiate and direct the reshaping of the world order. These movements also shape and support the evolution of theory and social analysis.

INDIVIDUALS AND SOCIETY

Identity can be seen as a kind of existential crossroads between a person and society, a space in which both are mutually constituted. Identity formation is a process by which individuals articulate the set of references that guide their ways of acting and mediating their relationships with others, the world, and themselves. Identity is not only shaped by an individual's life experience but also by the representations of his or her community and by society's collective experience, both of which are absorbed in a person's interaction with others. Collective identity can be understood either as the set of references that guide the interactions of a society's members or as the set of references that differentiate a particular group from "others," or those that compose the rest of society. Hence, identity involves multiple dimensions, forms, and levels of operation. It is a complex process that occurs both at the core of an individual and in the central nucleus of his or her culture—"a process that establishes, in fact, the identity of these two identities."[1]

Brazilian philosopher Muniz Sodré revisits the main authors who explain the philosophical approach to identity. He begins with the etymological origin of the Latin term, *idem,* meaning "the same," which is the source of *identitas,* meaning "that which stays unique or identical to itself when faced with the pressures of internal and external change." In this sense, personal identity is the continuity of an individual's personality characteristics over time, rooted in memory and habit. It is also rooted in expressions of community, such as traditions, language, and faith. Identity formation is not a static system, but undergoes changes and variations in its relationship with society, in a manner something like the bed of a river that changes slowly and imperceptibly.[2]

In the past, societies were located geographically and their traditions supported and gave structure to individual and collective identity. The stability of representations grounded in tradition mediated language and culture, placing identity in the realm of the conscious. Two phenomena of the twentieth century drastically changed this scenario. The Freudian concept of the unconscious defied the idea of the autonomous individual guided by conscience and identity. Psychoanalytic theory suggests that the unity of self is always incomplete, and therefore there is no continued identity, but rather a flux of *identifications*. Heidegger introduced an element of volition into the concept of identity when he stated that people forge their relationships with being, social milieu, tradition, and community "in the free choice of common belonging."[3]

But population growth and the fluidity of migratory movements subverted stability. Other changes further undermined the geographical base of society: wars, famine, and the adverse conditions of increasing socioeconomic inequality, recently exacerbated by globalization, uprooted individuals and families, scattering them. Ever-increasing productivity, technical efficiency, and the development of transportation and telecommunications accelerated the passage of time. The substitution of identity as stability and permanence with the idea of a shifting process of identifications fit perfectly into the new contours of the postmodern world.

But the story does not end there. The portrait of the evolution of identity theory outlined here does not sufficiently consider the context of social action in which it was forged. Theory reflects, and is made from, concrete reality, without which it lacks meaning. I contend that the actions of feminist and anticolonialist social movements, and those of dominated groups in plural societies, have been of basic import to the evolution of the theory of identity, although their influence tends to go unrecognized.

The critique of patriarchy and Western ethnocentrism that came out of feminist and anticolonialist movements gives the issue of volition in identity building a new perspective. These movements questioned the white, middleclass identity standard that was endorsed and cultivated by Western society and was supposedly universal. In the wake of this questioning, psychoanalyst Erik H. Erikson developed his thoughts about identity in social context.[4] What distinguishes his approach is the emphasis Erikson places on *crisis*. Crisis is a moment of social transition marked by conflicts, uncertainties, and a sense of urgency. Society or culture, in Erickson's view, is not a fixed structure to which the individual must adapt. A process that generates new values resides within the dynamics of social flux. There is an intimate connection between this historical and cultural flux and the development of the personalities of individuals whose actions, in turn, may lead to cultural and social changes.

The innovative core of Erikson's thought is that he delved into issues brought to him not only by middle-class youth in personal crises but also by the global social cataclysm that led such youth to question dominant values. That global social cataclysm mainly involved decolonization, which was linked to the rebellion of minorities and dominated majorities in capitalist societies, most notably African Americans in the United States and black South Africans under apartheid. While often couched in the language of class struggle, the issues Erikson heard from youth in crisis refused to fit into that parameter and mobilized new dimensions of social action and change involving the issue of identity.

Erikson comes close to the idea of identifications in the plural when he notes that identity is never established or static. It is woven from the many threads of an ever-changing social fabric. Personal development cannot be separated from community change. Identity crises in individual life and in society are mutually dependent. The idea of identifications in the plural emphasizes the importance of social movements and recognizes their protagonists as actors on the stage of individual and collective human development.

In Brazilian psychology, there is a convergence of thought in the same direction. Antonio Ciampa states that identity "is the search for meaning, the invention of direction. It is self-production. It is life."[5] For him, identity is at the center of the dynamics involving culture, social environment, and individual subjectivity. It is a process of transition and metamorphosis, which both "represents and engenders the person."[6] Ricardo Franklin Ferreira, taking a constructivist approach, proposes identity to be a system of constructs in continuous flux, a "dialectics without synthesis" in the process of living.[7] He calls this system the *dynamics of identification*. Through this process, "the individual builds references and creates himself and his world with a *sense of authorship*."[8]

This notion of a sense of authorship seems more expressive than Erikson's "active role of choice initiative."[9] It also is forged with reference to social action. Ferreira studies identity building among social activists, emphasizing the interrelationship between the development of social actors' individual identities and the society they aim to change as "a continuous and dynamic process of mutual construction."[10] The sense of authorship takes on larger dimensions as a phenomenon of collective identity in national, regional, or global culture and civilization.

The issue of identity became more visible and, indeed, was raised to the status of paradigm in Latin American social psychology.[11] The Latin American approach was characterized by its emphasis on this aspect of social action for change, which is also expressed in the paradigms of *construction and critical transformation.* Identity thus became the "central axis of para-digms."[12] The reference to a critical position as a central core of any paradigm leads us back to the notion of *crisis.* While criticism induces the articulation of paradigms, it is *crisis* — criticism made tangible by social agents and move-ments and their impact — that creates the impulse for change in society and cultural environments.

IDENTITY IN THE GLOBALIZED WORLD

At the beginning of 1971, Yale University was going through a moment of cri-sis. It was rocked by the student movements against the Vietnam War, apartheid in South Africa, and especially the university's investments in what was referred to as the military-industrial complex, the economic interests of which spurred and sustained the first two issues. Yale was shaken by the trial of Black Panthers Bobby Seale and Ericka Huggins. This situation reflected the general climate on university campuses across the nation, but the Panthers' trial on the East Coast highlighted the national impact of this move-ment coming out of Oakland, California. It also underscored the political per-secution of social movements, particularly those of African Americans and Native Americans, in a country that prized its image as a confirmed democ-racy. The political persecution of social movements was embodied in Huey P. Newton, the Panthers' commander, who was arrested and accused of killing a policeman.

The aggressive, armed image of Huey P. Newton and the Panthers was an emblem of that moment of crisis. The Panthers pointed out the hypocrisy of a democracy that applied the constitutional right to bear arms in a highly selective way. The exercise of that right by black citizens was as intolerable as its exercise by whites was unquestionable, even if in the latter case, the spe-cific goal of using that right was frequently to terrorize the black community. The image of the Black Panthers also symbolized the need to push the limits of the gains made in the Civil Rights era, assert the African American's iden-tity as a right of citizenship, and challenge the society that repressed it.

Following the trial of Seale and Huggins, a public encounter between Newton and Erickson was held in New Haven, during which they discussed their theoretical perspectives in a dialogue as rich as it was revealing.[13] The expected confrontation between two generations gave way to an exchange of ideas in which Newton put forward his concept of "intercommunalism," and Erikson discussed his ideas about identity and "pseudospecies." Another series of meetings were held in Newton's apartment in Oakland. Even today, the transcripts of this dialogue are impressive in that the analyses and issues raised remain remarkably timely.

For example, Newton seems to foresee the emergence of neoliberalism, neoconservatism, and globalization when he asserts that the categories of colonialism and neocolonialism are outdated. He suggests that decolonization and nationalism mean little if the extraction of natural resources and the exploitation of labor occur in an integrated market in which a small and ever more concentrated elite dominates the world via the manipulation of technology and the revolution in communications media. According to Newton, the world had become "a diffuse collection of communities," and the goal for the future was to establish revolutionary intercommunalism, a kind of global socialism in which power and wealth would be distributed in an egalitarian way at the intercommunal level and communities would exercise decision-making power over their own institutions and development.[14]

Erikson speaks of the role of identity as a definitive social factor in the constitution of this integrated world, in which identity has to do with "tremendous struggles for power" to the extent that it becomes "a question of life and death." As the technological elite attempts to impose its pseudospecies identity, the awakening of consciousness and the communal resistance of peoples historically excluded from this standard of identity—those who have "preserved certain qualities that [economic] success could not preserve"—will configure a decisive social phenomenon in the formation of a new world.[15]

By struggling with such themes, this unlikely pair—Erickson the senior psychoanalyst and Newton the radical black activist—highlights the search for balance between the liberation, reconstitution, and assertion of specific identities on the one hand and, on the other, the creation of a broad and inclusive "humanist" identity. These approaches were posed as possible ways of preparing for the world of the future. The proposal and language of multiculturalism had not yet come on the scene, and without it both Erikson and Newton articulated their visions in terms of an ideal universality. The possibility of making real such a humanist ideal as they envisioned remained simply a matter of hope or a profession of faith in human beings.

Thirty years later, sociological analyses of the new contours of the globalized world have confirmed the emphasis that Erikson and Newton placed on identity and community. Identity has become a basic category of social analysis as well as a paradigm in psychology. An example is the work of Spanish sociologist Manuel Castells, who suggests that modernity and postmodernity have given way to what he calls *network society*, a result of the information technology revolution and the restructuring of capitalism. It is a society of global fluxes of wealth, power, and images in which "the search for identity, collective and individual, attributed or constructed, becomes the basic source of social significance."[16] Castells offers a typology of identities. The *legitimizing identity*, defined by mainstream institutions, expands and justifies their dominion. *Resistance identity* is created by actors belonging to undervalued or stigmatized groups with value references different from prevailing ones, who often build communities of resistance. *Project identity* comes into play when actors seeking to change the social structure create new identities that transform society. A political dimension is expressed in the self-construction of identity when subjects are mobilized to operate social changes. "To claim an identity is to build power," asserts Castells.[17]

In the network society, the power of domination is diffused not only in global networks of wealth and finance capital but also in constantly changing information and images that circulate in a dematerialized geographical system. The information codes and representational images around which societies organize their institutions and people build their lives become the objects of "a continuous battle for the cultural codes of society."[18]

Refusing to be dissolved, identities establish their specific relationships of nature, history, geography, and culture, fighting for the codes to define behavior and configure new institutions. In this context, the first and foremost task facing agents of social movements is the mobilization and manipulation of symbols. Acting on the virtual culture that delimits communication, the new collective agent—which is now the decentralized social movement integrated in a network of social change—subverts that culture in the name of alternative values and introduces new codes based on autonomous identity projects. The role of the individual agent is no longer that of the charismatic leader or brilliant strategist at the helm of organizations such as political parties, labor unions, and right-wing or left-wing social interest organizations. Rather, the individual agent is likely to be a symbolic personality who lends the decentralized movement a face. Social agents compete for power by producing and distributing cultural codes.[19]

Erikson's and Newton's ideas anticipate this contemporary sociological analysis. Newton emphasizes the decentralization of communities and autonomy in the formation of specific collective identities, capturing the central role of cultural codes. Erikson, in turn, speaks of "new communal images," a notion akin to that of cultural codes, and points out how the Black Panther movement incorporates this dimension.[20] The image projected by the Panthers, particularly by Newton himself, was a posture of contained, armed challenge, but shadowed by discipline and pacifism. Newton held his gun with its barrel pointed up, echoing the classic imagery of the 1776 revolutionary militiamen. He conveyed the notion of someone prepared and willing to defend an ideal of justice, rather than coming across as an uncontrolled aggressor. In real life confrontations, the Panthers showed their weapons defiantly, but waited for the first shot to come from the police. Their stance morally paralyzed the repressive authorities, who were used to dealing with a terrorized black community. By exercising a constitutional right that society granted only to whites—and denied to blacks by means of racist intimidation and violence—the Black Panthers' stance symbolized courage and human dignity. Their weapons were symbols not of violence but of resistance to injustice—a stance that counted the Panthers as part of a tradition of nonviolent civil resistance. And prior to Castells's analysis, Newton already was a symbolic personality, lending his face to represent the collective demands of his community.

I return here to the dialogue between Newton and Erikson not only to point out the timeliness of their ideas but also to demonstrate the historical continuum of the evolution of thought on the issue of the identity. This thought has emerged from social movements that gave new meaning to the concept through resistance to colonialist and patriarchal systems of domination. Concepts like identity gain new contours in psychological and sociological theory due to their elaboration in the practice of those movements. For this reason, I am not convinced by Castells's argument that "race is a very important factor, but one could hardly say that it is still capable of building meaning."[21] On the contrary, I contend that, particularly in multiethnic and pluricultural societies formed out of trafficking enslaved Africans, the articulation of racial and ethnic identities, interacting with the feminist and environmental movements, has forged deep and widespread intervention in social reality. As a result, assertion of these identities has also contributed to significant conceptual innovations, such as the paradigm of identity in the social sciences, and to the building of the critical multiculturalism that has in fact transformed society.

RACE AND DOMINATION: THE SORCERY OF COLOR

The concept of "race" and its utility as a category of scientific analysis have been contested with vehemence since the end of World War II, when the Jewish holocaust in Europe, one of the greatest human tragedies, provoked a broad consensus on the need to eliminate racial distinctions from social thought and practice. An attempt at universal color-blindness was introduced in the humanities and sciences; reference to racial differences became a dangerous mistake. At the same time, the scientific basis of race fell apart when researchers concluded that it was useless as a biological concept. The range of genetic variation proved to be larger within any one of the so-called races than between them.

Race came to be seen as purely fictional, the useless leftover from a sorry stage in the evolution of human thought that has been overcome, with the exception of a few backward steps that are widely rejected by the scientific community. Léon Poliakov, in his careful study of Aryanism, states, "Everything is done as if in shame or fear of being racist, as if the West had never been racist, and minor figures like Gobineau, H. Chamberlain and others are given the role of scapegoats."[22]

The simple relegation of race as science fiction, though, has not eliminated its continued discriminatory impact. Whether or not it is a valid biological category, race persists as a hard and undeniable socially constructed reality.[23] As much as intellectuals with noble intentions protest the invalidity of the division of the human species into races, they cannot prevent statistically demonstrated inequalities from continuing to exist according to socially defined racial differences. Nor can they make discrimination against individuals belonging to groups classified as inferior races disappear, no matter how fictitious this inferiority may be from a biological point of view. The reality of the social facts emerging from the popularized notion of race means that we must name it in our analysis of society. The idea of the social construction of race defines a new way of recognizing social reality without resorting to the illusion of euphemism. When we study the concept of race as a socially constructed category, what stands out is its plasticity, mutability, and diversity of expression over time, between one social context and another, and in the face of sociopolitical, cultural, and economic change.[24]

The case of Brazil and other "Latin" American countries is an outstanding illustration of this mutability. In general, the operation of racism is similar in countries and societies founded by Iberian colonization. That the region has been named Latin reinforces, via linguistic means that produce deep psychological effects, the domination of Latin Europeans over the Native American and African-descendant populations that outnumbered them.

All over the region, an ideology of antiracist pretense was long successful in obscuring the reality of race discrimination. Through a sort of white magic masked as scientific method, a racial hierarchy composed of a graduated scale of color and prestige—veritably a pigmentocracy[25]—was ideologically transformed into a racially neutral structure. Within this scheme attributed to Latin societies, race as a social classifier supposedly does not exist. In the United States, racial classification is assigned according to origin (so-called hypodescendancy): one drop of African blood makes you black. In Latin society, color classifies a person. "Mark" or appearance determines a plethora of categories and their associated levels of prestige. This criterion is supposed to be purely aesthetic, divorced from the notions of racial or ethnic origin, and therefore nonracist. The fact that black skin color and corresponding physical features are at the bottom of this hierarchy is supposed to have nothing to do with race or African origin as announced by color. Thus, while *mestizos* have a lower status than whites, this is considered to be merely a matter of aesthetic preference or a reflection of class standing with no racial implication. The pretense of this scheme was to erase race and racism from Latin American history and culture.

During and after decades of European immigration, darker-skinned groups stayed at the bottom of the social pyramid. While Europeans and Asians quickly climbed the social ladder, arriving at the top in a matter of decades, African descendants were left irremediably on the lowest rungs. As if by a magic spell, this fact was reduced to mere coincidence or a structural leftover from the slave system. It was understood to result from "social discrimination," meaning class discrimination, which reproduced colonial heritage in a racially neutral way.

I have called this process of ideological deracialization disguised as scientific analysis the sorcery of color. This doctrine contradicts reality by denying the racial content of hierarchies that are, in fact, based on white supremacy. Its efficacy illustrates how much the idea of race and the operation of racial categories can differ from one society to another. But there is a link that unites different modalities of race and its diverse forms of social operation: they all are based on white supremacy and Western ethnocentrism.

The function of the sorcery of color ideology is that it obscures this fact, exalting the color and ethnicity criterion that supposedly has prevailed over race, thus avoiding the pernicious effects of racism. For decades, black intellectuals and those associated with black movements have been contesting this thesis.[26] Twenty years ago I myself had the occasion to observe that there is no real distinction between prejudice of mark and of origin. The "'mark' is simply the sign of origin; it is by 'mark' that origin is identified and can be discriminated against. But the target of discrimination is origin, not appearance itself."[27]

The notion of race, firmly embedded in the hierarchy of color, is not biologically real but exercises a social function that has considerable impact on human life. This is the phenomenon of socially constructed race. Eliminating the word race from the vocabulary is fruitless, since physical differences continue to be typified and interpreted by the collective imagination that socially constructs symbolic races. Rather than erasing racism, the suppression of the word tends to favor the prevalence and normalization of its effects. This was the victory of the sorcery of color in Brazil, where substituting race with color allowed the nation to cultivate a pretentiously antiracist ideology that obscured the existence of an extremely efficient system of racial domination.

The idea of eliminating race from the social science vocabulary led to its substitution by the term "ethnicity," which emphasized the cultural dimension and was seen to be coherent with the conclusion that biological races do not exist. However I will show that in Brazil the slogan of ethnicity created a solid base for the continuation of practices based on of the old criterion of racial inferiority. Indeed, the cultural focus of ethnicity does not necessarily offer a "clean" exit from the terrain of race. Europe, for example, is now faced with large incoming waves of Arab, Asian, African, and Caribbean immigrants. As a consequence, mainstream European society has developed a racialized treatment of these immigrant cultures.

Thus, in a way similar to the biological notion of race, culture itself can be transformed into something fixed, essentialized, and "natural," a means of distinguishing groups and justifying the subordination of one to another.[28] Moreover, ethnicity is not an adequate substitute for race because groups designated as races are more inclusive. Groups that are considered races generally refer to geographical origin (Africa, Asia, Europe, the Americas) evidenced in aspects of physical appearance, which also denote commonality of historical experience, cultural matrix, and social life.

It seems that the theoretical emphasis on the biological definition of race obscures the broader, simpler, and more commonly understood social sense of race as "a group of individuals interconnected by a common origin"[29] or "a social identity, characterized by metaphorical or fictitious family relations."[30] The notion of family relations evokes a common origin or ancestry. The social sense of race appears to describe collectivities like African Brazilians, who constitute a social group defined with reference to racial identity, with commonalties such as the geographical ancestral origin and other historical, social, and cultural experiences. If the notion of race refers to origin, ancestry, history, culture, and social experience and excludes the reference to biological essence, then the proposal to substitute race with ethnicity makes no real sense.

Academic analysis does not close the subject, however, since the social movement is the collective actor that critiques, redefines, and transforms these concepts. In order to underline commonality among populations of African origin wherever they are found, the black movement coined the term *African descendant*. This phrase reflects the same idea that inspired adoption of *Afro-Brazilian*, *Afro-Uruguayan*, and *African American*. In

Brazil and Spanish-speaking countries, it replaced *negro*, a pejorative term originating in the slave system that refers to skin color in Portuguese and Spanish. Since "Negro" is not a word for color in the English language, though, it could only refer to some undefined biological essence of race and—also due to the action of the social movement—was exchanged for "black."

The word *negro* in Portuguese, or black in English, when it is a self-construction of identity, is a victory of the social movement and has an affirmative dimension. In this case of self-assertion, though, it is infused with references to history, culture, and social experience that are not intrinsic to the words themselves—which denominate only color—but are the social construction of identity with a sense of authorship. The full understanding of these names requires some familiarity with their history. *Afro-Brazilian* and *African American* are names that make explicit the reference to the common cultural, historical, and social experience of people who share African origins. *African descendant* goes a step further, placing this identity above national context and underscoring commonality between those of African origin that are in different countries. This approach is not based on a biological criterion, but considers the cultural and historical dimension of the African experience across the world.

"RACIALISM" AND NEGRITUDE

Forty years ago, faced with repeated allegations that black movements believe in biological notions of race, Abdias Nascimento asserted the following:

> We use the expressions *race* and *racism*, obviously, in the informal, popular, nonscientific understanding of the terms: as a synonym of ethnicity and never as biological purity. It is appropriate to emphasize, however, that the taboo against the word *race* has never prevented and will never prevent our engaging in all possible acts dictated by our sense of responsibility for black people's future in Brazil. And neither intimidation nor the infamous label of *racist* will stifle our rebellion.[31]

Nascimento's statement leads me to discuss the "reverse racism" supposedly cultivated by black antiracist social movements. In Brazil, if a group that is discriminated against organizes its own associations dedicated to combating racism, this in itself often is seen as a racist act. A classic expression of this reasoning is the 1950 declaration of Congressman Afonso Arinos, author of Brazil's first antidiscrimination law, that "the insistence on creating organizations for people of color is the reverse side of the coin, for it will be, in the last analysis, a manifestation of black racism."[32]

More subtle and sophisticated, as well as sympathetic to the social movement in question, is Jean-Paul Sartre's celebrated essay, "Black Orpheus." He proposes a dialectic in which the "antiracist racism" of black movements would function as an antithesis to the thesis of racism, creating a common meaning of struggle, a step necessary to the final synthesis: a society without racism.[33] Sartre's essay was the preface to a book of the poetry of Negritude, the anticolonialist movement of French-speaking African and Caribbean intellectuals led by three poets: the future governor of Martinique, Aimé Césaire; the poet, Léon Gontran Damas of Guyana; and the future president of Senegal, Léopold Sedar Senghor. This movement was accused of reverse racism, not only by its adversaries in the West, but also by Africans with leftist ideological positions and commitments. Sartre proposes a theory of antiracist racism and writes an eloquent and solid defense of Negritude. The idea of an "antiracist racism," however, does not fail to coincide essentially with the idea of reverse racism.

Half a century later, the issue is still relevant. To this day—especially in the conservative aftermath of measures implemented in the United States as a result of the civil rights and affirmative action movements—it is common to see the accusation of reverse racism hurled at black movements and affirmative action policies. In this context, the discussion sometimes turns to the concept of racialism, derived from an English line of sociological thought and revived by philosopher Anthony Kwame Appiah[34] in the United States and sociologist Antonio Sergio Alfredo Guimarães[35] in Brazil. According to their reasoning, racism is characterized by a set of institutional discriminatory devices that perpetuate racial inequalities, while racialism is the belief in the existence of biological races as subdivisions of the human species.[36] Thus, antiracialism does not imply antiracism, because one can maintain discriminatory structures without endorsing the notion of biological races, or even while combating it. This, indeed, would be the case in Brazil.

Thus, Guimarães corrects Sartre's expression and attributes to the Negritude poets, more precisely, a racialist antiracism. The fact that they "assume the idea of race" in order to fight racism is seen as equivalent to a demonstration of their belief in biologically defined races.[37]

The idea of antiracist racialism reveals a kind of symmetry similar to that of antiracist racism and is equally false, which in my view results from an overly mechanistic and abstract reading of racialism as a belief in the subdivision of the human species into racial groups. To divorce this racialism from white supremacy is an artificial exercise, the practical effect of which is to justify the description of black movements as racialist. Guimarães writes,

"Starting in the 1970s, the [Brazilian] black movement radically changes the basis of its policy, adopting a racialist posture."[38]

The distinction between racism and racialism is untenable, in my view, because biologically based racist theories are only one expression of one stage in the ideological development of white supremacy, which goes back much further than the biological criterion and has maintained its coherence through many stages of mutation. This narrow reading of racialism contributes to emptying white supremacy of its essence, which is the ideological process of dehumanizing blacks and defining them as inferior. Biologically based scientific theories contributed to this process, but they were neither necessary nor sufficient in constituting it. Erasing Africans from human history as the builders of civilizations, technologies, philosophies, economies, and political organizations another of its cornerstones, without which the power of white supremacy would wither. This exclusion of Africans from the stage of human history has been invested with the highest scientific authority.

Thus, it is not viable to make Negritude's concept of black identity equivalent to the racialism of white supremacy. If the poets of Negritude sang the joy of the race, it was in the sense of praising positive values like emotiveness and creative sensitivity, and thereby redeeming the humanity that racism denied African descendants. If the essence of racism is the denial of black people's humanity, then the gesture of assuming black identity as positive is diametrically the opposite: a statement of that humanity.

During the Cold War, African critics of Negritude reacted against what they understood as its implicit endorsement of biologically based racist theories. To attribute greater emotiveness and creative sensibility to Africans, for example, was itself based on the stereotype created by white supremacy.[39]

This critique lacked subtlety and failed to take into account the tone of polished irony with which the proponents of Negritude threw racist theories back at their creators. In this way, the Negritude poets implicitly contested such theories and transformed the platitudes of racism into weapons of resistance. A considerable part of the leftist critique of Negritude, however, is ideological. The proponents of class struggle's ascendancy did not stop at denying both biologically based and socially constructed race. They also denied the legitimacy of identity as a consciousness-raising factor in anticolonialist struggle. Pan-Africanism was transformed into a "racially neutral" scientific socialism of class struggle, defined according to Western historical, economic, and cultural criteria.[40]

This extreme denial of identity was short lived. Soon the hegemony of Cold War ideological constructs was dismantled as new international tendencies came into play, such as the Non-Aligned Movement and South-South

Dialogue. The Black Consciousness Movement, led by Steve Biko in South Africa, was marked by the mobilization against the institution of "Bantu education," and underscored the imperative of confronting racial domination and white supremacy with identity politics.

During the 1980s, then, the African world largely reconciled itself with the legacy of Negritude, recognizing its role in anticolonialist mobilization and its partnership with Pan-Africanism.[41] This reconciliation held a kind of world forum in 1987, when the First International Conference of African Communities in the Americas brought together twenty-five hundred representatives of the most diverse countries in honor of the historical example of the Negritude movement. Along with Césaire and Senghor, two Brazilians were present: Congressman Abdias Nascimento and anthropologist Lélia González.[42]

"RACIALISM" AND PAN-AFRICANISM

With his book *In My Father's House: Africa in the Philosophy of Culture*, Ghanaian philosopher Kwame Anthony Appiah embarks on the mission of demonstrating the racist or racialist essence of Pan-African thought. Analyzing the discourse of the movement, he constructs a line of reasoning that is pristine in its formalistic logic, but charged with clear ideological intent. This mission is not inconsistent with his effort to delegitimize the line of research that documented common elements of unity that allow one to speak of an African matrix of civilization.[43] Because he judges the study of pre-Socratic thought to be of little use,[44] Appiah endorses the notion that philosophy qua philosophy—and, by extension, scientific thought and Western civilization—sprang wholly out of the "Greek miracle," as if these things had no basis in four millennia of previous development by Africans in Egypt. He founds this argument on the distinction between "real" philosophy, that is, the formal discipline that begins with Socrates, and "folk" philosophy, or the domain of primitive peoples' intellect. Yet for ancients like Herodotus, considered the "Father of History," the continuity between Egyptian thought and that of Greek thinkers like Euclid and Pythagoras who made pilgrimages to Egypt in search of knowledge was obvious. Cheikh Anta Diop, the Senegalese chemist, archaeologist, ethnologist, and historian, began a line of research that has demonstrated, in several different scientific fields, the Eurocentric distortion of history that has been responsible for obscuring this fact and the continuity of the Egyptian legacy with many African cultures.[45] This work is complemented and reinforced by linguist and philologist Martin Bernal in his work, *Black Athena: The Afroasiatic Roots of Classical Civilization.*

Appiah concedes a certain historical interest to Bernal's thesis, but he notes that, in contrast to Diop's school of "Egyptianists," Bernal is not interested in the possible contemporary implications of his theory, but only wants to "correct the historical record."[46] Yet this is precisely the Egyptianists' goal. The Egyptianists recognize, though, that the correction of the historical record in itself has contemporary implications not only for African descendants' identity building but also for the discussion and critique of Eurocentric hegemony.

Returning to W.E.B. Du Bois and the Pan-African thinkers, Appiah evaluates the notion of race in their work. He cites Du Bois stating, explaining, and offering arguments in support of his position that Pan-African unity is based not on biological notions of race but on the historical, cultural, and social experience common to African peoples in their collective heritage of cultural values.

Applying the unflinching scalpel of his Cartesian logic, Appiah dissects Du Bois's arguments one by one, in each case reducing the solidarity of African peoples to a question of biological race and, therefore, one of racialism. Appiah simply refuses to accept Du Bois's option for a broader conceptualization of identity, demonstrating with formally impeccable arguments what he judges to be its logical incoherence. The philosopher thus endorses the classic Eurocentric argument that this and other African consciousness movements are definitive, irredeemable cases of reverse racism.

The dialogue between Appiah and Du Bois reenacts a quarrel that is both long familiar and still relevant: intellectuals who identify with antiracist social movements are labeled black racists; they then protest to the contrary, articulating their thoughts and arguments. Their accusers reinterpret their arguments in such a way as to reveal what is supposedly their true underlying meaning, which is said to be racist or racialist.

Here Castells's definition of the resistance identity asserted by social movements is notable: "they are what they say they are."[47] For him it is enough to accept the discourse of the protagonists as an expression of their goals and positions.

Since the 1930s Afro-Brazilian intellectual and activist Abdias Nascimento had been familiar with the accusation that black identity consciousness was based on biological notions of race. Writing more than twenty years ago, he underscored the need for emphasizing the contrary. He states, "I warn the intriguers, the malicious, those quick to judge: the word *race*, in the sense here used, is defined only in terms of history and culture, and not biological purity." Two pages later, he continues, "I reiterate here my warning to the intriguers, the malicious, the ignorant, racists: in these lines the word *race* is exclusively historical-cultural. Biologically pure race does not exist and never did."[48]

Nascimento's reasoning in these lines echoes that of Du Bois. Both foresee the concept of the social construction of race, which is currently in vogue in the social sciences. Indeed, black movements as a whole assumed a nonbiological idea of race and built the concept of socially constructed race into their actions for change long before sociology came to this theoretical conclusion.

GENDER AND RACE: DIOP, DU BOIS, AND FEMINISM

The notion of socially constructed race echoes the feminist critique of patriarchy. Simone de Beauvoir's classic statement that one is not born a woman, but becomes one through a complex and socially conditioned process, anticipated the concept of the social construction of reality by bringing to light the social construction of the category "woman" in patriarchal society. For Beauvoir, the final goal of the process of *becoming a woman* is to assume one's womanhood as a "project," in Sartre's sense. However, in order to articulate this identity as a project, one must forge a critical consciousness of the identity of "woman," which is socially constructed in patriarchal society. The project emerges from the deconstruction of this identity.[49]

The core of Beauvoir's theory is the critique of the ideology according to which social inequalities are defined as a consequence of woman's supposedly natural essence, her organic constitution. Thus, the biological difference between male and female—particularly with regard to maternity—is used to justify women's confinement to inferior social roles, the restriction of their legal rights and responsibilities, lower expectations of their success, as well as gender inequalities in income, education, employment, and remuneration. Childhood and secondary education imbued with the ideology of patriarchy can hinder the development of personality, self-esteem, and autonomy in women.[50]

There is a clear parallel between this process and the naturalization of racial inequalities. Psychological effects are reinforced by representations and stereotypes of congenital inferiority.[51] Racism is constituted and operates in many ways that are essentially the same as sexism. Discrimination results not only in statistically measurable social inequalities but also in a broader perspective that determines and conditions possibilities and perspectives in the lives of individuals and groups. Thus, in Brazil, two important studies on the race issue in psychology recall Beauvoir's expression: psychoanalyst Neusa

Santos Souza studies the process of "becoming black," and sociologist Matilde Ribeiro examines the process of "becoming a black woman."[52]

In the 1970s, some analysts focused on the idea of the reduction of the cultural to the realm of the biological as the essence of racism. Thus, racism existed whenever something that was regarded as prestigious or stigmatic was explained by the presence of a natural characteristic. Feminist criticism helped extend this analysis to sexism and classism: the supposedly scientifically proven hereditary basis of criminality, mental illness, and so-called weakness of spirit—which led to unemployment, poverty, and alcoholism—condemned the poor to a state of innate inferiority. The notion of such heredity with respect to race, class, and gender was the heart of the pseudoscientific theory of eugenics. Thus, techniques applied to optimize the population's genetic stock were instituted as public policy not only in the fascist countries of Europe but also in the United States, Brazil, and other parts of Latin America.[53]

However, the dimension shared by race and gender goes beyond making social inequalities natural. The commonalties between racism and sexism include the identification of targeted groups as a part of nature itself. They are represented as subhuman or animal, as opposed to being recognized as human. Western humanism, indeed, is based on a process of exclusion, as Sodré observes:

> Modern Western culture—in other words, the triumph of absolute humanity—comes into being with a spatial order centered in Europe. In this way, the "universal human being," created out of a cultural conception that reflected the realities of the bourgeois European universe, necessarily generated a universal non–human being, the other side of the coin, which included all the qualifications referring to the "nonperson": barbarian, black savage, and so forth.[54]

Jacob Pandian notes that the Enlightenment created the black "other" as "a distinct being, biologically and intellectually inferior to Western whites ... [who] came to represent the height of racial difference, the supreme contrast by which Western man could compare and define himself."[55] But neither of these authors speaks to the gender identity of this absolute humanity. It was feminist criticism that pointed out "the hidden perspective behind which the abstract being of metaphysics is, in reality, the extremely concrete point of view of the adult, white, property-owning man."[56] Once the model of the universal human is established as male and white, people diverge from being human to the extent that they "deviate" from that model. Thus, racism and patriarchy intersect to produce the dehumanization of subordinated groups, closely linked as forms of domination.

This interlinkage was identified in African world thought and social practice before Europe popularly embraced its poststructural and otherwise postmodern stances. I will examine two examples: Senegalese ethnologist, archaeologist, and chemist Cheikh Anta Diop, and the leading twentieth-century intellectual, W.E.B. Du Bois.

Diop articulated one of the most incisive critiques of the universal model of patriarchy in his study of the essential unity of precolonial cultures in Africa.[57] He finds that one of the main elements of this underlying cultural unity is matrilineal social organization.

Western science postulated a universal evolution of family and social organization in which all human groups progressed from the "primitive horde"—a concept dear to Sigmund Freud—through the primitive stages of matriarchy and matrilineal society into the higher stage of social development, which is patriarchy, the stage of light. Diop analyzes these theories in detail, demonstrating their lack of empirical support and their base in the distortion and subjective interpretation of observed fact and historical record. In the process, he anticipates both deconstructionism and the feminist criticism of Marxism.[58]

Far from being a primitive stage of social development, matrilineal societies include some of the most highly organized ones in history, such as Egypt and the empire of Ghana. Diop maintained that social, economic, and political development does not depend on the subordination of women. On the contrary, he asks which society is more fully developed: one that denies half its population their full humanity or one that recognizes and stimulates everyone's capabilities and contributions to collective life.

The interrelationship between racism and patriarchy is the focus of action and analysis of other Pan-African thinkers. One of the greatest intellectuals of the twentieth century, W.E.B. Du Bois, dedicated himself actively to the cause of women's suffrage, writing, organizing, and participating in countless public events between 1911 and 1920.[59]

The U.S. feminist movement at that time was composed almost exclusively of white women, many of whom espoused openly racist positions. Some used arguments based on white supremacy to campaign for women's suffrage. In a Jim Crow society, they argued that the female vote would help defeat black suffrage. When traveling south to advocate women's suffrage, Northern feminists tended to endorse such arguments or remain silent about them, even when they considered themselves personally to be antislavery and antiracist.

Du Bois understood that women's suffrage was an important advance in the direction of a democratic, nonracist society, and a necessary step toward the black vote. He maintained his advocacy of women's suffrage, and articulated a highly ethical argument in which he reestablished the philosophical link between the female vote and the black vote, which had been broken by the rhetoric of racist feminists. Du Bois did all he could to convince the black community to overcome its resentment and support the cause of women's suffrage. He did this by demonstrating that women's suffrage would have positive consequences for the black population. In this process, Du Bois entered into serious confrontations with African Americans who were understandably indignant about racist feminists and feminists who billed themselves as antiracists but lacked interest in black suffrage.

Recall that this is the black intellectual labeled an extrinsic and intrinsic racist by Appiah in his exegesis of what he identifies as the racialist foundations of Du Bois's Pan-African thought.[60]

I looked briefly at these examples in order to illustrate how the analysis of the entwinement of patriarchy and racism is an integral part of the critique of Western ethnocentrism. However, the critical perspective of black women was articulated later, in the context of social movements.[61] With decolonization, women of the so-called Third World began to articulate their own critique of Western feminist practice and rhetoric.[62] This critique targeted the supposedly universal reach of the category of woman, which was socially constructed in the context of Western society. In her challenge to this category, Nigerian anthropologist Oyeronke Oyewumi joins other writers who had questioned "precisely the presumption that there is an experience-of-being-a-woman that can be generalized, identified, and collectively consensual,"[63] asserting that the specific and heterogeneous nature of women's experience in peripheral societies places in question the theoretical models of unitary feminism that fail to take that experience into account.[64]

To the extent that it was capable of absorbing this critique in the process of worldwide social activism, feminism was transformed and recovered as a theoretical perspective. One could say that bell hooks, one of the most outstanding contemporary black female theorists of the United States, returned implicitly and symbolically to Du Bois's position by underscoring the need for black women to face the issue of patriarchy as a phenomenon intertwined with race.[65] Gender can be experienced "through" race and vice versa. In standpoint theory, the multiplicity of women's experience is articulated through race and class.[66] Finally, the concept of race and gender intersectionality, developed by Kimberlé Crenshaw and others, has become an important conceptual tool.[67]

Indeed, the concept of gender is a landmark in the recent evolution of feminist thought, which had formed a perspective of women, by women, about women. Gender analysis moved the focus to male–female relations and the impact of patriarchy on men and women. The notion of gender broadened the field of feminist theory, but it was forged more in the concrete dynamics of social action than in the abstract dominion of theoretical speculation.

In feminist thought, identity emerges as a process of identifications with a sense of authorship similar to that described by Ricardo Franklin Ferreira with respect to African descendants in Brazil.[68] In Simone de Beauvoir's phrase "we become women," the word "become" means not only that gender is socially constructed but also that women can intentionally take on and redefine this identity. Judith Butler observes, "not only are we culturally constructed but, in some sense, we construct ourselves."[69] Just as the concept of gender moves the focus of feminist theory from woman to gender relations, the movement toward a relational view of race—focusing on whites and blacks rather than studying "the Negro" or "the African"—raises the need for new approaches to the race issue. Feminist criticism of patriarchy and the ex-colonials' critique of Eurocentrism also coincide in pointing out the need for interdisciplinary approaches to deal with social issues. Interdisciplinary approaches are, indeed, a founding epistemological principle of both feminist thought and the critique of Western ethnocentrism.

In both cases, theoretical elaboration follows the social movement's initiative. Yet theoretical discussion tends to ignore or underplay the role of social movements in the evolution of concepts. An example is sociology's difficulty in seeing that black movements did work with an idea of socially constructed race decades before the concept was developed in theory. The insistence on characterizing these early theories as racialist originates in this implicit refusal to recognize the agency of black social movements in building theoretical constructs. Thus, one student of these movements in Brazil states that there have been few attempts to give the concept of race a sociological meaning,[70] though the language of the movements had done just that by basing the concept of race on factors like land, culture, history, and commonality of social experience.[71]

As in the case of gender, approaches to race are articulated in the context of the social movement and speak to the living experience of human rights and citizenship. It is in this context that the theoretical approach to identity makes sense. In Matilde Ribeiro's words, "For blacks and for women, the process of building identity is basically the effort to win full citizenship, legitimate our ways ... of exercising freedom, obtain the recognition of plurality."[72] There are parallels between gender and race in that both are seen as relational; they do not place the focus on the targets of discrimination. In the study of race as in gender there emerges the question of how to avoid the reification of a certain standardized definition of blackness or femininity, that is, how to avoid an essentialist discourse.

The critique of Western reason brings new dimensions to these issues, influencing the direction of postmodern thought and laying new bases of action for social change.

AGNES HELLER'S ARCHIMEDES' POINT

In an essay on hermeneutics in social sciences, philosopher Agnes Heller speaks of modern man being in a "prison of contemporaneousness" since the Enlightenment. She notes that the social sciences have been confronted with the dilemma of seeking "the true knowledge of a world" while also verifying that this knowledge is limited by its specific time and space. To overcome this paradox, it would be necessary to find an "Archimedes' point" outside this time and space. She writes:

> Let us suppose that we are able to converse with the actors of past ages or with members of alien cultures; let us suppose as well that we can read the mind of these peoples (or their texts) and come to know what they really meant (or mean). Finally, let us suppose that, due to all this, we can look back at ourselves, with those same alien eyes, from the cultural context of this "other." If we could make these "others" raise their questions, and evaluate and judge our history and our institutions from their perspective, in other words, from their historical consciousness, we will have established an Archimedean point outside our own culture.[73]

Yet quite an extensive literature has been written by non-Western authors in the vein that Heller suggests.[74] By proposing the need to provoke such manifestations, Heller underlines the invisibility of this literature and exemplifies how the academy fails to note them or, at best, pays them little attention. Yet the critique of modern rationality has been formulated in great part by the intervention of "others" who have articulated their outlooks on Western theory, deeply influencing its evolution.

A herald of this phenomenon was W.E.B. Du Bois of the United States. When he wrote in 1903 that "the issue of this century will be the problem of the color line," he was not referring superficially to skin color.[75] His work holds deep significance as the articulation of an "outside outlook" on

Western culture in the social sciences. Brazil gave us another prophet of this process, sociologist Guerreiro Ramos, who articulated a specific outlook on basic standards of Western social sciences.[76] His concept of *sociological reduction* attempts to provide a method of evaluating whether parameters said to be universal should apply to Brazil. Guerreiro Ramos's sociology was innovative in that he emphasized *praxis*, his inductive methodology in which social action informs theory. His stance was based on the conviction that "if one does not act, if one does not participate in the societary process, one cannot comprehend society."[77] In his case, the venue for engaged social action was the Black Experimental Theater (TEN).

TEN insistently questioned the posture of studies of blacks in which supposedly neutral observers took black people and their culture as objects, as a problem. Their methods implicitly denied black people as human beings, as members of society, and as holders of rights and duties—in sum, as citizens. TEN also anticipated the idea of perspectivism, which is summed up by Ramos when he wrote about Brazilian "blacks from within."[78] For him—writing as early as the 1950s, and this was audacious—the "life situation" that most favors understanding of the race issue is *niger sum* ("I am black"), which he explains is "a procedure of high scientific value, since it introduces the investigator to a perspective that allows him to see nuances that otherwise would go unnoticed."[79]

This position of TEN, carved out of its theatrical, artistic, and political practice, represents an enunciation of Afro-Brazilian resistance identity. This phenomenon is not unique to the contemporary network society but part of a continuum of historical tendencies that formed the global context in which TEN was created. The emergence of resistance identities became more clear and visible in the 1970s, and in the 1980s and 1990s erupted into a political demand for recognition of identities: multiculturalism.

MULTICULTURALISM

The basic proposal of multiculturalism corresponds, in many aspects, to the analyses of these Afro-Brazilian authors and their social movement. In the 1970s, Brazilian society generally refused to recognize the existence of racism and the legitimacy of specific collective demands. The demand for recognition of the ethnic and cultural plurality of Brazilian society was a theme basic to the search for citizenship of groups that are the targets of discrimination.[80] These social movements won the inscription in the 1988 Constitution of the Republic of an article stating the multiethnic and pluricultural nature of Brazilian society.[81]

The theme of multiculturalism arose earlier in Canada, Europe, and the United States than in Brazil and other countries in South and Central America. It was promoted not only by minorities (in number) but also by majority populations like Francophones in Québec, blacks in Brazil, and Native Americans in other South American countries. The multicultural demand was expressed in great part in the area of education. Communities insisted particularly on the reformulation of school curriculum content and prevailing teaching practices in order to respond to the needs of their children.

Charles Taylor explains multiculturalism as the politics of recognition, focusing on the subordination and exclusion of identities as a form of oppression and studying the interplay of ethnic and cultural assertions as a game of power.[82] There is a basic human need to be recognized, he asserts, and this need was articulated by social movements as a citizenship right. Multiculturalism thus brings the issue of identity into the public sphere. As the particularist and subjective interest of individuals or specific groups, it had belonged traditionally to the private sphere. The res publica, which transcends the interests of groups and individuals, now includes what before was private—body, affective life, desire. Identities are conceived as having a public dimension—specific expressions of nationalism, languages, and culture—within a social context marked by a larger identity taken to be "universal."

Taylor's text is eminently characterized by the author's identification with this larger dimension of the universal. At no point does the philosopher abandon his commitment to the "true" res publica that reigns above the identities competing in the political arena. Indeed, the tone of Taylor's discourse reminds one of a Caesar, observing the "game" of the gladiators and pondering from the heights of his uncontested authority to what point this competition is in the interest of the larger destiny of the Empire.

Postulating the recognition of the right to cultural identities, Taylor observes at the base of this right a "universal potential" of forming and defining one's own identity as an individual and as a culture.[83] This potential must be recognized in everyone. However, there arises a stronger demand—one that is problematic for Taylor—that equal respect be given to the different cultures as they have "evolved in fact."[84]

In Taylor's understanding, the act or intention of attributing equal value to all cultures is baseless. He recalls a polemical comment on the controversy over the canon in literature: "When the Zulus produce a Tolstoy, we will read him."[85] This phrase transmits a certain European arrogance, observes Taylor, by stating its insensitivity to difference. Moreover—and here resides the problem for him—many also understand that the phrase "reflects the denial of a principle of human equality."[86] For Taylor, this notion eliminates at the outset the hypothesis that the Zulus, despite having the potential of being equal to other peoples, may nevertheless "have *produced* a culture *less valuable than others*."[87] At the end of his essay, Taylor is busy with the theme of the relative value of cultures, concluding that "peremptory and unauthentic judgments of equal value" cannot be used to justify the insertion, for example, of non-Western works in the academic canon. The principle of equality among cultures requires of us only that we be open to comparative cultural studies and to the admission that "we are very far away from that last horizon from which the relative value of different cultures can become evident."[88] For Taylor, it seems, the issue of the canon revolves around the question of what contribution a culture judged to be of lower value could be capable of offering, or has already offered, to the constitution of universal knowledge. This is a paradoxical question when we consider that "universal knowledge" has been constituted unilaterally up to now by the dominant West, in a process that used non-Western peoples as their laboratory objects. This placed a priori limits on the conditions of these peoples' contribution to research that, with great rigor and objectivity as well as impeccable methodological procedure, created and gave sustenance to the scientific proof of their innate inferiority. As Oyewumi remarks, "What has Africa contributed to the disciplines? Following the logic of this question, let us consider what Africans contributed to craniometry—our heads; and to French anthropology—our behinds!"[89]

The political issue is not, then, the "relative value" of cultures, but the exclusion, repression, and distorted representation of the cultures of subordinated peoples. The concern with value judgment immediately brings to mind the question: who is to judge? Indeed, who is the "we" of Taylor's narrative? According to what parameters will the product of another culture be evaluated in the scenario imagined by the author when he states that "the act of declaring valuable the creations of another culture and the act of declaring oneself sympathetic to it, *even if its creations are not so interesting*, become indistinct"? Or when he says that "the demand could be: include these [works in the academy's canon] because they are ours, even though they *may very well be inferior*"?[90]

The liberal model presupposes a political arena in which everyone participates on equal footing. It seems the notion of the politics of recognition does not deal with the relative position of groups within the democratic regime. The recognition of a subordinated identity does not necessarily imply that it will be able to assert itself in the political arena. Peter McLaren sums up this point by noting that "the paradigms of multiculturalism repackage neo-liberal conservative ideologies under the discursive mantle of diversity." McLaren proposes "critical multiculturalism" as the imperative of considering the asymmetry of access to the multicultural arena established by the configuration of power and ideology.[91] To offer a subordinated identity equal footing to compete in this democratic game, it is necessary to break the hegemony of the dominant identity, Eurocentric whiteness, constructed so solidly and so well reinforced that it reigns silent without being perceived.

This point is fundamental in the Brazilian context, for perhaps the most outstanding characteristic of racism in Brazil is its unconscious nature. Racist attitudes and the privilege attributed to being white prevail in the underlying but unexpressed meanings contained in language and social convention. Most of the time, they simply go unperceived. It is not surprising, then, that a precocious contestation of the ideology of whiteness arose in the Brazilian context. Decades before the articulation of the critique of multiculturalism, Nascimento and Ramos anticipated this theme in the course of their artistic and political work in TEN. It was an important theoretical step forward, because only after the critique of whiteness is it possible to measure the relational character of race. In this sense, the advance corresponds to the concept of gender in feminist theory, which rests on the following principle, in which words about gender may be substituted for corresponding words regarding race:

> In all discussions about the standing of women, their character, their temperament, their submission and emancipation, the fundamental fact is lost from sight: that is, that the roles of both sexes are conceived according to the cultural framework that is at the base of human relations in which boys, as they develop, are modeled just as inexorably as girls, according to a particular and well defined canon.[92]

GENDER, RACE, AND WHITENESS

The gender approach implies moving the focus of attention from women to patriarchy as a cultural framework that affects both men and women. In a similar way, the intellectuals of TEN advocated moving so-called studies of blacks in the direction of denouncing the ideology of whiteness, a canon that conditions the lives of those who discriminate as well as those discriminated against. "In Brazil, whites have enjoyed the privilege of watching blacks, without being seen by them," observed Ramos, as he launched TEN into the project of inaugurating "a new phase of studies on race relations in Brazil, a phase that is characterized by looking at such relations from the act of building black people's freedom."[93]

Critical race theory's incursion into the area of critical white studies[94] has its precedents in W.E.B. Du Bois's two essays, "The White World" and "The Souls of White Folk" that are early examples of a critical look at whiteness in the United States.[95] It also has its counterpart in Brazil, where whiteness studies have come back into debate.[96] It posits the need, in order to comprehend race issues, to study whites as the creators, agents, and reproducers of the theory and practice of racism. Whiteness must be identified and understood as the silent and obscured implicit standard that conducts the reproduction of discriminatory race relations. Students of race relations move their focus of analysis from the dominated subject to the dynamics that constitute interaction between the groups, mediated surreptitiously by the ideology of whiteness.

From this point of view, in order to understand racism it is necessary to question and investigate the contours of whiteness and its impact on society and individuals, both white and black. White supremacy is the silent norm that prevails unspoken. Guerreiro Ramos writes: "In Brazilian culture whiteness is the ideal, the norm, the value, par excellence." He sees as a pathological form of alienation the Brazilian habit of "renouncing the induction of local or regional criteria for judging what is beautiful, because of an unconscious subservience to an outside prestige."[97] In the same way that Brazilians adopted colonial and neocolonial external standards, blacks are coerced into accepting the standards of whiteness. When blacks assume their true position, freeing themselves of this pathology, studies of blacks can evolve in another direction that looks out from the position of *niger sum*.

This possibility is contained in a viewpoint formed by the person's experience as a black person who is the protagonist of these studies not because of skin color but by virtue of his or her position of observation and analysis. When Joel Rufino dos Santos states that for Guerreiro Ramos black people are not a race, but a place, he captures the way in which Ramos and the Black Experimental Theater anticipated one of the basic principles developed in the theory of Afrocentricity.[98]

AFROCENTRICITY

The Afrocentric critique of multiculturalism builds on principles similar to those discussed by McLaren, and takes them further. For the Afrocentrist, the issue is not recognition, but empowerment for participation in the democratic play of power. Rather than plead for recognition from others, the Afrocentrist seeks to build the foundation for full self-recognition of his or her people and their culture, a necessary condition for this empowerment. Afrocentricity defines as its priorities the deconstruction of dominant notions of African history and culture, distorted by Eurocentrism, and the reconstruction of the content obscured by them.

The concept of place in Afrocentricity makes Joel Rufino dos Santos's comment all the more appropriate with respect to Guerreiro Ramos, whose work foreshadows the idea in Brazil. Like Ramos's thought, Afrocentric analysis coincides with postmodern approaches that emphasize the need to recognize and make explicit from what point of view the observer deals with an issue. This involves a critique of conventional ideas that tend to impose themselves as universal when they are actually specific. The idea is to look at phenomena from the viewpoint of Africans, an exercise that intrinsically involves a critique of the conventional Eurocentric approach. In this exercise, the idea of place is useful because it dispenses the focus on the subject's racial identity. Those located in the Afrocentric "place" are not necessarily African descendants, and by the same token not all African descendants inhabit this place.

Afrocentricity states explicitly that it has no pretense of hegemony; it contests the pretext of the hegemonic universality of the European center, but not the validity of a European center specifically for Western individuals. "The Afrocentric idea is projected as a model of intercultural agency in which pluralism exists without hierarchy and respect is freely conceded to the origins, achievements, and potential of others."[99]

The notion of place is related to a second major Afrocentric concept, that of agency. To look at history from the African place implies that one sees Africans as active agents of history, in contrast to the conventional portrayal of passive victims—from Stanley and Livingston forward, the Africa of whiteness is one in which Europeans are the actors. African agency needs to be asserted as it is necessary to the participation in multiculturalism's dynamics of identity as power. Communications media, schools and universities, and cultural institutions reinforce the representation of Africans as people who do not produce knowledge, technology, or civilization and their portrayal as authors only of "ethnic cultures" on the order of the substratum (samba, soccer, and cooking, for example). Such a conception of Africans leads to severe restriction of African descendants' access to the benefits of society and their possibilities of gaining power.

For this reason, the Diopian line of research is a point of departure for the Afrocentric approach. Ancient African thought and classical civilization, located in Kemet and the Nile valley, are emphasized as "references for an African perspective, in the same way as Greece and the Roman Empire are the references of the European world."[100] Extensive research has informed the debate around the suppression of Egyptian civilization as the origin of

Western civilization; the underlying unity of African cultures; the presence and influence of Africans and their culture in the building of human civilizations in the ancient world; the matrilineal nature of these civilizations and its implications for feminist thought and the issue of gender; and the implications of all these considerations for the formulation of educational curriculum content and teaching technique. Afrocentric research is also concerned with current themes of late modernity, neomodernity, and postmodernity.[101]

Criticized as a tendency to close off African descendant identity, on the contrary, this line of analysis brings a new, enriching, and more inclusive contribution, for it "expands human history, creating a new path for interpretation."[102] Molefi Kete Asante writes, "It is at this point that feminist critique converges with Afrocentric reasoning. What I try to do here is come closer to the post-Eurocentric idea that makes truly transcultural analysis possible; this can be achieved side by side with a post-male ideology on the way to freeing human potential."[103]

AN AFROCENTRIC CRITIQUE OF FEMINISM

Returning to non-Western women's critique of feminism, Oyewumi develops an analysis of gender relations in the Yoruba society of Oyo, which includes a critique of feminist thought and of academic approaches to non-Western cultures. In minutely detailed analysis, she examines how scholars and activists perpetuate the noncritical imposition on these cultures of presumably objective or neutral concepts whose anchor is the Western matrix.

The author points out the following principles that are basic to feminist thought:

1. Gender categories are universal and eternal and have been present in every society at all times.
2. Gender is a basic organizing principle in all societies and for this reason it is always salient.
3. There is an essential and universal category, "woman," which is characterized by the social uniformity of its members.
4. The subordination of women is a universal.

The category "woman" is seen to be precultural and fixed in historical time and cultural space in opposition to another fixed category—"men."[104]

Based on detailed linguistic and social analysis of traditional Yoruba society, Oyewumi shows that the application of these five principles "can lead to serious misconceptions when applied to Oyo-Yoruba society. In fact, my central argument is that there were no *women* — defined in strictly gendered terms — in that society."[105] Colonialism introduced Western, socially constructed gender categories to the Yoruba. The first tool of this process is language.

Oyewumi demonstrates that Yoruba vocabulary reflects a remarkable indifference to the sex of social actors. In Yoruba cosmology, the body part that is symbolically most significant is *ori*, the nongendered head, seat of individual destiny. Also, gender-neutral nouns were common. For example, *omo* means child or offspring, but before British domination there were no Yoruba words differentiating between *girl* and *boy*. The words *obinrin* and *okunrin* refer only to the anatomical difference; they did not refer to gender implications with connotation of social privilege or disadvantage. Oyewumi translates them not as "man" and "woman" but as "anatomically male" and "anatomically female."

To accommodate the English colonialists' concern with the sex of children, it was necessary to invent the words *omokunrin* (anatomically male child) and *omobinrin* (anatomically female child). Samuel Johnson, the first Yoruba historian, writing in 1877 — when English colonialism was in the process of establishing itself and traditional Yoruba society still maintained a greater degree of coherence — comments that, "Our translators, in their desire to find a word expressing the English idea of sex rather than of age, coined the ... words '*arakonron*,' that is, the male relative; and '*arabinrin*,' the female relative; these words always have to be explained to the pure but illiterate Yoruba man."[106]

Literary critic Olabiyi Yai identifies colonizers' linguistic impositions on Yoruba as the failure to acknowledge epistemological differences between the two cultures. Adeleke Adeeko seconds his observation, asserting that such a problem results from researchers' insistence on looking, in a noncritical way, for Yoruba equivalents to English terms, as if the latter signified constants in human experience.[107]

English translations of Yoruba imbued many neutral words with gender. An eminent example is the word *oba*, which means male or female sovereign, but was translated as "king." A fictitious male political power was built into the famous "lists of kings," based on oral tradition, which include the names of several women recorded as if they were men.

Yoruba society and language construct social differences among persons with reference not to sex but to age, or one's relationship to family by either domicile or lineage. The words *aya* and *oko*, erroneously translated as wife and husband, are gender neutral: *aya* denotes belonging to a domicile by marriage and *oko* denotes relationship defined by lineage. All those who belong by birth to the lineage of a woman who entered the domicile by marriage are *oko* in relationship to her, although only one of them, the husband, may maintain sexual relations with her. Women belonging to the lineage by birth, for example, would be her *oko* and would have inheritance rights when she became a widow. Social differences within the family structure are based not on gender but on age and chronological order of entrance into the domicile.

The translation of these terms as "wife" and "husband" engenders a series of confusions in the interpretation of family relations, inheritance norms, and cultural traditions. In the context of religious life and cosmology, these confusions multiply. One example is the notion of subordination of women in the Yoruba religious context. Anthropologist John Pemberton, for example, observes initiates in the worship of Shango, one of the important Yoruba deities, called Orisha. When these worshippers lie with head to the ground in *dobale*, a traditional gesture of reverence, Pemberton interprets the gesture as a sign of female subservience to men. Yet in this worship everyone, including the sovereign *alaafin*, the highest authority in the social hierarchy, venerates the deity Shango by prostrating themselves. Pemberton also cites the praise song in which women call Shango their "husband"—an inaccurate translation of the Yoruba *oko*—and remarks that "The unpredictable, capricious, self-serving Orisha [divinity] is also the one who imparts his beauty to the woman with whom he sleeps. He is the giver of children."[108]

The erroneous translation of the word *oko* leads Pemberton to allege that only women sing this song and to suggest that the initiates worship him as a male sexual figure. But Shango is *oko* to his followers because he is the owner of the house and they are outsiders. Both male and female worshippers are referred to as "spouses"—*oko*—of Shango. In sum, as Oyewumi points out, "the relationship between Shango and his congregation is neither gendered nor sexualized."[109] Nor is Shango the only deity who gives children. Oya and Oshun, both female, are worshipped specifically for their ability to give children. Another researcher interpreted the gender-neutral word *iyawo*, meaning initiate (literally "child of the secret") as masculine, and thus attributes symbolic or even practiced homosexuality to Shango worship. Oyewumi cites the step-by-step refutation of this interpretation by Wande Abimbola and other authorities.[110]

The sexualization of social relations in Yoruba religious worship is not a privilege of the aforementioned authors. Writers on Candomblé, the Brazilian religion of Yoruba and other African origins, also show a strong tendency to sexualize rituals, reflecting judgments about women of African descent that result from Western patriarchal standards and racial stereotyping. For example, the fact that women participate actively in the ceremonies, singing and dancing in a festive context, triggers the assumption that they are sexually accessible, a judgment confirmed, under such standards, by their racial identity as black or mulatto women. The works of Jorge Amado, one of Brazil's foremost writers, are exemplary: not only the women but also the ceremonies themselves are subjected to negative stereotyping of this sort. Among those whose research corroborates this conclusion are the English critic David Brookshaw[111] and the African American literary analyst Doris Turner;[112] they concur with Brazilian writers like Teófilo de Quiroz Júnior and Eliana Guerreiro Ramos Bennett.[113]

In traditional African societies like the Yoruba of Oyo, the body was not the basis of social thought, roles, or inclusion or exclusion. The gender map, in which biology determines social hierarchy, is not useful in understanding Yoruba society, whose social order instead demands understanding of societal relationships based on age and family relations. All such Yoruba definitions of social position are mutable; thus, one's social identity may change constantly.

The West's insistence on gender distinctions is grounded in its dichotomy between body and soul, matter and spirit, reason and sensibility. The Western value hierarchy that identifies the divine with soul and spirit and the diabolical with body and sensation produces an obsessive concern with the body—which is considered the debauched and degenerate side of human nature—a habit characterized by the attribution of essences to discourse around the body. Such "somatocentricity" leads Oyewumi to ponder, "Since in Western constructions, physical bodies are always social bodies, there is really no distinction between sex and gender."[114]

Before the imposition of Western categories and social forms by the colonial order, Yoruba society was characterized by a relational dynamic in which social identities were not determined by gender. When studying gender in contemporary African societies, then, the intervention of colonial domination must be taken into account. In the case at hand, Oyewumi concludes the following: "In Yorubaland, the transformation of *obinrin* into women and then into 'women of no account' was at the essence of the colonial impact as a gendered process. Colonization, besides being a racist process, was also a process by which male hegemony was instituted and legitimized in African societies. Its ultimate manifestation was the patriarchal state."[115]

CONCLUSION

The concern with essentialism—the idea of gender or race as biological or physiological essence—takes us back to Western culture, from which the attribution of essences to arguments around the body seems to sprout. It was the West that attributed negative essences to non-Western peoples and reserved the positive ones for its own. Yet it is now the spokesmen of the West who admonish others about the danger of defining and restricting identities around essentialisms. Such admonitions almost always are addressed to those who look for identity references in histories of antislavery and anticolonialist resistance. In Brazil, they are often directed to African descendants who seek historical and cultural references to Africa.

The proscription of these cultural and historical references reminds us that at the background of the multicultural scenario is the question of how, in an asymmetrical context of power, one can sustain the equal participation of people whose cultural references have been distorted or obscured by the process of domination. It is not enough simply to assert diversity, because diversity is charged with value judgments that differentiate and institute inequalities. Repression, distortion, and obfuscation of subordinated cultures' historical and cultural references has restricted the range of identifications available to those building identities with a sense of authorship. The opening of new possibilities of reference offered by Afrocentricity effectively expands the multicultural horizon.

The process of building identities is part of a broader phenomenon in which social movements have helped build, influence, and constitute post-modern thought. Specifically, the articulation of racial and ethnic identities has contributed to conceptual innovations and the development of paradigms in psychology and the social sciences. Black activists and intellectuals adopted a nonbiological, nonessentialist idea of blackness, anticipating the concept of socially constructed race in their actions for change. Like feminists who sep-arated gender from biology, they contributed to the theoretical formulation of the social construction of reality. Along with feminism, environmentalism, and other movements, African descendants and their organizations con-tributed to building critical multiculturalism as they helped transform society and theory. The tendency to leave this contribution unrecognized and the failure to attribute it to social actors and movements like the proponents of Negritude and Pan-Africanism are part of a broader denial of the social and historical agency of African men and women. Such a denial impoverishes the production of knowledge.

In the next chapter, I deal with the history of race relations in Brazil, in an effort to contribute to understanding the mechanisms by which the hege-mony of whiteness was established and maintained there. The hegemony of whiteness is expressed in the peculiar racial ideology that I call the sorcery of color. With local variations, it prevails not only in Brazil but in all of so-called Latin America.

2

BRAZIL AND THE MAKING OF VIRTUAL WHITENESS

RACISM IN BRAZIL is part of a larger social context of severe inequalities. In this chapter, I offer statistical documentation of the contours of racial inequalities as well as data on gender inequalities. I consider the historical roots of these inequalities, which prepares us for the study of their social and ideological aspects. The singularity of these aspects lies in the operation of the sorcery of color, which transforms domination into democracy and launches national identity on a permanent search for the simulation of whiteness, which I call *virtual whiteness*. The expression entails virtuality both in the sense of a faculty that has not yet been realized and in a sense analogous to the virtual reality of the age of information technology: the electronic image or impulse that is not concrete but becomes real because it generates effects.

If it is true that to speak of race relations implies an examination of whiteness, I suggest that in Brazil, to interrogate whiteness is to question miscegenation. A basic source for this exercise with respect to Brazil is Kabengele Munanga's 1999 study of the history of miscegenation ideology. For my part, I would observe that the sorcery of color means that being a light-skinned person of mixed race is *almost* equivalent to being white. Investigating the limits of this equivalence is important to understanding the relational aspects of whiteness in Brazil.

It is commonly believed that the notions of African inferiority and racial determinism were wiped away in Brazil by what I would call the white magic or sorcery of Luso-Tropicalism. Sociologist Gilberto Freyre expounded this doctrine, according to which Portuguese colonialism was characterized by a special form of race relations stamped on the ethnic and cultural face of the country by miscegenation. Its trademarks are said to be cordiality and nondiscrimination.[1] Freyre is widely credited with creating a new paradigm in Brazilian thought that is said to have substituted the biological criterion of race and the discourse of eugenics and racial degeneration with a new national ideal of antiracism. By rejecting biological race theories and adopting an anthropological approach based on culture and ethnicity, such an ideal is supposed to have left no vestiges of racist ideology's social operation in Brazil.

This set of ideas has gained a mass appeal uncommon to academic theories. It coexists in permanent tension with the testimony of African-descendant activists and intellectuals who have documented the active presence of eugenic notions in daily incidents that permeate the social fabric of the country. While rarely made explicit, such notions about the innate inferiority of blacks remain in force, indifferent to the supposed nonexistence of biological racism. The persistence of these eugenic notions, albeit obscured, is pervasive and generates social consequences that contribute to the maintenance of racial inequalities still today.

CONTEMPORARY INEQUALITIES

Though it ranks among the ten largest economies in the world, with respect to social development Brazil compares unfavorably with its neighbors. In 1995, its per capita gross national product (GNP) was significantly lower than that of Argentina or Uruguay. Though its GNP was three times higher than that of Paraguay, 43 percent of Brazilian households were at the poverty level, a higher proportion than in Paraguay and more than four times those in Argentina and Uruguay.[2] Brazil had the lowest literacy rate and by far the highest infant mortality rate: fifty deaths per thousand live births, in contrast to about seven deaths per thousand in the United States.[3] The value of the monthly minimum wage was about US$75, which is more than ten times lower than what is defined as poverty in the United States. According to the World Bank's World Development Report, in 1981 Brazil was behind only Haiti and Sierra Leone with the most unequal income distribution in the world. Since then, the concentration of wealth has increased consistently.

TABLE 1: EVOLUTION OF INCOME CONCENTRATION IN BRAZIL, 1960–2000* (PERCENTAGES)

YEAR/INCOME	1960	1970	1980	1990	2000
50% poorest	18	15	14	12	11
20% richest	54	62	63	65	64
Inequality index	3.0	4.1	4.5	5.4	5.8

*Projection.

Source: Institute of Applied Economic Research (IPEA) and Brazilian Institute of Geography and Statistics (IBGE). Compiled by Guido Mantega, Institute of Applied Economic Research (IPEA).[4]

The Brazilian Institute of Geography and Statistics (IBGE) and the Brazilian Census use two categories, *preta* and *parda*—roughly translating to "dark-skinned black" and "brown"—both of which identify African descendants. Researchers, technicians, and social actors, however, have found these categories to be so arbitrary and subjective that they are almost meaningless. For this reason, a consensus has developed around the technique of adding together the *preta* (dark-skinned black) and *parda* (brown) categories, the sum of which constitutes the category of *negros* (blacks). This group is also referred to as Afro-Brazilians or African descendants. Economist Roberto Borges Martins, a senior scholar in this field, observes that usage of this composite category in demographic and economic studies "has been consecrated by scholars and specialists in race relations ... the homogeneity observed, in several different thematic areas, in the indicators for these two groups reinforces the presumption of the adequacy of this aggregation. In the Census of 2000, these two broad classifications [whites and African descendants] comprehend 99,1% of the total population residing in Brazil (whites: 53,8% and blacks: 45,3%)."[5]

There is a strong tendency among African descendants to classify themselves as white or brown when interviewed by the census takers. Such a tendency results from the whitening ideal, which assigns higher social status to lighter skin color. As a consequence, official statistics have been notoriously distorted: the dark-skinned black group is undercounted, but the white and brown groups are considerably inflated.[6] While officially the sum of dark blacks and browns is 48.5 percent of the population, the estimates are as high as 70 to more than 80 percent when these distortions are taken into account. This official underestimation of the dark-skinned black population is a fact essential to the understanding of Brazilian racial statistical data.

In an effort to broadly measure the impact of public policies on people's quality of life, the United Nations carried out global research that resulted in the creation of the Human Development Index (HDI). This indicator brings together figures concerning education, life expectancy, median income, and access to social and material goods. In 1999, Brazil ranked seventy-ninth among the 174 countries studied.[7]

The racial dimension of inequality was revealed in a new expression by the work of economist Marcelo Paixão, who considered a hypothetical nation composed only of Brazil's black population and calculated that it would rank in the 108th place in HDI, a position twenty-nine places below Brazil and seven below South Africa. The white population taken alone as a hypothetical nation, however, would classify as forty-ninth, thirty places above Brazil and fifty-two above South Africa.[8]

The country is characterized by remarkable regional differences. Extreme poverty prevails in rural Brazil, while most of the country's considerable wealth is concentrated in a few large urban centers. The country is divided into six major geographical regions: the North, Northeast, Central, Central-West, Southeast, and South. Agrobusiness and urban industry are centered mainly in the richer South and Southeast. Poverty and hunger are particularly severe in the North and Northeast regions; seasonal droughts make this situation worse in the Northeast. Rural poverty induces migration to the urban centers, a trend that has progressively exacerbated inequality in the cities over many decades. At the same time, technology-intensive development of agricultural production has driven landless peasants out of the countryside, further increasing inequality in rural areas.

These inequalities correspond to the population's racial composition. The miserably poor rural populations, particularly in the Northern and Northeastern regions, have accentuated African-descendant majorities.[9] The rural backlands—*sertões*—are inhabited mostly by people of mixed African and indigenous descent, *caboclos*. They are such a large majority there that the word *caboclo* came to designate both the residents of those rural areas and their racial identity itself. The *sertanejo*, inhabitant of the *sertão*—the rural backlands—is almost by definition a *caboclo*. The Afro-Brazilian group, which comprises 48.5 percent of the general population, officially makes up 70 percent of the rural poor. In such regions, the practices of slavery and semi-slavery continue to reign unpunished. While the Afro-Brazilian population would rank 108th in HDI as a hypothetical nation, the black population in Maranhão, a major state in the Northern region, would rank 122nd, along with Botswana.[10]

For decades, the sorcery of color obscured the racial character of this regional inequality. The ideal of harmony among races so entranced social analysts that they attributed differences among color groups either to the so-called "social issue" (as opposed to the "race issue)" or to the historical legacy of slavery. Ultimately, they denied the significance of racial discrimination as a factor in creating those differences.

More recently however, the racial nature of inequality has been demonstrated progressively by quantitative research. Carlos Hasenbalg and Nelson do Valle Silva began a line of investigation demonstrating that racial discrimination, independent of other factors like education, contributes to the institution of inequalities.[11] Other studies have developed this theme further,[12] so that in 1998 Atila Roque and Sonia Corrêa observed that "two factors of disparity run across the different levels of reproduction of social inequality and have deep roots in Brazilian culture: gender and race."[13] Roberto Borges Martins was responsible for outstanding work in this field, in conjunction with his colleagues at the Institute of Applied Economic Research (IPEA).[14]

In Brazil, the gender distinction cannot be adequately understood without considering race. As a determinant of income, gender follows race. White women enjoy a privileged position in relation to black men, and Afro-Brazilian women are on the lowest rung of the income and employment ladder. White men earn over three times more than black women earn. Black women in turn earn less than half of what white women do.

In general, blacks earn about half, or less than half, of what whites earn.[15] Approximately 26 percent of blacks, as opposed to 16 percent of whites, earn less than minimum wage, while 1 percent of blacks, as opposed to 4 percent of whites, earn more than ten times that value. Educated African Brazilians earn less than whites with the same level of education, and in the higher income brackets the difference is more accentuated.[16]

The proportion of blacks living in poverty, earning less than R$38.00 (US$13.97) monthly, is twice as high as it is among whites. The inverse is also true: whites comprise higher income brackets at three to five times the rate of blacks.

TABLE 2: AVERAGE INCOME BY GENDER AND RACE IN MULTIPLES OF THE VALUE OF THE MONTHLY MINIMUM WAGE*

White men	6.3
White women	3.6
Black men	2.9
Black women	1.7

*Source: IBGE, 1994.

TABLE 3: AVERAGE MONTHLY INCOME BY GENDER AND COLOR IN REAIS (R$)

| COLOR | GENDER | | TOTAL |
	MALE	FEMALE	
White	757.51	459.20	630.38
Black	338.61	227.13	292.05
Brown	359.27	234.72	309.66
Total	589.89	370.33	498.57

Source: Brazilian Institute of Geography and Statistics (IBGE), Annual Household Sample Survey (PNAD), 1996.[17]

TABLE 4: PER CAPITA FAMILY INCOME BY RESPONDENTS' COLOR

PER CAPITA FAMILY INCOME	COLOR		
	WHITE	BLACK	BROWN
Up to 1/4 minimum wage	14.7	30.2	36.0
1/4 to 1/2	19.2	27.4	26.8
1/2 to 1	24.2	24.9	20.7
1 to 2	20.2	12.0	10.6
2 to 3	8.2	2.7	2.9
3 to 5	6.5	1.6	1.8
5 to 10	4.5	0.8	0.9
10 to 20	1.5	0.3	0.2
20 or more	0.3	0.1	0
Total	100%	100%	100%

Source: IBGE, PNAD 1988. Compiled by Nelson do Valle Silva / IUPERJ.

TABLE 5: RELATIVE INCIDENCE OF POVERTY* BY RESPONDENT'S COLOR AND THE GENDER OF THE HEAD OF HOUSEHOLD

GENDER OF HEAD OF HOUSEHOLD	COLOR		
	WHITE	BLACK	BROWN
Male	14.6	30.5	36.2
Female	15.4	28.9	34.9

* Per capita family income up to 1/4 the value of the monthly minimum wage

Source: IBGE, PNAD 1988. Compiled by Nelson do Valle Silva / IUPERJ.

The situation of Afro-Brazilian women embodies the feminization of poverty that marks the worldwide situation of the last few decades. As many as 80 percent of employed black women work in manual occupations; more than half that number are domestic servants or offer freelance domestic services (washing, ironing, cooking) for some of the worst pay in the Brazilian economy. Approximately one out of every four black female heads of households earns less than minimum wage.[18] These parameters have remained constant or worsened over time.[19] Unemployment rates are higher among blacks, a fact that suggests that Afro-Brazilian women suffer more than their share of the extraordinarily high unemployment rates among Brazilian women in general, as the following table shows.

Racial disparities in living conditions (sanitation, garbage collection, running water) are greater than can be accounted for by regional differences: in 2001, 23 percent of blacks, as opposed to 7 percent of whites, lived in areas with inadequate water supply; 48 percent of blacks, as opposed to 26 percent of whites, lived in areas with inadequate sewage facilities; and 7 percent of blacks,

TABLE 6: UNEMPLOYMENT RATES BY RACE, GENDER, AND REGION

	TOTAL	MEN	WOMEN	WHITES	BLACKS (PRETOS + PARDOS)
Brazil	6.9	5.7	8.8	6.6	7.7
Urban North**	7.7	6.0	10.2	6.8	8.2
Northeast	6.3	5.2	7.8	5.7	6.5
Southeast	7.7	6.2	9.8	7.4	8.7
South	5.4	4.5	6.6	5.1	8.1
Central-West	7.9	6.2	10.5	7.6	8.7

Source: IBGE, PNAD 1996.

* Population ten years of age and up, with or without income.

** Excluding the rural interior of Rondônia, Acre, Amazonas, Roraima, Pará, and Amapá.

as opposed to 2 percent of whites, lived in residences without electric energy.[20] While regional differences are great, in Brazil as a whole, according to data collected in 1997–1998, infant mortality among Afro-Brazilian children up to one year old was 82 percent higher than for white children: 53 deaths, as opposed to 29 per 1,000 live births.[21] In the United States, by comparison, in 1991 Asante and Mattson reported an infant mortality rate of 18 per 1,000 among African Americans in the United States, as opposed to 7 for the population as a whole.[22]

All these factors combine with others to make life expectancy shorter among blacks—66 years—than among whites—71 years—even when accounting for income and education.[23]

Among the poor, not only are black families disproportionately represented, but their per capita income is lower, which means that more people in the family must work in order to earn an equivalent family income. Children often leave their studies in order to complement their families' incomes by cutting sugar cane, working in agriculture or in mines, selling wares at traffic stops, or some similar activity. As a result, illiteracy rates among African Brazilians are more than twice as high as rates among whites, and the percentage of blacks with nine years of education or more is almost three times lower than among whites. An Afro-Brazilian child has about a 66 percent chance to obtain elementary education, while a white child has an 85 percent chance. Once out of elementary school, the chance of a black child continuing on to high school is about 40 percent, whereas the white child's chance is about 57 percent. African Brazilians who graduate from high school have about half the opportunity to go on to university as whites have.[24]

Together, these facts mean that the percentage of black men and women with eleven to sixteen years of schooling is about half that of white men and women. The percentage of whites with at least fifteen years of education is six times higher than that of blacks. Finally, differences in education levels are significantly higher between blacks and whites than between men and women in all regions.[25]

A very well defined and extremely rigid racial stratification tends to exclude African descendants from positions of power and prestige, keeping whites at the top of the hierarchy. In 1998, 110 years after slavery's abolition, there were

> no African Brazilians in the highest echelons of government, except during the [short] period when Pelé was Special Sports Minister. Of 594 Congressmen, 13 are African descendants. In the public universities, which are better quality and more prestigious in Brazil, "brown" professors are rare and dark black professors almost nonexistent. Among judges, there are almost no blacks, while today white women constitute the majority of newly admitted judges (*Jornal do Brasil*, 27.06.1999). In courts of appeals, there were no black judges until 1998, when Carlos Alberto Reis de Paulo was seated on the Labor Appeals Court.[26]

The sorcery of color, with its ideological pretense of antiracism, managed to obscure the reality of racial discrimination over a long period of time. One of its effects was to make statistical data unavailable by not including race and color differences in the collection of data. Today this is still a problem in the area of health services and information.[27] Only relatively recently, especially since the 1980s, have social scientists conducted research by using official statistical indicators, more fully demonstrating and documenting this discrimination. One early pioneering project was a set of studies sponsored by UNESCO during the 1950s, when such data were not available; outstanding among them were those carried out by sociologists Florestan Fernandes and Roger Bastide.[28] UNESCO's original objective in sponsoring this project was to elucidate what was perceived as the unique racial harmony of Latin American societies, with an eye to the possibility of formulating models for nonracist society. Brazil was chosen as the "laboratory" country, but the researchers' conclusions were unanimous in revealing a stark situation of racial stratification and prejudice.[29]

While such research played an auxiliary role in the later decades, during the twentieth century the black social movement was the one major agent responsible for whatever acknowledgment existed, inside and outside the country, of the existence of racism in Brazil. Fernandes and Bastide captured an early stage of this action and recorded the outcry of the black social movement. The movement's tireless efforts to denounce racism were truly quixotic, as it faced a mainstream society and a national popular consciousness imbued with the academic and intellectual tradition that cultivated the myth of racial democracy and the sorcery of color.

Later on, changes in methods and criteria furthered the utility of demographic research. Beginning in the 1970s, color categories, which had been discarded since the 1930s, were reintroduced into IBGE's statistics; in the 1990s, researchers began to adopt the inclusive criterion of quantitative analysis using the sum of the traditional dark black and brown categories. Both these developments were the result of pressure brought by the Afro-Brazilian social movement and by researchers sympathetic or linked to the movement.

A pioneer in English language work in the new approach to analysis of race relations in Brazil was Ghanaian political scientist Anani Dzidzienyo of Brown University, who broke away from the traditional discourse about appearance, "prejudice of mark" and the nonracial character of social discrimination in Brazil. Dzidzienyo showed that de facto racial discrimination brought about the same practical results as segregation based on the criterion of hypodescendancy, or the so-called one drop rule.[30] Another pioneering author was Thomas E. Skidmore, who documented the extent to which the whitening ideal permeated the articulation of public policy in Brazil in the formative years of the early republic.[31] The most recent advances have been linked to pressure brought by the social movement and also to the growing presence and activity of African-descendant researchers, although blacks are still extremely underrepresented in the Brazilian academy. The year 1995, Zumbi of Palmares's third centennial, was a watershed that marked a distinct and significant increase in the production and publication of works by Afro-Brazilian authors.[32]

Only at the threshold of the third millennium, then, did the antiracist movement's protests begin to bear fruit in the form of recognition of racial inequalities and the need for public policy to correct them. In particular, the research and publications of the Applied Economics Research Institute (IPEA) in the late 1990s and the first years of the new millennium, paved the way for broader acceptance of the principle of affirmative action and its implementation in certain federal government agencies, beginning with the Ministry of Agrarian Reform on the eve of the 2001 Durban World Conference Against Racism.[33]

Despite such progress, many elite intellectuals still contest the racial nature of inequality. Prominent writers and powerful media personalities have used their prestige to argue against affirmative action proposals and repeat the traditional discourse denying the existence of racism and citing multiple color categories as the major proof of this thesis.

GENOCIDE: HISTORICAL ROOTS OF INEQUALITY

During most of Brazil's history, African descendants formed the immense majority of the population. In 1872, the census recorded more than 6 million *pretos* and *pardos* compared with 3.8 million whites. The imminence of slavery's abolition caused veritable panic in the ruling elite, who rushed to design public policies erasing the "black stain" from the population and purifying the nation's racial stock.[34]

Raymundo Nina Rodrigues, a psychiatrist from Maranhão State whose name was inscribed in the title of Bahia's Institute of Forensic Medicine in 1906, is considered the founder of research on blacks in Brazil. He was perhaps the most prominent advocate of the inferiority of Africans, who were supposedly responsible for the degeneration that dictated the urgent need to "cleanse" the Brazilian race. His was a classic statement of the most rigorous precepts of racial determinism: "For Science this inferiority is nothing more than a phenomenon of perfectly natural order, [since] to this day negroes have not been able to make themselves into civilized peoples."[35] For this reason, he writes, "the negro race in Brazil ... will constitute forever one of the factors of our inferiority as a people."[36]

The then-prevailing scientific theory of race condemned racial mixing as a process that would lead inexorably to the degradation of the species. But the whitening of Brazil's black demographic mass was essential to the building of a state that could merit acceptance into the community of civilized nations. The solution was to create a new theory exalting race mixture by justifying it as a way to dilute the inferior African base of the Brazilian racial stock and strengthen the superior white component. The basic tenet of degeneration theory—which was African inferiority—stayed intact, but was construed to favor a particular public policy solution to the dilemma at hand. By encouraging racial mixing along with the mass immigration of Europeans, Brazil's leaders would gradually make whiteness prevail.[37] In 1911, the Brazilian delegate to the Universal Races Congress, held in London, announced that by the year 2012 this process would eliminate all vestiges of African descendants, both the black race and mixed bloods from the population.[38] In this way the goal of a totally white population could be reached, an objective expressed widely and eloquently in the literature of the time. It is not gratuitous that prominent writer Oliveira Vianna called this a process of Aryanization.[39] However, many skeptics who agreed with eugenic theory continued to believe that race mixture could lead to degeneracy.

Whitening policies had two cornerstones: mass European immigration— which was subsidized by the state and controlled by legislation that excluded the undesirable races—and the cultivation of the whitening ideal based on the subordination of women. White women served to maintain the "purity" of the genetic stock. Black women, whose sexual availability was compulsory as slaves, found their role as *mucama*—the enslaved concubine—perpetuated in domestic service after abolition.[40] In a society obsessed with the idea of "improving the race," the subordination and sexual availability of the *mucama* were then transferred from the maid to the *mulata*—the mulatto woman who evolved into a female mulatto samba dancer catering to the foreign and national tourist market. The *mulata* became "Brazil's most important export product."[41] Thus, contrary to the popular saying that mandates "marrying white to improve the race"—which implies the encouragement of interracial marriage—the norm for relationships that produced whitening was the concubinage of African descendants. Indeed, the driving principle of the whitening process is summed up in the proverb that the Brazilian man's dream is to "marry a white woman, get a black woman to do the work, and have a *mulata* to fornicate with."[42]

In its new role as a bearer of citizenship rights, the postabolition majority black population embodied a potential threat to the political power of the minority elite. The fear of this threat was expressed in the discourse of national unity. Enmeshed with the notions of pseudoscientific racism, this discourse considered Africanness and blackness extraneous to the national context.[43] Although Brazil had never existed without Africans, they were transformed into foreigners by a Eurocentric definition of national identity.

The majority of emancipated African Brazilians were progressively excluded from the labor market. Ironically, conventional histories record the lack of a qualified labor force for the new industrial sector as the reason for European immigration policy. But whether enslaved or free, blacks had operated each and every technological change in the Brazilian economy up to that moment. The real motive for the exclusion was to reserve jobs for the more desirable European immigrants, whose subsidized arrival was intended to contribute to the improvement, meaning the whitening, of Brazilian identity. Nina Rodrigues makes a classic statement demonstrating the justification for such a fact when he speaks of black people's "well-known incapacity for continued and regular physical work," a fact that "has its natural explanation in the compared physiology of the human races."[44] Given that Africans had worked continuously for four centuries to build Brazil, it seems the nation's spokesmen resorted to outright fantasy in their haste to justify the public policy.

Between 1890 and 1914, more than 1.5 million Europeans arrived in the state of São Paulo alone, 64 percent of whom had their fare paid by the state government.[45] Stigmatized not only as degenerate and unqualified but also as dangerous and disorderly, black men were excluded from the new industrial labor market. Many Afro-Brazilian women went to work for a pittance—when they received anything at all beyond housing and food—as cooks, nannies, and cleaners; others made their living as street vendors. But it was mostly black women who maintained the community. Afro-Brazilian religious communities such as Catholic brotherhoods or Candomblé houses—most of the latter under the leadership of women—made survival and human development possible in these conditions.

In 1933, Gilberto Freyre published his major work *Casa Grande e Senzala—The Masters and the Slaves*—in which he praised race mixture and proposed to substitute the biological paradigm of race for an ethnocultural or anthropological one. This substitution meant essentially that race mixture could be accepted as a link to whiteness rather than rejected as degeneracy, to the relief of a ruling class faced with such a large black population. Nina Rodrigues's caveat that this population would constitute forever a factor of the Brazilian people's inferiority could now be dismissed; but the goal of public policy remained improvement of the race—ultimately, the elimination of the black population. Freyre conjugated his celebration of miscegenation with a festive idea of parallel cultural mixture. Although it was based on explicitly racist principles and on sexual aggression toward black women, the miscegenation ideal was now set forth as the paradigmatic development of the Portuguese colonizers' generosity and lack of racial prejudice toward enslaved Africans. Freyre's theory of Luso-Tropicalism was based on the idea that the Portuguese were singularly nonracist in their colonial enterprise because they mated with black women, in spite of the fact that as a social phenomenon the act was actually rape.[46] Freyre himself described in detail the systemically violent coercion—which extended beyond rape itself—that was entailed in the process of miscegenation and sexual relations in the slave regime. Yet the premise of his theory was that such intimate relations between the races did not exist in other colonial systems and that the Portuguese were uniquely nonracist in this respect.

Freyre's theory allowed the Brazilian ruling class to celebrate and take pride in its penchant for miscegenation, which had earlier been a source of shame. This moral breakthrough soon intertwined with the ideological pretense of antiracism and welded into a denial of the existence of racial prejudice and discrimination in Brazilian society, forming the basis of the myth of racial democracy. The "fable of the three races" is underwritten by these theories and imprinted on the social imagination. It is the image of Africans, Native Americans, and Portuguese living happily together as they built the new nation and, through miscegenation, a new race of *morenos*—light-skinned mulattoes and mestizos. *Moreno* is a favored color identity in Brazil, but the term is so elastic and arbitrary as to be a common euphemism for blackness—used in place of the offensive term *negro*—as well as a popular designation of near-whiteness. Anthropologist Angela Gilliam compares this elasticity to attitudes in the United States about class. She notes that Benjamin DeMott identifies a situation in which both economic extremes are defined as middle class and as comprising the *imperial middle*, an all-encompassing ideological center. In Brazil, she observes, "there exists an analogous imperial *morenidade* [brown-ness], in which persons of many different physical appearances define themselves as *morenos*."[47]

Nevertheless, the notion of African inferiority remains the basis of the whitening ideal, which is the motor of miscegenation, and it has remained intact, if unexpressed, in the national consciousness. Also intact is the reality of de facto racial segregation and inequality. The ideology of white supremacy, silent in its operation, adaptable and flexible in its continuity, is always weaving new ways to perpetuate its domination.

Brazil was the last country to formally abolish slavery. No measure was taken to integrate the new African-descendant citizens into the national economy or society. Many stayed on plantations, in conditions of semislav-ery, or moved from the slave quarters to urban hills. Often such hills had for-mer roots as *kilombos*,[48] communities of Africans who refused enslavement. Like the maroon societies found in the United States, the Caribbean, and other South American countries—where they were called *cumbes*, *palen-ques*, and *cimarrones*—kilombos, found all over Brazil throughout its history, were more than the hideouts of runaway slaves. They were communities where Africans rebuilt and organized their lives in freedom, often according to African social, political, or economic norms and traditions, and who often negotiated treaties and engaged in commerce with colonial powers.[49] Thousands of them have survived to this day in Brazil, mostly in the rural regions, and as a result of Afro-Brazilian activism the 1988 Constitution pro-vides for the formalization of their land rights.[50]

In some cases urban kilombo communities located on hills became today's *favelas*; in others, such shantytowns have sprouted in peripheral urban areas receiving the influx of a black population excluded from the postaboli-tion economy's labor market. Economist Hélio Santos demonstrates that the nature of slavery's abolition in Brazil was the essential component determin-ing the circular nature of a chain of interconnected factors that caused and characterized the historical exclusion of African Brazilians.[51]

Beyond the vicious cycle of exclusion, Abdias Nascimento sees another characteristic of this historical process. He writes:

It was not the result of some romantic utopia to hope that those emerging from the servile regime would directly and easily find their place in post-abolition competitive society. Several public figures—including José Bonifácio and Joaquim Nabuco—brought to the attention of those who governed the country the need for effective support, concrete measures, to guarantee former slaves' effective integration into society. They were not heard, since those governing were either slave owners or their heirs and beneficiaries. And, in the apparent omission that followed, the governing classes put into action a conscious and strategic plan to liquidate blacks, exterminating them not only by leaving them to hunger and homelessness, but throughout our history creating a veritable system of veiled discrimination, all the more efficient because it dissimulated its true intentions and goals with respect to blacks. The bad faith, the guilty conscience of the fact that a crime was being committed against blacks—a genocide similar to the one practiced by the Nazis against Jews—can be found in several different moments in Brazilian life.[52]

This statement, in a nutshell, reveals the backdrop of stark racial inequalities that negatively affect African descendants in Brazil today.

WHITE SUPREMACY IN BED WITH RACIAL DEMOCRACY

In Brazil and in all of so-called Latin America, the culture of whitening—in Spanish, *blanqueamiento* or *mestizaje*—was based on the premise of black inferiority, the glorification of racial mixing, and the subordination of women in various ways depending on their race. Whitening proposals go back to the founding of the colonies and were underwritten by humanists and abolitionists in many parts of Central and South America and the Caribbean. The Catholic humanist tradition is well represented in the writings of Friar Alonso de Sandoval, who in 1627 was already advocating whitening as a solution to eliminate the "black stain."[53] José Antonio Saco, the eminent nineteenth century Cuban historian, exclaimed: "We have no other choice but to whiten, to whiten, to whiten, and so make ourselves respectable."[54]

In the entire region, the theory of whitening spilled over into the conviction that the Iberian elites had created a cordial and harmonious form of race relations based on miscegenation. Two corollaries were intimately associated with this notion. The first is that African enslavement in the region was a benign or benevolent institution, "ordinarily a mild form of servitude."[55] The second is that the absence of legislated racial segregation, along with the constitutional guarantee of equality before the law, was enough to characterize these societies as nonracist.

Contrary to the common supposition that the anthropological paradigm of ethnicity had introduced a widespread antiracist ideal in these societies, white supremacy remained in force, but with new trappings. The ideal of whiteness was ever present, although sometimes camouflaged, in the praise of racial mixing and the pretentiously antiracist discourse embracing the cultural criterion of ethnicity, which was held up as a guarantee against the existence of racism. The whiteness ideal was largely visible in society's triumphant transformation of light-skinned mulattoes and mestizos—*moreno* is the favorite term in Brazil—into virtual whites.

Indeed, the history of Brazil and its neighbors is in great part a chronicle of the violent imposition of a European identity on populations that were composed mostly of indigenous and African people. The Iberian takeover of the subcontinent, billed as the "discovery" of lands that had been inhabited for millennia, unleashed against their populations a process of genocide from which emerged an America that is Latin to the extent that a numerical minority, its ruling elites, has been successful in suppressing the identity of the indigenous and African-descendant peoples. The whitening policy was the cornerstone of this enterprise, but the "whites" it fabricated are generally acculturated blacks, Native Americans, or *caboclos*—those with mixed African and Native American heritage.

A Latin or Iberian identity is applied routinely to mixed—*moreno*—populations. This habit is traditionally as commonplace among leftist elite intellectuals as it is among conservatives. Darcy Ribeiro embodies an outstanding example of the contrast in many leftist intellectuals between their reactionary discourse on Latin racial mixing and their progressive political activity in other spheres. Although he fought against social injustice and authoritarianism,[56] his writings on the race issue reproduce the most authoritarian standards of patriarchy and the ideology of whiteness. He refers to the "majority mixed population" of the region, "whose ideal of inter-racial relations is fusion" in the sense of the "whitening" and "homogenization" of the population. In the same line of thought, the major Cuban intellectual, José Martí, identified "our America" with its "autochthonous mestizo" race, Nicolas Guillén praised "Cuban color" in his *Mulatto Poems*, and Mexican intellectual José Vasconcelos coined the term "cosmic race" in yet another eulogy of miscegenation. The sorcery of color, in the end, transforms black, Native American, and mixed race—*moreno*—populations into "Latin" or "Iberian" ones in a simulation of whiteness, the best expression of which is perhaps Darcy Ribeiro's conclusion that "we are the new Rome." He writes: "We are the largest Latin mass. The

French went around jerking off, the Italians drank Chianti, and the Romanians were afraid of the Russians; it was the Spanish and Portuguese who went out in the world fucking and we made a mass of people who number 500 million."[57]

This idea of the "New Rome" ultimately expresses the paradigm of empire. As Léon Poliakov and Muniz Sodré demonstrate in rich detail, this paradigm is the highest expression of European identity as white supremacy, with the Nazi dream of Aryan rule being only one expression of this phenomenon.[58] Building a Latin identity for all the different variations of race mixture—morenos—puts in practice the ideal of virtual whiteness: individuals of mixed race may enjoy a "white" identity by virtue of being Latin, and Latin people can populate an empire of millions. To restore Rome is to renew the Aryan myth.

Darcy Ribeiro's vulgar language does not fail to reflect a relevant dimension of such ideology—a hypersexual, patriarchal one—rephrasing the popular saying about the Brazilian man's desire for a white, a black, and a mulatto woman to perform distinct functions. Indeed, as Helena Bocayuva Cunha points out, Freyre's 1933 work establishes the standard of "sexual excess" as a factor crucial to the formation of the Brazilian racial ethos that has characterized national identity.[59]

Such hypersexualization of racial mixing is grounded in the biological and genetic discourse on race, but is also planted firmly and without contradiction within the anthropological criterion of culture that has substituted race with ethnicity. After all, the theory of Luso-Tropicalism was built around the idea that the Portuguese colonizer had a "natural propensity" for miscegenation involving the outlets that the slave regime offered for his sexual prowess. Anthropologist Angela Gilliam has referred to it simply as "the Great Sperm Theory of National Formation."[60] It metaphorically violates black women again in retrospect, as if the historical rape it documented were not enough, by crediting the formation of Brazilian national culture—and of the mulata herself—to Portuguese men and their predilection for black women. In this way Freyre's legacy obscures or implicitly denies black women's role as agents of the transmission of culture in Brazilian colonial society—as anthropologist Lélia González points out, they were mothers to white children, teaching them speech, culture, and customs, and in the process they transformed the Portuguese language in Brazil.[61]

In the context of such discourse, to construct the new criterion of ethnicity meant to transpose biologically based racial mixing directly onto the cultural plane. Arthur Ramos observed that: "If, in Nina Rodrigues's works, we substitute, for example, the term 'race' for 'culture,' and 'miscegenation' for 'acculturation,' his ideas and concepts come completely up to date."[62] Freyre himself put it this way: "Only ... the Portuguese and the Spaniards seem to be able to develop relations not only reciprocal but also of amply cultural and freely biological interpenetration, free from the Anglo-Saxon dread of 'mongrelization.'"[63] Thus, the anthropological criterion is so fully identified with the biological one as to indicate that not only mulattoes and *morenos*, but also culture, are made in bed.

The cultural criterion, permeated with patriarchy, is stated in classic terms by Darcy Ribeiro when he affirms that "we Brazilians" are "a mixed race people in flesh and spirit, since here race mixture was never a crime or sin." This mixed-race people "is defined as a new ethnic-national identity, that of Brazilians," which is "in fact, a new Romanness."[64] This identity is nothing more, nothing less than virtual whiteness, worthy of the Aryan myth. Indeed, Oliveira Vianna observed that

> Aryanized mixed bloods ... have signed up bravely as whites, disguised in the euphemistic garb of "morenos." Only characteristically dark *pardos* and *caboclos* really are placed in the *mestizo* class; even so, this is when they are part of the teeming hordes of plebian countrymen who pull the hoe or do servile work; because, if it happens they are "colonels" or "doctors"—which is not rare—there is no considering them "mulattoes" or "caboclos": they are none other than "morenos."[65]

In Brazil, this Romanesque whiteness is viscerally linked to the fable of the three races and is expressed in constructions like "metarace," "syncretism," and Luso-Tropicalism itself, all summed up in what Angela Gilliam has called "imperial *morenidade* [brunetteness]."[66] The ideal of imperial *morenidade* is a logical consequence of this mixture of the cultural realm with the sexual/genetic one, which creates a culturalization of race that is accompanied by a racialization of culture, both of them founded on the idea of biological race disguised as ethnicity.[67] This composite permeates Iberian American intellectual discourse, the pretension of which is an antiracist culturalism that simply is not sustainable.

Allegations that miscegenation took place in interracial marriage or as a result of cordial relations between the races are historically unfounded, but they continue to exercise enormous impact on the Latin and Brazilian popular consciousness. One example is interesting for its irony in the face of historical fact. Brazilian diplomat José Sette Camara made the following statement before an audience of predominantly African diplomats at a time when the international authorities were evaluating the abundant evidence of racist atrocities committed by the Portuguese in their African colonies that were fighting for independence: "Portuguese colonialism is different. The absence of racial discrimination, the ease of miscegenation, the willingness of colonizing whites to stay, grow, and prosper with their new lands, exist in the African colonies as they did in Brazil. Africans themselves recognize all these positive peculiarities of Portuguese colonization."[68]

In Brazil, such discourse seeped into the national personality in the form of an implicit, unspoken consensus on norms, values, and ends, which is stated in underlying meaning and language interpretation. Thus, the Latin flavor of sexism emerges in the rosy version of miscegenation presented by French ethnologist and photographer Pierre Verger to a largely African audience at the University of Ife, Nigeria. Verger described how the white sons of plantation owners "would have their sexual initiation with the colored girls who worked in the big house or the fields, thereby infusing elements of sensual attraction and mutual understanding into relations between what one has chosen to call persons of different races."[69]

Miscegenation as the fruit of the sexual abuse of subjugated females reveals little about mutual understanding among human beings, but does speak eloquently of male colonizers' violent control over women. The genius of the Brazilian ideology was to make this violence the core of a self-serving discourse in which the white elite purges itself of any responsibility or guilt in the violence inherent to racism and patriarchy. Freyre, the master of such discourse, left pearls, like the following, to shine against the background of inequality and the subordination of women in Brazil:

> The cross-breeding so widely practiced here corrected the social distance that otherwise would have remained immense between the big house and the slave quarters. What the slave-owning plantation monoculture produced in terms of aristocratization, dividing Brazilian society into classes of masters and slaves, ... was in great part neutralized by the social effect of miscegenation. Native Brazilian and African women, at first, then mulatto women, then lighter-skinned ones, the octoroons and so forth, by becoming domestic servants, concubines, and even legitimate spouses of the white master, had a powerful impact in the direction of Brazil's social democratization.[70]

Lourdes Martínez-Echazábal observes that it is not surprising to find a son of the Northeastern sugar oligarchy such as Freyre writing a Proustian apology for miscegenation in 1936, but that it is certainly depressing to find a progressive intellectual like Darcy Ribeiro, overcome by his Latin machismo, declaring in 1995 that "miscegenation here was never a crime or a sin." At a time when many are making efforts to deconstruct narratives that legitimized the patriarchal order, Martínez-Echazábal writes, "By ignoring the means of extreme violence and sadism with which, at times, the 'masters' submitted women of 'inferior races,' Darcy Ribeiro not only makes all Brazilians accomplices to a collective crime but also places himself in the counter-stream of contemporary criticism."[71]

The sexualization of Brazilian mulatto women is part of the context of patrimonialism, a social form of power relations dating from the fourteenth century in Portugal that was expounded and instituted by Infante Dom Pedro (1392–1449) in his *Book of the Virtuous Favor*.[72] The volume is the eulogy of a system in which the prince, all-powerful and benevolent, selectively bestows favors upon his subjects in return for their permanent loyalty and submission, including payment of tribute. Functionaries and bureaucrats compete for the privilege of receiving favors, while the toiling masses labor to maintain the pleasures and privileges of the sovereign and the aristocrats. According to Muniz Sodré, such a form of power relations prevails to this day in Brazil.[73] The mulatto woman's compulsory sexual availability can be seen as part of this tradition, since women's subordination guarantees to the "prince" his prerogatives of possession, privilege, and pleasure over her. It is also part of the erotization of inequalities noted by Marianne Hester in her study of patriarchal domination.[74] Perhaps singular to Brazil, the role of the mulatto woman became a card-carrying profession and she herself was explicitly considered an export product at the end of the twentieth century, making Brazil a unique actor in the current international trade of trafficking in women, adolescents, and children.[75]

The sexualization of female mulattoes—*morenas*—has roots in the racist theories of Nina Rodrigues and his followers, whose notions of degeneracy were not limited to the individual's organic constitution, but reached definitively into the sphere of morality. Nina Rodrigues describes the "depraved influence of this singularly Brazilian type, the mulatto woman, in the malleability of our moral character" and observes that "the sensuality of negroes may reach the limits of morbid sexual perversion. The genetic excitation of the classic Brazilian mulatto woman cannot but be considered an abnormal type."[76] Such a stereotype is exalted and celebrated by the "genetic sociology" of Freyre's culturalism. In other words, white supremacy goes to bed with racial democracy. Their offspring is the hegemonic *moreno* of virtual whiteness.

JECA TATU AND THE DE-AFRICANIZATION
OF THE "BRAZILIAN PEOPLE"

Miscegenation as a whitening process implies the de-Africanization of color. Freyre made it clear that the recognition of African cultural values would occur "without ever implying repudiation of the predominance of European cultural values in Brazilian development."[77] Africanness is traditionally seen as "exotic" in the sense of being foreign, anti-Brazilian, and exogenous in the national social context.[78] As ethnologist Édison Carneiro observed, "the opus of what we call 'the civilization of Brazil' was precisely the destruction of black and indigenous peoples' particular cultures."[79] While the indigenous peoples of Brazil were portrayed as noble savages representing the natural purity of the land, black people were considered non-Brazilian and their culture foreign. They were viewed as a problem. Indeed, this theme was considered a research topic in the social sciences; many essays were written on "the black problem," which had been stated simply by Nina Rodrigues when he wrote that blacks would stand forever as one of the factors of the Brazilian people's inferiority.[80] In his classic essay on the black as a subject or theme of research, Guerreiro Ramos cites the outstanding authors in Brazilian sociology and anthropology and notes how "all of them, however, see the black as something strange, exotic, problematic, as non-Brazil."[81] At the First and Second Afro-Brazilian Congresses, for example, papers were presented on the following topics: "Customs and Practices of Negroes," "blood types of the Negro race," "Mental Disease among Negroes in Permambuco," "The Negro and his Culture in Brazil," "Negro Cultures, Problems of Acculturation in Brazil."[82]

Contrary to the traditional notion that cultural syncretism prevailed in Brazil, the predominant tendency was to carefully extirpate Africanness from national identity. One way this was accomplished was through repression of religious houses of worship, which until 1974 were obliged to register with the police. They were frequently victimized by violent police raids, and the Police Museums of Rio de Janeiro and Salvador, Bahia, housed until very recently the confiscated objects used in Afro-Brazilian religious worship as evidence of the abnormality of black people and their culture.[83] In some very specific instances, such as music, cooking, folklore, and sports, the African or Afro-Brazilian tradition is recognized and celebrated, but it is defined and appropriated by those outside Africanness and is exhibited as proof of racial harmony and tolerance. Vaguely considered throughout the Latin region as a threat to national unity, reference to Africanness is often avoided as a question of civic loyalty. We frequently witness protests that someone is *not* black or of African descent, but is rather Brazilian, Cuban, Mexican, or Dominican. Thus, the simulation of whiteness remains the basic reference of Latin identity, which is generally overtaken by acute Afrophobia.

Anticipating the clash between racist and culturalist theories, the beginning of the twentieth century witnessed the birth of the sanitarist movement, a series of public health campaigns that mobilized the medical profession and moved its focus from the defects inherent in race to those resulting from sickness and inferior hygienic conditions, especially rural endemic diseases.[84] Now it could be seen that the backwardness or alleged inferiority of the Brazilian people was due not to congenital deformity but to disease. Thus, the sanitarists helped elevate Brazilian self-esteem and mend the national identity. Belisário Penna, for instance, described Brazil's population as suffering from a "state of latency." It was bestialized from the time of the Proclamation of the Republic, and "the bestialization remained, aggravated daily by miserable poverty, generalized disease, and the uncontrollable alcoholism of the ignorant masses."[85]

An episode symbolic of this clash involved the story character Jeca Tatu, who embodied the image of the *caipira*—the humble country farmer. His creator was writer José Bento Monteiro Lobato, a prominent author of children's literature who was a proponent of nationalism and defender of the consolidation of Brazilian industrial development. Monteiro Lobato opposed the idyllic image of the countryside promoted by a romantic literature that exalted the exuberance of nature and the innate vigor and generosity of Indians and frontiersmen.[86] This image of the countryside as the home of robust and healthy men prevailed in the literature emerging from the centers of intellectual production of the nineteenth century, as well as in the creative works of writers like José de Alencar, Bernardo Guimarães, and Franklin Távora.[87]

The singular mark of this eulogy of the countryside is the process of de-Africanization that accompanied and characterized it. The image of the "noble savage" is attributed to Native Brazilians, while the "frontiersmen" mentioned above are Portuguese *bandeirantes*.[88] The *sertanejo* (inhabitant of the rural backlands who is a *caboclo*—of mixed African-indigenous descent) is depicted as something akin to a *virtual Indian*. The Brazilian identity ideal portrayed in this romantic literature, with its idyllic image of the countryside, did not entail the encounter of the three races. In contrast to the demographic reality of the time, which was the overwhelming presence of Africans and their descendants, what characterizes this literature is the almost absolute exclusion of black people.[89]

Monteiro Lobato embarks on the civic task of belying this idyllic image of the countryside. In the major daily *O Estado de São Paulo*, in 1914, he published two articles in which he presents the *caboclo*—African-indigenous denizen of the rural backlands—as a major national plague: "woeful parasite of the earth … barren man, unadaptable to civilization."[90] Jeca Tatu is the character he created in contrast to the romantic image of the rural hero in Indianist literature. Monteiro Lobato's expression is significant: "Poor Jeca. How handsome you are in novels and how ugly you are in reality."[91] This is not the noble and generous Indian, but a *caboclo* of "ugly" appearance. The intimate association of "ugly" with African origin and appearance is abundantly documented in the literature on racism and racial prejudice in Brazil.[92]

The sanitarist campaign would come to convince Monteiro Lobato that his judgment of Jeca Tatu was mistaken. Instead of congenitally inferior creatures condemned to stagnation, the people of the interior were victims of abandonment to disease and poverty. In 1918, Monteiro Lobato made peace with Jeca, redeeming him. Monteiro Lobato returned to *O Estado de São Paulo* and published a series of articles in which Jeca emerges not as lazy and indolent by birth but as a worker who has taken ill: "Jeca wasn't born this way—he just needs help!" Treated and cured, Jeca becomes a farmer, and then a prosperous rural entrepreneur, modernizing his property and surpassing his Italian neighbor by introducing new technologies.

Jeca reappears in children's magazines and books as a main player in the public health campaigns. By this time, though, Jeca Tatu is no longer a dark-skinned *caboclo* or a black ex-slave. In the illustration for the book *Ideas of Jeca Tatu*, he is portrayed as a healthy white farmer with "good hair."[93]

Although the sanitarist campaign counterposed the disease thesis to that of racial determinism, the African genetic stock in the national population was still not valued. The reconciliation with Jeca Tatu and his redemption as a straight-haired white farmer left the stigma against Africans and their descendants entirely intact, and to this day the *sertanejo*—dark-skinned *caboclo*, inhabitant of the rural backlands—is not considered black. Similarly, in flagrant disregard of ethnic reality, the term *nordestino*—"Northeasterner"—does not indicate blackness. One might say that Northeasterners have exercised a sense of authorship and constructed their identity as nonblack. This tendency results from the anti-African racism that reigns in the region—a brand of inferiority complex that was the pathology of Brazilian whites identified by Guerreiro Ramos;[94] I have called it the search for virtual whiteness. Walter Salles's 1998 film *Central Station*, which was nominated for the Academy Award for best foreign language film in 1999, illustrates the racial-ethnic reality of the region. It tells the story of a boy's return to his home in the Northeast. Filmed in loco, it shows the Africanness of the huge majority of Northeastern pilgrims and market hawkers, whose blackness is generally "forgotten" in the national imagination about Northeasterners and about *sertanejos*—dark-skinned inhabitants of the rural backlands—in general.

Himself from Bahia, sociologist Guerreiro Ramos focuses on this pathology when he questions the region's "well-born" elite, whose pretension to whiteness is characterized by an anxiety bordering on obsession. The members of the "white" minority in the North and Northeast, he demonstrates, "are very sensitive to anyone who tries to question their 'whiteness'":

> Bahia, the State of the Union with the largest contingent of colored people, has an Institute of Genealogy. One hardly need mention that the Institute specializes in discovering the white origins of members of the "light" minority. This paranoic trait ... characterizes the behavior of Brazilian "whites" in general, but especially of "whites" in the States that make up the North and Northeastern regions.[95]

The research of sociologist René Ribeiro also showed that family "pedigree" is a major factor of prestige in the North and Northeast.[96] But the demographic reality is such that whiteness retains its strong appeal, but remains unattainable. The solution to the problem of making the ideal of whiteness viable is to transform it into a goal whose achievement is possible: the de-Africanized mestizo. Thus, in his essay Guerreiro Ramos italicizes the word white "because our *white* person is, from the anthropological point of view, a *mestizo*, since among us only a tiny minority of *whites* do not have black blood."[97]

The sorcery of color thus operates an identity transformation in which the mestizo—more popularly the *moreno*—comes to be considered *almost* equivalent to the white person. Yet the limits of the near equivalence are inscribed in a more or less narrow social margin in which rejection of whiteness looms threateningly, leaving the mestizo never completely secure in the enjoyment of social privilege. Examples of this fact abound in research on race relations. René Ribeiro records such a case when he interviews a Catholic intellectual in Pernambuco. The Catholic describes himself as someone who, "educated into the doctrine of the Church, does not, could not, and should not have racial prejudice." But the interviewee speaks not as a Catholic intellectual, but as a "man, a grandson of sugarcane plantation owners":

> I never felt any violent reaction against a colored man riding with me on the same transport, sitting at the same table or in the same movie theater, etc. What irritates me is psychological mulattoism ... it's the mulatto

wanting to take the place of whites, dressing like them, trying to marry white women, going out in their own cars. It's mulattoes who think they can think, trying to act like people. Then my reaction is strong. I have an invincible antipathy for this kind of mulattoism.[98]

Another interviewee states "I don't like blacks who try to be white, I detest mulattoes who talk fancy. I have always thought that black people are mentally and morally inferior. Mulattoes are even worse. They have all the defects of blacks and none of their virtues. Sexually, though, I think that a tipsy and well-washed little black girl is better than many a French lady."[99]

Always potentially at the mercy of judgments like these, the light-skinned mulatto or mestizo—the *moreno*—has no way of knowing when a similar reaction will emerge from someone who holds decision-making power over aspects of his or her life. This uncertainty becomes a permanent social dilemma for African descendants, who may even be the target of discrimination within their own families for countering the general aspiration to whiteness. In the labor market, uncertainty is total when facing the subjective preferences of a hiring employer, who might well be a "Catholic intellectual who entertains no prejudice" but who feels "an invincible antipathy" against the idea of mulattoes exercising positions of leadership, directorship, or superior station. "In this country," the Catholic intellectual goes on to say, "there are still enough whites to govern and give orders. I think that blacks and mulattoes cannot and should not govern or command white people."[100] It is not surprising, then, when René Ribeiro writes, "Capping his racial opinions, one informant, who was obviously an Indian mestizo, which he confirmed by saying his great grandmother had been 'hunted down by dogs,' told us that if any blacks appeared in his family genealogy he would kill them historically."[101]

The ideal of whiteness tactically retreats and contents itself with an anti-African mindset. Thus, the Northeastern elites, who pride themselves on being virtually white mestizos—*morenos*—reject blackness to compensate for the fact that they cannot attain the ideal of purebred white ancestry. Indeed, many Brazilian intellectuals who are proponents of miscegenation may be so vociferously averse to the one drop rule of racial identity because under it, they all would be considered black. Such sentiments are the essence of the pathology observed by Guerreiro Ramos, who writes, "they use whatever resources they can to camouflage their racial origins."[102]

One of Guerreiro Ramos's greatest innovations was to identify in the scientific posture of certain Northeastern social scientists "one of these processes of ethnic disguise: the thematization of blacks." He writes that by taking blacks as an object of study, such social scientists separated themselves from blackness, "approaching their aesthetic archetype—which is European" and reinforcing their own identities as virtual whites.[103] In this way, "the studies in question that call themselves sociological or anthropological are nothing more than illustrated documents of the ideology of whiteness or lightness." Guerreiro Ramos speculates that such a fact is the reason that the researchers are mostly intellectuals from the North and Northeast regions of the country. To this posture, the present sociologist responds with his proposal of a new epistemological outlook—'Niger Sum.'"[104]

The innovation of the intellectuals of the Black Experimental Theater (TEN) was their commitment to reverse the process of de-Africanization by recovering and placing value on black Brazilian identity with the African matrix. It would be mistaken, then, to suppose that an "abrupt" break occurred between the supposedly universalist or integrationist position of TEN's generation of black activists and a movement in the 1970s that claimed a "racialist" identification as blacks with African roots.[105] On the contrary, we can observe remarkable continuity and coherence between the two generations in a move toward African identity that in no way can be characterized as racialist.

With respect to the sociological analysis of race, what distinguishes Guerreiro Ramos from his colleagues is his identification of African descendants not as a minority population in a nation of whites, but as the *people* of Brazil.[106] In this way, he prepares the path for an important advance of the post-1970 Afro-Brazilian movement. If African descendants are the people of Brazil, then the race issue can no longer be characterized as a "black problem" but becomes a national issue of citizenship and human rights.

"IT'S IN THE BLOOD": THE LIVING LEGACY OF RACIAL DETERMINISM

There is a broad consensus that, since the publication of Gilberto Freyre's works in the 1930s, the Brazilian social fabric and national personality has incorporated not only antiracism but also a positive valuation that has elevated the image and acceptance of African descendants and their culture. Antonio Sérgio Alfredo Guimarães expresses this consensus neatly when he states that "Brazilian modernity ... found a common national destiny in overcoming racialism and valuing the cultural heritage in use by Brazilian blacks, mulattoes, and caboclos."[107] The idea of overcoming racialism reflects the common sense that Brazilian society's repudiation of racial determinism is an inextricable part of the national social fabric.

In Brazil, the ideal of "antiracialism" is not incompatible with the reproduction of racial inequality. Guimarães explains this apparent paradox by referencing the distinction between racism and racialism. He states that antiracialism consists only in demoralizing and combating the belief in the biological concept of race, while an antiracist program would go beyond this, fighting racial inequalities and mechanisms of discrimination. For Guimarães, the Brazilian national ideal reduced its program of action and ideology only to the first dimension, practicing an antiracialism announced as antiracism. This confusion of the two ideas prevails not only in Brazil but in other countries as well and has the effect of obscuring the reality of racism in its concrete social operation.

However, the distinction between racism and racialism is not sustainable, since the social effects of racism are linked viscerally to the ideology of white supremacy, which is broader than—and inclusive of—the biological criterion. An antiracist program geared toward overcoming statistically measurable inequalities without taking into account the broader impact of white supremacy—which includes the living legacy of racial determinism—would be equally destined to fail.

The idea of repudiating racialism or racial determinism is almost always accompanied by the affirmation of a substantive difference between race relations based on the color criterion and those founded on the criterion of hypodescendency. In Brazil, the belief in such a difference is strong and dear to both social scientists and the majority of the population. Psychologist Edith Piza writes:

> I would like to alert the reader to the fact that everything said here with respect to classification, nomination, and attribution of color in Brazil passes without appeal through the filter that Oracy Nogueira called the "appearance rule," as opposed to the "rule of origin" that prevails mainly in the United States of America. In the appearance rule, color is a social determinant that carries no connotation of ethnic-racial origin in the context of inter-subjective relations.[108]

Those who are part of such consensus agree that, since color does not denote origin, no social criterion of race defines people's opportunities in life, whether in the labor market, in terms of social prestige, or in terms of power.

In the Brazilian social sciences, vast reserves of energy have been, and still are, dedicated to the hypothesis that there exists an essential difference between the rejection of African appearance and the rejection of African origin. Researchers have stated that by disassociating the African phenotype from African ancestry, Latin people developed a more benign form of prejudice of a nonracial nature. The preference for whiteness and for lighter colored appearance is then supposedly purely aesthetic and devoid of any racial connection, that is, devoid of any reference to ancestry or origin. Guimarães offers a succinct expression of this conclusion:

> For Brazilians, "race" came to mean "determination," "will," or "character," but almost never "subdivisions of the human species" These came to be designated only by a person's color: white, brown, black, and so forth. Colors that came to be considered objective concrete realities, unquestionable and *without moral or intellectual connotations*, which — when existent—were rejected as "prejudice."[109]

The testimony of Afro-Brazilian voices indicates that their experience of Brazilian social reality differs significantly from such an evaluation.[110] In their experience, the antiracialist ideal is less a social reality than a self-serving and self-congratulatory pretension on the part of the minority elite, built up as an integral part of the ideology of "racial democracy" that has obscured, reinforced, and contributed to the mechanisms of exclusion. Moreover, it is certain that strong moral and intellectual connotations inform color categories. Such perceptions are engrained in the Brazilian conscience to such an extent that they are hardly perceived at all. The negative implications of blackness seem so natural that they are silently implicit. The presumption of national antiracism has been used as a tool to muffle the voice of Afro-Brazilian protest and to reinforce the whitening ideal. After all, why listen to black protest if white society is already committed to an antiracist ideal? Why should African Brazilians articulate their own values and perspectives if the prevailing intellectual milieu already incorporates them? The presumption of antiracism is deeply entrenched in the national self-image, but it is also closely accompanied by an equally entrenched, long-standing current of racist ideas, a fact that Guimarães himself articulates when he speaks of "the persistent and surreptitious use of the erroneous notion of biological race, which sustains discrimination practices and whose main mark and metaphor is color."[111]

The weight of biologically based, traditional racism is visible in daily life in black subordination and stereotype in schools, the workplace, social relations, and cases of police repression. In daily experience, racist principles founded on the biological notion of race are perfectly compatible with the ideology of racial democracy, which blames African descendants themselves for race-based inequalities.

The popular consciousness retains notions of the subdivision of humans into color categories that are anything but neutral in social practice. Moral and intellectual connotations are intimately associated with these categories and have been so consistently over time. Writing in the nineteenth century, Sylvio Romero refers to the "component that came to us from Africa enslaved, and which contributed so much to our material progress and to our moral degradation."[112] Confirming the continuance of such attitudes, psychologist Edith Piza records at length the moral connotations associated with blackness by white women she interviewed a century later.[113]

It seems that, rather than building an antiracialist ideal, the great feat of Brazilian racial ideology was to repress the notions of racial determinism. Racism based on those notions continued operating by means of color categories without making itself explicit. In the same way as white ethnicity, racial determinism reigns silently and invisibly as an unnamed and implicit force. It is the glass door described by Piza when she spoke of whiteness as ethnicity: a door that is transparent and seems not to be there, but effectively shuts out those on the other side. Its transparency in no way reduces its solidity as a barrier.[114]

Many of those who espouse the theory that color categories in Brazil have no moral or intellectual connotations allege, to support that theory, that miscegenation was made a national ideal along with antiracialism. Indeed, the two ideals are often treated as if they were one and the same. An eminent example was when Guilherme Figueiredo, former Minister of Education and Culture, spoke at a seminar on apartheid held in Kitwe-Lusaka in 1967 about Brazil's "antiracist formation, its miscegenation," which he contrasted with the United States, where blacks are "almost without mixture, almost always pure."[115]

Indeed, miscegenation was raised to the level of a national ideal, but this was done not as an antiracist proposal opposing biological determinism but as a tool of social engineering grounded firmly in the racist idea of African inferiority. Moreover, the preference for whiteness and the principles and social engineering of eugenics that allowed it to prevail were formally inscribed in the 1934 Constitution[116] and in immigration legislation. Promulgated in September 1945, Law-Decree 7967 maintained the criterion that had regulated the entrance of foreigners into the country since the nineteenth century: "The need to preserve and develop, in the ethnic composition of the population, the more desirable characteristics of its European ancestry."[117]

To this day in Brazil, the popular conscience expresses racist ideas of biological inferiority in many ways, one of them being a perennial concern with what is "in the blood." Such a concern is evidently reminiscent of state-promoted efforts in the direction of whitening that have been in force since the end of the nineteenth century. It was, after all, the massive infusion of the "robust, energetic, and healthy Caucasian blood"[118] that was supposed to improve the nation's inferior racial lineage.

In my own first experience of Brazil—which took place when I was an adolescent in a high school exchange program—it was explained to me that there was no discrimination against blacks in the country. I asked why the rich young members of the São Paulo Yacht Club were almost all blonde, blue-eyed second-generation Europeans, while the urban beggars and rural peons who lived in semislavery on the farm I had visited were almost exclusively black. The response was unforgettable: "There's nothing to be done about that; it's in the blood."

Twenty-five years later, after I had lived for some years in Rio de Janeiro, I was redoing my apartment and needed some qualified plumbing services. The specialist I found was a Scandinavian type, blonde and blue-eyed. Admiring the quality of the work in progress, he spoke to the contractor, a Portuguese gentleman, and threw a glance of complicity in the direction of the white homemaker, me: "Of course. Without European blood in the veins, you don't get quality work."

Stereotypes concerning the indolence, intellectual backwardness, and criminal tendencies of African descendants populate the social imagination in the form of the idea that such characteristics lurk in the blood of these populations, just as a special talent and vocation for rhythm, samba, and football are said to "flow in their veins." These beliefs unmistakably reflect the biological criterion of racism, which is alive and active, though repressed and unstated.

The idea of "cleansing the race" has held enormous weight as a kind of call to civic and social responsibility for young black women. This fact emerged clearly in a series of interviews I conducted with black women, most of whom were educators, in Rio de Janeiro in 1999. Though it perhaps is not as prevalent today, black women are still expected to take care to have a "clean womb," meaning lighter-skinned progeny.

Nina Rodrigues's research on the *Abnormal Collectivities*[119] and his theory of the criminal nonimputability of the "inferior races"[120] had their roots in the most rigorous Brazilian scientific tradition. His work inaugurated the method in criminal anthropology, the efficacious use of which won Rio de Janeiro's Cabinet of Criminal Investigations the Lombroso Criminal Anthropology Prize, which was conferred by the Royal Academy of Medicine of Italy in 1933.[121]

It is no news that the Italian school of positivist criminology, founded by Cesare Lombroso, turned biological notions of racial determinism into concrete social policies and was responsible for legitimizing ideas like criminal atavism and the existence of born criminals and degenerate criminal types. Lombroso was celebrated for associating race and phenotype with innate tendencies to commit crimes. His method involved measuring the cranium and other bodily parts and using those measurements to identify physical characteristics that supposedly would denounce "suspect" racial origin and the consequent degeneracy of an individual in custody. Based on this identification, it would be determined whether such individual belonged to one or another criminal "type."

What may be surprising to those less familiar with the operation of such ideas in Brazil is the enthusiasm of the praise of Lombroso that emanated from Nina Rodrigues's pen. In his preface to Nina Rodrigues's book on penal responsibility, Afrânio Peixoto noted that Lombroso himself had consecrated Nina Rodrigues the "Apostle of Criminal Anthropology in the New World."[122]

According to Lombroso's apostle, "Aryan civilization" was represented in Brazil by a "small minority of the white race" responsible for defending that civilization against the antisocial acts of the inferior races, including the mestizo population, whose innate indolence was a cause of crime. Thus, the author's enthusiasm for the penal measure that punished vagrancy is clear in the following statement: "The latest Penal Code, which happily found along with the general consensus that the indolence of mestizos is a manifestation of free will in not wanting to work, rushed in with its Article 399 to offset this damage."[123]

Hédio Silva Jr. observes that Nina Rodrigues was not content merely to transpose his master's ideas to the tropics. He also introduced a new and audacious standard into the Brazilian collection of techniques to identify degenerate criminal types. To the measurements of crania, middle fingers, and forearms, Nina Rodrigues added the measurement of the width of the suspect's nostrils.[124]

The continued impact of the Lombrosian legacy on Brazilian criminology can be seen in several contemporary studies on the discriminatory operation of the criminal justice system.[125] Black men who are well dressed and driving fancy cars—and therefore not the victims of social discrimination against the working poor—are arbitrarily arrested much more frequently than whites. The probability of conviction is much higher for black defendants, who are by far the favorite victims of police for abuse, persecution, and torture. These facts are not the innovations of a police force trained in the dungeons of the 1964 military regime. In his open letter to the police commissioner in 1949, Abdias

Nascimento made a statement that is still valid today: "One would say that the police consider people of color to be born criminals and is creating the crime of being black."[126]

The Lombrosian legacy perpetuated by Nina Rodrigues can be found in the writings of contemporary jurists in the field of criminology. One example, published in 1996, explains why the criminality of the mestizo type is comparatively much higher than that of the white population:

> One century after [slavery's] abolition, blacks have not yet adjusted to social standards; and our mestizo, our caboclo [African-indigenous mixture], in general is indolent, has a propensity to alcoholism, makes a living from primary activities, and is unlikely to prosper in life. It is this *type* that normally migrates and forms the *favelas* of the large demographic centers. It is a vast contingent, with no education or technical know-how, unable to stabilize socially, resorting to marginality and crime.[127]

The text reflects the evolution of criminal anthropology in the same direction as social anthropology, which substituted cultural for biological determinism. The focus shifted to social groups and their cultural milieus. Rather than being the fruit of heredity, criminal tendencies would now be determined by social ecology.[128] In another text, published in 1995, the authors state that "the Africans and Indians conserve their uses and customs and combine them and new ones into an insoluble amalgam. In their actions there must be the powerful influence of conscious or unconscious reminiscences of the savage life of yesterday, very poorly counterbalanced by the new emotional acquisitions of the civilization imposed on them."[129]

Truly instructive is the declaration of Colonel Élio Proni, commander of metropolitan policing in São Paulo, who spoke in 1996 about police training in that city and was quoted by Veja newsmagazine (February 7): "There is no preference for stopping blacks because there are no suspect persons, but only suspicious situations." An example often used in the Military Police Academy of a suspicious situation, the Colonel continues, is that of "four coons (*crioulos*) in a car."[130]

Another incident illustrates the contemporary presence of the racist legacy in Brazil: Until 1999, the Faculty of Medicine of the Federal University of Bahia had on display an exhibition featuring sacred objects of Afro-Brazilian worship displayed side by side with homicidal weapons, defective fetuses, and the heads of rural criminal strongmen whose throats had been slit, all of which eugenic theorists showed as "monsters of degeneracy." The same exhibition was later transferred to the Secretariat of Public Safety's police museum. Its lesson in both venues was the silent and implicit endorsement by scientific authority of the theories it illustrated. Anthropologist Ordep Serra writes of the exhibition's eventual closing:

> It is often said that the racist perspective and approach of Nina Rodrigues has been overcome, that it was limited to the narrow bounds of a remote past, now duly buried and excommunicated.
>
> But it was only in 1999 that the Estacio de Lima Museum closed the exhibit that illustrates these theories in a brutal way, having resisted for more than a decade against the pressures brought by civilian society seeking to close it down.
>
> Yes: until 1999, public schools of Salvador took their primary and secondary level students to visit a show where objects used in Candomblé worship were presented alongside weapons of crime and what medicine classes as monsters.
>
> Thus the Faculty of Medicine of the Federal University of Bahia and, later, the Bahia State Secretariat of Public Safety, over half a century, ministered frightening and systematic, scheduled classes in racism to an audience made up in great measure of children.
>
> How many seeds of prejudice has this strange pedagogy of discrimination probably planted? We should recall that it invoked the authority of Science: Psychiatry, Ethnology, Law, and Forensic Medicine.[131]

The living legacy of such science in schools, in the operation of the criminal justice system, and in countless other facts of daily life constitutes the other side of the sorcery of color: a national consciousness that carries the stereotypes and prejudices of the racist tradition of biological determinism into contemporary social practice.

CONCLUSION

The notion of a national identity forged out of the rejection of biological racism and based on color categories divorced from racial origin and moral attributes is entrenched in the Brazilian consciousness and articulated in the national discourse. It sustains the ideas that make up the sorcery of color, which transforms a social system composed of profound racial inequalities into a supposed paradise of racial harmony. Although racist ideas are obscured and denied, they have a daily impact on life in Brazil. Invisible and mute, notions of biological determinism intimately accompany the pretense of antiracism, composing an integral but repressed part of the ideology of racial democracy. But just as important as notions of racial determinism is the set of ideas—or constructed ignorance—about the history of African peoples. Denial of African agency in the building of human civilization and of the Brazilian nation is a component of racism that sociological analysis underestimates by restricting its focus to biological determinism. In this respect, and in its refusal to listen to the actors of Afro-Brazilian social movements who define their identities in terms of history, culture, and social experience—not in biological terms of race—such analysis has contributed, in my view, to the unique operation of racism that I have called the sorcery of color.

A major characteristic of the sorcery of color is the confusion of race and culture in a national ideal of miscegenation that masks the aspiration of whiteness. The fusion of patriarchy and white supremacy created an ideal of imperial *morenidade* at the expense of black women, relegating their agency and that of the black population to the status of folklore and recreation. Education is a major terrain in which the sorcery of color operates daily with its repressed set of racist notions. By omitting or delegitimizing African and Afro-Brazilian historical and cultural references, and by perennially identifying blackness with enslavement, schools have cordoned off the road to building positive black identities. But in this respect schools only reproduce the national ethos, built over centuries, which cultivates the aspiration of whiteness by rejecting and symbolically erasing the African matrix. Surrendering to the impossibility of attaining de facto whiteness, Brazilian society has contented itself with the goal of simulation, imbuing the de-Africanized mestizo—the hegemonic *moreno*—with an identity of virtual whiteness that is the national ideal.

In the next chapter, I look at the discipline of psychology and explore its role in the sorcery of color. Like other Western sciences, psychology does not fail to be marked by the influence of white supremacy and theories of African degeneracy. I point out that, as black professionals consolidate their practice a new clinical and analytic approach is emerging, which I call the "Afro-Brazilian ear."

3

CONSTRUCTING AND
DECONSTRUCTING THE
"CRAZY CREOLE"

HE TITLE OF THIS CHAPTER is comprehensible only when one is familiar with the Brazilian expression *samba do crioulo doido*, which can be roughly translated as "the dance of the crazy Creole." While the word *crioulo* sounds like "Creole," in Brazil it has a pejorative connotation like the word "coon" in the United States and indicates a dark black person born in Brazil. The phrase may refer broadly to various kinds of confusion, but more commonly it specifically denotes a convoluted process of reasoning.

The stereotype of the crazy Creole is only one of many images associating blackness with mental or emotional unbalance. In this chapter, I reflect on the paths Brazilian psychology has forged with respect to race. Only very recently have psychologists here—who generally are considered and consider themselves white—paid serious attention to this matter. There are, of course, the usual exceptions, a notable one being the pioneer work of black female psychoanalyst Neusa Santos Souza, whose 1983 *Becoming Black* is a basic reference on race in Brazil. But the discipline has increasingly encountered the need to come to grips with the issue of racism due to social and human rights demands and in the name of appropriate therapeutic relationships.

I entertain no pretense of definitive analysis or finished solutions to the questions raised, but the reflections that follow seek to propose a point of departure for broader discussion within the discipline in Brazil. The analysis also records some recent approaches by a very small but growing group of African-descended professionals concerned with black identity issues in psychology from both the clinical and the theoretical points of view.

THE GENESIS OF PSYCHOLOGY IN
THE UNIVERSE OF WHITENESS

One of Brazil's foremost authors in the history of psychology, Luiz Claudio Figueiredo shows the "self-contradiction" of psychology as a science derived from Western epistemology.[1] He notes the "marginal gestation" of the space psychology would occupy in the wake of the epistemological tradition[2] and attributes the multiplicity of psychological currents and approaches to its inherent contradiction as a scientific project.

From its inception, Western scientific tradition established man's distrust of himself, judging that his subjectivity would interfere with his knowledge of "truth" and the correct identification of what is real. In the sixteenth century, Francis Bacon's empiricism established the inductive method of modern science in lieu of the a priori approach of medieval scholasticism. This innovation ushered in the doctrine of the "idols of knowledge" that would have to be tamed in order for man to apprehend truth. Bacon insisted on full empirical investigation and the avoidance of theories based on insufficient data. But with René Descartes and the age of reason, the empirical subject came to be seen as a factor of error and illusion. Now the guarantee of scientific objectivity was to be obtained by the method of beginning with universal doubt and following rigorous rules of reasoning: The scientist became "not someone who attains the truth, but someone who conscientiously submits to the discipline of the Method."[3] Descartes' method is at the service of the utilitarian interest of science, which had not changed. As in Bacon's empiricism, man was the master and owner of nature and the task of knowledge was to permit and to execute nature's control.[4]

Descartes' method involves insurmountable distance between investigator and object of investigation on one hand and the procedures and techniques of control, calculation, and testing on the other. The object of science, then, is whatever can be submitted to these processes. More than this, for science what is "real" is that which can be measured and technically manipulated by them.

Psychology's constitution as a natural science involves an a priori contradiction, then, because its object—human subjectivity—does not fit into the scientific conception of what is "real." Figueiredo maintains that the terrain of psychology

came to be the "place of what is excluded or purged by the Method, consisting of the negative of the full subject that returned in the form of symptoms
and malaise."[5] Psychology's inherent dilemma can be understood, in part, as
a conflict between its nature as a scientific discipline and the principles of
ethics, free will, and emotion as faculties proper to human subjectivity.
According to the imperatives of Descartes' method, psychology as a science
must reduce subjectivity to something measurable and subject to manipulation, thereby denying it the faculties of free will, ethics, and emotion. Such a
science must recognize its object—subjectivity—and at the same time ignore
its essence, which is characterized by the very faculties—free will, ethics, and
emotion—that science denies it.

Placing psychology's roots in the social theater of Europe, Figueiredo
mentions the polyphony of diverse voices sounding in the sixteenth century,
including those of "African and American savages" who were exhibited in
that theater as slaves or as exotic specimens.[6] His expression reflects the common belief that Africans, like Native Americans, were always considered savages by Europe. However, at that time, the legacy of the Moors' sovereign
presence in Europe was still recent. As Shakespeare's character Othello wit-
nesses, the Moors were Africans. They were the authors of important
advances in scientific and technological knowledge. Albeit identified with
the enemy in the Crusades, these civilized Africans inspired the respect of
their contemporaries in Europe, a fact well demonstrated in European literature and iconography.[7] While the view of the sovereign and civilized Moor
coexisted with that of the barbarian in the Middle Age's religious conflicts,
only later would the attribute "savage" be fixed on Africans in the context of
mercantile slavery.

Figueiredo notes that since the sixteenth century African and Native
American peoples have constituted "radically distinct forms of difference."
They became, in the European popular imaginary, "external threats" to be
conjured away by the force of arms and by the "reaffirmation of a European
cultural identity."[8] This reassertion of Western identity involves its contrast
against the identity of the savage "Others," who come to be part of it, their
image incorporated into Western identity by contrast as a negative imprint.
But despite being part of Western experience and society, and despite being
incorporated into Western identity, these peoples and their descendants
hardly appear again in the panorama of psychology's history. It is as if the
European confrontation with the phenomenon of difference embodied in
these peoples, through this initial reaffirmation of European cultural identity, had resolved the issue definitively. Figueiredo's own work is no real
exception in this sense; however, his mention of these peoples as part of the

historical scenario is a considerable advance in relation to the silence that generally reigns in texts on psychology's history and evolution.

In the same way, histories of philosophy and epistemology generally take apparently neutral routes, dealing with scientific ideas as if they floated high above any suspicion of involvement with race. Yet this difference that confronted Europe in the century of light was a fundamental, recurring issue in the development of Western philosophy and science. The construction and reaffirmation of European cultural identity was carried out in contrast to its opposite, the negative image of Africans built by this philosophy and science. In this process, the representation of Native Americans was not fused with that of Africans in the role of savage, but instead had a distinct and singular role of its own.

In the sixteenth century, Paracelsus and other scholars speculated that Native Americans, whose existence had not been foreseen in Biblical tradition, could only have descended from another Adam. This Pre-Adamite hypothesis caused sensation and influenced the thought of Thomas Hobbes and Baruch Spinoza, among others.[9] It was soon honed into a scientific theory, that of polygenesis, which introduced the demonstrability of the pre-Adamite hypothesis in accordance with Descartes' method. In this way, scientific objectivity came to endorse a theory earlier based only on academic theological speculation.

In the debate on Native Americans, the humanists followed the reasoning of the Greek master Aristotle, writing centuries earlier, who classified them as barbarians. Therefore, they were born to be enslaved. However, Bartholomé de Las Casas argued that they were part of Adam's progeny and therefore free men. The outstanding fact is that when the Catholic Church officially adopted Las Casas's position, in Papal Bull *Sublimis Deus* of 1537, it did not extend the new status to enslaved Africans. Pedro d'Anghera, author of the first book on the Americas, *De Orbe Novo*, had already established in 1516 the contrast between "white" American Indians and "black" Ethiopians—referring to Africans generically. François Bernier's work reinforced this classification in the seventeenth century.[10] In its terms, the blackness of Africans became the mark of contrast par excellence with Europeans and "civilized" peoples. For Bernier, the darkness of the Egyptians and indigenous Americans was accidental, the result of exposure to the sun. As for sub-Saharan Africans, blackness for them is essential to their natural condition, and not an effect of circumstantial factors.[11] Africans were considered different per se, the absolute other: the nonhuman.[12] Faced with the Africans who were exhibited after the first explorers returned from the "black continent," Jean-Jacques Rousseau posed the question "whether these simians might not be men" and François Voltaire remarked that these men were very much like simians.[13]

Native Americans were instead a kind of counter-image of Europeans: they were seen as the pure human, not yet corrupted by civilization. The age of light considered first nation peoples to be the natural man—a fact that did not spare them from genocide when the Europeans took their land.

This differentiation between the distinct groups of "savages" is not exactly arbitrary. Before the Enlightenment, theology reigned almost absolute in the constitution of Western knowledge. The monogenetic theory of racism began as part of the ancient Biblical tradition that all men descend from Adam. Noah's progeny, the descendants of Japheth, Shem, and Ham, branches out as the three races that correspond to Europe, Asia, and Africa. The curse of Ham,[14] launched against his son Canaan, is at the base of negative representations of Africans rooted in Judeo-Christian tradition centuries before the Enlightenment. The exegesis of this text is found in Christian and rabbinical scholarship, as in the following example from the sixth century:

> And since you've disabled me ... doing ugly things in the blackness of the night, Canaan's children shall be born ugly and black! Moreover, because you twisted your head around to see my nakedness, your grandchildren's hair shall be twisted into kinks, and their eyes red; again because you neglected my nakedness, they shall go naked, and their male members shall be shamefully elongated![15]

In the anthropology of the century of light, the race issue was hotly debated, and zoological themes predominate in the discussion:[16] perhaps monkeys and Africans were desperately backward men;[17] simians might be closer to the lowest individuals of our species and, if they could speak, perhaps they would demand the category and dignity of the human race by the same right as the savage Hottentot,[18] and so on. Voltaire generously observed that whites are "superior to these negroes, just as the negroes are superior to monkeys, and the monkeys are superior to oysters."[19] Recalling the Pre-Adamites, Voltaire and his colleagues joined in believing that the origin for Africans was a different Adam; their theory of polygenesis coexisted as a minority current, while monogenesist theories were defended by Comte Georges-Louis Leclerc de Buffon, Denis Diderot, and others.[20]

A core issue in the history of psychology as a discipline is that during the course of its formation as a science—and until very recently—Africans and first nation peoples were not subjects. They were not characterized as human and their persons, societies, and cultures were relegated to the status of objects to be tamed, measured, manipulated, and controlled by instrumental reason. In this sense, Léon Poliakov questions Sigmund Freud—stating, "just this once, he was a poor psychologist"—about his notion that science inflicted a great defeat on the naïve ingenuousness of men with its discovery that the Earth is not the center of the universe. Poliakov points out that such a discovery did not make a dent in European pride. On the contrary, this pride was nourished from then on, immeasurably, as Western man went about the world conquering and occupying new terrain, subjugating its inhabitants, and creating a world order in which Progress was attributed to white men, "in whom the triumph of Reason had chosen its domicile, a congenital bio-scientific superiority."[21]

Far from being absent from the evolution of Western epistemological tradition, then, black Africans, and the difference they embodied, were a basic reference in the building of European cultural identity and white supremacy, an ideology constructed out of the notion of scientifically proven congenital superiority.

In the nineteenth century, biological theories of race encouraged and supported the scientific endeavor to erase black Africans from the record of human development and civilization. Subdivisions of the human species were invented and manipulated to prove that a "white Paleo-Mediterranean race" was the sole author of Egyptian civilization and therefore of the first foundations of Western culture. By this simple eradication of the fact that most clearly demonstrates Africans' capacity to build civilizations, it was possible to condemn so-called black savages to a timeless inferiority.[22]

The dimension of the supposedly scientific process of proving the black race's inferiority tends to be minimized or glossed over in analyses that reduce racism to an issue of skin color or biological essence. The denial of Africans' capacity to create civilization is a crucial and essential factor in the construction of racist theory. In Brazil, one such example is clearly present in the 1930s debate between the famous ethnologist Oliveira Vianna[23] and the eminent psychiatrist and anthropologist Arthur Ramos: Oliveira Vianna embodied the racial determinism that still prevailed on the scene of social sciences at the time while Ramos defended the cultural criterion of anthropology.

Oliveira Vianna responds to public criticism of his theories by Ramos in a lecture at the Oswaldo Spengler Center of Rio de Janeiro.[24] Ramos had accused Oliveira Vianna of basing his work on "the science of a century past" and of emitting "false opinions about the civilizatory aptitude of the Afer,"[25] since recent research—with Leo Froebenius at the forefront—had found "in the hidden corners of African jungle, highly reliable vestiges of civilizations identical to those that our culture considers superior."[26] Promptly admitting the existence of such civilizations as an accepted fact, Oliveira Vianna goes on to contest "the conclusion that is taken from there—that these ancient civilizations, which flourished in the central zones of Africa, were created by men of the black race."[27] In his view, the empire of Ghana was "the creation of white people—not black."[28] The "civilizatory elements ... were, in fact, these princes of Berber or Arab origin and the masses there affluent were Hamites, not pure black men but men of the 'red' race [probably fixed mixtures of Semites with blacks]."[29] The Empire of Songhay also was the creation of Semitic chiefs: "Blacks represented, in this new great empire, the material base of labor—and not the agents of civilization."[30] The founders of the kingdom of Bornu "were of the red race of the Sudan and not the black race *per se*."[31] By the same token, the "Negroids of the Bantu group ... are not pure blacks; but the dosage of Berber blood in them is smaller than in Sudanese blacks and Moor mixed-blooded people. However, the presence of a small *quantum* of Semitic blood is enough to make them superior to genuine black populations."[32] As for them, "pure blacks, living in the forests of the Congo or of Angola, they never created any civilization at all."[33] In sum, according to Oliveira Vianna,

> What the study of ancient African history demonstrates, then, is that the great centers of civilization, found in the interior of the African continent, were not organized by peoples of the black race; but rather by foreign peoples, by Arab or Berber conquerors, who mixed with the primitive black population, forming a mass of mixed-bloods of whom they made themselves the educators and guides.[34]

The Arab and the Berber—considered Semites belonging to the white race—played "the role of fermentation agent" in Africa, since they "prepared, by mixing their blood with the blood of pure blacks, the necessary conditions for progress and civilization of those barbarized populations."[35] The conclusion, Oliveira Vianna announces, "is that, until now, civilization has been the attribute of other races and not the black race; that, in order for blacks to exercise any civilizing role at all, it is necessary first that they mix with other races, especially with the Aryan and Semitic races."[36]

Oliveira Vianna is only one among countless authors who adhered to these theories, which have not entirely lost their impact. Contrary to common understanding and to sociological theories that deny the biological base of race prejudice in Brazil after the supposed triumph of the culture criterion in the 1930s, the denial of the "civilizatory aptitude of the *Afer*"—taken from the theories of biological racism—is at the base of broadly documented discriminatory attitudes prevalent in the Brazilian educational system today. Such denial is translated into the stereotype of blacks as having "learning difficulties," particularly in the exact sciences. Expectations of student performance are lower with relation to black children, as is incentive toward higher achievement.[37] I also maintain that the tendency to focus on racism purely as a question of essentialism and melanin and the lack of importance attributed to the denial of African civilization as a basic dimension of racism are two factors that give sustenance to the antiblack discriminatory system in Brazil.

While in the field of education there are authors and groups engaged in the task of giving priority to this issue, it seems that psychology tends to suffer from a certain blind spot with respect to the discipline's involvement with racist theories. Figueiredo, alert to the question of "cultural differences," declares the following:

> It is even more necessary to listen to what is repressed and left unsaid when, as happens in Brazil and especially when attending a population that is just beginning to join the modern world and still remains rooted in a pre-modern culture, what does not have a voice audible to the institutionalized ear is everything that comes from that culture and does not fit into the set of demands and services legitimized by modern institutions. In these cases, however, there is a risk of psychologizing and pathologizing the excluded; to avoid that pitfall it is necessary for the psychologist's listening to be trained also in the fields of anthropology and sociology.[38]

I believe that before resorting to anthropology and sociology psychologists might benefit from a renewed listening to their own discipline, in particular because there have been occasions where psychologists who turned to anthropology fell precisely into the pitfall pointed out by Figueiredo, as I will discuss further on. While his objective is laudable, the path he suggests seems to take the direction of learning from other disciplines the patterns, standards, or elements necessary to understand another culture, a premodern one, in the sense of training the psychologist in a new, more inclusive way of listening. With respect to the black population in Brazil, I am not sure to what extent this path will yield effects, partly because most African descendants today are integrated into the modern Brazilian culture. If the premodern culture to which Figueiredo refers is to be found in part in the houses of Afro-Brazilian religion, I would suggest that these communities tend to provide more therapeutic resources than sources of anguish.

Of greater urgency, in my view, is the psychologist's task to become familiar with white supremacy's patterns and standards that affect African descendants' lives since they are the factors often most apt to throw a person's subjectivity into crisis. The "forbidden" or the "unsaid" in Brazilian race relations are the standards of white supremacy, denied and repressed by the sorcery of color and the ideology of racial democracy. Such repression is reinforced by negative representations of Africans and the lack of positive references for Afro-Brazilian identity outside the bounds defined by traditional discourse and stereotype—folklore, eroticism, and recreation. Silence and denial become the normative patterns that guide parents and children, teachers and students, employers and employees in dealing with race relations. This only reinforces the traditional patterns; a fact that is expressed in the title of Eliane dos Santos Cavalleiro's pioneering work *From the Silence of the Home to the Silence of the School*.[39]

Singular indeed, then, was Ricardo Franklin Ferreira's incursion into recent psychological literature.[40] His survey demonstrated that in a total of 4,911 works—including master's, doctoral, and postdoctoral theses and dissertations defended in the field of psychology at the two major universities in Brazil's largest city, São Paulo, between 1987 and 1995—only 12 included material referring to African descendants. Of these, only three were published. When he consulted a colleague with a doctorate in psychology about how to interpret these data, the response was that they might suggest that psychologists don't have any race prejudice.[41] Such a statement is a classic example of repression in Brazilian racism: the racist is anyone who mentions, studies, or otherwise is concerned with issues of race.

Ferreira notes that the absence of attention to race favors "experiences of disconnection." By denying the impact of racism on a person's life, one denies the person recognition of the singularity of his or her experience, a situation counterproductive to therapy. Ferreira concludes that "psychologists, with very rare exceptions, seem to be concerned with their methodologies and concepts, maintaining a 'politically correct' position of not getting involved with issue [of race]."[42] He warns against "a possible risk that with its silence Brazilian psychology will fail to contribute to diminishing discrimination."[43]

In the discussion and constant reformulation of methodologies, psychology exercises a function common to systems of knowledge defined as sciences, elaborating its *competent discourse*.[44] In addition to establishing the person who claims scientific knowledge as the only actor authorized to apply it, the elaboration of competent discourse also, to some degree, constitutes its object. Thus, psychology helps "create" pathology and "establishes subtle relations of power with respect to the object of its essentially normative and imposing speech."[45] Other actors and influences also contribute to this process in the social and political context, which in turn reflects and acts upon the making of competent discourse. Thus, relations of domination and hierarchy infiltrate and are revealed in the constitution of the object of knowledge, in this case pathology and madness. I do not hesitate to suggest that in Brazil psychology has participated in the construction and maintenance of the stereotype of the crazy Creole.

I suggest also that familiarity with how the competent discourse of psychology was articulated with respect to race would contribute to the development of the new kind of listening idealized by psychologists like Figueiredo who are sensitive to the issue. A brief visit to Brazilian psychology in its dealings with race might favor such a possibility.

PSYCHOLOGY AND THE EVOLUTION
OF THE RACE ISSUE IN BRAZIL

In Brazil, psychology as a discipline was constituted in an intellectual milieu deeply influenced by positivism,[46] racial determinism, and social and cultural evolutionism. One of its outstanding voices was Raymundo Nina Rodrigues, who declared that "the general laws of mental development in their philogenetic mechanisms constitute the basic and fundamental principles of modern psychology, which the manly efforts of the English school detached from Comtist biology to give it the forums of a distinct science."[47]

Nina Rodrigues was a psychiatrist, a criminologist, and an expert in forensic medicine. His work is an illustrative example of psychology's development as a discipline in Brazil under the aegis of social medicine and the theory of degeneracy. His work contributed to a profound identification of madness with crime and supported the consolidation of racial stereotypes like the crazy Creole and the degenerate criminal, two images closely associated in a web of mutual interlacing.

Nineteenth-century medical science was marked by the victory of organicism, a tendency wedded to racial determinism that attributed the origin of mental and emotional disorders to the individual's organic constitution. In Brazil, the triumph of this tendency in the latter half of the century brought about the institution of a new field of medicine, alienism, perhaps the first in a series of disciplinary technologies emerging from the urban milieu and concerned with its "hygienization" and "organization." The goal was to tame the masses of poor and marginalized urban populations, seen generally as a horde of free Africans and disorderly types—including strikers, *capoeiras* (black men who practiced the African-derived martial art of the same name), drunks, prostitutes, and degenerates—who were rapidly becoming a major threat and danger.

Alienism comes to the foreground, then, in a context in which medicine was associated with hygienic engineering and urban planning to treat the "social organism": the city and society vulnerable to the contagion of both moral and physical vices. What unified all the techniques of social control articulated to this end was the theory of degeneracy.

The theory of degeneracy allowed the psychiatrist to extract the etiology of madness from the sphere of reason and the soul and instead define it as a hereditarily transmitted organic condition, a pathological deviance from the normal type of humanity.[48] To separate madness from reason and the soul made it possible, among other things, to conceive of madness without delirium. Such a distinction is exemplified in behavior interpreted as antisocial manifestations of degeneracy including drug addiction, alcoholism, idleness, prostitution, and gambling. Emerging from the theory of degeneracy was the notion of "moral madness," viscerally linked to crime. The criminalization of mental illness and the medicalization of supposedly antisocial behavior were facilitated by the fact that degeneracy theory allowed for the concept of progressive pathology, recognizing intermediate stages of madness like the *demifou*, the degenerate on the way to madness, the "pervert" who carries an invisible disease. These moral madmen were taken to be born candidates for the world of crime.

Criminality and madness, then, ride the same rails of degeneracy. In 1903, legislation on the subject defined the alienated person as "an individual who, by congenital or acquired malady, compromises public order or people's security."[49] Juliano Moreira, director of the National Asylum for the Alienated, commented in 1905 on the relation between criminality, madness, and the growth of the cities, observing the long succession of "epileptics, hysterics, and other degenerates with which, progressively, the vast culture broth of national criminality is being thickened."[50]

Nina Rodrigues does not let us forget that a decisive factor in this theoretical scheme is racial determinism. His writing assumes that blacks are born degenerates whose race is deviant from a standard of normality that presumed whiteness. They were on the lowest rungs of the ladder of degeneracy—close to animals or very early stages of human evolution—and therefore more inclined to criminality.

When Nina Rodrigues observes that "the study of the inferior races has furnished science with well-observed examples of their organic cerebral incapacity," he treads the grounds of tension between the science of subjectivity and the principle of free will. For him, the solution is simple: with respect to inferior populations, the "spiritualist presumption of free will" has no support in science. His theory of the criminal nonimputability of Africans and their mixed-blood descendants is based on what he describes as

> The material, organic impossibility that representatives of the inferior stages of social evolution will pass suddenly on in only one generation, with no slow and gradual transition, to the superior stages' level of mental and social culture; for modern psychology the postulate of free will as a basis of penal responsibility can be applied only to homogeneous social groups that have achieved the same standard of median mental culture.[51]

The propensity to criminality was supposed to originate in inadequate psychic development, which was the result of an innate and involuntary tendency to impulsiveness. The African, the *crioulo* (our Creole, the dark-skinned black person born in Brazil), the mulatto, mestizo and *caboclo* (African-indigenous mixed heritage), all are psychologically unstable "types." Nina Rodrigues writes: "The Negro does not have bad character, but an unstable character, like a child, and as in the child ... his instability is the consequence of incomplete development of the brain. In an environment of advanced civilization, where he has full freedom to act, he will be out of place."[52]

Nina Rodrigues believes that the adaptation of these backward types to superior civilization results in psychic disturbance. He reasons that mestizos receive in their genetic heritage the impulsiveness and improvidence that characterize the emotional state of savages. To avoid being caught in contradiction, Nina Rodrigues explains that apathy, another characteristic he attributes to Africans, is not incompatible with impulsiveness.[53]

Oliveira Vianna confirms Nina Rodrigues's thesis by observing that mulattoes, forced to conciliate the two ethnic tendencies colliding inside them, "always end up proving themselves morally disorganized, psychically unharmonious, functionally unbalanced."[54] Sociologist and historian Clóvis Moura analyzes Euclides da Cunha's classic work *Os Sertões*, a basic text used in many Brazilian studies courses and an exemplary exposition of the constituted knowledge on race that prevailed during the first part of the twentieth century. Moura sums up the representation of mulattoes in Brazil that occurs in *Os Sertões* and in other pseudoscientific theories of miscegenation: "[Mulattoes] are unbalanced. An incurable unbalance, because there is no therapeutic remedy for this battle of antagonistic tendencies inside the soul."[55] Such evaluation of African descendants prevailed in

Brazilian psychology and social sciences over a long period of time, infiltrating the popular consciousness.

According to Oliveira Vianna, from the physical type of an individual it "can be inferred, with a very high coefficient of probabilities, what are his *pathological predispositions*, what are the probable modalities of his *temperament* and his *intelligence*," by using "contemporary bio-typology."[56] Such an idea is the founding principle of Lombrosian criminology based on racial determinism: The psychological type of the degenerate corresponds to his physical type, which "not only determines the emotional state of the individual, but also his intellectual condition."[57] On the psychological type of the *Homo Afer* and its descendant, Oliveira Vianna cites Federico Muller: "The negro is, in all things, a sensitive creature in whom fantasy dominates.... The life of the negro is spent in contrasts; the most opposite feelings find place in his heart. From the most intense and foolish joy he switches to the most bitter desperation; from boundless hope to extreme terror; from thoughtless prodigality to sordid greed."[58]

Contrasting the mental value of blacks with that of whites and Native Americans, Oliveira Vianna surveys the respective literature and concludes that "the Negro, indeed, does not seem to me capable of competing with the white or yellow races. This is what observation demonstrates and the results of researches in experimental psychology seem to confirm."[59] Oliveira Vianna's profile of the Native American, however, "is somber, reserved, recalling greatly, in his affective constitution, Bleuler's 'autist.' Observing his attitudes and ways of life, one feels that, in the general run of things, he behaves as a typical schizoid."[60]

The effect of such ideas on therapeutic psychological treatment in Brazil was broad and profound. The ways in which these effects were manifest emerge in a singular way in Maria Clementina Pereira Cunha's 1988 study of the asylum of Juquery, the model psychiatric institution of Brazil. She identifies the social and historical context of the asylum's creation and development, which she documents in some detail, recording a rich and fascinating body of information on the institution and its day.

Juquery's founder, Francisco Franco da Rocha, was considered the Brazilian Philippe Pinel; a pioneer in psychiatry, he advocated the modern philosophy of therapy and cure instead of the former standard of the early and mid-nineteenth century, limited to assisting, caring, and consoling. The move from asylum to hospital was the journey from exclusion and quarantine to treatment and cure. A man of his time, Franco da Rocha was not unaware of the so-called urban threat, on which he commented the following: "Those declassified by society aggregate themselves very naturally to the group of degenerates. We can call those declassified by society a series of special types that do not fit, whether into society or the asylum.... They are in the streets, everywhere. Shake up society a little, for whatever reason, and they will crop up in a minute. They are constant candidates for the hospital." [61]

This discourse illustrates that Juquery was one example of a new idea that would be ushered in with the new century: the mental hospital as institution. This innovation was in part a response to the growth of the cities in which, supposedly, hordes of degenerates and delinquents presented the danger of psychological epidemics and contagion. Couched in the language of therapy and cure, the idea of the psychiatric hospital was conceived along with another mission: to intercept such an urban threat to social order.

Steeped in social evolutionism, Franco da Rocha's ideas coincide completely with those of Nina Rodrigues; he states, "Lombroso's born criminal can be taken for a moral madman in all his particulars." The moral madman could be a marginalized poor person, a bourgeois rebel with a "lawless life," or an anarchist agitator. "The revolutionaries are companions of the paranoid," explains Franco da Rocha, "with whom they are often confused, with the difference that the paranoid reveal intellectual disturbances that exclude them more quickly from social communion, since they are more visible to everyone."[62]

According to Franco da Rocha, the moral madman is weak in spirit. Weakness of spirit was indeed a basic symptom of certain types of madness. Madness is also identified with weakness of the brain, and so symbolizes the opposite, the "Other," of progress and civilization. As a positivist, Franco da Rocha assigned phases to mental and psychological evolution, which progressed "from fetishism to the scientific stage." Weakness of the brain could also be classified as regression to the individual patient's earlier stages of development.[63]

Alienists at the helm of these new psychiatric institutions did not diverge from Oliveira Vianna and Nina Rodrigues in locating blacks at the lowest rung on the ladder of degeneracy. The extremes of this ladder held two types of patients: the inferior degenerate, "incapable of supporting himself," and the superior one, with an intellect that was well developed "at the cost of a deficiency in the general equilibrium of spirit." Thus, "the idiot, the imbecile, the weak degenerate ... and the superior degenerate, even a genius (it seems incredible), meet each other, come to the same level, to the extent that they are brought together by a common trait—perversion of character."[64]

As born inferior degenerates, black people wear on their bodies the "physical stigmas of degeneration common to their race,"[65] duly registered in the hospital records: full lips, flattened nose, flat feet, or the set of traits that sums up to a "perfect simian type."[66] The record of the so-called black imbecile or idiot was very small in size as a result of both the patient's indigence and the lack of scientific interest due to the condition being thought of as determined by biology and therefore not bringing new questions to psychiatry. While the superior degenerate, or the moral madman, who was often rich, merited much more detailed diagnostics and treatment, the so-called black inferior degenerate—idiot or imbecile—frequently was admitted to the hospital, waited a few years to be evaluated, and would not see the doctor again before discharge or death.

Once again, it is silence that reigns eloquent in Brazilian racism, saying much more than any discourse. As Cunha observes, "the thousands of records on black patients are practically blank, filled out almost telegraphically with diagnoses that point in the majority to 'idiocy,' 'imbecility,' and other shorthand for the inferior degeneracy inscribed in their racial identity itself."[67]

The degeneration of Juquery's degeneracy theories begins with the victory of eugenics in the campaigns of sanitarist medicine. A series of public health campaigns carried out all over the nation were led by Leagues of Sanitation, founded in 1918 with Miguel Pereira and Belisário Pena at the forefront. The sanitation and public health movement was marked by a shift of emphasis from degeneracy theory to the engineering of eugenics, which proposed to turn the uncertainties of natural selection into "a rational instrument consciously employed."[68] In these campaigns prevailed the public spirit (doctors, other health professionals, and lay people engaged, often without extra pay, in the improvement of hygiene and health conditions for the population as a whole); popular mobilization (involvement of the resident population in campaigns to improve health conditions); and ambulatory treatment (broader access to health care through treatment without hospitalization). This tendency took on the taste of a veritable civic mission and had an authoritarian and coercive dimension that sparked the Revolt of the Vaccine in Rio de Janeiro.

A major urban reform designed to eliminate narrow, rat-infested streets in the name of hygiene and sanitation followed a series of smallpox and yellow fever epidemics that had killed hundreds of European visitors. The authorities demolished whole residential areas in the central city and replaced them with broad avenues modeled on those of Paris. In the process, they displaced the local—mostly black—population. Homeless ex-residents flocked to the hills, accelerating the expansion of favelas. The General Public Health Department created the civil service post of rat purchaser, paying three hundred *réis* per rat captured, and instituted the Health Brigades, a police force that spread rat poison and sprayed insecticide in the streets. Faced with a smallpox epidemic in 1904, Oswaldo Cruz, director of the Health Department, renewed an 1834 law making the smallpox vaccine compulsory and sent out his Health Brigades to apply it by force. People already skeptical about the idea of yellow fever being transmitted by mosquitoes were horrified at the prospect of a police brigade injecting an unknown liquid into their bodies. They destroyed street cars and stores. Rio de Janeiro, then the country's capital, was at civil war for a week when parts of the Military School of Praia Vermelha supported the rebellious population and sectors of the military conspired to stage a coup d'état. President Rodrigues Alves repressed the revolt and restored order, arresting more than a thousand people, most of whom were condemned to forced labor and sent off to Acre Territory in the Amazon region. Official statistics report a toll of 23 deaths and 67 wounded, but historians agree that this is severely undercounted.[69]

Presiding over the noble efforts of the public health campaigns were the principles of eugenics mixed with the waning but still vigorous discourse of degeneracy. Psychology was by no means absent, engaging in this virtuous movement in the person of the "hygienists of the spirit" organized in their Leagues of Mental Hygiene. Proselytes of the new order, the alienists dedicated themselves to the propagation of sanitation: "The study of cerebral functions, of psychology, became not only the doctor's prerogative but that of all men who think and act."[70] The encouragement of eugenic education and the creation of technical councils and public agencies designed to look out for the "perfection of the race" were among the items defended in the National Constituent Assembly of 1934 by Congressman Antonio Carlos Pacheco e Silva. The congressman was also founder of the Brazilian and the São Paulo Leagues of Mental Hygiene as well as director of Juquery and director of the Department of General Assistance to Psychopaths from 1930 to 1938.[71]

In this period, the early 1930s, the paradigm of a cultural view of race was emerging timidly in the social sciences and struggling to establish its ascendancy over that of racial determinism.[72] But, it is naïve to think, as do many Brazilians who pride themselves on the national antiracist ideal, that the publication of Gilberto Freyre's work in 1933 meant that the postulates of racial determinism were suddenly and definitively replaced, as if by magic, with a cultural or anthropological approach free of such postulates. Social Darwinist notions continued strong in the ideas of assimilation associated with the new anthropology of culture. There was a tradition and a history of work in this field, deeply imbued with racial determinist ideas, and the controversy was intense. From our perspective and with a focus on psychology, it is useful to note the intersection of these two disciplines. Anthropological research on

Afro-Brazilian culture—beginning with Nina Rodrigues—focused on religions of African origin from the viewpoint of psychology, using the same evolutionist model that dictated the innate inferiority and mental imbalance of the population of "inferior degenerates" who practiced these religions. A look at the chapter titles and subtitles in Nina Rodrigues's book is informative: "'Negro Criminals in Brazil,' 'The Fetishist Animism of Bahian Negroes,' 'Epidemic of Madness in the Canudos Rebellion,' 'Negro Paranoia,' 'Miscegenation, Degeneracy, and Crime.'"[73] Psychiatrist Nina Rodrigues's detailed research in Candomblé houses is an important source of ethnographic data on African religions in Bahia to this day.

In solidarity with Candomblé communities—despite their members' innate inferiority—Nina Rodrigues was concerned with the violent police repression against them. His democratic response was to propose psychiatric—instead of police—control of the houses. This proposal was justified by the same criminal nonimputability that Nina Rodrigues judged to be a result of the inferiority of the black devotees. He was not able to implement this project at the time, but it was put into practice later in Recife under Ulysses Pernambuco and in Salvador during the administration of Juracy Magalhães.[74]

Psychiatrist and anthropologist Arthur Ramos, although a follower of Nina Rodrigues, turned away from his teacher's racial determinism and took new directions in social psychology and cultural anthropology. He criticized the "linear evolutionism" that then still influenced and, in his opinion, deformed the psychological perspective in ethnology. He made it clear, however, that social psychology and cultural anthropology did not reject evolutionism itself, "as some hasty culturalists suppose.... It is just that, instead of considering evolution to be linear, we now study the evolution of *structures*."[75]

In his scientific work, Ramos's priority was the study of African cultures, particularly religious culture, in Brazil and in the Americas.[76] For him, as for his forerunners and contemporaries in this line of psychological analysis of religion, the most intriguing matter was spiritual trance. Research on Voodoo in Haiti took directions similar to research on Brazilian Candomblé. Elie Lhérisson, a physician writing on Voodoo, saw the candidate for initiation in that religion as "almost always hysterical" with "very evident stigmas of neurosis." Dr. Justin Chrysostome Dorsainvil defined trance as "a religious, racial psycho-neurosis characterized by a doubling of the self, with functional alterations of sensibility, motility, and the predominance of hysteria, encompassing all the phenomena of possession."[77]

Nina Rodrigues placed religious trance in hysteria as a "hyster-hypnotic monodical delirium of suggestive verbal somnambulism." However, his hypothesis on trance as hypnotic suggestion suffered an experimental setback when, in his consultation room, he hypnotized a female initiate. When she was asleep, the psychiatrist told her she was in a religious festivity and commanded her to dance. The young woman, from the depths of her hypnotic trance, responded that she could not dance to receive the saint because she was not dressed in the appropriate vestments. There arose, then, the need for a conceptual distinction, since hypnotic somnambulism had not been confirmed.[78]

For Ramos, the hypnotic suggestion was more complex, linked to different psychological conditions. Such conditions could vary from somnambulistic, hypnotic, oeniric, schizophrenic, or magical-catatimical states—"those processes, akin to hysteria, where the motor mechanisms of ancestral reaction are verified"—to the state of mental automatism: "they range from simple xenopathic phenomena to the most complex influence-based delirium."[79]

In his 1953 essay, French sociologist Roger Bastide follows the evolution of these psychological evaluations of trance in Haitian Voodoo. Dr. Price-Mars, using Dupré's theory of the five basic constitutions, "thinks that the possessed person is a mythomaniac endowed with hyperemotivity." In contrast, Dr. Louis Mars makes use of the psychoanalytic method and "defines the deity that has possessed the initiate as a projection of the Ego in the symbolic form of an already familiar mythical entity; the mystical trance of Vouduns externalizes the individual's deep impulses, inhibited in daily life by social censorship or by the superego."[80]

Continuing this line of interpretation decades later and taking what seems to be a moderate position, Dr. George Alakija, is a psychiatrist of Nigerian origin from Bahia, a member of one of the families who returned to Lagos after enslavement.[81] He participated in the official Brazilian delegation to the Second World Festival of Black and African Arts and Culture, held in Lagos, Nigeria, in 1977. As spokesman for the Brazilian delegation, he presented to the Festival's intellectual forum a paper on the state of trance in Candomblé in which he applied the methods and concepts of sophrology, "a new scientific discipline that originated in Madrid in 1960." Alakija reached a groundbreaking conclusion: trance for him is a sophronic state that "can be classified neither as normal nor as pathological."[82]

Decades earlier, Bastide had covered a long road of research and critique of Western methodologies. He broke with the pathological focus and was initiated into the Candomblé. Bastide dispensed with traditional methodological canons: "We will study the Candomblé as an autonomous reality. ... We will not be concerned with placing descriptions into conceptual systems taken from traditional ethnography or cultural anthropology." He set out to "show that these religions are not a network of superstitions; that, on the contrary, they imply a cosmology, a psychology, and a theodicy; in sum, that African thought is erudite thought."[83] In a formally sociological expression, Bastide concluded that trance was the vital power of "the mythical model society gives to the individual."[84]

Bastide engaged in a critical exploration of the frontiers between sociology and psychoanalysis, starting from the observation that neither Freud's "Oedipian fable" nor his theory of the primitive horde, pillars of his sociology, withstood contemporary analysis.[85] He found reprehensible the notion shared by Freud, Jean Piaget, and others, of primitives as children in the evolutionary development of peoples: "One should not compare the primitive adult to a civilized child. ... We need to stay within the same cultural context."[86] In Bastide's understanding, "Freud's work consisted of 'naturalizing the cultural' as well as 'culturalizing the natural,'"[87] similar to the process of racializing culture and culturalizing race observed in the preceding chapter. Convinced that the psychological approach was not appropriate to the understanding of different cultures, Bastide asserts that "the social is not extracted from the psychological."[88]

His recognition of the importance of psychoanalysis, however, survived these criticisms. The emphasis Jacques Lacan placed on the symbolic, on meaning, and on language redeems psychoanalytical theory for Bastide and inspires him to compare Lacan's psychoanalytic approach to the structuralism of Claude Lévi-Strauss.[89] Bastide wrote the prologue to Georges Dévereux's pioneer work, *General Essay on Ethnopsychiatry*, which reports on extensive field research, clinical work, and a landmark seminar held at the Sorbonne's École Pratique des Hautes Études.[90] Work in this field has since continued in an active school of ethnopsychiatry in Paris, offering clinical treatment to immigrants from different corners of the French ex-colonies, particularly North Africa. In Brazil, a series of exchange initiatives was organized by Professor José Flávio Pessoa de Barros of the State University of Rio de Janeiro with Tobie Nathan and other professionals associated with this school of theory and therapy.

Ethnopsychiatry fuses anthropological and ethnographic tools with those of psychoanalysis, obtaining highly positive clinical results. Respect for the African cultural matrix as "erudite thought" is one of its basic tenets. The clinical approach is based on the results of extensive field research in Africa, where religious cultures are experienced in living dynamic by researchers and therapists. The technique's controversial innovation "legitimizes" "prelogical" therapeutic techniques (so-called shamanism or witchcraft), to the extent that it collects them, studies them, and incorporates them into its field of knowledge. Their role is one of consultancy, revealing therapeutic needs arising from the clients' cultural contexts. The clinical approach involves listening that is "initiated" in the cultural language of the patient. The goal is to interact with the person on terms proper to the ethos of his culture.[91] Such technique comes close to Figueiredo's suggestion of incorporating anthropology and sociology into the listener's training.[92]

While ethnopsychiatry implicitly legitimizes non-Western therapies by consulting them, anthropologist Ordep Serra of Bahia observes that it avoids looking for analogies or equivalencies between these therapies and modern techniques of psychotherapy. Serra recalls that in his prologue Bastide congratulates Dévereux for not falling into this temptation. It would be a mistake, because "the similarity sometimes found is only apparent, since the methods of shamans and witchdoctors belong to the realm of *the mystical* and not *the rational*." In Serra's view, non-Western therapeutic practices are subjected to an "almost merely 'symptomatic' reading, if you will"—the idea being to unveil pathologies that otherwise would go unknown. "If in this Ethnopsychology there is a questioning of the pathos of medical systems," says Serra, "it is entirely unilateral: it is concerned only with the domain of what Bastide would call 'pre-logical medicine.'"[93]

By taking non-Western cultures' therapeutic techniques as an object, ethnopsychiatry does not abandon its center, the place from which it observes its object of study. Western knowledge might identify useful techniques by studying these cultures, but the observer keeps his distance and his legitimated approach as "competent discourse." Serra observes that "sovereign reason interrogates, explains, comprehends what is on the other side, which comes on the scene only as the silenced subject of scientifically authorized reflection. Even possible analogies between the iatric procedures of scientific psychotherapists and the curing techniques of 'others' ... must be rejected as illusory because of the essential difference."[94]

Perhaps Figueiredo's recipe will be useful still, for anthropology seems to help identify some forms of Afro-Brazilian listening—including attention to such possible analogies. Other forms of that listening are developing within the discipline itself.

AFRO-BRAZILIAN LISTENING:
THE RISE OF A NEW APPROACH

Instead of focusing on the Afro-Brazilian religious matrix as a place for revealing pathologies, Serra proposes another way to understand the concept: "When I speak of 'Ethnopsychiatry of Afro-Brazilian Rites,' I mean that these rites involve knowledge and practices, strategies and values applied in mental health treatment; I also say that by studying them in a certain way (with methods adequate to this end) we can attain a certain knowledge about mental health in the field in which these rites are carried out."[95]

The author warns that in traditional religion the idea of therapy does not exist as something detached or separate from the larger context of the rites. With this caveat, several authors have identified *terreiro* communities—houses of Afro-Brazilian religious culture—as a place of psychological therapy and complementary treatment of chronic illnesses like epilepsy.[96]

Such is a novel proposal to bring before psychology as a scientific discipline whose outlook reserves the therapeutic function to those initiated in the competent discourse, meaning therapists trained in the academy. Thus, recalling Nina Rodrigues and his colleagues at the Bahia Faculty of Medicine, Serra comments,

> perhaps the Bahian luminaries of Nina's school would not be more shocked by the expression "therapeutic practices in the Candomblé" than were many illustrious psychiatrists (and ethnopsychiatrists) when some anthropologists began to make analogies between shamanic procedures and Western psychotherapies: one may recall the uproar that Lévi-Strauss caused, the ferocious protests he provoked, when he dared to compare psychoanalysts to shamans in a famous article.[97]

It is not my task in this work to explain the forms or report examples of therapeutic practices studied in such literature. However, I do think it important to note the change that a new listening approach would imply on the subject-object relationship between psychologists and the non-Western cultural milieu. Perhaps such a change could move in the direction of dialogue, which means an exchange between two subjects. Instead of trying to hear in the culture of "others" the marks of specific pathologies, perhaps a listening founded in dialogue could surpass the limits of the subject-object relationship and apprehend new therapeutic possibilities. More likely, this dialogue could indicate treatment alternatives in cases of individual crisis where the issues brought to the consultation room point to the need for a different interlocutor.

The analysis taken from the field of white studies might help to elaborate some of the issues implied in the question of the nature of this relationship as subject-object or subject-subject in this context. The invisibility of white identity, unnamed and unmarked, underlies the consideration of who is the therapist and who is the patient. When we speak of this relationship, the unarticulated but practically universal presumption will be that the therapist, who masters the competent discourse, is white. The suggestion of psychology's dialogue with other disciplines, for example, implies the idea of preparing the "therapist" for a richer and more viable encounter with the "patient" in which the therapist will not run the risk of pathologizing the patient's culture. In other words, the therapist versed in the competent discourse of psychology is implicitly identified as white, while the patient is presumed to be black.

The protest to such an argument will be that the issue is not skin color, but the representation of a Western form of knowledge. Precisely: The maintenance of this knowledge as the almost exclusive domain of whites is part of the interdicted material that we are trying to hear. In other words, to approach issues of race by defining the therapist as neutral or without color would obscure the privilege that race confers upon whites in terms of access to the competent discourse. The idea of privilege here does not mean class position, possessions, and wealth, but the favored status that whiteness confers on an individual in daily situations and decisive moments in life. The privilege can be purely symbolic but may have concrete consequences, as in competing for a job or the differentiated treatment that a student might receive from a teacher (who may also be black). In the case at hand it refers to privilege in access to professional training.

The pretentiously colorblind attitude also leaves untouched the possibility that the intellectual training of a white therapist, and his or her life experience marked by privilege, might interfere with the therapy itself, which may, for example, lead to the "disconnection experiences" that Ferreira points out.[98] In listening to a client whose personal crisis involves issues of racism, for example, the white therapist's life experience could lead the therapist to resist the idea that a situation brought to the clinic involves the impact of racial discrimination on the client's life, thus failing to recognize the singularity of the client's dilemma. The white therapist's life experience could interfere also with the interpretation of silences. It might be easy, for example, to misinterpret a person's hesitation to speak about his or her experience of race issues when the reason for silence is that the client wonders whether the therapist will listen with sympathy and understanding.

The pretense of colorblindness also obscures the implications of a therapist's blackness for a patient whose crisis of subjectivity is shaped by race issues or other factors of his or her identity as an African descendant. In a revealing statement to this effect, psychologist Marilza de Souza Martins refers to a demand for black therapists:

[Black] people didn't feel they were being understood about the doubts and issues that concerned them.... Either the theme [of racism] was dealt with in the past tense, or there was a deviation or a distortion, or it wasn't even touched upon. It was as if it was not a black person that was there as client. So people wanted black therapists who emphasized the same issues, who had lived through the same kind of anguish.[99]

The relative unavailability of Afro-Brazilian therapists is a logical consequence of the racial inequalities in access to education and in the labor market that are amply documented in the work of the Institute of Applied Economic Research — IPEA and the *Map of the Black Population in the Labor Market*.[100] To the extent that Afro-Brazilian psychologists earn their degrees and exercise their profession, their perspective on race is leading some of them to develop relevant issues in the discipline. This is an extremely incipient phenomenon in Brazil, but both in theory and clinical application there is emerging what I have called an Afro-Brazilian ear. What differentiates this listening, I think, is expressed in Serra's following warning: "It is time to take racism seriously as pathology. To discuss it is indispensable when one wishes to understand the 'Ethnopsychiatry of Afro-Brazilian Religions': this pathology is precisely one of the maladies it treats, a source of disturbances that challenge the medical efforts of the *terreiro* communities in their role as health care agencies."[101]

In the early 1950s, sociologist Guerreiro Ramos discusses the "social pathology of 'white' Brazilians" and develops therapeutic practice in the form of psychodrama in the Black Experimental Theater (TEN). This practice was based on psychoanalytical theory but did not entertain any pretense of carrying out clinical work in psychoanalysis. Ramos was a sociologist and looked at this project as one of social action; he even referred to it as "sociatry" (as opposed to individualistic psychiatry) in order to emphasize this aspect.[102] Another landmark in the evolution of this issue the work of psychoanalyst Neusa Santos Souza, *Becoming Black*. She coined the phrase "white ego ideal," endowing the Freudian ego with a specific racial reference.[103] According to outstanding psychoanalyst and Brazilian intellectual Jurandir Freire Costa in his preface to Souza's book, she challenged "the flaccid omission with which psychoanalytical theory has treated this issue up to now."[104]

Souza analyzes the statements she collected from ten black subjects who were improving their class status. She concludes that blacks who desire a better socioeconomic position "pay the price of a more or less dramatic massacre of their identity"[105] because of the "multi-racial, racist society of white hegemony that paradoxically touts the ideology of racial democracy."[106] Identified by their former status as slaves and made to turn away from their original cultural values—which are "represented fundamentally by their religious heritage"—black Brazilians "assume an identity entrenched in white emblems, in the effort to overcome the obstacles presented by being born black." Such an identity "puts them in conflict with their historicity, given that they must deny both their past and their present: the past with respect to black tradition and culture and the present with respect to race discrimination."[107] Such a dilemma is acted out in the body itself, whose color and physical traits link them inescapably to everything that society rejects, not only as an "ugly" body, but as an only partly human being incapable of creating civilizations or positive human values. Negro (black) means dirty, bestial, monkey, ignorant, criminal, drunkard, inferior degenerate; it refers to the object's hair being rotten. The negro body is the indelible mark of identification with negative values. The subject is imprisoned in ceaseless "suffering of her own body" pointed out by the black psychiatrist, psychoanalyst, and philosopher Frantz Fanon of Martinique.[108]

The contrast is great if we compare this painful and moving situation to the stereotype of the sculptural black body—athletic, exuberant, and hypersexualized—that symbolizes a strength and freedom supposedly reserved to blacks. This is the local version of the eroticization of inequality unequivocally demonstrated in Marianne Hester's work.[109]

Costa observes a process of self-persecution against this body, whose impossibility of mutation is felt as a persecution against the self. The person's potential future identity depends on the possibility of "un-blaming" the body; this possibility is denied; an impasse is created.[110] "I feel race as a wound, it's something I think and feel all the time; it's a thing that never heals," says one of Souza's interviewees.[111] Souza writes:

> This narcissistic wound and the ways of dealing with it constitute the psychopathology of black Brazilians in social ascension and its nucleus is the relationship of continuous tension between Superego, actual Ego, and Ego Ideal. At the clinical level, this tension takes the form of guilt feelings, inferiority, phobic defense, and depression, affects and attitudes that define the identity of black Brazilians in social ascension as a structure of un-acknowledgment / recognition.[112]

Only two alternatives are open to this person: to "become black" or to "consume oneself in the effort to fulfill the impossible verdict—the desire of the Other—becoming white."[113] Souza concludes the following:

The possibility of constructing a black identity—a task that is eminently political—demands as a necessary condition the contestation of
the model received from the first figures—parents or substitutes—who
taught the person to be a caricature of whiteness. Breaking with this
model, the black person organizes the conditions of possibility that will
allow him to have his own face, ... to construct an identity that gives
him his own features, founded, therefore, on his own interests, and
capable of transforming History—individual and collective, social and
psychological.[114]

Judging by the definition of the matter and by Souza's terms of analysis,
the issue of black identity is on the table only with respect to blacks "in social
ascension." Such an idea reflects a slant common to intellectual approaches
to social issues in the 1970s and early 1980s. Marxist structuralism oscillated
between the pure denial of the race issue in favor of class struggle and the
recognition of its legitimacy qualified by the insistence that racism was the
exclusive monopoly of capitalist bourgeoisie.[115] Thus, it was presumed that
there was no prejudice among the working class or the poor, in which case
there would be no suffering by virtue of racial identity problems among poor
working blacks. I look at a classic example of this kind of reasoning in
Chapter 5.

The analysis exemplified in Marxist structuralism is founded on a
Western model of class society in countries with industrialized capitalist
economies, and its problems are patent when we introduce colonial domination, which is hardly a negligible definer of reality. Theoreticians who promote such a line of reasoning apparently are not aware of the analysis of colonialism's effects on the psyche by authors like Algerian philosopher Albert
Memmi. Like Fanon, Memmi analyzes the psychological dynamics of colonialist domination and demonstrates how the ideal of whiteness acts on the
identity-building process of dominated peoples.[116] In Brazil, recent extensive
literature exists that records the experience of black children in public schools
in poor communities. Such children suffer incisively from the effects of
racism and the racial discrimination that is characteristic of their education.[117]

The psychoanalytic approach from an Afro-Brazilian perspective was
given new expression by Isildinha Baptista Nogueira. She writes:

As a psychoanalyst, I proposed to explore the way in which the socio-his-
torical-cultural reality of racism and discrimination is inscribed on the
black person's psyche. That is, I dedicated my efforts to the question of
how this process of constituting oneself as a subject is experienced by

black people, to the extent that they have always been affected by these issues. As a psychoanalyst and, particularly, as a black person, my listening has always been placed in that direction.[118]

Given the new abundance of available statistical data demonstrating that racial domination affects blacks in all social classes, the author can make such an assertion without constraint, a possibility not so readily available when Neusa Santos Souza wrote her book.[119]

Nogueira proposes a model of the psychic processes of this domination in Lacanian terms that involve, beyond the operation of the white ego ideal, narcissistic dissociation in the body image; the lack of whiteness experienced as privation; and the envy of whites as those who have what the black subject lacks. She focuses on the notion of the persecutory relationship with the body observed by Costa,[120] for whom this persecution is triggered when someone becomes conscious of racism. Emphasizing that the marks of this process are "inscribed" on the psyche,[121] Nogueira suggests that such an experience functions as a superimposition: "The encounter with racism as a conscious experience superimposes itself on a real rejection of the black body that corresponds to an archaic memory."[122] The archaic memory is the mother's desire for whiteness, in an analogy to Lacan's theory, by which "desire is articulated for what the mother lacks: the phallus."[123]

Nogueira's theoretical innovation invites us to reflect, from a gender perspective, on Freudian and Lacanian theory of psychic structure and the symbolic order based on sexual difference. One might begin by recording the fact that psychoanalysis is conceived precisely in the process of interrogating the feminine nature. Regina Neri observes that psychoanalysis "is inaugurated giving credit and ear to hysteria as the bearer of a truth that subverts the scientific and philosophical rationality" built over the previous centuries.[124] Such a truth is the female "other," who comes on the scene deconstructing the universal and installing in the heart of psychoanalysis the question of sexual difference. Neri writes:

> The richness and singularity of psychoanalysis lie in the fact that it is constituted precisely in the discursive tension—present in Freud's work—between giving voice to this singular other and reasserting the male as universal in culture. Referred to a phallocentric *telos* that is held up as a universal, a-historic symbolic context, phallic construction is an expression of this current of reassertion, a male version of difference, in continuity with the philosophical and scientific discourse of a metaphysics of the sexes.[125]

In the Lacanian universe, the intervention of the symbolic father as the third party shatters the illusion of union in the relationship between mother and child, introduces language, and makes possible the individual's process of psychological differentiation, allowing the subject to perceive itself as a being distinct from others. Such intervention also institutes *logos*, thought and speech, which arise from the discernment of difference and the process of differentiation. The symbolic is fundamental to the maintenance of sanity; its only alternative is psychosis.

The phallus symbolically represents this rupture caused by the intervention of the third party and constitutes the mark of absence, that is, the fact that the subject is not complete in itself. Theoretically, such symbolic structure does not imply male dominance, since the phallus is a neutral sign and both sexes could occupy either the male or the female place in the symbolic world. However, there are two planes on which the linkage of symbolic to sexual difference determines that the link between phallus and penis exists and persists, structuring the Freudian–Lacanian symbolic world as fundamentally patriarchal. The first is the operation of socially constructed gender roles, given that generally women care for children and that the intervening third party generally is male. Moreover, men are socially valued, a fact that reinforces the necessity of the male being the intervening third party. At the same time, the third party is associated with language and *logos*, and therefore with power of action in the world—traditionally considered the prerogative of men. The second is that in linking the body to symbolic process, we depend on a visual representation of sexual difference; the penis then represents the phallus. The female, on the other hand, is identified as absence or lack, something that exists only in opposition to the phallus.

In Freudian phallic construction, penis envy is supposed to arise at the moment the child discovers the anatomical difference between the sexes, whose meaning for the girl—absence—is made essential and universal, in a classic example of the naturalization of social inequalities. Feminist critique of psychoanalytical theory focuses on this thesis of the sexual nature of the preference for what is male. Irenäus Eibl-Eibesfeldt writes:

> A plausible explicative hypothesis is taken, in an excessively glib way, to be the *per causas* explanation and discourse is built around the Oedipus complex, the fear of castration, and the girl's envy of the penis, as if one were dealing with demonstrated facts. But this is not so. It is true that, in isolated cases, a girl might want to be a boy and a male child might experience precocious conflicts with his father. But all this can be explained outside the sexual field and equally plausibly as a struggle for social position.[126]

As for the moment of discovery of anatomical difference, Elena Gianini Belotti maintains that this is a social phenomenon, for it is enough that the child witness the relations of power that prevail within the family to understand the superiority of the male position.[127] The child might observe the anatomical difference either before or after such a moment but it would not matter; in any case, the child will learn to identify the penis with the symbolic phallus. The identification flows, however, not from the knowledge of anatomical difference but from power relations and patterns of family organization in patriarchal society.

The problem of elevating the Freudian–Lacanian symbolic construction to the status of universal psychological structure, though, is not only essentialism. By focusing only on the social sphere, the critique neglects the real psychoanalytic difficulty, which is the need for the symbolic in order to maintain sanity. In other words, if the alternative to the symbolic is psychosis, it is in the context of clinical treatment that the major import of feminist critique emerges.

Following the logic of phallocentric construction, some have come to the conclusion that men have more capacity for psychological differentiation, which would explain the empirically greater incidence of psychosis among women. "The paradox arises here," observes Teresa Brennan, that "the patriarchal symbolic is a condition of sanity for both sexes, with the exception of women." Therefore, feminist criticism is concerned not only with neutralizing patriarchal language and modes of thought, but with intervening in psychological discussion of the symbolic from a clinical point of view and dealing with the specific problem of the organization of the psyche and sanity.[128]

For Brennan, real changes in patterns of parenting and in social relations of gender should have consequences for the symbolic. Taking into consideration the influence of the symbolic on the organization and sanity of the psyche, the question becomes *what would a nonpatriarchal symbolic world imply?* In this perspective, for example, explicit attention of some authors to the female body "can be read not as a celebration of the body in itself, but as a psychoanalytically informed argument destined to counterbalance the centrality of the penis in the differentiation of the psyche."[129]

Returning to Nogueira's theoretical innovation, I do not know whether considerations analogous to those of feminist critique could be articulated in relation to her characterization of the envy of whiteness. She superimposes the rejection of black identity on the archaic remembrance of the mother's desire for what she does not have: whiteness. It seems that a universalization of this absence would run parallel to the sexualization of the absence of the phallus, placing in the order of the symbolic issues that more appropriately speak to racial power relations.

On the other hand, one can contemplate the possibility that social relations of race, like those of gender, have consequences for the symbolic world. If effects of the social dynamics of racism and white supremacy on personality formation influence the experience of the symbolic in a way analogous to gender relations and identification of penis with phallus, the question may be asked, "what would a symbolic world untouched by Western ethnocentrism imply?"

Afrocentric thought complements feminist critique of psychoanalysis by pointing out its basis in the myth of Oedipus, which comes out of a specific and eminently patriarchal ethnocultural matrix: ancient Greece. Afrocentrists question the tendency to naturalize patriarchal structures. If the symbolic structure of language defines the phallus as symbol of the power that resides in the father, and if the father is constituted as a moral authority "by the name that designates him and that posits behind him a genealogy, a tradition,"[130] we could ask (with Cheikh Anta Diop) what happens when the genealogy is traced through the mother and when women and men both wield power.[131] We could ask the same when, as Oyewumi points out, the linguistic structure—language—does not support the singular investment of power in the male figure. If the father's authority derives from ancestry, it will be "signaled in life by something pertaining to *another order that is not the order of life*"[132] only if the symbolic system that conducts life defines it so. In Yoruba cosmology, ancestry is present as an aspect of the order of life, represented symbolically in male *egungun* worship as well as the female orders of *géledés* and *èléèkó*, not to mention the female power of the *iyami* and *iyaba*. This female spiritual power is reflected in the social power structures of *terreiro* communities,[133] a fact that may carry implications for the symbolic and for the structure of the psyche in such a cultural context.

Considering a different facet of the possible influence of gender and race relations on the formation of psyche, another Afro-Brazilian psychologist, Maria Aparecida da Silva Bento, points out the need to introduce into psychology a consideration of rights taken from a critical understanding of power relations. For Bento, by naturalizing power relations symbolized in its signs of the structures of the psyche, psychoanalytical theory obstructs a critical approach to power relations and risks blaming the dominated people. Bento relates:

> I think that if you want something that has been expropriated from you, you don't want to be white, you want that thing that was expropriated,

and you have a right to that thing. [The idea in psychoanalysis is] that I don't want to be white if I am in the *favela* and have a pushcart; then I'm fine with being black. If I want to live in the Gardens and have a BMW, does that mean I want to be white? No. [If psychoanalysts think so, they must] believe that these things belong to whites. I think that these things do not belong to white people; they are what I pay for. They are the fruit of usurpation.[134]

The implicit culpability lies in attributing to structures of the psyche an envy that supposedly marks the subject's organism, having been inscribed on it.[135] Such analysis restricts the possibility of agency, making the status of being oppressed seem immutable, and for Bento can contribute to the naturalization of social inequalities. She told me:

There are two things, two separate things. One is to see a situation of loss or inferiority related to what you can do to change it and to your own efforts to change the situation. That is a positive thing. But when you discount a whole history, when you focus only on the oppressed, then you are going to say: oh, blacks are in that situation because they haven't figured out how to turn the boat over.

She concludes:

Psychology needs to redefine envy and desire and learn to introduce the concept of rights into its vocabulary. Rights are present today [in some] areas of social psychology, but rights are not present in clinical psychology. There, what we have is the reassertion of a place reserved for whites. There is indeed in psychology a dimension that says: the best man wins.[136]

Bento's observation seems to fit, in a certain way, with Nogueira's conclusion, which is pessimistic about Afro-Brazilian political action. According to Nogueira, such action "can be compromised and limited by the lack of consciousness ... of the process of forming, in the psyche itself, the imaginary and symbolic representations of the black body," and the action might "end up failing, for example, because of the unconscious survival of the myth of whiteness in the very forms in which political action is expressed."[137] Nogueira's conclusion seems, then, more pessimistic than that of her colleague Neusa Santos Souza, also a psychoanalyst, who asserts that "The construction of a new identity is a possibility that this dissertation indicates, generated from the voice of black people who, in a more or less contradictory or fragile way, struggle to build an identity giving them their own features, founded, therefore, on their own interests, and capable of transforming History—individual and collective, social and psychological."[138]

The theoretical discussion does not affect the quality of practice by psychotherapists like Bento and Nogueira, whose reports of cases they treat reveal commitment and competence in the sense of unveiling and redirecting anomalies aroused by the living experience of race in a context of domination. They share the formulation of theory and practice with reference to the history of usurpation, since Nogueira asserts, "It seems that the structures of power and domination are not strangers to the psychoanalyses practiced in consulting rooms."[139]

The theoretical debate highlights, instead, the incipience of a process of dealing with race in Brazilian psychology. The process is made possible by the entrance of a small group of blacks—mostly women—into the profession. Mainstream psychological theory—with few laudable exceptions—either maintains the traditional silence or recognizes the problem of race but exempts itself from the task of solving it, focusing instead on other priorities that psychologists perennially judge to be more urgent. Still a minority, but I think a growing one, some professionals in the field tend progressively to recognize the problem but remain uninformed and unequipped to deal with it. Psychologist Marilza de Souza Martins comments: "There is a total ignorance of how to deal with it. There is ignorance when there is not denial ... or when not denial, total ignorance."[140]

Recently, though, the number of professionals capable of dealing with the race issue has been growing. For the most part, they are psychologists who had firsthand experience of the demand for black therapists trained for addressing the issue, as Maria Lúcia da Silva recounts:

> I did my analysis with an orthodox psychoanalyst on the couch, in 1982, and at the time I was going through real, concrete situations. For example, I would take a bus to go to therapy at lunchtime, it was packed, and there was this group, a real gang, I knew them, they mugged people in the bus. It was a period when there were a lot of muggings on buses and they made me a kind of accomplice to them, because when they started to mug people, they would look me right in the eye and start to approach other people.
>
> I arrived at therapy one day going crazy, because in the first place how could I turn them in? If I turn them in I'm a goner, because it was a heavy scene. This was one part of it, because the other part is that since this bus route had a tradition, any black person inside that bus

was suspect, so a lot of times when they saw me go by on that bus, people would put away their purse, hold onto their bag, put their hands in their pockets. A lot of times I came into therapy with these issues and my therapist would always say that it was an inferiority complex and that things weren't exactly like that. And I would argue with her. "No, you're not black, you don't know what it is to get on the bus and have people think you're the one who's going to rob them, that you are a thief and a mugger," and so on and so on. Not to mention other things that the race issue generates. And this psychoanalyst, whom I like very much, who helped me a lot, couldn't understand, until one day the time arrived that she gave in and said, "Alright, okay, what do you suggest I read? How can I begin to understand where this is coming from?" So she was able to be humble enough to say: "I don't understand this stuff you are bringing me; how can I prepare myself to be able to see you in a different way?"

Now, I was also bold and intrepid enough, and I knew about race issues. I was already part of the black movement. I was studying psychology. So I could say to her: You are wrong. This is not an inferiority complex. I might well have an inferiority complex, but this part here is not inferiority complex. You're wrong. You have to see it another way. And so we can see from what people tell us, that things go differently with other people, partly because they don't have the same willingness to confront. After all, it's an authority that's there in front of you; it's hard for the person to confront this authority with respect to what they are feeling and say, "No, that's not true!" How can this young woman disqualify a therapist! So these are the kind of complaints that came to us.[141]

Since approximately the middle of the 1990s, groups of psychologists have formed with the goal of filling this gap in the understanding of racial issues in psychology. A pioneer among them is AMMA—Psique e Negritude of São Paulo. The name of the group refers to the African mythological principle of the "divine breath that represents the spiral movement of the world's creation."[142] Its core is a group of psychologists, Ana Maria Silva, Maria Lúcia da Silva, Marilza de Souza Martins, and Sílvia de Souza. Their work includes individual and group therapy complemented by community service, consultation, and participation in events, seminars, and workshops, and publication of texts for the public like the book *Liking Ourselves Better*, described as "a manual, indeed a survival kit."[143] They use a mix of clinical approaches that vary from Freudian, Jungian, and Reichian to holistic techniques. Their following statement about their work recalls Serra's exhortation about the urgency to be alert to the pathology of racism:

> We share the idea, which is a fruit of our life experiences and professional lives, that racism produces different ways of being sick, in addition to causing distortions in the construction of our identity. We believe in the need to create working strategies that take racism into account as one more element that structures our psyche's apparatus and, therefore, unleashes attitudes and behavior peculiar to those who are subject to discrimination. Our perspective is to investigate differentiated alternatives that can reflect on black experience taking into account our history and our singularity. To understand how racism acts on our psyche and find ways to overcome it is a task and one of the stages of reconstruction of the dignity of the black individual and people.
>
> We hope, also, that society will contribute its share of responsibility in the search for solutions that can eliminate social and racial inequalities affecting the majority of the Brazilian population.[144]

Organized groups within the Afro-Brazilian social movement have made several initiatives in this direction. Another example is the Instituto Negro Padre Batista (Father Batista Black Institute) also in São Paulo, which offers a program—operating under an agreement with the State Prosecutor's Office—of legal services with psychological assistance for victims of racial crimes.[145]

In Rio de Janeiro, the Health Troupe and the Afro-Reggae Cultural Group develop a broad experience from their location in Vigario Geral, the community where the massacre of dozens of people triggered the effort to organize alternatives for youth and all residents.[146] In the health area, their priority is work with HIV/AIDS and sexually transmitted diseases, an activity that necessarily involves the reflection, intervention, and development of approaches in the area of psychology. One of the coordinators of the Health Troupe, psychologist Marco Antonio Chagas Guimarães, formulates an approach to clinical work with reference to the religious culture of African origin and to the work of Donald Woods Winnicott, the British psychoanalyst whose influence in Brazil, Argentina, and Uruguay has been substantial.[147] Guimarães focuses his research on the traditional role of *mães criadeiras*— caring mothers—who see the *iyawos*—initiates—through their period of reclusion and rebirth. He evaluates this role in the *terreiro* community as one of "good enough mothers" who create and sustain a "holding environment" in Winnicott's terms.[148] In another research work in *terreiro* communities,

Guimarães studies three community health projects and proposes the notion of "networks of support" as a model for intervention in collective health.[149]

Marta de Oliveira da Silva, psychoanalyst and researcher for the Palmares Human Rights Institute, observes how violence, which brutally befalls the black population, returns in symptoms treated as mental health disturbances. She shows that the system of classification of these disturbances "makes exceptional, excludes, and covers up the true factors unleashing the symptoms presented, and makes people who look for help feel individually responsible for their illness."[150] In her evaluation, the state of continuous violence experienced by the black population results in the need to "think about a wartime economy of the psyche, which alters subjective attitudes toward life because it perverts the possibility of thinking about the future with pleasure; and toward death because death is banalized."[151] The need for public mental-health policies adequate to respond to such a situation has been recognized in various contexts, including reports by the Ministry of Health.[152]

In 1998 in Florianopolis, Santa Catarina, the Nucleus of Black Studies (NEN) Justice Program created a program of Psychotherapeutic Consultation for Victims of Racism, whose goals express in a very representative way those of other psychological counseling programs, services, and initiatives created by black organizations and therapists. Their goals read as follows:

> 1. To understand how racism acts on the psychic structure, how it alters attitudes and behavior of individuals subjected to discriminatory practices; 2. To make theoretical and experience-centered discussion possible by means of a group psychotherapeutic process; 3. To allow victims to understand aspects related to the justice system, social inequalities, discrimination, self-esteem, identity, and social participation.

The hope to go beyond overcoming individual suffering expresses, perhaps, the major objective common to these initiatives. NEN states: "If in our experiences we include a process of self-knowledge and contextual evaluation, we can become a tool for change, to the extent that knowledge broadens the possibilities of independence and creativity."[153]

AMMA—Psique e Negritude, the group of Afro-Brazilian psychotherapists in São Paulo, has the same kind of objectives. Maria Lúcia da Silva, AMMA's coordinator, uses a clinical approach supported by bioenergetics. Her theoretical discussion coincides with the psychoanalytical one when it finds the same open wound, exposed and subject at any moment to all types of attack that Neusa Santos Souza observed. Based on her clinical experience, she suggests "the hypothesis ... that the historical life process experienced by black people imprinted on them some traits of the psychological dynamics of the schizoid individual."[154] The absence of identification of the ego with its body leads the individual to not perceive it in a living way; "he [or she] feels unconnected to the world and to people ... the sense of conscious identity is unlinked to the way the person feels about himself." She observes that phrases such as "I discovered I don't have a body" or "I pretend I have no body" are commentaries often to be heard among black people in the consulting room. The identity is shattered, fragmented. This fact, in schizoids, is "due to a story of rejection, an absent, cold and hostile mother, who did not look at the child with affection ... making it difficult for this child to establish a relationship with his own body." Or the child might have suffered a real threat of death in the first moments of life, "or even in the intra-uterine period (the mother or even the baby might have suffered some kind of accident), [and might] carry this bodily and emotional memory into life."[155] Maria Lúcia da Silva offers a unique analogy:

> Let us take Brazilian Society as a great mother, or stepmother some might prefer, and let us see how this mother cared for this child, her Afro-Brazilian offspring.
>
> A totally rejecting mother, she does not recognize blacks as her children, on the contrary, since they were "slaves they could be the objects of buying, selling, loan, donation, pawning, sequester, transmission by inheritance, embargo, deposit, bidding, adjudication, like any other merchandise."
>
> Not only does this mother fail to shelter, but she attacks this child with corporal punishment, which often leads to death even before being "born" in the new land: "The causes of death were physical abuse, malnutrition on board [the slaveships], overcrowding, disease ... mortality would continue on Brazilian soil, where the slaves arrived exhausted and exposed to diseases for which their immunological system was not prepared."
>
> This is a mother who allows her child's body to be abused, as in the rape of black women and the use of men as reproducers. This is an inhuman and hostile mother who sees her child as something akin to an animal and stamps him with an image of worthlessness....
>
> In order to withstand physical punishment it was necessary to "leave" this body.... Any demonstration of affect, be it hate or love, would put the child's life at risk.
>
> On the other hand, the punishments and humiliations constantly undergone, plus the encouragement of animosity among blacks, contributed to installing conflict in their identity as well as the desire not to be black.[156]

Maria Lúcia da Silva writes, "society takes it upon itself to reinforce [the metaphorical mother's historical rejection] by means of racism." She does not fail to note the atavistic inscription of these historical marks "engraved on our bodies, as a kind of 'emotional genetics'" that racism renews and reinforces. However, this process is not linked to the Lacanian symbolism of the phallus, nor is it expressed in terms of envy as an archaic memory of the psyche. Rather, it is "a constant process of annihilation" that leads some black individuals, like the schizoid individual, to close themselves off in an internal world, where they "are protected and can create, dream, spiritualize. ... It is the only place of freedom." The annihilation of one's own identity favors "difficulties of coexistence, violence among blacks," which is the "fruit of not being able to recognize the other as an equal. To look at the other is the same as looking at a broken vase, shattered, worthless."[157]

The mainstay of the articles in the AMMA psychologists' book, which was written for a lay audience, is the theme of self-esteem. In various ways and in different contexts, the authors think through alternatives for building black people's self-esteem. They propose that to achieve self-esteem, blacks must redeem their own bodies as well as their historical legacy and cultural matrix. "To me, redeeming Africa is to rescue and recover self-esteem," Maria Lúcia da Silva states, "and we need to do this, we need to work on self-esteem." Nevertheless, she admits that there are serious difficulties, not the least of which is the lack of "agile information" to support this proposal.[158]

Maria Lúcia da Silva confirms that an identity based on the single image of enslavement as a historical reference has little chance of building self-esteem. To recover the African and Afro-Brazilian ancestors as historical agents and the creators of civilizations and technology is important to counter the weight of negative representations that encourage belief in their inferiority and that of their descendants.

Psychologist and scholar Ricardo Franklin Ferreira is an important contributor to this endeavor with his study of African-descendant identity. His research focuses on a long-term interview—carried out over a period of several months—with João, a member of the black movement in São Paulo.[159] The main characteristic of Ferreira's methodology is a dialogic relationship forged with his subject, in which Ferreira avoids the posture of outside observer and embarks on a "journey" with João in which they build the research and conclusions together. Using theoretical references offered by William E. Cross[160] and Janet. E. Helms,[161] Ferreira identifies four basic stages in the construction of the African-descendant identity: submission, impact, struggle, and articulation. The process of identity building is not static; it will differ from one individual to another and elements of the different stages will overlap and coexist at different moments in the person's life.[162]

In the first stage—submission—the individual accepts mainstream society's convictions about his or her racial inferiority, submits to them, and tries to avoid identifying as black.[163]

The second stage—impact—corresponds perhaps to the injunction against blackness in Costa's model. But for Costa, the impact of the injunction is to install persecutory conflict with the body, maintaining and even intensifying the state of submission.[164] Ferreira's study involves a subject whose consciousness of racism inspired him, on the contrary, to rebellion and activism. João's consciousness of racism impelled him to search for information and for contexts of collective action in which he could exercise agency in the fight against racism.

The third stage—struggle—is itself activist, as it is characterized by the subject's immersion in political engagement and value identification.

The fourth stage—articulation—involves the consolidation of an African-centered identity developed through activism and the search for new partners and broader alliances to engage in dialogue, exchange, and solidarity with others.[165] The identity evolves "in articulation with other matrixes and references."[166]

Ferreira's model seems to pick up where Souza left off: "The possibility of building a black identity ... founded on black interests, transforming History—individual and collective, social and psychological."[167] In such a political dimension resides Ferreira's innovation that focuses on identity built through social activism and with a sense of authorship.

Ferreira's second innovation is the idea that an African-centered identity can be articulated with an identity based on other matrixes. In such an idea the essence of the Afrocentric concepts of centeredness and agency arises. The subject needs to be secure in his or her own center in order to engage in a dialogic activity with others. Ferreira describes such a stage as the following:

> Little by little, the person develops a nonstereotyped African-centered perspective, with more open and less defensive attitudes that seek to value qualities referring to a broader, more expansive notion of blackness.... Psychologically, from the moment in which the individual stops considering the values associated with different ethnic-racial sources to be antagonistic, their internalization is no longer a conflict, which makes the person calmer, more relaxed.... This "new" identity, with the African

quality as one of its important dimensions, begins to have a protecting function. ... The African matrix then can be effectively asserted.[168]

Undoubtedly, Ferreira's advance is great when he recognizes the possibility of an African-centered identity in dialogue with other matrixes. The blind spot of mainstream miscegenation discourse in Brazil is the absolute inability to perceive this possibility, so it is discarded before it can actually be raised. An African-centered identity is assumed to be intrinsically racist and incapable of interaction with other matrixes, much less the internalization of them. Ferreira seems to affirm the contrary: By centering his or her identity over a located axis, the subject not only can engage in dialogue with other values but also absorb them and integrate them in a balanced way. It seems that the dialogic method, based on the interview with João, allowed Ferreira to understand this.[169] Such an understanding is exceptional among Brazilian intellectuals.

In the final chapter, however, the researcher reevaluates his model and this second innovation cedes in favor of a new goal, a fifth stage of "integration" in which "the identity of the African-descendant Brazilian stops being African-centered and becomes Afro-including [*afroincludente*]." Ferreira goes on to discuss João: "Still fixed in a stage of activism, but now in articulation with other cultural roots that he also possesses, João—the 'black' who became 'African descendant'—is on the way to becoming an '*African-European-Native Brazilian descendant*.'"[170] Here it seems that Ferreira has remitted the stage of African-centered identity in articulation with other values and interacting with other groups to the stage of activism, where it is left somehow submerged in the identity characteristics of that stage: a militant, defensive or aggressive attitude that values Africanness *as against* other references. The final stage, now emphasizing integration as opposed to articulation, is defined in the classic terms of race mixture.

In an e-mail, kindly responding to my query about this change, Ferreira explained that the term "Afro-including"

allows for the idea of a black and white and Native Brazilian, *without any emphasis on Africa*, because I believe that, as a function of the historical process undergone by enslaved Africans, today the identity of black Brazilians is built upon European and Indian [Native Brazilian] roots, and [blacks] are rescuing and recovering their African matrixes, independently of the value one might attribute to that process (in my case, I consider it a perverse process).

The author adds that "Brazilians of African descent, independently of their 'degree' of blackness or amount of melanin, harbor in the construction of their identity white European, African, and Native American, and, in the future, Japanese values, because this last one is an influence that is participating more and more in citizenship formation."[171]

The African-centered identity in articulation with those of other groups was an original proposal, emerging from the dialogical methodology that is one of the outstanding features of Ferreira's work. His intimate contact and conversation with the subject João had allowed the psychologist to surpass the bounds of the fable of the three races and comprehend the basic notion of Afrocentricity: that a centered identity favors interaction with others. However, expressions like "degree of blackness" and "amount of melanin" point to the familiar fear of essentialism. It would appear that the pressure of the mainstream ideology led him to reevaluate the notion of African-centered identity interacting with other values and resulted in his giving preference to the new formulation "Afro-including."

The term "Afro-including" immediately inspires the question of what criteria—and who defines them—determine the new identity. Ferreira's response indicates that the proposal does not embrace, for example, "an emphasis on Africa," which seems to have been left to the stage of activism.

We might also ask what exactly one is included in; if the including identity is supposed to be the fusion of Brazilian ethnic and cultural matrixes, then African identity already *is* Brazilian identity and there would be no need to "include" it as the capping stage of the process. On the other hand, if the identity has been excluded or destroyed then only an African-centered approach will be able to recover it.

In Brazilian daily life, the European component of the Afro-including identity is emphasized constantly, or detached and developed separately, with enormous richness of detail; no one raises the red flag of white essentialism. One does not speak of "including" European references since the defining slogan of Brazilian civilization has always been its characterization as Western. In turn, Africanness has always been "included" on the terms that Western hegemony defines—an Africanness irreducibly identified with slavery, bereft of the image of Africans as sovereign peoples and actors on the stage of human history. Such an image is what might be called "recreational" Africanness, limited to the spheres of dance, rhythm, football (soccer), and cuisine.[172]

Ferreira recognizes that the substitution of the African-centered for the Afro-including reflects and reproduces the process of de-Africanization that characterizes Brazilian cultural ideology; he judges that process to be perverse. His disapproval, though, does not resolve the issue because it leaves hanging the source of the Afrocentric identity notion: his dialogic relationship with the subject João. It seems that in the writing, João convinces Ferreira of the possibility of an African-centered position that allows for articulation with other identities and cultures. However, when Ferreira reevaluates the model and hopes that João will surpass the Afrocentric stage and go on to a fifth "Afro-including" stage, the possibility seems to elude them. The path that the dialogic relationship takes implies a certain curtailment of the subject's exercise of a sense of authorship in building his identity. Ferreira returns to the premise that only by moving forward to another identity—the Afro-including one—will João truly be able to engage in articulation with other groups. In other words, he returns to the mistaken notion that an African-centered identity is by definition a closed and exclusive one.

Afrocentricity merely locates the center of identity. Nothing prevents a centered identity from absorbing and internalizing other values in a balanced way except the rigidity of the discourse that proposes the disappearance of African identity in a so-called synthesis inevitably centered on Western values. In such a discourse a double-blind spot exists: on one hand there is a refusal to recognize Western centrism and on the other there is an insistence on denying that non-Western centrism has the capacity for solidarity and balanced dialogue with other identities.

I believe that the example of Ferreira points to the relational dimension of racism. All the approaches we have seen have one characteristic in common: They take as their object the pathologization of racism but they look at it only in terms of its impact on blacks. Perhaps such a fact derives from the clinical position, which deals with identity issues and emotional disturbances brought to the therapist by black patients.

Another approach emerges from the work of the Center for Study of Ethics and Inequality in Labor Relations (CEERT) of São Paulo, a nonpartisan, nongovernmental, nonprofit organization founded in 1990 "with the objective of conjugating production of knowledge with programs of intervention in the field of race and gender relations, seeking to promote equality of opportunities and treatment and the effective exercise of citizenship."[173] CEERT also works with applied psychology in the labor union context. For over a decade, the organization has been offering training courses and consultancies on race relations. These courses helped to push forward the challenge to the traditional Marxist position that denied the legitimacy of specific issues of race and gender in favor of a unitary view of the working class. In this view, as Maria Aparecida da Silva Bento observes, "All possibilities of trade union action were geared to the totality, which was understood as nondifferentiation. Thus, the problem of discriminatory practices was not understood

as a problem for trade unions, just as racial differences and inequalities provoked fears of rupture, of harm to the totality."[174]

Spurred on by black activists, trade union work against racism developed
despite these obstacles. Trade unions formed committees against racial discrimination and approved position papers at conferences of trade union federations and specific categories. On November 20, 1995, National Black
Consciousness Day and Third Centennial of Zumbi, Brazil's three major labor
union federations—Unified Labor Federation (CUT), General Labor
Federation (CGT), and Força Sindical—together founded the Inter-American
Institute for Racial Equality (INSPIR) with the support of the AFL-CIO of the
United States and the Inter-American Labor Organization (regional office of
the International Labor Organization) seated in Caracas, Venezuela.

The objective of CEERT's workshops and training programs is to contribute to this development by working on racism in its relational aspect—its
impact on both whites and blacks. Thus, they start from the following premise expressed by Ruth Frankenberg:

> Any system based on differences shapes those to whom it accords privi-
> lege just as much as it shapes those it oppresses. White people are
> invested with "race" in the same way that men are invested with "gen-
> der." And in a social context where white people see themselves too fre-
> quently as nonracial or racially neutral, it becomes crucial to observe the
> "raciality" of the experience of being white.[175]

The social dynamic of the labor union training programs confirms
research done by social psychologist Edith Piza in São Paulo,[176] which showed
that whites tend not to identify themselves racially. Moreover, among whites
and blacks

> it is not an uncommon tendency to deny, escape, forget that one is a dis-
> criminator or a victim of discrimination. In discussing racism, people
> expect to talk about a kind of oppression that is "out there" in society, but
> not something that involves them directly or that involves their institution.
> If they are white, they are not always avid to come into contact with the
> fact that at some point they have benefited from racism. On the other
> hand, being discriminated against, being associated with failure, incompe-
> tence, and inferiority, is not always something people will quickly admit.[177]

Relational analysis underscores the fact that both the privileges of some
and the deficits of others are the fruit of discrimination. "Privilege" here does

not necessarily refer to wealth or assets but rather to social advantages, which are often purely symbolic in nature. Racial inequalities are seen and often accepted by recourse to platitudes that are unsustainable by facts or by logic but allow whites and blacks to avoid entering into conflict and maintain the system of privileges. Denial of discrimination implies both the exemption of whites and the culpability of blacks.[178]

To admit that racism brings them privilege undermines whites' self-image of competence and merit. It is difficult to recognize that "blacks under the same conditions as whites tend not to have the same opportunities or the same treatment,"[179] because such a fact shows that it is not always merit that determines the winning of superior positions by whites. For this reason, "a great resistance to overcome is the belief, which many want to preserve, that individual effort is recognized with impartiality."[180]

CEERT offers a reformulation of the official history that attributes basic references in trade union training courses to whiteness. Such concepts include the struggle and resistance of the proletariat. Europeanization of such concepts led to the idea that "work and struggle in Brazil began only a century ago, with the arrival of European immigrants."[181] Looking at this process helps trade unionists understand how the people who were the sole producers of wealth throughout over 80 percent of the country's history—African-descendant workers—have been divested of their historical agency. The reclaiming of such agency is more than simply a revision of history or a deconstruction of myth, "since it allows us to re-signify racial groups" and offers references for the redefinition of social places. "In other words, a process of education and training on race relations can always become an eminently political process."[182]

Revising identity concepts with the tools of psychology complements this approach. Citing authors like Theodor Adorno, Frantz Fanon, and Edward Said, CEERT's texts examine the function of racism in the psyche of racist personalities, the construction of the absolute "other" with reference to the self, and the function of what Freud called "cannibal love" articulated with "narcissistic hate." In the last analysis, whites invent the white man's black person and instill the image they have invented in the Other.[183]

CEERT's essays also contribute to the study of whiteness as an identity matrix. In her pioneering essay, Edith Piza uses the magnificent image of the glass door to describe white identity:

> In the beginning it was like this: walking into a glass door. Anyone who has come up against a glass door knows what I am talking about. The impact is staggering and after the fright and the pain comes the

astounded realization that one had not seen the contour of the glass, the doorknob, the lock, the metal hinges that kept the door closed. Everything seems accessible, but in reality there is an invisible frontier that stands between what one knows about the Other—which is quite a lot—and what very little—almost nothing—one knows about oneself.[184]

Racial nonidentification is the trademark of whiteness. "To be white … is not having to think about it. … The meaning of being white is the possibility of choosing whether to reveal or ignore one's own whiteness. [It is the privilege of] not having to call oneself white."[185]

Piza proposes the concept of a "place" of race as the "social locus of identification of the 'other' as a subject in relationship, in which race defines the terms of this relationship." And she offers an example:

If the person is black and is parking a car in a prohibited spot, someone might always recall that "only a black person would do that!" However, if a white person does the same thing, certainly someone will curse them behind their back with a word that might, at most, offend their mother, but will never curse the population of whites as a whole, the group to which the person belongs. The behavior expectation for the two subjects is not determined by their race, but only one is racialized and his behavior extended to the whole group of his racial belonging—the black person. The white person simply has a mother.[186]

In its relational aspect, racism generates for blacks an intense visibility of their bodily features accompanied by certain behavior expectations. For whites,

"Neutrality" and nonexplicitness make race a dispensable datum of their own identity, but support "daily confirmations" of the prescriptions of a "racial geography of the other." They become, in reality, a glass door. They generate the transparency of a universe that is experienced as something unique, universal, unchangeable. It is the "others" who must change. It is the "others" who are seen, evaluated, named, classified, forgotten.[187]

Whiteness unnamed may generate powerful consequences when it influences decisions like choosing among candidates for a job. Faced with two equally qualified people—one black and one white—when the objective criteria do not determine the choice, what decides the case is the employer's subjectivity. Imbued with stereotypes built over the course of five centuries, the "natural" reaction, that is the one taken without thought, is to prefer the white candidate.

Discrimination often occurs in these moments of subjective evaluation. In a process of selection, the black person may have higher results on all phases of written exams or other tests and be eliminated by the interview or the psychological test. The decision made by racial criterion may not be conscious, much less intentional, but the result is the same. The discussion of the subject in the context of the labor market, therefore, may be considered an important initiative.

It is important to recall that in Brazil whiteness is viscerally linked to the ideology of racial mixture. Its standard has become virtual whiteness, which is expressed as what one might call an ideology of tropical *morenidade*—the hegemonic preference for light-colored mixed race. Such an ideology is contained in ideas like Freyre's "metarace" and the "cosmic race" of Vasconcelos—the eulogy of miscegenation that is supposed to result in a homogeneous light-skinned *moreno* population.[188] The "euphemistic garb of *moreno*" that Oliveira Vianna mentioned[189] is the dress of our virtual whites, and they are the ones that define the terms of the fable of the three races.[190] But the Brazilian commitment to whiteness remains, disguised in the language of miscegenation and syncretism or tropical *morenidade*. This is why I consider it fundamental to a critical analysis of race relations in Brazil to refer, in a kind of constant vigilance, to the technique of critical white studies. This is not as new an idea as it would seem; it was already being discussed among black intellectuals in the 1940s and 1950s, first as an ironic reference to the studies of the black "problem" in vogue at the time.[191] Later, sociologist Guerrreiro Ramos made significant incursions in the field with his work on the social and psychological pathology of "white" Brazilians, a veritable treatise on what I have called virtual whiteness.[192]

CONCLUSION

I hope that the brief visit we have made to the history of psychology's handling of race in Brazil can contribute to a broader and more in-depth understanding of racism as a relational phenomenon affecting blacks, whites, and society as a whole. Psychology's role in making and reinforcing negative representations of African descendants in Brazil has been powerful and active. It has helped raise whiteness to a position of superiority and whites to that of the legitimate holders of knowledge and masters of the competent discourse.

Only in the last decade of the twentieth century did there begin to arise an "Afro-Brazilian ear" with the intention and capability of listening to issues appropriate to an identity that was massacred over the course of centuries, thus opening new perspectives for black Brazilians to realize their potential for human agency and to reclaim their history.

In Chapters 4 and 5 I explore some expressions of this Afro-Brazilian historical agency in the contours of twentieth-century black movements in São Paulo and Rio de Janeiro. The collective exercise of historical agency means black people acting as the protagonists of their own history. Such an instance has remained largely obscured by the anti-African slant that underlies the sorcery of color and the fable of the three races as well as the considerable gaps in the country's historical and sociological records.

The goal of this research is to contribute to restoring some historical references on Afro-Brazilian agency, not only to set the record straight, but also to support the building of Afro-Brazilian identities with a sense of authorship. Another aim is to fuel the preparation of curricula for the teaching of Afro-Brazilian culture and history.

4

ANOTHER HISTORY: AFRO-BRAZILIAN AGENCY (SÃO PAULO AND RIO DE JANEIRO, 1914–1960)

> *We no longer need to consult anyone to come to the conclusion that we have legitimate rights, that the reality of our situation is an anguishing one, and that various forces are conspiring in the commitment to despise us and, indeed, to create the conditions for our disappearance!*
>
> —MANIFESTO OF THE NATIONAL CONVENTION OF BRAZILIAN BLACKS (A GAZETA, NOVEMBER, 1945)

PART OF THE sorcery of color is the magic of erasing blacks as protagonists from the available record of history. This chapter is an exercise in the opposite direction. I found through my research that the historical record shows the agency of black movements creating resistance identities whose assertion was an important part of the continuum that anticipated and helped build the critical multicultural demands of later movements. The scant sketch of Afro-Brazilian activities here is limited to the states of São Paulo and Rio de Janeiro between 1914 and 1960.

This is a little-known history, almost entirely absent from teaching curricula. Schools teach lessons on Zumbi of Palmares[1] and certain heroes of the abolition movement, but these figures appear to be the only recognized African descendants who are actors in and creators of their own history. Even so, these names are remembered only on commemorative dates like May 13, the anniversary of slavery's abolition, or November 20, National Black Awareness Day. The first step in reinforcing

African-descendant identity in schools is to teach more recent examples of African Brazilians as subjects of the country's history. Both this chapter and the following one seek to address this need.

ANTECEDENTS AND CONTEXT

The black movement emerging at the outset of the twentieth century was really the continuation of a process that had been in motion since the country's very beginnings. Kilombo resistance, which is most forcefully expressed in the example of Zumbi and the Republic of Palmares, is not restricted to a particular historical period or geographical area, but permeates the entire colonial period and the period of the Empire of Brazil, shaking the foundations of the slave economy until it finally collapsed.[2]

The fight to abolish slavery was led by black personalities like Luis Gama, José do Patrocínio, and the brothers André and Antonio Rebouças. It was fueled and fed by the Revolts of the Tailors, the Malês, the Cowrie Shells, and others, whose anonymous heroes were mostly African Brazilians. After abolition, the same antiracist struggle took different forms, such as the Revolt of the Chibata—led by sailor João Cândido in 1910—which was diligently hidden from official history and unveiled only decades later.[3] Finally, the *terreiro* communities of Afro-Brazilian religion were a major mainstay of black resistance throughout the nineteenth and twentieth centuries. Catholic brotherhoods also played an important role in the resistance and development of the black community.

The record of the black movement in the first half of the century following slavery's abolition is very precarious. Most books, folders, newspapers, and documents relating to Afro-Brazilian community organizations and activities are out of print, kept in private archives, lost, or otherwise inaccessible. This situation reflects the life experience of a community devoid of economic and political power and a movement composed of organizations constantly subject to instability and lack of resources, infrastructure, physical space, and the support of other sectors of civil society. One consequence of the sparse record of— and research on—the black movement is the reinforcement of the belief that African Brazilians have no specific history. Brazilians generally think of their history as one in which black people collectively played only passive roles as, for example, the victims of slavery or the beneficiaries of its abolition. The actors in Brazilian history are not seen as black; very few exceptions confirm the rule. Moreover, the notion of a black community with little tradition of antiracist struggle prevails naturally among supporters of the racial democracy theory, for whom there would be no reason for such struggle since they deny the existence of racism. Intellectuals in general, sociologists in particular, and some participants of today's black movement, also tend to believe that black political consciousness and Afro-Brazilian activism in the twentieth century really began in the 1970s.

Very few sources have yielded most of the material I used in the present effort to partially exhume this history. The major works of sociologists Florestan Fernandes[4] and Roger Bastide[5] are rich with excerpts from primary sources in the period from the 1920s to the early 1960s. They record a plethora of texts taken from newspapers and from original documents of the black movement. Another important source in my research was the catalogue of black press publications for an exhibition held at the São Paulo State Pinacoteca Museum in 1977 as a result of Professor Eduardo de Oliveira e Oliveira's dedication and perseverance.[6] Members of Quilombhoje, the black literature group, offer two published records of the Brazilian Black Front, an outstanding black organization of its time.[7] Also crucial to this study are Abdias Nascimento's personal archives, which include his collection of the *Quilombo* newspaper[8] and of other original documents of the black movement (pamphlets, magazines, journals, newspapers, newspaper clippings, manuscripts, essays, and interviews). I also had occasion to interview several black-movement participants, including Ironides Rodrigues, Sebastião Rodrigues Alves, Léa Garcia, Guiomar Ferreira de Mattos, Marietta Campos Damas, and Abdias Nascimento.

BLACK PRESS AND CONTEXT (1914–1931)

At the beginning of the twentieth century, African Brazilians created many associations from which emerged a dynamic black press. In São Paulo, these associations grew out of burgeoning musical and recreational pursuits among African descendants, many of whom left the poor rural interior in search of a better life and converged in the capital city. Kim Butler compares the development of these associations and their cultural output to the Harlem Renaissance.[9] I agree with her that such associations are expressions of Afro-Brazilian self-determination and that commonalities in the African Diaspora cross national boundaries.

These São Paulo groups were mainly social or recreational, but they also espoused broader public objectives expressed in names like the Palmares Civic Center and the Afro-Campinas Civic Center; today, one might define such aims as community mobilization for human and civil rights. The black press denounced what it called "prejudice" (meaning racism and racial discrimination) and sought to overcome the exclusion of blacks from the labor market, the educational system, political activity, and civil society. A recurrent theme in these writings was the need for a second abolition of slavery, since the decree of 1888 had not promoted life in liberty, but rather had condemned blacks to a state of privation. These organizations and their newspapers combated the identification of blacks with slavery and contested the notion of their congenital inferiority. This notion was reinforced by the Brazilian State's adoption of eugenics, a principle inscribed with the blessings of science in public policy[10] and, later, in the 1934 Constitution.[11]

Only shortly before these turn-of-the-century associations were formed, enslaved blacks had been released and left to their own fate in a false freedom that Abdias Nascimento characterized as a "civic lie."[12] The Afro-Brazilian population remained mostly illiterate and without jobs, housing, or health care. Society was hostile to blacks and desired their elimination. Alcoholism, tuberculosis, and other diseases swept through the community. Observing this social context, Florestan Fernandes comments that

in spite of insoluble limitations, ... [these organizations of the black movement] were successful on three points. They brought to the scene a new state of spirit, which impelled integrationist and assimilationist aspirations in the direction of demands for equality. They raised people's interest in the objective knowledge of "Brazilian racial reality," as a condition for enlightening the "population of color" and for its conscious action on the historical scene. They mobilized the "black element," trying to insert it directly into the debate and solution of "Brazilian racial problems," which represented, in itself, a revolutionary event.[13]

In general, black-movement organizations aimed to achieve the effective participation of formerly enslaved blacks in the mainstream society that excluded them. They considered education to be the best means for attaining this goal and therefore it was their main focus. Several offered night school courses[14] and the Brazilian Black Front, the largest and most outstanding black organization of its time, had its own school.[15] In addition to denouncing "prejudice" and exhorting the community to fight against it, their periodicals played a role in furthering education. French sociologist Roger Bastide observes in his study of the São Paulo black press: "These newspapers first seek to bring men of color together, give them a sense of solidarity, set them on a path, and teach them to fight against the inferiority complex."[16] The black press was, in the first place, an educational tool and, in the second place, a voice of protest.

An interesting example of this relationship between education and protest is the Palmares Civic Center, which emerged in the 1920s from the unique proposal of Antonio Carlos to form a library for blacks. José Correia Leite, cofounder of the newspaper *O Clarim d'Alvorada* and longtime activist in the Brazilian Black Front, spoke in the 1950s about this history:

> At that time, when blacks were beginning to become aware (a cloudy awareness, confused, full of contradictions) of their social situation, there appeared a black man, Antônio Carlos, who is now a major in Barbacena, with the idea of forming a library just for blacks. From this idea arose an institution called the Palmares Civic Center, which soon took on a unique role among black movements. The clearly cultural objective it began with (the organization of a library) was overcome by the force of the conditions in which we lived, and this association came to take on a role of defending black people and their rights. It is enlightening, in this sense, to recall the campaign it waged against an administrative order by the Chief of Police, Dr. Bastos Cruz, which made whiteness a prerequisite for acceptance into the [São Paulo] Civil Guard. The Palmares Center prevailed on Assemblyman Orlando de Almeida Prado to make a speech, which was widely publicized and discussed, and the order was revoked.[17]

Roger Bastide identifies three phases in the development of the black press of São Paulo. The first, beginning in 1914, coincides with World War I and the national policy of developing gratuitous public primary education. He writes that the war, "publicizing the ideas of freedom and equality, presenting itself as the great democratic combat, awakened in the masses of colored workers aspirations for a better life."[18]

The city of Campinas had actually come out ahead of the capital city, São Paulo, by publishing the first black newspaper of São Paulo State, *O Bandeirante*, in 1910. It continued with newspapers such as *A União* (1918) and *A Protectora* (1919). One of the foremost black papers—*O Getulino*, founded by poet and essayist Lino Guedes, writer Benedito Florencio, and others—had been launched in Campinas in 1919 and continued to be published until 1924. Over a decade later, in 1935, the newspaper *Escravos* was published in Campinas. The city was also significant to the black movement, because the Afro-Campineiro Congress was held there in 1938.

Other towns in the interior of São Paulo State were similarly active. In Piracicaba, the 13th of May Beneficent Society had been on the scene since before 1924. When the newspaper *O Patrocínio* (1925) reached its fifth year and fiftieth issue, it lamented "the unjust prejudices that unfortunately still exist" and exhorted the new generation to issue the call for a First Congress of Black Youth.

In the city of São Paulo, the periodical *O Menelike* was founded in 1915. The title was in itself an educational gesture, invoking the royal ancestral lineage of Ethiopia. The *Princess of the East* came out that same year, and *O Bandeirante*, the Kosmos Recreational Club's journal, was founded in 1918 under the directorship of Antonio dos Santos. Its editorial stance was announced in the subtitle "Monthly Vehicle for the Defense of Men of Color." Other organizations and journals of the time included the Federation of Men of Color and the Friends of the Fatherland Beneficent Society, *O Alfinete* (1918), *A Liberdade* (1919), *O Kosmos* (1924), *O Elite* (1924), and *Auriverde* (1928). In its first issue, *A Liberdade* defines itself editorially as "one more newspaper to take on the defense of men of color."

A salient aspect of this first phase identified by Roger Bastide is the ostentation of a certain social status. *O Bandeirante* declared on the front page of its second issue, "Our Club has progressed considerably and imposed itself in the eyes of the social circles of this Capital, an imposition that is also successful among those in the interior of the State—where we work to further the interests of the class of black men."[19]

Rather than reflecting a fantasy of social prestige, this type of assertion expresses the rejection of stereotypes of black indolence, laziness, criminality, and lack of initiative—in sum, inferiority. Such stereotypes had the endorsement of scientific theories and of official government policies based on the state-sanctioned theory of eugenics. The journals of the black press condemned alcoholism and called for morality and dignity in social relations. They emphasized the need to assert a clean and positive image of honorability and polish to counter the stereotyped image of blacks as savages.

The educational aspect of the periodicals is also apparent: they sought to teach ways of promoting greater possibilities for success in the modern world. In order to improve their living standards, blacks had to compete, which meant they needed to master not only technical training, but also the social tools demanded for professional performance. To this end, the journals of these associations emphasized good behavior and demanded their members' impeccable presentation according to the prevailing rules of society.

In considering the emphasis on presentation, it is important to be cautious in interpreting these attitudes. For example, some writers characterize them as typical of the "stage of submission" in the development of identity, in which "carefulness in dressing, adoption of socially correct behavior, sometimes excessively, reveals a struggle to overcome the supposed ontological inferiority that these people are led to believe they have."[20]

Without contesting the applicability of this observation in individual cases, it does not seem to fit these black associations. In contrast to internalizing the belief in their own inferiority, I suggest that they rejected this attribution, that is, they were convinced otherwise. The posture the journals advocate is one that projects equality, contesting racist discourse by making the falsehood of the inferiority stereotype evident.

Roger Bastide identifies a second phase in São Paulo's black press as beginning with the foundation of the newspaper *O Clarim* (*The Bugle*)— which later became *O Clarim d'Alvorada* (*The Bugle of the Dawn*)—in 1923, by Jayme de Aguiar and José Correia Leite. *O Clarim* reminded readers of the black ancestors' resistance and called on the community to organize and continue the fight. It also waged a battle against the racist undertones of current use in language. In *O Clarim*'s fourth issue, published in 1924, Correia Leite wrote the following:

> If we analyze the bravery of our ancestors, we will see, throughout history, the sublime courage of a race that, even while enslaved, did not allow itself to be brought down in battle, in the winning of its rights. ... How many teardrops did the freedom of those poor martyrs cost, those who were the first workers and makers of our fatherland's progress and order. The good name of our class depends on our procedure. It is our duty to introduce the value of our race into the country's social evolution. We must work hard in endless accord in order to see the fruit of our efforts shine in the progress of our land. For this we must issue a general call to all black men, elect a directorate, send manifestos to all the States of Brazil, and, in sum, create the society "Confederation of Black Men," as several of our countrymen have suggested.

It is notable that Correia Leite cites not the "slave," but a race that was enslaved. This language confronts the underlying tenor of the word "slave," which implies a condition that is inherent and immutable. The slave *is* a slave, while the enslaved ancestor is a person who was once free.

Another change in language characterized this era: the expressions "men of color" and "population of color" were exchanged for *negro* (black). Correia Leite records that the outstanding Afro-Brazilian orator of the time, Vicente Ferreira, introduced this word "to substitute the then empty and overused 'men of color.' Yellows and Indians are also men of color; Vicente Ferreira put a stop to this nonsense about men of color, which doesn't really mean anything at all."[21]

Also in the fourth issue of O *Clarim*, Moyses Cintra makes the following appeal to the black community:

> Oh! You, heads of family, do not lose heart before the miseries and difficulties that we are going through and that face us. Wake up! Fight with fervor, tell your loved ones that we must be more powerful, taking away from our race the terrible emblem that time and again leaves us disconsolate: "Slave." ... Friends and readers, do not despair, if we unite we will do everything we can.

This was already a more explicit call to arms than was found in earlier papers. By the time O *Clarim* became O *Clarim d'Alvorada*, it had been the voice of the black movement for a decade, appealing for unity and organization against discrimination. It was a crucial part of the organizing efforts that led to the creation of the Brazilian Black Front. In 1933, on the anniversary of the abolition of slavery, O *Clarim d'Alvorada* echoed the secular phrase of W.E.B. Du Bois when it declared, "Every century has its caption, and the caption of the twentieth century is that of the Black Race." According to the newspaper, blacks are "part of the determinism of contemporary transitions because the Black Race is the last hope of a Brazil shaken by the turmoil of new ideologies in the affirmation of its origin and that of the Fatherland." This statement signals the desire to participate in the national destiny and influence its direction. African Brazilians asserted their origin as the basic source of a national identity that could be composed without reference to imported ideologies and without the need for subsidized European immigration. The origin of the Black Race is associated, then, with that of the fatherland, in the hope to gain the sense of authorship of a new Brazil.[22] According to O *Clarim d'Alvorada* the nation should move in "A direction that can prevent the great ruin that a policy without national objectives ... has been causing the Nation created by Our Dead Ones, by Our Ancestors, whose powerful and painful Blood struggled, worked, and produced without reservation and without sectarianism to build Our Fatherland."

The largest mass organization of Brazilian blacks was in the making—the Brazilian Black Front—and it was born in the midst of this effort to rethink the issues of the nation. Raul Joviano do Amaral maintains that the Brazilian Black Front "is the result of a new consciousness of a new black generation in Brazil in the observation and study of the national environment in relation to the problems that concern Humanity within new life perspectives."[23]

The formation and development of the Black Front was a crucial component of this second phase, and several newspapers were instrumental to it. Such periodicals included O *Progresso* (1931), *Promissão* (1932), and *Cultura*,

Social e Esportiva (1934). A *Voz da Raça* (1936), though, was the Black Front's official newspaper. The *Tribuna Negra* was another important paper, whose subtitle "For the Social and Political Union of the Descendants of the Black Race" expresses the aim of these periodicals. The paper was directed by Augusto Pereira das Neves, and the prominent writer and poet Fernando Góes was its secretary. Manoel Antonio dos Santos was chief editor and Aristides Barbosa, a major figure in the Brazilian Black Front, was among the founding members. The first issue features an article by Henrique Antunes Cunha, later an outstanding member of the Black Cultural Association, in honor of Luis Gama, the major black abolitionist of the nineteenth century.

BRAZILIAN BLACK FRONT AND CONTEXT (1931–1937)

O Clarim d'Alvorada enunciated in 1924 the cry of protest that would crystallize with the foundation of the Brazilian Black Front in 1931. The black population in the State of São Paulo was still predominantly rural; while it formed the huge majority of the rural poor, it composed only about 11 percent of the population in the capital. A great majority of people generally were illiterate. Excluded from the labor market of the new industrial economy, blacks took odd jobs or temporary and ephemeral employment and lived in tenements, *cortiços*, or squalid basements. They suffered from many health problems. Historian Márcio Barbosa observes that, in contrast with the case of European immigrants, there were no public policies "intended to give African descendants any chance to attain a better quality of life. ... The situation was so serious that the disappearance of the black population was foreseen and one of the causes would be tuberculosis."[24]

The Black Front was a mass movement of protest against the race discrimination that excluded blacks from trade and the industrial economy. It spread to several different corners of the nation. It targeted the exclusion of blacks from employment and the education system, as well as the segregation of movie theaters, barber shops, hotels, restaurants, and other public places. It was the most significant expression of Afro-Brazilian political consciousness of the time period.

The Brazilian Black Front's proposal was not new. It could be summed up in the slogan "To Congregate, Educate, and Guide."[25] As in earlier decades, the goal was to bring the countless Afro-Brazilian associations together in a united force, achieving the transition from "fragmentary associationism to global solidarity," in Roger Bastide's words.[26]

The Front established its goals in its "Manifesto to the Brazilian Black People," published in the O Clarim d'Alvorada (June 8, 1929) and reproduced as a pamphlet for distribution (dated December 2, 1931):

> The Brazilian black problem is that of the absolute, complete, integration of blacks in all of Brazilian life (political, social, religious, economic, labor, military, diplomatic, and so on). Black Brazilians must have education and acceptance in all aspects and in all places, given the competent physical, technical, intellectual, and moral conditions (which need to be favored) demanded for "equality before the law."[27]

With respect to the priorities of action toward this end, the consensus of the previous decades was still intact, that is, that the first battlefront was in the field of education and the second in that of citizenship rights. The Front writes: "And thus the Brazilian black question, according to former and contemporary opinion that we have collected among Black People, is first and foremost a *problem of education*, intrinsically; and extrinsically it is one of respect for all the human, social, civic, and political rights of blacks, on the part of society as well as the Public Authorities."[28]

This is why the Front had a school for children in its headquarters, with teachers appointed by the government, and why it offered literacy courses and adult education. The teachers in adult education were members of the Front who lectured for free. Among them were Lino Guedes—one of the founders of O Getulino—Salatiel de Campos, and Raul Joviano do Amaral.[29]

With more than twenty local nuclei and affiliates spread throughout the state—boasting more than six thousand cardholding members in São Paulo and two thousand in the port city of Santos—the Brazilian Black Front can be characterized unequivocally as a mass political movement. Its appeal radiated to other states, including Maranhão, Pernambuco, Bahia, Sergipe, Rio Grande do Sul, Minas Gerais, Rio de Janeiro, and Espírito Santo. The Front mobilized thousands in parades, street demonstrations, public conferences, seminars, and other events protesting racial discrimination. Two of the main orators were Vicente Ferreira and Alberto Orlando, and the leadership included, among others, José Correia Leite, Raul Joviano do Amaral, Francisco Lucrécio, and the brothers Arlindo and Isaltino Veiga dos Santos.[30]

The Front was also the center of a kind of honorable lifestyle, an example of dignity for its members and associates. The group demonstrated its discipline as it organized around countless well-defined activities. Francisco Lucrécio, its former Secretary General, observes the following:

The Black Front functioned perfectly. There was the sports department, the ladies' department, and the departments of music, education, and moral and civic instruction. All the departments had a directorate, and the Greater Council supervised all of them. They worked very well. This way, many black organizations that were dedicated to recreational activities became Black Front affiliates.[31]

In addition to promoting sports events, social functions, and balls, the Front made it a point to encourage and praise the institution of family, earning the nickname of "Marriage Front."[32]

Women, Francisco Lucrécio tells us, "were more assiduous in the struggle for black rights, which meant that in the Front the majority were women. It was a very large contingent; they were the ones who made things happen."[33] Undoubtedly, it was due largely to the efforts of these women that the Front achieved concrete gains in the fight against employment discrimination. For example, the Front won domestic service jobs by gaining employers' trust and respect. Lucrécio asserts: "Many families wouldn't accept black domestic servants; they began to be accepted when the Brazilian Black Front was created. It came to the point that a lot of employers demanded that black women show their Black Front membership cards."[34] In 1932, the Front won the admission of two hundred blacks to the city's Civil Guard—a victory that had a great impact on the community—after a committee made its case before President Getúlio Vargas.[35]

During the Constitutionalist Revolution of 1932, when São Paulo State attempted to secede from or bring down the Vargas regime, the Black Front officially adopted a neutral stand. But a dissident group was formed within the Front, which, under the name of the Black Legion, went to the trenches in support of the São Paulo rebels. This episode of the participation of organized black movements in Brazilian history is not well known. Correia Leite notes the following: "It was truly a Legion. If anyone fought in that Revolution of 1932, it was those black men, and they went at night, by truck, they paraded through the city receiving flowers. Today the 1932 Revolution is celebrated, but no one mentions the Black Legion, they don't mention the participation of blacks, it's funny, isn't it?"[36]

Other groups splintered from the Brazilian Black Front, such as the Socialist Black Front, founded in 1933 by a group with a leftist bent that disagreed with the monarchist tendencies of the Black Front's prominent leader, Arlindo Veiga dos Santos. Another contingent of socialists left the Front under the leadership of José Correia Leite and founded the O Clarim d'Alvorada; later they created the Black Social Culture Club.[37] But the first objective of all these organizations was to advance specific issues of the black community; the groups were not based on the ideological positions of the right or the left and they were not primarily concerned with party politics. Marcello Orlando Ribeiro recalls, with respect to the Brazilian Black Front, that "we never led anyone to support this or that politician or political party. We always were looking out for our own recovery, our own social integration and for union among ourselves. The goal was for blacks to move forward."[38]

With respect to the monarchist position of the Black Front's leader, Francisco Lucrécio comments, "That was irrelevant, because Arlindo Veiga [dos Santos] always said that in the Black Front he was blackfrontist and outside the Black Front he was a convinced patrianovista."[39] As for the Integralist, Communist, and Socialist ideologies, the same former director states, "The Black Front did much more without those ideologies ... than the groups that took that kind of radical position."[40]

This zeal for political independence was fully expressed when it was decided that the Black Front would become a political party. Organized in this way, the Front commanded some weight in the São Paulo political scenario and was broadly supported in the Afro-Brazilian community. Aristides Barbosa recalls the following:

> The Black Front was unique and respected by everyone, so much so that in 1937 it had its own candidate. At that time, if I'm not mistaken, it was Raul Joviano do Amaral, very young then. The Front was going to present a candidate, so no other group in São Paulo tried to present one. You can see that the consciousness was so high at the time, of that process, that if you went to [the Black Social Culture Club] and asked: "Why aren't you going to present a candidate?" the answer would be: "I'm not going to present one because Black Front is going to present one." The most opposing group, the Front's biggest rival, was the Black Legion. ... The two groups were ideological adversaries, but even so, during the time of that effervescence of everyone presenting candidates, the Legion refused to present a candidate, which would have been Lieutenant Arlindo, because the Black Front was going to present its candidate. So there was this consciousness.[41]

The posture of the Front as a political party had a didactic aim, symbolic of the general search for black civil rights. Lucrécio articulates this, referring to another election:

> I was candidate for deputy, and Arlindo was too. But our goal was to show that, in fact, blacks could be candidates and could be elected, because

there wasn't an understanding by blacks or by whites about voting for a black candidate. We knew perfectly well that we wouldn't be elected, but it was necessary to raise this banner to raise the consciousness that we were also Brazilian citizens, with the same right to be candidates and be elected. At that time it was a step forward.[42]

In 1937, President Getúlio Vargas staged a bloodless coup that ushered in the authoritarian New State regime. One of its first acts was to declare illegal all political activity. The Black Front was closed down along with all other political parties. Its name changed to the Brazilian Black Union, and as such it celebrated the fiftieth anniversary of slavery's abolition in May 1938. But it wasn't successful in restructuring with the same breadth and dimension as before. Later, it became the Palmares Recreational Club.[43]

A year after the Black Front was closed, the racism that brought it into being remained intact. The São Paulo police chief, Commissioner Alfredo Issa, issued an order prohibiting *footing*, an important traditional black community social event on Rua Direita, a street in the commercial center of São Paulo. Footing took place every Sunday and consisted of young men and women walking up and down the street and socializing. White storeowners on this main urban artery battled this black presence on their territory and demanded that it be banned. In protest, black citizens organized a committee to take the issue to Rio de Janeiro, which was then the nation's capital. The protest had little effect because of the rigid press censorship enforced at the time. The only news item that got past the censors was Osório Borba's piece in the *Diário de Notícias* of Rio de Janeiro.[44]

In the same year, despite the continued political climate of repression and censorship, African Brazilians managed to organize another major event. The Afro-Campineiro Congress was held in Campinas in May 1938, organized by a group including three names that would be evident in black affairs over the following decades: Aguinaldo de Oliveira Camargo, Geraldo Campos de Oliveira, and Abdias Nascimento. They were joined by Agur Sampaio, Jerônimo, José Alberto Ferreira, and others. This Congress was convened to fight racial discrimination and segregation, which were ingrained in Campinas, and, more generally, to evaluate the situation of black people in the country.[45]

Contemporaneous with the Congress, black organizations, such as the Brazilian Movement against Racial Prejudice, appeared in Rio de Janeiro. Also at that time, the Association of Brazilians of Color was active in Santos. In 1942, the *Phylon*, a journal founded by W.E.B. Du Bois, published a message from the National Union of Men of Color, based in Rio de Janeiro.

The message called for "closer cultural community with our North American brothers" and made a moving statement about society's abandonment of black Brazilians.[46]

Despite their lack of resources and means of communication, these movements maintained contact—to the extent of their ability—with the African world and international black struggle. O Clarim d'Alvorada quoted news and articles written by members of the Universal Negro Improvement Association and African Communities League (UNIA), which encompassed black communities in several different countries of the Americas. UNIA was founded by Marcus Garvey, the Jamaican leader who also mobilized millions of African Americans in New York. Abdias Nascimento observes that the Brazilian Black Front "remained alert to all the emancipationist gestures that took place in other countries."[47] Lucrécio points out that the Black Front did not agree with Garvey's "return to Africa" proposal.[48] Serious research, as well as UNIA's own literature and path of action, show that his message was broader than such an alleged proposal; Garvey's slogan was "Africa for the Africans, at home and abroad." His idea was that everyone would contribute to the development and welfare of Africa, which would be a base of strength for those in the Diaspora.[49]

CONSCIOUSNESS AND IDENTITY (1914–1937)

Afro-Brazilian political consciousness from 1914 to 1937 took an integrationist position, reacting against discrimination in the labor market, education, and civil society. It demanded black participation in all levels and aspects of Brazilian life but did not question the economic and social structures of society; it also did not make claims directly to a specific Afro-Brazilian cultural identity.

Some analysts interpret this integrationist approach as a naïve acceptance of the values of mainstream white society. Social activists in the contemporary black movement have expressed such an idea to this author. A recorded example is the subject João who participated in Ricardo Franklin Ferreira's study of African-descendant identity in 1999.[50] João is an activist in the São Paulo branch of a national organization called Unegro. In a dialogic approach to the issue of Afro-Brazilian identity, João became Ferreira's partner. Together they fleshed out the contours of the process of building African descendant identity in Brazil by conducting a long-term interview that Ferreira recorded, transcribed, and later discussed with João in the context of theoretical considerations. Their dialogue focused on the dynamics involving groups and individuals in the identity-building process, with reference to certain stages, the first of which is the stage of submission.

In this stage, writes Ferreira, "it is common for African descendants to absorb and submit to the beliefs and values of the white dominant culture, including the notion synthesized in the ideas of 'white is right' and 'black is wrong.' This internalization of negative stereotypes occurs unconsciously."[51] He points out that this mechanism of adapting to white European values operates not only on the individual plane, but also on the collective level. For João, the black movement has gone through characteristic phases, the first of which Ferreira associates with the stage of submission. Such was the case of the Brazilian Black Front, which suggested "adequate" forms of behavior and personal care to its constituents.[52] João defines this period as the black movement's "age of innocence," in which it tried to eliminate any mark that could associate it with negative values. He explains that Unegro considers this period an age of innocence because "we believe in the impossibility of insertion in the Brazilian social structure by mechanisms of noncontestation, of natural absorption."[53]

In my view, to observe the integrationist nature of this period's black consciousness does not reduce it to merely an internalization of maintream values. João's and Unegro's identification of this period as one of innocence characteristic of the stage of submission does not seem to be supported by the facts. Brazilian historian Eduardo Silva made an observation as he embarked upon his research about an outstanding African-descendant personality of pre-Abolition Brazil, Dom Obá II of Africa. I believe that the approach Silva suggests can and should be applied to this and other periods of the Afro-Brazilian social movement. Silva writes, "to penetrate this era ... requires a methodological respect for difference." He advocates the need to "put oneself in the place of the people involved, ... understand their intentions in principle and, tuning in to their rhythm, perceive an era ... as a meaningful whole."[54]

The historical period we have examined, 1914 to 1937—the Brazilian Black Front existed formally from 1931 to 1937—was the height of the age of whitening policies based on the scientific decree of the black race's innate inferiority. Public policy founded on the theory of eugenics stamped its influence vividly and profoundly on everyday life in Brazilian society. Nina Rodrigues—recognized to this day as the highest authority on blacks in Brazil—identified African blood as the basis of the Brazilian people's innate inferiority.[55] Such a notion was solidly anchored in the scientific production of the day. Physical anthopologists were busy measuring African Brazilians' crania and nostrils. These heralds of Aryanism announced the mental and psychological deformity of the *Afer*, not to mention the degeneracy of people with mixed blood. Statesmen, intellectuals, and politicians were calling on

Brazil to mobilize itself in favor of the noble objective of "improving the race" by eliminating the "black stain" as quickly as possible, that is, with the greatest possible amount of civic dedication. In 1934, when the Black Front's mass demonstrations were occupying the public squares, the second edition of Oliveira Vianna's *Race and Assimilation* was being published and Gilberto Freyre's thesis was just coming off the press.[56] In other words, the culturalist perspective in anthropology, just out of the crib, was still crawling on all fours in a direction opposed to that of the general march of ideas. What prevailed was still the discourse of degeneracy and racial determinism. The principle of eugenics was inscribed in the 1934 Constitution of the Republic; the hope for a white future for Brazil shone high and bright. In sum, the elimination of the black race was the nation's goal.

When we view them in this context, the black movement's language of universal equality and its rejection of the negative stereotype gain new contours. Against the official discourse on the desirability of whitening—which was publicized in books, classrooms, theater, magazines, propaganda, newspapers, and by means of countless daily incidents making race discrimination explicit—these spokesmen of the race were raising a vigorous protest. They did not do this from a position of submission, soliciting the white paternalist to grant a generous favor; they demanded respect for the *rights* of blacks and their language was largely one of battle. Thus, the discourse of the black movement does not confirm the hypothesis that the actors were motivated by a belief in the possibility of "entrance into the Brazilian social structure by means of the mechanisms of noncontestation, of natural absorption," as João and his Unegro colleagues imagine.[57]

I believe that the action of these movements reflects the priorities of struggle defined by its protagonists. Antiblack societal conditions gave the black movement two clear priorities: to reject and combat the predominant stereotype of inferiority founded on the science of the time, showing it to be mistaken; and to overcome the miserable status of pariah to which the Afro-Brazilian population had been relegated as it was excluded from the labor market of a new economy on the way to industrialization.

In my view, the most outstanding characteristic of the early black movement resides less in its ideology and discourse than in its establishment of the African-descendant community's ability to stand as the maker of its own history and to positively assert its identity. Fernandes observes, with respect to the first phase of this period, that

> The movements that made these demands also encouraged an internal moral reevaluation of "blacks" as such. They presented a new measure

of the creative capacity of "blacks," including in their sphere of social consciousness the conviction that they are just as capable as "whites." ... They helped, therefore, to configure new psycho-social impulsions, which gave "blacks" the incentive to trust "blacks" themselves and their capacity for action as human agents of the historical process.[58]

If this voice of black protagonism lacked resonance, it is because it lacked mainstream society as a welcoming—or unwelcoming—audience. Fernandes underscores this fact, commenting on "inclusive society's" indifference to the black movement's appeal.[59]

In the effort to perceive this era as a meaningful whole, we might observe in the black movement's language and in its press an eminently critical position on the issues that concerned African descendants—one which does not sound naïve. This is the case, for example, of its critique of the policies of whitening, the invention "of the great immigrations that came to Aryanize Brazil by the initiative of the illustrious statesmen of stupidity," writes Arlindo Veiga dos Santos in A Voz da Raça.[60] Commenting on the new language of medical sanitarists who approached the Afro-Brazilian poor population in a highly authoritarian way with their public health campaigns, the same author comments as follows:

> Miguel Pereira and Belisário Pena have said that Brazil is a vast hospital. And we do not fear to say that this vast hospital derives from the most serious disease, which is race and color prejudice, in sum the headache of the mentality of our leaders, allowing a whole people to perish because they must be substituted, because they are mixed-blood, because they are black and must be made white at any cost, even the cost of Brazil being torn apart by the rush of immigrated international Aryanism.[61]

Where other interpretations detect the introjection of the mainstream society's values characteristic of a stage of submission, I find here, on the contrary, a sharp critique of the imposition of white values and the tendency on the part of some blacks to adopt or advocate them. The psychological effects of this introjection are denounced, for example, by the journal Senzala when, "on the occasion of Christmas and New Year festivities, it exhorts blacks to offer to their children not blonde blue-eyed dolls with pink cheeks, but a black doll, with kinky hair, the only toy admissible for children of color." Considering this, Bastide asks, "But is not this appeal ... a reaction against the acceptance of the superiority of white values?"[62]

The insistence of these movements on attention to personal presentation does not seem to be a naïve acceptance of white values; rather, it shows that they contested and rejected antiblack stereotypes. We can heed the warning of Dalmir Francisco, an outstanding intellectual and black-movement activist from Minas Gerais, when he challenges the

> familiar verdicts that judge race club or black socio-recreational associations to be whitened, based on the observance or simple description of their moral and ethical behavior, their adoption of etiquette and indumentaries of nonblack or white origin. These analyses, which are present even in the pretentiously radical discourse of black movement activists, end up ignoring that the race club is still a black people's club, even though it presents, both in content and forms of expression, the cultural plurality to which all members of societies with different ethnic-cultural groups are submitted.[63]

The criticism of the acceptance of white values is a constant in the black press of the period. In another example, A Voz da Raça "denounces the desire of blacks to look like whites and thus deny their origins instead of being proud of them"[64] when it publishes the following text on the "current fashion of whitening the skin and straightening the hair": "The newspapers of America go to the extreme of dedicating entire pages to suggestive illustrations on the matter. But, what result is there in this metamorphosis? [The use of] this cream may give whites the idea that all our social improvement efforts are based, simply, on the ridiculous dislike of our having black skin."[65]

Similarly, mulattoes and morenos—mixed-blooded people—who aspire to be white and move away from the community receive acidic commentaries, whose irony targets the simulation of whiteness, the ideology of miscegenation, and the government's policies:

> Robbed of positive black values by the whitening of the epidermis of formerly wealthy black esquires who escaped the company of blacks through miscegenation and prejudice (for the greatest enemy of blacks is the white person who is a grandchild of blacks!!!), black people were left without natural leaders and hanging over them is an anti-racist government concerned with the general Aryanization of the Brazilian Nation of the past.[66]

The discourse of these periodicals is often directed to an internal audience, and sometimes couched in almost didactic terms. It did not escape the perception of these authors and organizers that mainstream society turned a deaf ear on their "clarion sounding the call to all men to pursue the ideals of fraternity and racial democracy."[67] They were well aware that their message rarely penetrated the wall surrounding the discursive space of mainstream society.

Given the historical, social, and economic circumstances in which they were working, the fact that these heralds of the black community managed to create their own discursive space by distributing, albeit precariously, their own means of communication, and creating and maintaining their groups and organizations shows courage and persistence. They succeeded in their assertion of a positive identity, constructed and sustained at high cost, which confronted the whole ethos of the discourse on race that was endorsed and supported by the science of the time. The black press and the organizations it represented said "no" to the racist ideology that reigned, diffusely permeating Brazilian society, by praising positive-identity values and the deeds of black heroes of yesteryear, by demanding access to education, demonstrating that it was the denial of this access and not lack of intelligence that caused black people's "backwardness," and by raising a social consciousness of cohesion and self-defense of their community. Their refusal to agree with society's view of them is a gesture that constitutes identity and denotes the historical agency of African descendants in this period. Their activities were part of the continuum that anticipated and helped build the critical multicultural demands of later movements.

NEW PHASE (1945–1960)

The third phase of black activism identified by Roger Bastide began with the political agitation that came with the end of the New State regime in 1945. Bastide remarks: "From 1937 to 1945 there is a gap. One must wait for the democratic regime in order to see the press of color return, with *Alvorada* and *Senzala*."[68] However, since the race issue did not disappear during the authoritarian regime, the black community did not fail to find ways to organize. It continued to aggregate in social groups, dancing clubs, religious brotherhoods, and particularly in the *terreiro* communities of Afro-Brazilian religion. Underground and violently repressed by the police, society, and the official religion (Catholicism), the *terreiro* communities formed the foundation of Afro-Brazilian resistance, not only in this period but throughout the nineteenth and twentieth centuries.[69]

In 1941, the José do Patrocínio Association was founded. It dealt with problems of domestic servants, protesting against the rejection of black candidates made explicit in want ads that asked only for white applicants or demanded "good appearance," a euphemism for being white.[70] This Association formed the basis for MABEC, the Afro-Brazilian Movement for Education and Culture, and remained active up to the end of the 1950s.

In 1945, Brazilian society was mobilized to discuss the great national issues, preparing for the election of the National Constituent Assembly that would shape the democratic state in the postwar period. The National Convention of Brazilian Blacks was the culmination of several initiatives that year, including the creation of the Afro-Brazilian Democratic Committee in Rio de Janeiro.[71] In São Paulo, the Association of Brazilian Blacks (ANB) was founded by the former leadership of the Socialist Black Front, another fruit of the untiring dedication of José Correia Leite. The ANB published the newspaper *Alvorada* and in 1945 it launched a *Manifesto in Defense of Democracy*, signed by José Correia Leite, Francisco Lucrécio, Raul Joviano do Amaral, Fernando Góes, and others. This document contains an incisive criticism of the Vargas regime and the race perspective is explicit when it makes the following call to organizing the community: "In the past, black Brazilians resisted against enslavement by means of insurrections and revolts, the most notable one being the democratic and anti-racist Republic called Palmares. ... [Today,] once again very much slandered black people must take on the task of eliminating the tendency on the part of whites, with few exceptions, of discriminating against blacks."[72]

Among other items on its program, the ANB demanded criminal laws against race discrimination. It is, then, one of the "forgotten" organizations whose action has been suppressed in the conventional history of the "Afonso Arinos Law," discussed later in this chapter. Because of its name, this law is still seen as a gesture of paternalist generosity from a son of the ruling elite, but its passage was largely the result of the black population's organized action.

The ANB also fought for measures to protect the interests of domestic servants, coinciding with the action and objectives of the Black Experimental Theater (TEN) and other groups. These two demands — antidiscrimination legislation and the rights of domestic workers — were to be central points in the program launched by the National Convention of Brazilian Blacks, held six months after the founding of the ANB, and the action of TEN in Rio de Janeiro leading up to the First Congress of Brazilian Blacks in 1950.

In addition to the ANB, which was still active in 1950, there were many other Afro-Brazilian associations in this period. With no pretension of compiling an exhaustive list, we could mention some of these groups in a superficial inventory.[73] In São Paulo, active groups included the Frente Negra

Trabalhista (Black Labor Front), the Luis Gama Cultural Center, and the Social and Cultural Crusade of Brazilian Black Men. In Porto Alegre, the Union of Colored Men and the Literary Center of Afro-Brazilian Studies were active. In Minas Gerais, organizations included the Turma Auri-Verde and the Grêmio Literário Cruz e Souza. Rio de Janeiro listed, among other associations, the Center of Afro-Brazilian Culture—whose leadership included the poets Solano Trindade, Aladir Custódio, and Corsino de Brito.[74] The Union of Colored Men—with headquarters at the Jesus do Himalaya Spiritualist Center in Niterói—published the newspaper *Himalaya*. The group was led by José Bernardo da Silva and Joviano Severino de Melo. José Bernardo, whose action was notable as the head of this organization, ran for State Assembly in 1950.[75] The Cultural Union of Colored Men of Rio de Janeiro, under the leadership of José Pompílio da Hora, made efforts to offer technical and literacy courses that were in considerable demand, particularly by domestic servants.[76] In 1949, the National Union of Men of Color was created in Rio de Janeiro; it advocated the formation of cooperatives and schools to improve favela dwellers' lives, gratuitous health-care services, and Afro-Brazilian literacy campaigns. Like other organizations it took a position against the obvious discrimination practiced by Itamaraty, the Ministry of Foreign Relations, and denounced the hypocrisy of a white Brazilian delegation to the United Nations, which pretentiously spoke out against South African racism while "forgetting that blacks suffer here in Brazil itself."[77]

The black press of São Paulo remained active with *Alvorada* and *Tribuna Negra* [*Black Tribune*], mentioned earlier, as well as *O Mundo Novo* [*New World*], edited by Armando de Oliveira Castro. Arnaldo de Camargo, Aristides Barbosa, and Ovídio Pereira dos Santos founded *O Novo Horizonte* [*The New Horizon*], one of the few newspapers of the black press that was published independently, not by a club or association. This paper published contributions by writers Lino Guedes, Oswaldo de Camargo, and Carlos Assumpção, and longtime black activists like Geraldo Campos de Oliveira. Inspired by U.S. magazine *Ebony*, it reported on Africa and Diaspora affairs.[78] Continuing the tradition of black recreational associations, the famous Elite Club of São Paulo published *Hyphen*, which reported the results of studies on race prejudice and discrimination in Brazil as well as news of its associates, visitors, and events.

The organizations and press of this period display a keener international consciousness. One of the objectives of the Frente Negra Trabalhista [Black Labor Front], for example, was the "defense of the equality of peoples and of international relations, without color distinctions."[79] All the black journals contained articles about world events and the recently created United Nations. The *O Novo Horizonte*, in October 1947, published a piece on the United Nations' positions

on racism at its meeting in Lake Success. *O Mundo Novo* printed an in-depth arti-
cle in its first issue on August 26, 1950, entitled "Creation of the United States of
Africa under Study: Solution to African Problems Difficult based on Current
Borders."[80] In Rio de Janeiro, *Quilombo*, published by the Black Experimental
Theater, TEN, maintained correspondence with Alioune Diop and his *Présence
Africaine* in Paris and Dakar, and with personalities like Langston Hughes,
Josephine Baker, Ralph Bunche, Katherine Dunham, George S. Schuyler, and
others. It frequently published articles on events and people in Africa—Uganda
and Ethiopia (Abyssinia)—as well as in Haiti and Cuba, as shown by reports on
Antonio Maceo, the "Bronze Titan of Cuba." It also printed stories on the Ku
Klux Klan in the United States.[81] Thus it is clear that black movements and press
consistently followed the international scenario of the African world.

In Brazil, the discourse of racial democracy was gaining ground, reinforced
by the victory of the Allied forces and the end of the Second World War. This
theory and the sorcery of color worked against black activism by helping to
convince society that there was no racial discrimination in Brazil. Antiracist
advocates were discredited before they could articulate their arguments.

José Correia Leite summed up the difficulties of this period in São Paulo,
where black activists were attempting to rebuild a mass movement on the
scale of the Black Front. With the fall of the Vargas regime and reinstatement
of the democratic process, hopes were high:

> In 1945, we intended to recover our position, with Mr. Abdias do
> Nascimento here in Rio de Janeiro with the Black Experimental Theater
> (TEN) holding a political convention, but that broad consciousness, that
> positioning of blacks before 1938 just wasn't the same anymore. And
> there was the danger of the word "racism" too. Blacks couldn't open their
> mouths without being denounced as racists.[82]

Sebastião Rodrigues Alves confirms this statement, writing, "We know that
blacks are relegated to a status of social inferiority and every time they rise
up against this state of things, they are labeled subversive, audacious, and
particularly black racists."[83] This accusation of "reverse racism" would consistently pursue African Brazilians working in favor of their community,
who were also accused of trying to import a foreign problem, one that
belonged to the United States or to South Africa but not to Brazil. Critics
called them un-Brazilian and antipatriotic. Their insistence on asserting
their resistance identity, built at considerable cost through these decades,
continued to move African Brazilians toward the critical multicultural
demands of later movements.

THE BLACK EXPERIMENTAL THEATER AND *QUILOMBO*

At a time when the theater was a place of social action and debate, the Black Experimental Theater (TEN) was outstanding in its success as an expression of black culture and consciousness. Founded in Rio de Janeiro in 1944, it was the first group to link political activity with the recovery and reassertion of Brazilian culture of African origin, a connection it made in both theory and practice. Its founder, Abdias Nascimento, explains this double dimension, cultural and political, in the following terms:

> Founding the Black Experimental Theater in 1944, I intended to organize a kind of action that at once would have cultural meaning, artistic value, and a social function. ... At the outset, there was the need to rescue black culture and its values, attacked, denied, oppressed, and disfigured. ... Blacks do not want isolated paternalist help as a special favor. They want and claim a higher status in society, in the form of collective opportunity for all of them, a people with irrevocable historical rights. ... The opening of real opportunities for economic, political, cultural, social improvement for blacks, *respecting their African origin*.[84]

One often hears that black movements at this time did not seek collective civil and human rights for the Afro-Brazilian population, but only advantages for individuals. This criticism was sometimes made against the movement by its contemporary critics. Abdias Nascimento makes it clear, however, that for TEN, the goal was collective improvement for all black people, not merely that of specific individuals, and those who climbed the social ladder individually, without working to benefit the group, merited criticism:

> We are not asking for a deputy's diploma or a title of Baron for all blacks. I hope that my words will not be distorted or interpreted maliciously. Discrimination affects mainly the humble occupations. ... Our "invisible negroes" constitute a tiny black and mulatto middle class and bourgeoisie, dependent on the ruling classes, and they have a cautious attitude of tamed ones. They do not involve themselves with the human promotion and social valorization of people of color; on the contrary, they function in the area of security and maintenance of the status quo.[85]

Like all the movements we have studied, TEN identified education as the first priority of action for black people. Its first activities were literacy courses, and those who signed up were favela dwellers, workers, domestic servants, and people of generally humble origin. The literacy process was complemented by classes in culture and lectures by invited speakers. Since it identified as essential factors in black oppression the exclusion of blacks from the system of education, their inferior socioeconomic status, and the characterization of their culture as inferior, TEN's objective in its theater work was to offer alternative education as well as rehabilitate and revalue black people's heritage and human identity.

Complementing this artistic work, TEN organized visual arts and beauty contests that highlighted Afro-Brazilian aesthetic standards. It sponsored and organized several sociopolitical events including the National Convention of Blacks (1945–1946), which first considered the idea of specific antiracist Constitutional measures and legislation. TEN also organized the National Black Conference of 1949 and the First Congress of Brazilian Blacks, which took place in 1950. In 1955, TEN organized the Black Studies Week and the Fine Arts Contest on the theme of the Black Christ. The contest was characterized by the major Rio de Janeiro daily, *Jornal do Brasil*, as "an attack against Religion and the Arts."[86] In the same year, TEN conceived and presented the Castro Alves Festival, in which the work of the abolitionist poet was staged as a work of dramatic interpretation.

TEN also published the newspaper *Quilombo*, which recorded "Our Program" in each issue. It is worth transcribing as an expression of the aspirations and objective of the day:

OUR PROGRAM

To work toward valuing and raising the value of Brazilian blacks in all sectors: social, cultural, educational, political, economic, and artistic.

To attain these objectives QUILOMBO proposes to:

1. Collaborate in the formation of a consciousness that there are no higher races or natural servitude, as theology, philosophy, and science teach;

2. Make it clear to blacks that slavery is a historical phenomenon that has been completely surpassed, and it should not, for that reason, be a motive for hate or resentment, nor for inhibitions caused by the epidermal color that constantly reminds us of the ignominious past;

3. Fight for the admission of black students, financed by the State, to all private and public institutions of secondary and higher education in the country, including military establishments, as long as education is not made gratuitous at all levels;

4. Combat prejudice of color and/or race and the discrimination practiced on their basis, which are an attack against Christian civilization, the law, and our Constitution;

5. Demand that the crime of race and color discrimination be foreseen and defined in our laws, as is done in some states of the North American and in the Cuban Constitution of 1940.

Among the aspects of Brazilian race discrimination denounced by *Quilombo* was racism among charities, many of which demanded "white color" as a condition for providing services to the poor. *Quilombo* carried a major report showing that the official government Catalogue of Social Work in the Federal District (Rio de Janeiro) of 1948 listed this requirement in the cases of the Brazilian Legion of Assistance, Good Pastor Asylum, Santa Marta House, Santa Teresa Retirement (part of the Santa Casa da Misericórdia), Immaculate Conception School Orphanage, and the Pestalozzi Society of Brazil.[87] It also denounced discrimination in schools and in teaching, documenting institutions that did not accept blacks. The "Student Tribune," a column in *Quilombo* signed by Haroldo Costa, listed examples of these schools, which included Notre Dame de Sion, Andrews, Bennett, Santo Inácio, N. S. de Lourdes, and "so many others," in addition to the Rio Branco Institute of the Ministry of Foreign Relations and the military academies.[88]

Quilombo maintained permanent contact with and manifested public support of other Afro-Brazilian organizations throughout the country, publishing interviews with their leaders and publicizing their activities. Articles appeared on Solano Trindade, Édison Carneiro, José Correia Leite, José Bernardo, and others, as well as groups like the Frente Negra Trabalhista [Black Labor Front] of São Paulo, Floresta Aurora of Porto Alegre, and the Union of Colored Men.[89]

FOLKLORE AND PEOPLE'S THEATER

In 1949, Haroldo Costa and Wanderley Batista of TEN formed the Grupo dos Novos [New Youth Group], a revue theater company.[90] Later, the group debuted as the Brazilian Folklore Theater. The show included a scene conceived by the poet Solano Trindade. Soon after this, Solano Trindade would create his own Brazilian Folk Theater, while the Folklore Theater became the Brasiliana Ballet, directed by Miécio Askanasy. Both Brasiliana and the Folk Theater toured Europe.[91] Another group founded with the same focus on folklore was the Center of Afro-Brazilian Culture, led by Aladir Custódio, Corsino de Brito, and Solano Trindade.[92]

These groups reproduced on stage what was referred to as popular culture, or folklore, based on dances and music that came from traditional festivities in the interior of different regions of the country. It was "people's theater" without reference to race.[93] This representation of folk culture contrasted with the emphasis on black culture of African origin in TEN's work. The position of the people's theater and folklore groups reflected an ideological focus on the pre-eminence of class over race. TEN's leadership was quite isolated in its position asserting the value of African culture. The perspective of class analysis and racial democracy, denying the impact of race, predominated in intellectual and artistic circles and among leftist political leaders who spoke in the name of the "people." Certain black leaders who adopted this position, among them Solano Trindade, sometimes agreed with the mainstream society and communications media that judged TEN's position defending black culture and identity to be racist. Yet the "people's" folklore that groups like Trindade's enacted on stage—supposedly without reference to race—was of African origin and its protagonists all belonged to what was then called the "class of men of color."

Recalling countless debates with Solano Trindade about this issue, Abdias Nascimento underscores the solidarity that united them.[94] In *Quilombo*'s special report on Solano Trindade, Nascimento made the following remark: "One can disagree—as we do—with some of Solano Trindade's ideas, but it is indisputable that he is one of the relevant personalities of the current generation that has managed to make black people's cultural values known, little by little, in an unfavorable atmosphere. Solano is always a poet, whether he is writing poetry, painting, or just living."[95]

AFRO-BRAZILIAN DEMOCRATIC COMMITTEE

In Rio de Janeiro in 1945, contemporaneous with the launching of the Association of Brazilian Blacks (ANB), the Afro-Brazilian Democratic Committee, which had parallel objectives, was founded. Under the leadership of Abdias Nascimento, Aguinaldo de OliveiraCamargo, and Sebastião Rodrigues Alves, the Committee worked with the National Student Union (UNE) and held its meetings and activities at UNE's headquarters. Leftist student activists supported the Committee's campaign for amnesty for political prisoners—most of whom were white upper-class intellectuals—and reinstatement of democracy. But once amnesty was won and political prisoners were freed, such leftist activists refused to support political work against race discrimination, raising the specter of "reverse racism" and division of the working class. They demanded public self-criticism from the Committee's founders, who were expelled, and the Committee soon disintegrated since it had no more reason to exist. Prominent black writer Raimundo Souza Dantas, who was later appointed Ambassador to

Ghana, declared publicly that he had been sent to the Committee with the purpose of recruiting the black activists to the Brazilian Communist Party (PCB). Later, Souza Dantas left the PCB, refusing to be manipulated.[96]

Leftist activists, in sum, enthusiastically accepted an Afro-Brazilian committee to be used for their own political ends, but rejected it as "racist" when it went on to address the ends for which it had been created. This episode deeply marked the nature of the relationship between the left and the black movement. It is still current practice among certain intellectuals to argue the danger of dividing the working class and to allege that in Brazil there exists no race issue because races do not exist, only colors.[97] This fact has been a major obstacle to the building of alliances with leftist forces.

Also during this period, there was an effort to create a Black Labor Directorate within the Brazilian Labor Party (PTB) of Rio de Janeiro. Sebastião Rodrigues Alves, Abdias Nascimento, Guiomar Ferreira de Mattos and others formed the nucleus of this initiative and held a series of initial meetings. However, the idea of a black group with autonomy inside a political party was entirely new and the group was not able to move forward effectively for lack of support within the party.[98]

THE NATIONAL CONVENTION OF BRAZILIAN BLACKS AND THE NATIONAL CONSTITUENT ASSEMBLY OF 1946

In 1945, TEN organized the National Convention of Brazilian Blacks, which held its first meeting in São Paulo and its second in 1946 in Rio de Janeiro. Among those who participated in the event's organization were Aguinaldo de Oliveira Camargo, Sebastião Rodrigues Alves, Abdias Nascimento, Geraldo Campos de Oliveira, Arinda Serafim, Marina Gonçalves, Guiomar Ferreira de Mattos, and José Pompílio da Hora.

The Convention was consistent with the efforts of the black movement in earlier periods, when the effort to unite different community organizations around common goals was repeated and persistent. In São Paulo, several hundred people participated in the Convention, representing a large number of organizations. Hundreds participated in the Rio de Janeiro session as well. At the end of its deliberations, the plenary assembly voted to publish the *Manifesto to the Brazilian Nation*, directed to "Our Black Countrymen," in which the Convention states the following:

It is imperative that, above all, we become more and more deeply conscious of the fact that we must be united at all costs, that we must have the audacity to be, first and foremost, black, and as such solely responsible for our destiny, not consenting that it be sponsored by or made the tutelage of any one at all. We no longer need to consult anyone in order to come to the conclusion that we have legitimate rights, that the reality of our situation is an anguishing one, and that various forces are conspiring in the commitment to despise us and, indeed, to create the conditions for our disappearance!

The *Manifesto* called on black people to unite around the following six concrete demands:

1. That in our Country's Constitution explicit reference be made to the ethnic origin of the Brazilian people, composed of three fundamental races: indigenous, black, and white.
2. That color and race prejudice be prohibited by law, as crimes against the State.
3. That crimes based on the prejudice cited above, in private businesses as well as civilian associations and public and private institutions, be prohibited by criminal law.
4. As long as education at all levels is not gratuitous, that black Brazilians be admitted, with State support, to all private and public secondary and higher education institutions in the Country, including military establishments.
5. Exemption from federal, state, and municipal taxes and fees for all Brazilians who wish to establish themselves in any commercial, industrial, or agricultural enterprise, with capital under or equal to Cr$ 20,000,00.
6. To consider an urgent need the adoption of governmental measures seeking to improve the Brazilian people's economic, cultural, and social living conditions.[99]

The *Manifesto* was sent to all the political parties, and the Convention received letters of support from each of the major political parties, signed by their presidential candidates, including Eurico Gaspar Dutra of the Social Democratic Party (PSD), who won the election. The National Democratic Union (UDN) sent a letter from its candidate, Brigadier Eduardo Gomes, and the PCB's letter was signed by its famous leader Luis Carlos Prestes, who wrote: "The Manifesto was read carefully, and merits our Party's full support for the demands expressed."[100] During the deliberations of the National Constituent Assembly of 1946, the organized black movement under TEN's leadership requested Senator Hamilton Nogueira to introduce a constitutional provision against race discrimination. The senator presented a bill that, had it been approved, would have included in the Brazilian Constitution a provision establishing the equality of all races that constitute the country's people and considering the violation of this principle a crime against the nation and its people.[101]

The presentation of this bill was an unprecedented moment in the history of the Brazilian Congress in two ways. For the first time, the organized black movement intervened, albeit indirectly, in the national legislative process, and for the first time the operation of racial discrimination was taken to the Congress as an issue requiring public policy measures. This fact is even more significant if we consider that only twelve years earlier the nation's Parliament had approved and included in the Constitution three clauses that officially adopted the principles of eugenics.[102] In his speech introducing his constitutional amendment, Senator Hamilton Nogueira asserted that racism "may not exist in our laws, but it does exist in fact ... [there are] restrictions against the entrance of blacks in the Military Academy, the Naval Academy, Air Force Academy, and principally in the diplomatic career."[103]

The only black representative in the Constituent Assembly was Congressman Claudino José da Silva of the PCB, who was personally in favor of the proposal.[104] Nevertheless, he voted against it and made a statement justifying that position under the allegation that such a measure might restrict the broader meaning of constitutional democracy. Later, he acknowledged at a public meeting of the National Convention of Brazilian Blacks that he had acted under strict orders from the Party.[105]

THE GENESIS OF THE AFONSO ARINOS LAW

Those who opposed the constitutional measure alleged that there was a "lack of concrete examples" of racial discrimination to justify it. The daily exclusion of blacks—who were banned from theaters, nightclubs, barbershops, clubs, schools, and jobs, as well as the political process—was not considered sufficient. This was partly because discrimination was so normal and commonplace as to merit little or no attention from the press and partly because its existence was simply denied by the general consensus of the sorcery of color.

It is important to emphasize the role of Afro-Brazilian organizations in making these incidents visible by taking them to the press. A year after the Constituent Assembly, in 1947, African American anthropologist Irene Diggs was barred at the Hotel Serrador in Rio de Janeiro. The Black

Experimental Theater's leadership denounced the incident, and as a result the prominent journalist Raimundo Magalhães, Jr., challenged the hotel to host a black couple for an evening. Abdias and Maria Nascimento not only stayed at the hotel, but also held a reception there, attended by many personalities prominent in the city's political, social, and cultural scene, with coverage by local newpapers.[106]

Another "example" arose in 1949, four years after the *Manifesto* was issued, when a group of TEN actors were barred by the police from the Artists' Ball at the Gloria Hotel despite holding invitations from the hotel's owner and from the Brazilian Society of Actors. Abdias Nascimento's open letter to the police commissioner protesting against this prohibition became a landmark document of the black movement, in which he stated that "it seems the police has decided all blacks are delinquents and is creating the crime of being black."[107]

But only in 1950, when Katherine Dunham, the prominent black choreographer from the United States, was barred at the Esplanada Hotel in São Paulo—an incident that TEN and other black organizations reported to the press—did sectors of the national political elite begin to recognize the existence of concrete examples.

Congressman Afonso Arinos presented a bill of law in the Chamber of Deputies that only partially revived the proposal of the National Convention of Brazilian Blacks. It defined racial discrimination in certain contexts as a misdemeanor. This measure, which came to be known as the Afonso Arinos Law,[108] made very little impact against race discrimination. It was far narrower in scope than the convention's proposal. By listing a series of acts that would be considered discriminatory, it severely restricted its range of coverage. Moreover, it required proof of discriminatory intent, something almost impossible to present in court.

When Arinos introduced his bill, he made a speech in which he justified the measure by reference to the case of Katherine Dunham as an "example" of race discrimination that had moved him to take action.[109] Later, it seems the congressman changed his mind and cited another incident involving an employee of his.[110] However, it was evident to all who followed the case in the press that Arinos was reviving the spirit, but not the full content, of the measure proposed to the Constituent Assembly in 1946. Given the congressman's well-articulated position against black associations, which he judged to be racist, it is predictable that he would be reluctant to invoke incidents in which such organizations had played an important role, as did TEN in the Dunham incident, in order not to give them visibility. This incident exemplifies how white leaders of mainstream society are credited with achievements of the black movement as a way of obscuring and hiding Afro-Brazilian agency. One could call such a habit the Princess Isabel syndrome, since an emblematic example is the exclusive attribution of the abolition of slavery to the imperial pen.[111]

Afonso Arinos was, in fact, hostile to the black social movement. In the year the law was approved, he declared,

> I have already had occasion to state my opinion on this particular aspect of the racial problem, ... the appropriateness of officializing the existence of Negro organizations or associations of Negroes. During the parliamentary debates of my bill, I sought to show the pernicious side of such congregations, the spirit of which the bill opposed with its concern to establish more positive foundations for the integration of the black element in Brazilian social life ... the insistence on creating groups of colored men is the reverse side of the coin, for in the last analysis this will be a manifestation of black racism.[112]

Congressman Gilberto Freyre, another spokesman of the theory of "racial democracy," stated the following soon after the incident involving Katherine Dunham:

> It is clear that two kinds of racism are arising in Brazil, as rivals: the "racism" of Aryanists who, in general, are under the pressure of the current supremacy of Anglo-Saxon paragons in half the world, and the "racism" of those who, for political or party-related ends, seek to oppose the racism of the "Aryanists" with that of a Brazilian Negro caricatured as North American. This second "racism" is, in general, inspired by individuals who are under the pressure, in Brazil, of the Communist mystique, not always easy to separate from the power of a Stalinist Russia, just as imperial as that of the United States.[113]

The identification of "black racism" with Russian Communism is quite ironic, in view of the fact that black movements had been accused of racism by the Communists themselves, along with the liberal left and the conservative right. It is an accusation that overrides political ideology.

OTHER MOVEMENTS (1950–1960)

Still with no pretense of being exhaustive, our overview of organizations composing the Afro-Brazilian social movement includes a few notes on the 1950s and 1960s. In 1956, the Black Cultural Association (ACN) was founded during a convention held in São Paulo. Those inspiring its creation include José de Assis Barbosa, José Correia Leite, Geraldo Campos de Oliveira, Américo dos Santos, Américo Orlando, Roque da Silva, Adélio Alves, Otávio Tavares, Nestor Silva, and Pedrona Alvarenga. Henrique Antunes Cunha presided over the ACN between 1963 and 1964. In 1958 the ACN created a student department newspaper, O Mutirão, directed by Gerson F. de Brito. Perhaps its main legacy was a compendium of literary works, which was published in its journal Cadernos Culturais [Cultural Notebooks].

In 1957, the ANC published the book Fifteen Black Poems, edited by Carlos Assumpção and Oswaldo de Camargo. Assumpção's poem "Protest" exemplifies the tone of this black literature. The poem was first published in 1954 in the newspaper O Novo Horizonte, after the author read it at a session of the São Paulo Abolition Week organized by Geraldo Campos de Oliveira. After that reading, the poem came to be a kind of slogan and symbol of the Afro-Brazilian movement on the Rio de Janeiro–São Paulo axis.[114]

PROTEST
Carlos Assumpção

Even if they turn their backs
To my words of fire,
I will not stop shouting,
I will not stop
I will not stop shouting.
Sirs!
I was sent to the world
To protest
Lies, ouropéis, nothing,
Nothing will silence me. ...
Sirs!
The blood of my grandparents
That runs in my veins
Are cries of rebellion.[115]

THE FIRST CONGRESS OF BRAZILIAN BLACKS (1950)

In May 1949, on the eve of anthropologist Arthur Ramos's departure for Paris, where—as chief of the research division of the United Nations Educational, Scientific, and Cultural Organization (UNESCO)—he would set in motion the process of making decisions about the idea of sponsoring major research on race relations, TEN was holding the National Black Conference. It was the preparatory meeting for the First Congress of Brazilian Blacks. At the invitation of the organizing committee, Ramos gave a speech at the closing session of the Conference. It was his last public appearance before going on to Paris, where eventually he would die, having just begun the process of making the research project a reality.[116]

With the Conference, TEN intended to create an encounter among intellectuals, social science researchers, and social movement activists whose goal was defining a program of action for the improvement of black people's condition. It was to be an alliance subsidized by scientific knowledge, but its main objective focused on concrete attitudes and actions rather than on theory. *Quilombo* printed the following statement on its methods: "The Conference is going to make a survey of the aspirations of black people by means of investigations carried out in the Federal District [Rio de Janeiro] and in the States, interviewing not only researchers and students, but mainly the leaders and the associations of people of color and the people themselves."[117]

The Conference organizers set out to inform the popular consciousness about the ethnocentric nature of the anthropological and sociological investigations that focused on blacks on display as a "show" or a research object. Such investigation was represented by the Afro-Brazilian Congresses that had been held in Recife in 1934 and in Salvador in 1937. In both the literature and the convening call, the Conference described itself as a sociopolitical event, in contrast to the academic-scientific nature of the congresses in which blacks were taken as an object of investigation. Its academic-scientific side would focus on TEN's criticism of such a method, which focused on "exotic" aspects of blacks' culture, ignoring their concrete living conditions and their situation as human beings. Such indifference had been denounced by an anonymous black person from the plenary audience of the Second Afro-Brazilian Congress of 1937, who said the following:

> The Afro-Brazilian Congress should show how the living conditions of blacks in Brazil are horrible.
>
> The Afro-Brazilian Congress should say to blacks that social lynching is worse than physical lynching.
>
> The Afro-Brazilian Congress should break the chains of oppression.
>
> The Afro-Brazilian Congress should tell blacks that they are dying of tuberculosis, of overwork, of carrying loads, and of miserable poverty.

The Afro-Brazilian Congress should remind blacks that they are chosen and preferred for the lowest occupations.

The Afro-Brazilian Congress should ask blacks how long they want
to go on being slaves.[118]

According to the activists and intellectuals of TEN, a response to this scientific procedure was in order. The response needed to be articulated by
organized blacks as the protagonists of their own destiny, who were gathered
to deal with the social needs of the Afro-Brazilian community and were open
to alliance with scholars as agents of history rather than as objects of study.

Several scholars who were sensitive to the issues raised by TEN's intellectuals responded to the convocation; one was Roger Bastide, who sent a written
contribution. There were representatives from different regions of the country,
including Minas Gerais, Rio Grande do Sul, São Paulo, Rio de Janeiro, and
Bahia. Among the organizations represented were the National Union of Men
of Color, Floresta Aurora, Turma Alvi-Verde, and Gremio Cruz e Sousa.[119]
Many speakers contributed to the Conference, among them Aguinaldo de
Oliveira Camargo, Sebastião Rodrigues Alves, Ironides Rodrigues, Guiomar
Ferreira de Mattos, Elza Soares Ribeiro, Mercedes Batista, Nilza Conceição,
and one of the country's rare black female physicians who worked for the
National Department of Children, Maria Manhães.[120]

Many of the Conference's papers and debates addressed issues of education, a fact consistent with the emphasis on education observed in other
movements in this chapter. Arinda Serafim, who was part of TEN's founding
group, spoke on the need to organize the professional group she created, the
Association of Domestic Workers. Maria de Lourdes Vale Nascimento analyzed the need to develop specific educational approaches capable of dealing
with the social and psychological problems arising from the imposition of
prostitution on black women. José Cláudio Nascimento, founder of two
schools in the communities of Parque Arara and Morro da Favela, spoke on
the need for literacy campaigns. Haroldo Costa, leader of secondary school
students at the time, spoke on race discrimination in schools. Sebastião
Rodrigues Alves, founder of the Afro-Brazilian Literacy Crusade, suggested
concentrating the energies of the black movement on the education of adults
and children in the favelas.[121]

The Conference elected a committee to organize the First Congress of
Brazilian Blacks, composed of Abdias Nascimento, Guerreiro Ramos, and
Édison Carneiro. During the process of organizing the Congress, regional
committees were formed. In February 1950, committees were functioning in

the states of São Paulo, Rio de Janeiro, Rio Grande do Sul, Rio Grande do Norte, Bahia, Pernambuco, Pará, and Minas Gerais, in addition to the Federal District.[122]

Quilombo printed the following objectives of the First Congress of Brazilian Blacks:

> The Black Congress intends to give a very special emphasis to the practical and current problems in the life of our people. Whenever blacks have been studied, it was with the evident or poorly disguised intention of considering them a distant, almost dead being, or else like a stuffed museum piece. This is why the Congress will give secondary importance, for example, to throbbing ethnological issues, it being less urgent to verify what is the cephalic index of blacks, or whether Zumbi really committed suicide, than to ask what means we can use to organize associations and institutions that can offer opportunities for people of color to improve their place in society.[123]

In the academic vein, the organizers intended to discuss the standards of social sciences in their dealings with research on blacks. The First Congress

> Recognizes the existence of a population of Color in the country, conscious of its importance as a factor of national progress, and attempts on the one hand to fill the gaps in the study of black people's past and, on the other, to find ways and means to provide social welfare to the thirteen million blacks and mulattoes of Brazil. Thus, the Congress will achieve two goals—one passive and the other active, one academic and the other political, one technical and the other practical. This duality of objectives is very clear in the Agenda of debates.[124]

TEN's critique of traditional scientific approaches that presented "blacks on display" became a pivot around which hot debates were waged. Sociologist Luiz de Aguiar Costa Pinto participated closely as a sympathetic observer in the preparatory work and the proceedings of the Congress. Later he made claims to the authorship of TEN's critique and published a book in which he completely omitted TEN's role in organizing the Congress. This incident became an illustrative instance of how white intellectuals make invisible the intellectual actions and initiatives of African descendants, appropriating their discourse and ideas, as we shall see in the next chapter. The heart of the issue is expressed in Abdias Nascimento's following statement about the First Congress of Brazilian Blacks:

Brazilians of color are taking the initiative of reopening the studies, researches, and discussions initiated by various intellectuals, mainly those who promoted the First and Second Afro-Brazilian Congresses in Recife and Bahia, respectively, this time not merely as a strictly scientific concern, but associating to the event's academic side a dynamic and normative direction leading to practical results. ... *Blacks are moving from being the raw material studied by scholars to shaping their own conduct, their own destiny.*[125]

A detailed look at the proceedings of the First Congress of Brazilian Blacks will illustrate the complex relations between academic work, ideology, and activism and how they all affect the record of Afro-Brazilian agency. One current of thought in the Congress was represented by ethnologist Édison Carneiro, anthropologist Darcy Ribeiro, and Costa Pinto. Édison Carneiro was an ethnologist who had participated in the First and Second Afro-Brazilian Congresses in Recife and Salvador and had published works on black culture, but neither Darcy Ribeiro nor Costa Pinto had yet produced works in the field of what was referred to as "studies of the black problem."[126] Darcy Ribeiro at that time was an ethnologist for the National Indian Protection Service; his already prodigious body of work focused on Brazilian Native Americans.[127] Costa Pinto had followed Arthur Ramos's work on the UNESCO project and was seeking to substitute the recently deceased Professor Ramos in the coordination of that research.

This group of participants in the Congress identified themselves as scientific researchers. They shared a Marxist theoretical orientation and were interested in giving the Congress an academic direction since, in their view, black people could not legitimately make specific political or social demands without endangering the unity of the working class. Édison Carneiro, for example, stated that the idea of black-community political organization was an attempt to "import the North American solution" and that the notion of black or African culture in modern Brazil as a living and dynamic value was no more than illusory nostalgia.[128] In his book *The Negro in Rio de Janeiro* (1953), Costa Pinto's "scientific" evaluation is that black movements had a "false consciousness" about color discrimination, which really was a feature of economic structure and therefore should be the target of working-class consciousness. Costa Pinto describes the Afro-Brazilian social movement, including the Congress in which he participated, as the promoter of a dangerous "reverse racism."[129] However, it was only later that he would make these positions public. At the time of the Congress, he was interested in obtaining its public manifestation of support for the UNESCO project on race relations, so he posed as an ally of the Afro-Brazilian social movement. He would later retract from that posture, but in his book he made it quite explicit that the fundamental mainstay of his research methodology was based on his active participation in the First Congress of Brazilian Blacks.[130]

The other major current in the Congress was espoused by the group of black intellectuals that proposed an independent critical outlook capable of sustaining the direction that the social movement itself articulated. Abdias Nascimento and Guerreiro Ramos were joined by Aguinaldo de Oliveira Camargo, Ironides Rodrigues, Sebastião Rodrigues Alves, Guiomar Ferreira de Mattos, Arinda Serafim, Marietta Campos, Maria de Lourdes Nascimento, and others who shared their focus on Negritude, Afro-Brazilian agency, the need for black organizations, and the need for policies to improve black people's living conditions. These were black leaders seeking to create conditions for the black population to act on its own behalf. Above all, their approach criticized the ethnological bent of research that focused on folklore as a set of exotic and curious customs—blacks on display—without taking them into account as people. This current of black intellectuals was associated with the majority of the Congress participants, who proposed to deal with what they defined as the specific social, political, and cultural needs of the black population.

Until the closing session, the divergence between the groups remained latent. The debates focused on several themes. Guiomar Ferreira de Mattos detailed the need for regulation and organization of domestic servants and proposals of several sorts were made for such organization. Proposals were made regarding methods to be used in literacy and adult education campaigns in the black community, particularly in favelas. Several papers were presented on manifestations of racism or race discrimination in different parts of Brazil. The record of the debates shows the active participation of people from many walks of life and segments of the country's African descendant population. Audiences numbered from two hundred to four hundred people at each session.

By democratic process, the plenary assembly of the Congress composed a Declaration of Principles that was approved by unanimous vote. In order to appreciate the later sequence of events, the following, which is the whole text of the document, is important:

Black Brazilians, gathered in their first Congress of national scope, promoted by the Black Experimental Theater, identified with the destiny of their Nation in all its vicissitudes, as an integral part of its people and in solidarity with them, and in the desire to be united increasingly into this whole of which they are a part, declare:

The main causes of Black peoples' current difficulties are the abandonment to which they were relegated and the Country's economic and social structures. The problems of black people are only a particular aspect of the general problem of the Brazilian people, from whom it is not possible to separate them without denying historical and sociological truth. Thus the Congress considers necessary, in order to remedy their situation, the development of the associative spirit of people of color; increased access to instruction and to technical, professional, and artistic education; protection of the people's health and, in general, the guarantee of equal opportunities for all on the basis of aptitude and ability.

The Congress recommends, especially,

a. Stimulation of the study of African reminiscences in the Country and of means to remove the difficulties faced by Brazilians of color, and the formation of public and private Research Institutes with this goal.

b. Vigilant defense of the healthy national tradition of equality among the groups that constitute our population.

c. Use of indirect means to reeducate, reverse the masses' process of repression, and transform attitudes, such as theater, cinema, literature and other arts, beauty contests, and techniques of socio-psychiatry.

d. The periodical realization of international, national, and regional cultural and scientific Congresses.

e. Inclusion of men of color in political parties' lists of candidates, in order to develop their political capacity and train and educate thinking leaders who can express colored peoples' demands in ways adjusted to national traditions.

f. Government cooperation, by means of effective measures, against the remnants of color discrimination that still exist in some social agencies.

g. Study, by UNESCO, of successful attempts at effective solution of race problems, with the objective of honoring them and recommending them to countries in which such problems exist.

h. Realization, by UNESCO, of an International Congress of Race Relations, at the earliest date possible.

The Congress vehemently condemns, considering them to be threats to the tranquility of the Brazilian family

a. Political exploitation of color discrimination.
b. Associations of white or Negro citizens organized by the criterion of racial exclusiveness.
c. Racial Messianism and the proclamation of race as a criterion of action or as a factor of physical, intellectual, or moral superiority or inferiority among men.
d. Violent processes of dealing with problems arising from inter-ethnic relations.

For the best execution of these measures, the enforcement of the public liberties assured by the Constitution is necessary. And, to overcome the unprepared condition in which the Negro masses were introduced into Republican life after Abolition and allow them to gain the behavioral modes of citizens in a democracy, this Congress recommends official and public support for all initiatives and organizations that intend to raise Brazilians of color to the broadest, richest, and most active possible participation in national life.[131]

The nature of the orientation that emerges from this document is unmistakable: it is an integrationist position, rejecting explicitly and repeatedly any suggestion of "racial separatism." At the same time, the document makes it clear that there is a need to act effectively for true integration of blacks in Brazilian society and to improve the living conditions of the people in general.

What is remarkable in the Declaration is the obvious pressure of the fear of the taboo "reverse racism" that surrounds the idea of working for integration of blacks into mainstream society. The Declaration repeatedly apologizes for itself, and actually gives more emphasis to the rejection of imaginary dangers of black racism and the possible political exploitation of the issue than to real antiracist measures. Despite the volume of the evidence of discrimination against blacks that had been presented in the participants' contributions, the Declaration carefully omits racism or race as a factor of discrimination. This detail may be interpreted as reflecting the diffuse effect of the ideology of racial democracy, illustrating why racial democracy has been characterized as a "subtler and more cruel form [of racism] than in the United States, because it does not allow its victims the opportunity to defend themselves."[132] The document's omission of race can also be seen as the expression of self-censorship as political strategy, since it avoids battling racism in an open, overt, or "radical" way.

After the agenda was closed, and the Declaration adopted by a large majority, the scientific-academic group presented a second declaration, proclaiming itself exempt from what it perceived as the racist implications of the Declaration approved by the assembly. The tachygraphic transcription of the debates[133] makes evident the perplexity that this second document evoked in the great majority of those assembled. For many participants faced with the tenor of the Declaration, the appearance of this other document revealed the paternalistic attitude of the academic-scientific group, which claimed the right to stand in judgment of the democratic manifestation of the plenary. In addition, it revealed the ideological tendentiousness of a presumably leftist position that found the document, however timid in its assertion of Afro-Brazilian struggle, to be separatist and capable of disaggregating the unified working class. The applause was long and intense when Aguinaldo de Oliveira Camargo made the following statement about the historical basis of the suspicion expressed by Sebastião Rodrigues Alves that there was "something subterranean" in the appearance of the second declaration:

> Congress Participants! It is deeply regrettable that now, during the solemn closing ceremony of the First Congress of Brazilian Blacks, where all the papers were debated with the maximum liberty of thought, with the maximum frankness; in which all of us worked together in democratic process up to the Final Declaration of the Congress; in which all these actions were perfectly addressed and signed by all the members, that this declaration should now appear as an appendix. ... We have always rejected political racism; that is a moot point.

Camargo then reviewed the history of Afro-Brazilian political struggle, in which he had been intimately involved over the previous decades, showing that this tactic was not new.

> When the Afro-Brazilian Democratic Committee was founded, there appeared subterranean elements. When we founded the National Convention of Brazilian Blacks, in São Paulo, these elements appeared. And now, as our Congress comes to such a brilliant end, once more at the last minute they appear in this declaration. ... In the black movement, last-minute elements with motions of this type always appear. In 1945, Raimundo Souza Dantas, before converting to Christianity, entered the movement with an order to take all the blacks to a certain place. ... In São Paulo there appeared an identical last minute declaration brought to the floor by Mr. Luiz Lobato. And now, here it comes again, brought to us by Messrs. Édison Carneiro, Costa Pinto, and others.[134]

When anthropologist Darcy Ribeiro tried to advocate acceptance of the second declaration, the plenary assembly's reaction was a resounding collective cry of "Not supported! Not supported!" thrice repeated during his short speech. After other speakers made their statements, the second declaration was rejected by the vote of the assembly's majority.[135]

The full import of the ideological nature of this second declaration is comprehensible only in retrospect, taking into account Costa Pinto's scientific procedure. During the preparatory organization phase of the Congress as well as its deliberations, the Congress organizers had cooperated with Costa Pinto in his research efforts. At that time, he was acting as an "ally" of the movement. With the objective of carrying on in Arthur Ramos's place at UNESCO, Costa Pinto wanted to be sure that UNESCO's research on race relations would be done in Brazil; a declaration of support from the First Congress of Brazilian Blacks would be a strong point in his favor. During the Congress deliberations, at Costa Pinto's request Guerreiro Ramos presented a motion proposing that UNESCO carry out its study of race relations in a Latin American country "in the effort to identify possibilities for positive experiences of racial coexistence." His motion also called for an International Congress of Race Relations under UNESCO sponsorship. The Congress record transcribes Costa Pinto's grateful support of Ramos's proposal: "If approved, it will reinforce the arguments presented in Florence that Brazil is the appropriate field for these investigations."[136] The plenary assembly approved the motion; the UNESCO research project became a reality and produced a series of works considered classics in the field of race relations.[137]

The UNESCO project also financed Costa Pinto's own research in Rio de Janeiro. With this history in mind, it is ironic that, in the book published as a result of this research, Costa Pinto uses his authority as a scientist to take an ideological position labeling the initiatives and positions of the black movement as "false consciousness" and "reverse racism" of "an intellectualized and pigmented petty bourgeois elite."[138] This extends to the black movement in general, and particularly the initiatives and positions of TEN— including the Congress in which Costa Pinto participated. Moreover, the Congress organizing committee loaned Costa Pinto the originals of a large portion of the annals of the First Congress of Brazilian Blacks for use in his research project, and Costa Pinto never returned them.[139] The book O Negro Revoltado [Blacks in Revolt] (Nascimento 1982 [1968]), which contains the annals of the Congress, suffers from important gaps resulting from the loss of these documents. In the list of papers and works presented at the Congress, some one-third of the texts are marked with asterisks as "lost documents."[140] In particular, the record of the closing ceremony is prejudiced by the absence of several written contributions, read at the session, which could not be reproduced in the annals.

Guerreiro Ramos, Abdias Nascimento, Sebastião Rodrigues Alves, and other black intellectuals addressed UNESCO by telegram, noting the tendentiousness of the research it had financed in Rio de Janeiro and underscoring the difference between the procedures used there and in other investigations carried out, for example, in São Paulo.[141] The content of the message sent to UNESCO was made public in a conference held at the Brazilian Press Association (ABI) in which Sebastião Rodrigues Alves noted the manipulative nature of certain researchers' relations with the social movement and concluded that "'scientists' and 'scholars' have tried to turn our work into an ideological bird trap."[142]

Perhaps the most eloquent expression of the nature of his scientific approach and his relationship with the black movement was Costa Pinto's own response, published in an important Rio de Janeiro daily: "I doubt that any biologist after studying, say, a microbe, has seen this microbe get offended and come out in public to write nonsense about the study in which it participated as laboratory material."[143]

CONCLUSION

I close this chapter with the quoted statement because it addresses issues that are fundamental, in my view, to understanding how the invisibility of African Brazilians as actors in their own history is constructed and reproduced. TEN's leadership—Abdias Nascimento, Aguinaldo de Oliveira Camargo, Sebastião Rodrigues Alves, Ironides Rodrigues, and Guerreiro Ramos in particular—interrogated a methodological procedure grounded in Marxist structuralism that imposed its expectations on the social movement it studied, then made value judgments according to those expectations, and passed this procedure off as an exercise in scientific objectivity. Their challenge to this method spoke directly to the question of Afro-Brazilian agency in two spheres: the movement itself and the making of its historical record.

Similar considerations are valid with respect to the historical record of the Brazilian Black Front and its antecessors. It seems that one obstacle to the comprehension of these movements has been researchers and observers' difficulty—because of their own ideological standards—to conciliate the monarchist position of Black Front activist Arlindo Veiga dos Santos with the leftist political position that the observers themselves judge to be more convenient, correct, or coherent with the movement's goals. Márcio Barbosa observes this phenomenon in his introduction to the book of interviews with Black Front leaders.[144]

This fact shows the analytical difficulty of researchers who do not recognize black historical agency to understand the principle noted by Guerreiro Ramos that for African descendants—who experience firsthand the social consequences of race and color in multiracial societies—the perception of their reality may differ from the set of presumptions that social science researchers bring to their analyses.[145] From the point of view of the black intellectuals involved in TEN and the First Congress of Brazilian Blacks, for example, the most important social condition is race, not class. Their priority is the issue of African descendants' individual and collective human dignity. Similarly, the discourse of the black press periodicals indicates that the majority of Brazilian Black Front participants were less interested in monarchism than in the fight against race discrimination. On the other hand, the emergence of various dissident groups, including socialist ones, indicates that not everyone engaged in the movement shared the rightist tendencies of part of its leadership.

Costa Pinto's study is exemplary in its practice of emitting opinions and omitting relevant or even decisive facts in favor of subjective value judgments. Simulating the presentation of facts, he weaves a novelistic scheme in which he accuses black leadership of reverse racism and manifests his contempt for the social subjects he studies. In the case of TEN, the "analysis" comes down to an exercise of personal demoralization against its leadership, as we will see in the next chapter. In his zeal to "proletarianize" Brazilian blacks, the scientist ignores the facts and numbers—widely announced by the organizations that are the objects of his study—that indicated the exclusion of this population from the working class during the formation of the country's industrial economy. The reason for the researcher's refusal to recognize this fact is purely ideological: it documents race discrimination and not class discrimination. The state policy that prohibited the entrance of "men of color" into the country at the same time that it subsidized mass immigration of white Europeans was not motivated by the need to import a working class for the nascent industrial economy. For that purpose, the formerly enslaved workforce was amply available. The policy had a racial goal: to whiten the nation's population, cleaning it of the black stain.

Costa Pinto's rejection of historical fact led him to a conclusion that is one more repetition of the denial of legitimacy to social movements that address specific forms of oppression like racism and patriarchy based on the caveat that they divide the working class. But perhaps more important from the perspective of Afro-Brazilian agency, Costa Pinto arrogates to himself a false identity as herald of a new sociological viewpoint that was already being elaborated by TEN's intellectuals: the critique of the conventional treatment of "blacks on display." This fact, by itself, would not be of great importance, except that his work remained in sociological literature a compulsory reference on the black movement and thus influenced or served as a model for a series of other studies.[146] Costa Pinto's book was republished by the Federal University of Rio de Janeiro in 1998, thus receiving the stamp of academic approval on the edge of the new milennium. Apparently, TEN's fate was sealed and its image fixed as a gathering of racist petty bourgeois "Negroes" who were "the captives of their own contradictions."[147] This is one instance of the white elite's appropriation of the knowlege and intellectual work produced by African descendants in Brazil.

Costa Pinto's version did not go without response.[148] In this discussion, what is at stake is more than TEN's fate. The nature and epistemological implications of the place from which—and from whose viewpoint—social phenomena and their actors are taken as "objects of study" are important. Guerreiro Ramos has said that some brown-skinned "whites" from the Northeast took blacks as their object of study in the effort to move away from them, reinforcing their own identity as virtual whites. This reflection is relevant to the issue of the subject-object relationship in science in general and in the humanities in particular.

These are questions that have been the material of rich and complex discussion in the critique of modern reason and the construction of postmodern thought. In this context, there is also a process of appropriation by Western intellectuals of the discourse and intellectual production coming out of non-Western social movements. Reading the literature, one would think that the building of postmodern thought emerged from a spontaneous process of self-contemplation by the West on its own terms. I suggest that the feminist critique of patriarchy and non-European intellectuals' critique of Western ethnocentrism are basic and necessary elements in the construction of postmodern thought.

The black movements whose stories emerge in this chapter created resistance identities whose assertion was an important part of the continuum that anticipated and helped build the critical multicultural demands of later movements. In this process, the Black Experimental Theater introduced a new dimension by emphasizing and building the theoretical base for the promotion of African cultural values as a part of the resistance identities being developed by these movements. The next chapter explores aspects of TEN that were largely obscured by the "scientific knowledge" produced about that organization and considers the nature of its activities and intellectual production.

5

THE BLACK EXPERIMENTAL THEATER: PLOTS, TEXTS, AND ACTORS

T HE BLACK EXPERIMENTAL THEATER (*Teatro Experimental do Negro*, or TEN), came into existence at the end of the Second World War. Its debut took place on Armistice Day at the Municipal Theater of Rio de Janeiro. The creation of TEN coincided with the demise of Brazil's New State dictatorship, which ushered in a period of political turmoil through which the country had to journey on its way to building a true democracy. This political struggle was acted out partly in the National Constituent Assembly of 1946, which produced a Constitution that was the point of departure for consolidating the new regime, and in the preceding election campaign that determined who would be the members of that Constituent Assembly. A key ingredient igniting the flame of democracy was the intellectual debate about breaking with the prevailing preference among cultural actors for an apolitical "neutrality" whose conservative nature was exposed.[1] As people threw off the bonds of dictatorship, they searched for more radical forms of political participation. At the same time, they engaged in a significant discussion of Brazilian culture in which the crucial notions of "national identity" and "the Brazilian people" were to be broadly reformulated.[2]

Created in 1944, TEN made its stage debut in 1945, the year of the First Brazilian Congress of Writers. Such a coincidence is symptomatic of a moment in which intellectuals proposed to "imagine Brazil" in the sense of creatively conceptualizing its culture in a new way in order to effect real change. Artists and writers challenged the institution of censorship and placed the issue of national identity front and center, along with ideas like "the people" and "nationality," as vital issues in a vigorous debate about the future of Brazil. The goal of building a new democracy led them to view Brazilian culture through the prism of politics.

The Black Experimental Theater burst on this cultural scene with an unprecedented and audacious new perspective, placing Afro-Brazilian identity in the limelight on stage and in society. Part of a wave of critical views of the conventional notion of national identity, the intellectual and political proposals of TEN, as well as its artistic work, inserted the issue of race into the cultural debate. Before this, "Brazilian" artists and intellectuals had left race unexpressed or couched in the terms of an increasingly repressed mixed-race evolutionism that was spilling out into racial democracy. Whitening was still the goal, but the focus of improving the race had shifted ostensibly from black inferiority to the self-exaltation of a pretentiously antiracist elite. The clarion call of earlier black intellectuals and activists simply was not heard or heeded by the body of Brazilian—implicitly white or virtually white—artists and intellectuals.

In the present chapter, I continue to uncover the historical agency of African descendants by looking at previously obscured aspects and achievements of the Black Experimental Theater. My primary focus is on the political-pedagogical initiatives of TEN as an organization of the Afro-Brazilian social movement, since it would be impossible in the space available to deal adequately with its theatrical work.[3] Yet one cannot separate TEN's theatrical work from its sociopolitical initiatives. The Black Experimental Theater's theatrical proposal—its artistic work—was based on a broad political objective: furthering the human rights of African Brazilians.

Another dimension that one cannot ignore is the international scope of the organization's work. Its political objective was part of a larger concern about human rights in the African world, at that time concentrated in the fight against colonialism. The Black Experimental Theater witnessed the creation of the United Nations Organization (UN) and participated in events and initiatives sponsored by the UN in Brazil. It made its debut in the same year the fifth Pan-African Congress was held in Manchester, England.

The Black Experimental Theater's artistic work has its place in the context of African theater on the Continent and in the Diaspora, sharing similar purposes, forms of expression, and sociopolitical dimensions in different societies. A symbolic landmark of this African Diaspora theater is Aimé Césaire's play, *Tragedy of King Christophe*. In the United States, theater groups and generations of dramatists had been composing this movement since the nineteenth century.[4] This black theater movement in the United States has much in common with black theater in Brazil, and both of them have much in common with black theater in Cuba.[5] Black movements in the western hemisphere and throughout the world at this time in history possessed a richness of cultural, historical, and political detail, but delving into that subject would take us beyond the scope of the present chapter.[6] Nonetheless, given the interconnections, we certainly need to place the Black Experimental Theater of Brazil in this international context in order to understand the nature of its political and cultural activity.

Brazilian sociological literature on TEN almost entirely ignores this phenomenon and omits or mischaracterizes the international dimension of the Negritude movement. Literary analyses, such as that of Afro-Brazilian critic Leda Maria Martins,[7] take a more integrated approach to the broader sociological and political aspects, a procedure that favors a more comprehensive and informed perspective. I hope to combine the two dimensions, pausing for a detailed consideration of the play, *Sortilege (Black Mystery)*. Published in English, both as a book and in two anthologies of African Diaspora literature,[8] this play is doubtlessly part of the larger international context of black theater in Africa and its Diaspora.

In the attempt to approach different aspects of TEN's work as an integrated whole, I start with the issue of identity: the way this organization articulated its assertion of blackness and culture of origin was unprecedented in the Brazilian context. As an alternative education project, TEN used aesthetics in a didactic process of identity consciousness, not only for African descendants, but also for all Brazilians. With respect to social issues, I examine the ways that TEN embraced the defense and promotion of domestic servants' rights; and how women played an outstanding role in the organization. A consideration of Negritude, both in the world and in Brazil, will characterize TEN's participation in African world events. Finally, taking off from the proposal to engage in sociology seen as *praxis*, I also offer a critical appraisal of some major works and ideas in sociology concerning TEN. All these topics of investigation open the way for a discussion of *Sortilégio*, which returns us to the issue of gender as the fulcrum for understanding race in Brazil—in this case, TEN's innovation in social thought and theater.

DEFINITION OF IDENTITY

The first battle faced by TEN was the controversy around the organization's name, which caused uneasiness in the cultural and artistic world. Editorials of important newspapers like the major Rio de Janeiro daily, *O Globo*, censured the idea of a theater "of blacks," reflecting the common notion that a black theater could mean nothing other than segregation. To define black identity and culture as national values was a proposal so preposterous as to be unthinkable; it was not even addressed.

But there was a larger meaning of the project, one shared by black theater the world over. It is both "enunciation" and "a thing enounced."[9] TEN practiced "enunciation" inasmuch as it was the act of appropriating words to one's own purpose and expression, and the "thing enounced" by TEN was the combination of the content, history, and identity that inform black drama. The proposal was to transform blacks from *object enunciated* to *enouncing subject*. The organization's name was the first thing enounced.

The explicit assertion of TEN's ethnic or racial identity in its name announced a challenge to the Brazilian elite, who were comfortable in their ignorance not only of the "black problem," but also of black people themselves and their culture. Certain friends of TEN advised that it would be wiser to choose another name. Abdias Nascimento, TEN's founder, observed:

> By the response of the press and other sectors of society, I could tell when we first announced the movement's creation that its very name appeared in our midst as a revolutionary ferment. The public mention of the word "black" provoked whispers of indignation. The polemical fate of TEN was foreseeable indeed in a society that had tried for centuries to hide the sun of the true practice of racism and race discrimination behind the window screen full of holes that is the myth of "racial democracy." Even the most apparently open and progressive cultural movements, like São Paulo's Modern Art Week of 1922, always avoided even mentioning the taboo of our race relations between blacks and whites and the phenomenon of an Afro-Brazilian culture relegated to the margins of the country's conventional culture.[10]

For its part, the leftist intellectual elite denied the relevance of race, which it saw as a diversionist illusion created by class domination. It was far more comfortable with titles like Popular Theater or Folk Theater. Symbolically these names repressed the African identity of these groups, even though their casts were black, in favor of staging an ideologically colorless version of folklore.

Thus, Nascimento's first pleas for support for his black theater project fell on deaf ears. The proposal was "politely rejected by São Paulo's celebrated intellectual of the day, Mario de Andrade," and found sympathy only in Rio de Janeiro among black intellectuals such as attorney and police commissioner Aguinaldo de Oliveira Camargo, sculptor and painter Wilson Tibério (who later moved to Europe), Teodorico dos Santos, and José Herbel. They were soon joined by "longtime black activist Sebastião Rodrigues Alves; domestic workers Arinda Serafim, Ruth de Souza, Marina Gonçalves; the young and valiant Claudiano Filho; Oscar Araújo, José da Silva, Antonieta, Antonio Barbosa, Natalino Dionísio, and so many others."[11] Rio de Janeiro's major daily, *O Globo*, heralded TEN's creation with the following editorial, the tenor of which it repeated six years later on the eve of the First Congress of Brazilian Blacks, when *Quilombo* announced black candidacies in the coming elections. These texts are instructive reminders of the context in which TEN was born and conducted its work.

THEATER OF BLACKS

A current of thought that defends national culture and the development of Brazilian theater is propagating and legitimating the idea of forming a theater of blacks, in the illusion that this will bring more advantages for art and development of the national spirit. It is clear that such an idea should not merit the applause of those responsible for these areas, since there is nothing among us that would justify such distinctions between white scenic arts and black scenic arts, as much as they may seem to be established in the name of what are supposed to be cultural interests. In the United States, where the principle of race separation is practically absolute and the process of historical formation unique, it is understandable that one and the other would be divided in the dominion of the arts, just as one can understand that in the yearning for originality of countries where all the arts evolved to the maximum, as in France, for example, their painters and sculptors would look to the Negro or the exotic isles for inspiration.

But the truth, indeed still largely unexplained, is that among us these distinctions are not even historically based, and despite the protest of universal antislavery consciousness, the human drama of abolition, and the voice of the slaves' poet, almost all works of art that explore the time of the slave quarters would be artificial because, generally, black slaves throughout the country were better treated than many of today's homeless. Crimes and tortures were exceptions, because the rule was always our Brazilian tenderness, the phenomenon of the black mammy, the slaves who, even after Abolition, remained almost everywhere at the service of their masters, and died beloved by all.

Without prejudice, without stigmas, mixing and fusing in the melting pot of all bloods, we are building our nationality and affirming tomorrow's race. To speak of defending a theater of blacks among us is the same as stimulating sports for blacks, when the grounds of our Olympics, even abroad, gather everyone together, or creating schools and universities for blacks, black regiments and so on. And in the case in point, the artificial creation of the theater that is being propagated is even more lamentable when it is certain that the distinction established would live, falsely indeed, in the suggestive and impressive spheres of theater, which should be a reflection only of the life of our customs, tendencies, sentiments, and passions.

ECHOES AND COMMENTARIES

—*EDITORIAL*

O GLOBO, OCTOBER 17, 1944

RACISM, IN BRAZIL! ...

The spirit of imitation has always been a bad counselor. And right now its influences are trying to create a problem that has never existed among us. In Brazil, the evil effects of the racist prejudice that divides other peoples and brings about deplorable conflicts are not known. From the earliest times of our development, blacks and whites have treated each other cordially. Many descendants of the imported races have occupied important posts in politics, in letters, in all branches of national activities, in perfect fraternity with the descendants of the conquering races who founded our nationality. Nevertheless, for some time now there have been currents concerned with giving blacks a situation apart. With this they seek to divide, with no laudable results. Black theater, black newspaper, black clubs ... But this is pure and simple imitation, with pernicious effects. Now they are even talking about black candidates in October's election. Can one imagine a worse movement, one more damaging to the indisputable spirit of our democratic formation? It is worth the effort to fight this, from the beginning, without damaging the rights that men of color claim and which were never denied them. Otherwise, instead of white people's prejudice we will have, paradoxically, prejudice from blacks. These are the extremes to which not racism (which does not exist among us) but the spirit of poorly digested imitation will lead us and whose most nefarious consequence will be, perhaps, the establishment of a system abominable in all ways: individuals would come to be this or that, to occupy certain posts, not by their personal value which recommends them, but because they are black or are not black. Skin pigmentation would come into play as proof of entitlement ...

—*EDITORIAL*

O GLOBO, APRIL 13, 1950, P. 1

Indeed, the Black Experimental Theater's assertion of black identity without euphemism fell like a sacrilege on the ears of many Brazilians. It came across as vaguely defamatory of the national culture. By consciously employing the word "black," the group was openly challenging the mixed-race *moreno* hegemony that paraded as a simulation of whiteness. But more than this, TEN's founders were also transforming the tenor of the word itself.

They were reversing the negative connotation given the word *negro* (black) by a society that had turned it into a nefarious insult. Using a strategy similar to the poetry and action of the Negritude movement, TEN made the word their own by infusing it with a new meaning. Brandishing this name as a symbolic weapon denouncing the hypocrisy of the insult, they also positively redefined what it means to be black in Brazil. Like restoring a long-lost antique found in the attic of an abandoned mansion, they infused the term "Black" with positive meaning by drawing upon historical and cultural content that had been systematically covered over by the standards of whiteness.

In Brazilian theater before TEN, the norm was to blacken the face of white actors when a black character was dramatically important. "Black actors were used only to give the set a certain local color, in ridiculous or impish roles or ones with pejorative connotations," writes Abdias Nascimento in his essay on the Black Experimental Theater.[12] The objective of founding TEN was, according to Nascimento, to create,

> A theater group open to black protagonists, where blacks could rise from the adjective and folkloric position to one of subjects and heroes of the stories they interpreted. Rather than a demand or a protest, I understood the change intended in my future action as defending Brazil's cultural truth and contributing to a Humanism respecting all people and diverse cultures with their unique qualities. The meaning would be to challenge, unmask, and transform the bases of that objectively abnormal situation of the 1944, because to say Genuine Theater—the fruit of human imagination and creative power—is to say delving into the roots of life. And Brazilian life with blacks excluded from its vital center, can be possible only through blindness or the deformation of reality.[13]

The first goal of the movement would be to rescue the cultural and human legacy of Africans in Brazil, since "What was then valued and publicized as Afro-Brazilian culture, baptized with the epithet of 'reminiscences,' was merely folklore and Candomblé rites served up as an exotic dish by the tourist industry. ... TEN was not content with the reproduction of such platitudes, because it sought to give proper dimension to the deep and complex dramatic truth of Afro-Brazilian life and personality."[14]

But an initial barrier was the absence of dramatic texts adequate to this end:

> What national repertory was available? It was extremely scarce. A few outdated dramas in which the black person would be the comic, the picturesque, or the decorative background item: *The Family Demon* (1857)

and *Mother* (1859), both by José de Alencar; *The Social Cancers* (1865),
by Carlos Antonio Cordeiro; *The Slaver* (1884), and *The Dowry* (1907),
by Artur Azevedo, the former with the collaboration of Urbano Duarte;
Calabar (1858), by Agrário de Menezes; the comedies of Martins Pena
(1815–1848). And nothing more. Not one single text that reflected our
dramatic existential situation."[15]

Thus, it became a priority to stimulate the creation of dramatic literature on
themes coming out of Afro-Brazilian experience and culture. In the opinion
of the playwright now recognized as Brazil's most important dramatist,
Nelson Rodrigues, producing such works was essential to developing the
authenticity of Brazilian theater.[16] TEN embarked on the "creation of
Brazilian dramatic pieces for black artists, surpassing the repetitive rudimen-
tary repetition of folklore, of the *autos* and *folguedos* reminiscent of the slave-
holding past. We aimed for dramatic literature focusing on the most profound
questions of Afro-Brazilian life."[17]

The mission of TEN was to break out of black art's habitual confinement
to recreation, Carnival, and local festivity, and to work with black aesthetics
in original art of quality. Another mission, according to Nascimento,
addressed the social issue: "Our theater would be a laboratory of cultural and
artistic experimentation, whose work, action, and production openly and
clearly confronted the elitist Aryanizing cultural supremacy of the ruling
classes. TEN existed as a systematic unmasking of the racial hypocrisy that
permeates the nation."[18]

AESTHETICS AND EDUCATION, ART AND POLITICS

The outstanding characteristic of TEN was its multifaceted work in several
dimensions of artistic expression and political activism: theater, dramatic literature, the fine arts, social sciences, journalism. Permeating all these aspects
of the project was the educational dimension; this was so deeply enmeshed in
TEN's work in theater and the arts that its implications were unavoidable.[19]
Abdias Nascimento described this aspect in 1946, in an interview granted to
one of Rio de Janeiro's major dailies:

When we founded the Black Experimental Theater, it was established
from the beginning that the show, in the sense of pure dramatic art,
would be a secondary matter. The main thing for us was education: to
make things understandable to the people. We intended to give blacks

the chance to learn how to read and write with general knowledge about history, geography, mathematics, languages, literature, and so on. Thus, as long as the National Student Union (UNE) offered us some space in one of their many rooms, we could put this program into practice, at least in part.[20]

The group felt the immediate need to do literacy training partly to enable people to read and memorize texts for staging. But this was not the group's only educational goal, as Nascimento made clear in the following two statements:

The first step in founding the Black Experimental Theater was the understanding that the process of freeing the masses of black people from their state of social marginalization would have to be based on education and on creating the social and economic conditions for this education for life in freedom to be effective. We started from zero: initially we organized literacy courses where workers, domestic servants, people from the favelas with no defined profession, low-level public servants, and so on, would gather at night, after their daily work, to learn to read and write.[21]

About six hundred people, men and women, registered for TEN's literacy course, which was taught by writer Ironides Rodrigues, a law student whose cultural knowledge was extraordinary. Another basic course, an introduction to general culture, was taught by Aguinaldo de Oliveira Camargo, an incomparable personality and intellect in the black community. While the first notions of theater and dramatic interpretation were my responsibility, TEN opened up the debate to other matters of interest, inviting many different lecturers, among them Professor Maria Yedda Leite; Professor Rex Crawford, cultural attaché to the United States Embassy; the poet José Francisco Coelho; writer Raimundo Souza Dantas; Professor José Carlos Lisboa.[22]

The educational dimension of TEN's work had definite sociopolitical overtones. Literacy was part of the general goal of "elevating black people" by making it possible for them to exercise the right to vote, which was denied to illiterates in Brazil until the 1988 Constitution, and by giving them the minimum tools for survival in the labor market and society in general. Beyond this, however, TEN proposed to teach people about their cultural matrix and encourage their critical evaluation of the society and social environment in which they would act. A kind of ever-present implicit goal was to inform the public about several related aspects of black culture: (1) the ethnocentric nature of the anthropological and sociological lines of research on blacks represented in the two Afro-Brazilian Congresses held during the previous decade, (2) the syndrome of studying "blacks on display," and (3) being alert to the need for blacks to take the lead and make their own history in the academic field as well.

> At one and the same time TEN taught its first participants to read and write ... it also offered them a new attitude, a criterion of their own that allowed them to see, to understand what place the Afro-Brazilian group occupied in the national context. We began a practical phase of black studies, the opposite of the academic and descriptive nature of the mistaken line of studies [represented by the Afro-Brazilian Congresses]. TEN had no interest in increasing the number of monographs and other writings, or deducing theories, but rather in qualitatively changing the nature of social interaction among whites and blacks. We found that no other situation had ever called more than ours for Bertolt Brecht's concept of distance. A web of impostures, jelled by tradition, hung between the observer and reality, distorting that reality. It was urgent to destroy it. Otherwise, we would not be able to free the treatment of the issue from all the red herrings, paternalism, vested interests, dogmatism, sentimentality, bad faith, obtuseness, good faith, and various stereotypes. There was an irreducible need to do everything as if it were being done for the first time.[23]

This educational activity was carried out initially at the headquarters of UNE, located in Flamengo. After some time, for ideological reasons—nonacceptance of the specific nature of the race issue and fear of dividing the working class—UNE decided to suspend the authorization for TEN to use its rooms. At this point, the continuity of reading and writing classes was jeopardized. But the cultural consciousness and pedagogical work in the broader sense stayed alive and dynamic in TEN's activities.[24]

The Black Experimental Theater's support of community educational projects is recorded on various occasions, as for example in the following report in the *Labor Daily*:

> Some sincere idealists have been creating literacy courses here and there for adults and children, which are entirely unsupported by government authorities and operate only thanks to the spirit of true apostles that drives them on.

One of these abnegated activists is Professor José Claudio do Nascimento, whose love of the cause of illiterates in the Rio de Janeiro hills led him to create several courses, among them the José do Patrocínio School and the May 13th School, the first being located in Parque Arara and the other on Favela Hill.[25]

In addition to establishing more solid material and educational foundations, not only to tend to the needs of the schools mentioned but also other courses to be founded in the future, Professor José Claudio decided to create the May 13th Institute and invited Professor Luiz Lobato to be its technical director.[26]

The Black Experimental Theater was represented at the inauguration of the Institute by Aguinaldo de Oliveira Camargo and Ruth de Souza, respectively the President and the Secretary for Women's issues of the National Convention of Brazilian Blacks. They reinforced the request of the May 13th Institute for support from Congressman Hermes Lima, who was also present.

Quilombo, TEN's newspaper, published several articles on community literacy and education efforts in Rio de Janeiro and in other states. All the issues of Quilombo, with the sole exception of the second issue, carry news items, reports, or commentaries on education, teaching, or community education. Children's programs in dance, voice, music, and puppet theater, kindergarten, literacy courses up to the eighth grade, orientation courses for mothers, cutting and sewing, knitting, swimming, physical education, and typing were part of the National Council of Black Women's activities. Once more, however, the project did not last very long, for lack of space, since the building where they held classes was ceded to TEN and soon was taken back by the landlord. The same process occurred with other provisional headquarters.

The Black Experimental Theater's educational project merited the following evaluation from O Jornal, an important local daily at the time:

One could say that TEN is sponsoring a "spiritual May 13th [abolition of slavery]." ... Its leaders intend not only to improve the intellectual background of black people, but all of us. Their intention is not racist. They do not want cultured and well spoken black people to protect them from white people's contempt. ... What they want is for blacks to lose, for their own good and for the good of all of us, the mental backwardness that is the compulsory inheritance of slavery, and come into step with their brothers. They [TEN leadership] think that by lapidating a parcel of the population—precisely the most backward, for historical and social reasons—they will contribute to the improvement of the nation. On the other hand, they know that only by valuing black people will they be able to bring reactionary color prejudice to its death. And like all idealists, I believe they aspire someday to see all men with arms linked.

However, with no physical space to work in, TEN has not been able to reorganize its courses, which are geared to the formation of a large scenic arts school: a) Literacy—normal and permanently functioning, for children and adults of both sexes; b) Languages; c) Diction, Voice Projection, Public Speaking; d) Music and Choral Singing; e) Dance; f) Dramatic Interpretation, Decoration, Costumes, and Sets; h) Direction; i) History of Theater and Dramatic Literature; j) Lectures on Matters of Theater and General Culture.[27]

The phrase "mental backwardness" in this context means illiteracy and lack of access to education. This commentary reflects another side, a kind of mirror and complement of this work, which made TEN's educational project even broader: raising the consciousness of society in general and of "white" intellectuals (i.e., potential allies) in particular, about the race issue. It was partly an appeal for the socially aware to help improve the Afro-Brazilian people's degrading situation. More than this, however, TEN defended the thesis "according to which it is necessary to 'reeducate whites,' in the sense of preparing them for democratic coexistence with people of color; undermine and undo their stereotypes and their racially discriminatory ideology, which is manifest even in their unconscious behavior, for example, when they associate black with pejorative meanings elaborated in historical contexts that are now surpassed. Reeducate whites to perceive black beauty and appreciate it as an intrinsic reality."[28]

Here is the understanding of the relational dynamic of race, looking at its effects on both blacks and whites. TEN's critique of the traditional studies of the Negro expressed its leadership's understanding that the so-called "black problem" was also a problem of *Brazilian whites*. They anticipated the current relational focus in social psychology, particularly in labor relations, which comes under the heading of white studies in social psychology.[29] Guerreiro Ramos and Abdias Nascimento often cited the ironic commentary of Afro-Brazilian writer Fernando Góes when he said that "now we need to hold a Congress of researchers of color to study whites, and we mixed-race blacks will be there to measure the crania, noses, ears, and eyes of whites and study, among other things, their cooking and their religion."[30]

In Brazil in 1944, whites' lack of preparation for a democratic coexistence with a social movement organized by African descendants is recorded in the editorials of powerful newspapers, examples of which (*O Globo*, 1944 and

1950) are transcribed in these pages. Such texts express the climate of the broader society within which TEN was doing its work: an environment hostile to any initiative identifying blacks as a social group, since this was seen as reverse racism. But in spite of this climate, the quality of TEN's artistic work and its competence in communicating its innovative message managed to prevail and guaranteed a certain degree of success to its efforts to persuade the public. One of the results was that TEN attracted a large number of allies from the intellectual and artistic world to collaborate with its project. The list of renowned artists and intellectuals who worked with TEN is too extensive to record here.[31]

A superficial reading of press coverage of the time reveals that TEN, with this strategy of denouncing and elucidating the society at large, was considerably successful in breaking through the barrier of mainstream society's seemingly impenetrable deafness to the race issue.[32] Before TEN the issue had not gained the volume of debate and polemics that this institution opened up in the intellectual and cultural milieu of Brazilian society.

At some points, these two objectives—education of blacks, reeducation of whites—came together in the same project. One of these was election politics. In the same way that the Brazilian Black Front had presented its candidates for political office in the 1930s, with the didactic intention of showing that blacks could and should also participate in the nation's political leadership, several black candidates entered the 1950 elections. TEN was not absent from this context. Abdias Nascimento registered as a candidate for city council and got his first taste of political deception when at the last minute he discovered that, contrary to the negotiated understanding, the Social Democratic Party (PSD) had placed him on their ticket for Federal Deputy (Congressman), making his candidacy unviable.[33]

But TEN offered space in its publication *Quilombo* to all black candidates, above and beyond party affiliation, by means of a letter sent to all political parties. In the letter, TEN asked the parties to send information on their black and mulatto candidates to *Quilombo*'s editor. The newspaper would then contact the candidates "in order to publish their propaganda in its pages, gratuitously."[34] *Quilombo* asserted that "Up until yesterday Brazilian blacks were pawns, tools of party activists, unconscious of their own potential to act and enact improvements for their people. But that was yesterday. Today they refuse the harness. Today they know that their vote can decide many things."[35]

This statement is from *Quilombo*'s introduction to the "Political Manifesto by Blacks of Rio de Janeiro State to Political Parties," in which the Democratic Committee to Improve the Moral and Material Condition of Blacks and to Combat Prejudice Against Men of Color in the State of Rio de

Janeiro advises that "men and women of color affiliated to this Committee shall never vote, in these elections, for candidates whose parties do not include at least three names of Brazilians of color, of recognized competence."[36] *Quilombo* reported about the following candidacies: José Bernardo (State Assembly, PTB), Isaltino Veiga dos Santos (City Council, PDC), Geraldo Campos de Oliveira (Federal Chamber of Deputies, party not specified, São Paulo), José Alcides (City Council, PSD), José Correia Leite (party not specified, SP).[37]

Another case where the two goals came together in one project was TEN's beauty contests, which were meant to "value women of color," exalting their own standard of beauty. On one hand, these events underscored and gave a concrete response to the racist criterion by which beauty contests admitted only white candidates. A report on the Tar Doll contest of 1948, for example, observes that the powerful newspaper *O Globo* was organizing the Miss Brazil competition to choose the Brazilian candidate for Miss Universe. Recalling previous Miss Brazil events, reporter Doutel de Andrade observes, "In these contests there has never been a candidate of color. All of them were white, within the best and most rigorous classical standards, taking the statue of Venus of Milo, kept in the Louvre Museum, as their model, her measurements being strictly observed."[38]

The Black Experimental Theater sought to offer African descendant women a chance at the self-esteem this exclusive standard denied them. This mission was not articulated in the current language of identity construction, but TEN was using a psycho-pedagogical practice that anticipated recent literature on identity and self-esteem. Several studies have shown how Brazilian children learn from the earliest age that blackness is ugly, which interferes severely with the building of self-esteem in personality development.[39]

Whiteness as the single standard of beauty and its perverse effects on black women and men were TEN's targets in these contests. They fit into a larger intent to unleash a process of mass de-repression. Yet the risk of physical beauty being linked to the stereotype of black women as "hot" and sexually accessible was not lost on them. At the time of these contests, such an issue would not be dealt with explicitly in public debate. Instead, it would be restricted to the language of morality. Thus, *Quilombo* rejects this stereotype by announcing that candidates would be judged not only on the physical aspects of their beauty, but also on their qualities of personality and character: "The candidates for the title of 'Tar Doll of 1950' were presented: lovely girls and worthy representatives of black beauty in our land. The contest, with the goal of promoting the social valorization of women of color, could not be limited only to the candidates' physical beauty, but required moral qualities, predicates of intelligence, requisites of grace and elegance."[40]

This intention of guaranteeing that Afro-Brazilian women were valued by their qualities as human beings and not only as erotic objects is reflected also in the following chronicle from O Cruzeiro magazine (similar to Life magazine in the United States) on the Tar Doll contest sponsored by TEN:

> Born in a humble cradle, it was nevertheless a just and opportune initiative. The seductive jet-black beauties were mobilized, registering for the contest, all of them yearning not only to be popular, but also to appear with dignity before the public's eyes, displaying their physical virtues and making known their moral gifts. In the days before the contest closed, the general headquarters of the sinuous carbon-colored little ones unexpectedly opened their doors, and employer-housewives tolerated with patient resignation the temporary absence of their cooks, nannies, and cleaning ladies, enthusiastically obliged to have their presence recorded at meetings at a luncheonette in center city, where, as candidates, they were advised of partial poll results and settled accounts on coronation ball ticket sales.[41]

The beauty contests were short-lived in TEN's history, partly because with time it became clear that it would be difficult to maintain the standard of seriousness demanded by the educational intent of the effort. As the popularity of the contests grew, the media and the public tended to distort this dimension of the original goals. Seeing that these distortions were inevitable despite their efforts to the contrary, the organizers suspended the contests.[42]

Martins suggests that the titles of these contests "reproduce social discrimination to the extent that the terms 'mulatto' and 'tar' (sic) exhibit gradations of color and features, ... [which] manifests certain ambiguities and conflicts that marked some of TEN's activities."[43] Yet Martins herself describes the strategy of taking words that "exist in the mouth of others ... and serve their intentions" and making them our own, "adapting them to our own semantic and expressive purpose."[44] This was TEN's aborted intent with "Tar Doll" and "Mulatto Queen." Rather than producing ambiguity or conflict concerning its conception of black women, the episode seems to reveal that the positions held by those who dare to innovate and adapt evolve based on experience.

Abdias Nascimento's own evaluation was that "There were leftist critics confusing these contests for the opportunity [for them] to exploit black women sexually. These people did not understand, could not comprehend, the distance that separated us, like an electric fence, from such concerns. For

the target of these contests was precisely to put a final end to the Brazilian tradition of seeing black and mulatto women as nothing more than an erotic
object, which has been in force ever since the remote times of colonial Brazil."[45]

But the discussion of "what is Brazilian beauty," i.e., the issue of aesthetics, was still one of TEN's priority goals after the beauty contests were suspended. Its work continued building support for the black population's self-
esteem and also the "reeducation of whites" in the challenge of rethinking the
deeper racist and exclusivist implications of the aesthetic standards then in
force. For Nascimento, "Brazilian art, to be authentic, must incorporate the
black canon that has permeated our formation from the first."[46]

The First Congress of Brazilian Blacks was held in 1950, sponsored and
organized by TEN. One of the resolutions passed by the plenary assembly
concerned the need for a Museum of Black Art. TEN adopted this project as
part of its work with the issue of aesthetics, engaging white and black artists in
the exploration of Afro-Brazilian cultural values and themes. Afro-Brazilian
sculptor José Heitor of Além Paraíba and painter Sebastião Januário of Dores
de Guanhães, both from the state of Minas Gerais, are among those who
developed their artwork in the context of this project.[47]

In 1955, when the thirty-sixth World Eucharistic Congress was held in
Rio de Janeiro, the Black Experimental Theater organized a visual arts
contest on the theme of the Black Christ. It seized the opportunity of a
world gathering to point out how the portrayal of Christ as a blue-eyed
blond was historically inaccurate and inappropriate in a country like
Brazil, where it "reflects aesthetic alienation, self-contempt, an attitude of
subservience in which we renounce an immediately tangible community-
based criterion of beauty and excellence in favor of one that is strange to
our national life."[48]

The idea of a black Christ was truly an anathema to the traditional sectors of Catholic society, provoking the irate reaction of important Rio de
Janeiro newspapers like the *Jornal do Brasil*, whose editorial of June 26, 1955,
is a classic expression of the discourse of the time. The text is prefaced by
invoking the image "of abnegation, of renunciation, of goodness—the Black
Mammy, who rocked us to sleep, who gave us her milk, who was the great
shaper of our heart." In this discourse, the Black Mammy is the example of
the African descendant who "knows her place" and demands nothing from a
society that benefits from her exploitation. However, her portrait does not
serve as a reference for the aesthetic standard, much less the identity model,
of the Son of God. A metaphor that identified Jesus Christ as the son of a
Black Mammy or of an Uncle Tom was considered not only subversive, but
veritable blasphemy:

This exhibition that has been announced should be prohibited as highly subversive. The occurrence of such an event on the eve of the Eucharistic Congress was prepared deliberately to cause a scandal and ignite repulsion. Our moral lack of control, our great lack of respect and good taste, the sorry state of our soul, cannot be given over as a spectacle on display to those who are visiting us. We sound our cry of alarm. The Ecclesiastical authorities should, as soon as possible, take steps to prevent this attack against Religion and the Arts from taking place. The Brazilian people themselves will feel shocked by the affront.[49]

In spite of protests from conservatives, however, the exhibition was held with great success, in partnership with the arts journal *Forma* and with the support of then bishop Dom Hélder Câmara (Archbishop Dom Jaime Câmara opposed the contest). More importantly, the event inspired a broad debate on the aesthetic standards of Brazilian art in relation to national identity as represented in the faces of its people. In the words of Quirino Campofiorito, an outstanding artist and intellectual of the day,

When registration had been closed, on the eve of the judges' deliberations, we found that the event's success had surpassed even the most optimistic expectations of those who had already guaranteed us an appreciable number of contestants. At least eighty paintings, in the most diverse techniques and aesthetic styles, will give a fine impression of art that is interested in a controversial theme, the conception of a Christ of color. Controversial, audacious, even reckless, given that it will not be easy to overcome the general conviction about a white Messiah.[50]

In this same year, TEN also organized the Week of Blacks of 1955, another political-pedagogical initiative that took place at the Brazilian Press Association and whose objective was to put black people at the helm of an effort to rethink what directions the study of race issues should take.[51] At this seminar, Guiomar Ferreira de Mattos presented a paper on "Education and Prejudice," speaking of the subtle processes of inculcating racist stereotypes in the souls of children that were still operating in Brazilian schools. Once more, education was a central theme of the black movement's discussions; this time not only did they announce the need for access to education, but they also critically analyzed racism in teaching and curriculum.[52]

Continued work on the Museum of Black Art project was another part of TEN's broad pedagogical effort. In addition to artistic activities themselves, this project involved events like the Introductory Course on Black Art and

Theater offered in 1964, whose main theme was "The Meaning of Africa's Re-awakening for the Modern World."[53]

The inaugural exhibition of the art collection was held in 1968 at the Museum of Image and Sound of Rio de Janeiro. In addition to the work of Afro-Brazilian artists like painter Sebastião Januário and sculptors José Heitor and Agenor, it included works donated by renowned artists like Manabu Mabe, Iberê Camargo, Volpi, Ivan Serpa, Lóio Pérsio, Nélson Nóbrega, Anna Letícia, Anna Bella Geiger, Bess, Aldemir Martins, Darel, Darcílio, Djanira, and others who donated their works and energies.

However, since TEN had no headquarters, they lacked the physical space to house the Museum collection permanently. The climate of political repression and censorship made it difficult to establish any innovative cultural and intellectual initiative. TEN's founder and curator of the Museum, Abdias Nascimento, traveled to the United States a few months before the Fifth Institutional Act of December 1968, which closed down Congress and propelled the military regime to its height of repression. Nascimento remained in exile for the next thirteen years, and the Museum of Black Art was unable to consolidate the collection and maintain its project. The artworks were held by Nascimento under precarious conditions until 2003, when they were inventoried and restored by IPEAFRO, the Afro-Brazilian Studies and Research Institute, and exhibited in Rio de Janeiro, Brasília, and Salvador.[54]

THE ISSUE OF DOMESTIC WORKERS

Throughout TEN's history, black women actively participated in the organization's programs. Among the first causes that TEN embraced, at the time of the National Convention of Brazilian Blacks in 1946, was the rights of domestic servants. The Association of Domestic Servants was born in the heart of TEN, with newly debuted actresses like Arinda Serafim and Marina Gonçalves at its helm.[55] In an initiative parallel to the convention's manifesto,[56] the Association of Domestic Servants issued a memorial, which it presented to Congressman Hermes Lima, in which domestic servants "come forth to present the members of the National Constituent Assembly with the facts of our situation, which is not sufficiently understood as a whole." This memorial was handed to the Congressman at the inauguration May 13th Institute founded by José Claudio do Nascimento, which supported the José do Patrocínio School and the May 13th School.[57] The Congressman promised to take the issue and the demands contained in the memorial to his colleagues in the Constituent Assembly.[58] The first demand was for professional registry, since, as the domestic servants pointed out in the memorial, "look how our work is considered: we must present not a work booklet from the Labor Ministry, but a police record to show we are not thieves."[59] The rights to organize as a union and to regulate these workers as a profession came next:

> Only the most backward prejudice can be opposed to the existence of Labor Laws for domestic servants.
> We demand union rights, which means for us the first step to social progress, because they will give us the advantages of Labor Law.
> To show how absurd the prohibition of our union organization is, it is enough to say that if we, cooks, cleaners, clothes washers, parlormaids, nannies, governesses, and so on, were working in hotels, we could have a Labor Ministry work booklet and belong to the Hotel, Pensions, and Similar Commerce Union; but since we do the same work in private homes, we do not have this right. ...
> We want to contribute to Social Security, so that we can have access to sick leave and maternity leave, pension, and retirement. ...
> We believe we have the right to an eight hour day, like all workers, earning, as they do, time and a half for overtime. We believe we cannot continue to be let off without notice and without compensation when there is no just cause.[60]

If Congressman Hermes Lima in fact raised these demands before the National Constituent Assembly, the effort produced no results. In her column, "Women Have Their Say," in *Quilombo* three years later, Maria Nascimento records the fact that the National Congress of Black Women, held in Rio de Janeiro, "decided to include in its resolutions the need to win legal norms that define the duties and advantages of this enormous class of workers":

> It is incredible at a time when social justice is so often cited, that thousands of women can be working as domestic servants, with no time defined for beginning and ending their work day, no support in sickness and old age, no pregnancy and postpartem protection, no maternity leave and no day care to shelter their children during work hours. For domestic servants the situation is the same servile regime of centuries past, worse than during slave times.
> In addition to this purely economic aspect, there is another, even more painful one: the moral violence of which domestic servants frequently are victims.[61]

In 1950, *Quilombo* published a major report returning to the subject of professional regulation for domestic servants and denouncing the major newspapers and press reports that were busy with a campaign in which they published interviews with housewives complaining about domestic servants' "lack of dedication to their work." *Quilombo's* reporter comments that "contrary to what one should have been able to expect, given certain Rio de Janeiro newspapers' and magazines' past dedication to the people's causes, our colleagues in the daily editions have criminally supported (partially or entirely) the slavist, fascist, and decrepit viewpoint of the 'mistresses.'"

As the report shows, the situation described in the 1946 memorial presented to Congressman Hermes Lima had not changed: "Domestic servants, rather than being registered in the Labor Ministry or any other competent organ that regulates professions, are given police records, like any common criminal." The need for unionization, professional regulation, and social benefits is pointed out in the same terms as the 1946 memorial. The difference seems to be that in 1950 the *"madames"* (employers) were complaining about their maids' lack of loyalty when they entertain higher aspirations and "abandon the profession (?) and go off to look for factory jobs." *Quilombo's* reporter comments: "Indeed, this abandonment is logical and praiseworthy. To stay in a profession with no security, with the inconveniences cited above, with no stability, represents sacrifice or conformity to the situation."[62]

On August 10, 1950, TEN swore into office another Association of Domestic Servants governing board, with Arinda Serafim and Elza de Souza in the leadership. Guiomar Ferreira de Mattos, the association's permanent consultant and attorney, presented a paper on the need for regulation of domestic work to the First Congress of Brazilian Blacks in 1950. It was one of the main subjects of debate at that event.[63]

WOMEN IN TEN

From its inception, women had an outstanding role in TEN. Arinda Serafim, Marina Gonçalves, Elza de Souza, and Ruth de Souza were among the first members active in the organization. Ilena Teixeira, Mercedes Batista, Léa Garcia, Guiomar Ferreira de Mattos, Marietta Campos, and many others continued their activities.

Quilombo published a column entitled "Women Have Their Say," in which Maria de Lourdes Valle do Nascimento (Maria Nascimento) sought to establish a dialogue with her readers: "From this column I will chat with my countrywomen of color. ... I ask my female friends to write me. Don't worry about grammatical errors, since this is not the Academy of Letters but a democratic platform for discussing our ideas and problems."[64] One can see the kinds of problems raised in the following excerpt from one of the "Women Have Their Say" columns:

> Do you know, my friends, what was the coefficient of infant mortality in the Federal District [Rio de Janeiro] between 1939 and 1941? You will be amazed: according to statistics from the National Department for Children, for whites it was 123.30 and for blacks and mixed race — 227.60! This means that almost two children of color die for each white one. In the city of São Paulo, between 1938 and 1940, the situation was even more serious: whites — 120.59 and blacks and mixed race — 275.39. This means that for each white child who died, more than two colored ones died!
>
> It is up to all of us, black women, to change this dismal situation. How? Waiting for the government to come to our help, waiting for the pity of charity institutions? No. We need to use prenatal and children's health posts, get places in maternity hospitals, learn to adequately prepare our babies' food, and maintain a clean environment, even with the little bit of money we might have.
>
> No giving up when a maternity clinic, for example, denies us entry. We need to go to the director of the establishment and insist, use all means and remove all difficulties, even though they may be motivated by color discrimination, as in many cases I know of. Our children's health is at stake, and they deserve every kind of sacrifice from us. Preconceptional, prenatal, and postnatal care are also decisively important. I know of many pregnant mothers who don't worry about getting treatment in time, sometimes because transportation is hard to find, sometimes because they think their child will be born strong or weak as fate commands, and not by the doctors' interference. This is ignorance, this is backwardness. If we want to have vigorous, intelligent, healthy children, we need to look for the help of science, of civilization. Don't you think that in order to move ahead we should be diligent and leave behind the ideas and habits of the past?[65]

Two black women's organizations were established in 1950 within TEN. In addition to the Domestic Workers' Association, the National Council of Black Women was founded on May 18, 1950. Maria Nascimento underscores in her inauguration speech: "Black women suffer from several social disadvantages because of their cultural lag, because of our colored people's poverty, because of the lack of adequate professional education. We cannot forget another reason for the social inferiority black women experience: the color prejudice existing among us."[66]

Among this organization's objectives was to offer social services to the black community, assisting in the solution of problems with basic citizenship rights, such as obtaining birth certificates, work cards, and legal services. It also intended to offer literacy courses and primary school for children and adults, in collaboration with the Rio de Janeiro Center for Recovery and Licensing. The program included children's theater and puppet theater projects, orientation courses for mothers, legal assistance, sociological orientation, professional training (cutting and sewing, embroidery, knitting, typing), physical education, and swimming.

The Council was conceived by TEN as a division "specialized in matters relative to women and children." In her column, Maria Nascimento left TEN's concern with this issue very clear:

> There is no need to go up and down the hills every day, go into cellars and tenements—as I do daily in my profession as a social worker—in order to understand the anguishing situation of Brazilian children. It is a well-known fact that in the cellars of Botafogo or Catete, the shanties of São Carlos or Salgueiro, or the tenements of Saúde or São Cristóvão, the drama, in any town in the country's interior, the scenario is always the same: undernourishment, filth, miserable poverty, and disease. ...
>
> These children, precociously adults because of the promiscuity in which they live, because of the need to go to work—ah, the agony of fire logs and cans of water on one's head!—nearly all of them are colored. Little black kids, redheaded with dirt, ragged and sick, form a kind of tragic procession of the afflicted. It is urgent to save our children, our sons and daughters, to recover these little lives in bloom that will be the men and women of tomorrow.[67]

Part of the attempt to provide programs for children, within the limits of its possibilities, was the creation of the Black Experimental Theater Children's Ballet, whose first class was given, in 1950, by African American choreographer Katherine Dunham of the United States.[68]

The loss of TEN's headquarters jeopardized the continuity of these activities. Despite its constant efforts, TEN was never able to settle in its own physical space. The fight for a headquarters was a constant battle, and the organization repeatedly borrowed office spaces from fellow theater people, business people, and other collaborators, which, for one reason or another, were taken back by their owners. One example that was covered in the press was the Phoenix Theater, occupied by actress and director Bibi Ferreira, who lent TEN her attic for their rehearsals and on Mondays allowed them to use the stage for their shows. When Bibi Ferreira's lease ran out, the owner revoked the authorization, even though the new occupant declared publicly that TEN's activities in no way interfered with her season. The owner's procedure was denounced in several reports in the Rio de Janeiro press.[69] One of these includes an interview with Abdias Nascimento in which he announces "the cession by the São Paulo Art Museum of rooms for TEN's courses and rehearsals, and its auditorium for TEN's plays."[70] This was one more initiative that did not bear fruit. There were other frustrated attempts to find a building, including a plot of land in Brasilia when the new Capital was being built.[71]

Despite the lack of quarters and all the energies expended in the effort to find one, TEN's initiatives, activities, publications, and concerns with the issues of domestic servants, black women, and children clearly marked the direction the organization intended to establish as its legacy.

THE POLEMICS OF NEGRITUDE

TEN carried on the tradition of African descendants' protest and political-social organization discussed in the previous chapter, which sought equal opportunity and human and civil rights for blacks. But TEN added another dimension to this struggle by demanding, in addition, the right to maintain difference. In the understanding of TEN's leadership, blacks were not seeking to integrate into mainstream white society without critically evaluating its values and standards. TEN demanded recognition of the value of African ancestral heritage and Afro-Brazilian personality. In other words, TEN worked with specific identity, showing that difference should not be made into inequality.

This new dimension of the struggle for Afro-Brazilian human rights was expressed in the language of Negritude. Founded in 1932 when African and Caribbean students in Paris published their *Manifesto of Legitimate Defense*, the Negritude movement was characterized essentially by its anticolonialist posture and its assertion of the value of African culture. The name Negritude derives from the 1955 epic poem *Cahiers d'un retour au pays natal*, by Aimé Césaire, a founding work whose impact as an indictment of colonial domination is still current and strong. In it, Césaire writes:

my blackness is not a stone
nor a deafness flung against the clamor of the day

my blackness is not a blotch of dead water
on the dead eye of the earth
my blackness is neither tower nor cathedral

it plunges into the red flesh of the soil
it plunges into the burning flesh of the sky
my blackness bores through
opaque despondency with its righteous patience.[72]

In addition to Césaire, the main leaders of the Negritude movement were the Senegalese writer Léopold Sédar Senghor and the Guayanese poet Léon Gontran Damas. Senghor helped lead Senegal to independence and became its first president.

In its early phase, the newspaper *L'Etudiant Noir* was their vehicle of communication. The movement spread quickly because it tapped a well-spring of experience, a deep vein in the colonized African descendant. It won the sympathy and adherence of outstanding intellectuals and instigated the creation of a vastly rich body of literature.[73]

In 1947 in Paris, Senegalese writer Alioune Diop founded the journal *Présence Africaine*, one of the movement's main means of communication. Through this journal, TEN made contact with the Negritude movement. *Quilombo* published notes and publicity pieces from *Présence Africaine*. In 1966, when Dakar held the First World Festival of Black Arts, *Présence Africaine* published TEN's note of protest against the use by the Brazilian Ministry of Foreign Relations, Itamaraty, of a so-called "criterion of national integration" to exclude from the Brazilian delegation any actor, author, or manifestation of black culture associated with Negritude, particularly TEN.[74]

TEN's focus on Negritude began with the international scene of the African poetic movement. In its third issue, *Quilombo* published the essay "Black Orpheus," by Jean-Paul Sartre, translated by Ironides Rodrigues.[75] Later, it published an essay by Roger Bastide on "The French Black Movement"[76] and the critical review "Prologue to Blaise Cendrars," by Nestor R. Ortiz Oderigo, translated by Ironides Rodrigues.[77]

However, the ideas and proposals that TEN and other contemporaneous groups in the black movement promoted as *Negritude* were not simply a transposition to Brazil of the concepts of the French movement. On the contrary, the debates and activities around TEN's Negritude were almost entirely concerned with the Brazilian context.

Negritude for the Brazilians was a matter of identification with African origin and ancestry as well as black people's position in national reality. There was little discussion about topical distinctions between Brazilian Negritude and the Negritude movement of the French-speaking Africans because they both dealt with fundamentally similar issues applying to African descendents in a world dominated by Western colonial power and the theories and practices of white supremacy. Black movement intellectuals agreed on the basic sameness of the two.

Their position holds up under critical examination. Some analysts have suggested differences between one context and another that are based, in my view, on erroneous assumptions about Brazilian race relations. Zilá Bernd, for example, alleges that there exists a basic difference between the French "négritude" and "negritude" in Portuguese. In French, she explains, négritude derives from the pejorative *nègre*, as opposed to the other French term *noir*, which has more positive connotations. The strategy of the French language African and Caribbean poets was to co-opt the pejorative sense, brandishing *nègre*, the anathema of whiteness, as an ideological weapon in favor of their embraced status of "other." Bernd claims that the term's use in Portuguese does not have such an aggressive quality because there is no opposition between two expressions for "black."[78]

However, the negative charge of this word in Portuguese is substantial and its use has a very aggressive quality. Guerreiro Ramos observes that "in the color black ... is invested the millenary weight of pejorative meanings. All imperfections are thought of in terms of black. If one reduced the axiology of the Western world to a chromatic scale, the color black would represent the negative pole. The suggestions are infinite, in the most subtle modalities that operate from infancy in men's conscious and unconscious, that the color black is negative."[79]

The black "other" is constructed as the ultimate contrast to the "Latin" virtual whiteness identity in Iberian American societies. To be considered black is to be associated with the negative side of "universal" dualities. According to the dictionary, which cites one of Brazilian literature's classical authors, *negro* (black) means "dirty, grimy; difficult, dangerous; very sad, lugubrious ('To think that his death could occur in Lisbon ... threw him into the blackest misery'—Casimiro de Abreu); melancholy, dire, funereal ('A black fate awaited him'); cursed, sinister ('It was a black hour when that bandit arrived there'); perverse, nefarious ('The black crime rocked the city'); slave."[80]

Such examples show that the Portuguese word indeed denotes an intense negativity similar to the aggressive *nègre* in French. Even today, to address someone as *negro*, rather than using preferred euphemisms such as *moreno* or *escurinho*, is considered insulting. Ricardo Franklin Ferreira records an example, recounting the state of malaise and perplexity created by an incident he experienced in an office of the University of São Paulo in 1997. He observes that such incidents are commonplace in everyday Brazilian life. This one involves someone hesitating, unsure of how to proceed, and then referring to another person as *morena*, avoiding the word *negra* for fear of insulting her. Another black woman intervenes and says, "You can call her *negra*. She is *negra*, that's her color." This statement creates a heavy uneasiness in the room, as everyone takes the word *negra* to be a degrading insult. The incident leaves the first person, who used the euphemistic *moreno*, entirely flustered, protesting that he didn't want to offend. His consternation is caused by the third party's intervention, saying "No! She is black! You can call her black!" The exclamation sounds like a clarion call to arms, given the weight of insult that the term *negro* carries and the extent to which the euphemistic *moreno* is ingrained as an imperative of decency and good manners.[81]

The social dynamic played out in this incident runs parallel to the one created by black activists who take a position asserting African identity. By publicly adopting the stigmatized identity *negro* as a positive value, they make the racist nature of the insult visible—it is only an insult because white society despises blackness. Hence the defensive reaction of a pretentiously antiracist virtually white elite, expressed in its horrified accusations of reverse racism. This is exactly what happened with the controversy over TEN's name.[82]

The Brazilian proponents of Negritude—basically the groups that composed and were close to TEN—were considerably isolated since both the ideologies of racial democracy and class struggle labeled their movement racist and divisive. It was difficult to build alliances because white political groups would condition their support on black groups' renouncing their distinctly black culture and identity. Some segments of the black movement that were associated with the left—and therefore enjoyed extensive press coverage— accused Negritude partisans of being racist. Indeed, the remnants of the reverse-racism accusation still influence sociological writings on TEN.

Compared to its potential political allies, TEN was ahead of its time when it proposed to combat the effects of the psychological dimension of racism— denial of the humanity and dignity of African descendants—which meant building self-esteem. Abdias Nascimento writes:

> The first step for the black person is to assume his blackness. He suffers and is discriminated against because of the skin color seen by others. The theoretical reiteration that scientifically inferior and superior races do not exist makes no difference. What is important is the popular and social concept of race, whose cornerstone, in Brazil, is founded—worse

than in declared war between races—on an embarrassed ornamental prejudice, a camouflaged aesthetic perversion. And this perversion is so strong in our midst that it has instilled in blacks themselves the bad conscience of being black.[83]

For TEN, the recovery of self-esteem necessary to a dynamic life of personal achievement depended on fostering such a recovery in the national culture as a whole. As long as a person exists in a culture that judges him or her as inferior, psychological damages will accrue. For this reason, TEN worked "to preserve and enrich the cultural personality of blacks, differentiated at the level of universality. This is not historical regression, but on the contrary, historical consciousness, historical presence." Such a take on Negritude clearly expresses the idea that in the 1990s would become known as multiculturalism, the assertion of identity as a claim to power. Such identities are based on history and tradition. Just as multiculturalism revives Negritude's meaning at a different historical moment, Negritude itself rearticulated an earlier assertion of African identity, as Nascimento recalls: "The kilombo fighters were the precursors of our struggle today when, risking their lives, they refused the imposition of forced labor, new cultural values, new gods, a new language, a new lifestyle. They—the kilombolas—are the first links in this chain of revolt that has crossed four centuries of Brazilian history."[84]

Such is an assertion of agency in an Afrocentric approach that TEN was already developing:

> Negritude, in its more well-known modern phase, is led by Aimé Césaire and Leopold Sedar Senghor, but it has secular forerunners like Chico-Rei, Toussaint L'Ouverture, Luís Gama, José do Patrocínio, Cruz e Souza, Lima Barreto, Jomo Kenyatta, Lumumba, Sekou Touré, Nkrumah and many others. It is black people assuming their historical protagonism, an outlook and a sensibility according to an existential position, and whose roots delve into the historical-cultural ground. Such roots emerge from their very condition as an exploited race. The values of Negritude will be eternal, perennial, or permanent to the extent that the human race and its historical-cultural sub-products are eternal, perennial, or permanent.[85]

Indeed, for the proponents of Negritude, Africanness is a value in itself, above and beyond revolt. Not limited to a reaction against oppression, it is a positive assertion on equal grounds with any other human achievement: "Black beauty is not, by chance, the cerebral creation of those whom circumstances dressed in dark skin, a kind of rationalization or self-justification, but an eternal value, which is worthy even if it is not discovered."[86]

The statement "Black is beautiful" supports individual and collective human achievement because positive identity makes it possible for African descendants to exercise their historical agency. Therefore, TEN's activity around the issue of aesthetics under the rubric of Negritude had an essentially political content: "The aesthetic rebellion we are dealing with in these pages will be a preliminary step in the total rebellion of people of color to become the subjects of their own destiny."[87]

Indeed, the impact of Negritude spurred forward the anticolonialist process. Aimé Césaire speaks of "this surge of faith and hope which raised up, at the time, an entire continent,"[88] and Kabengele Munanga shows that "Negritude gave a vigorous impulse to political organizations and African trade unions, enlightening them on their path to national independence."[89] He goes on to observe the principle of solidarity as one of the main tenets of Negritude: "Beyond the search for cultural identity and political action, the third fundamental objective of Negritude is repudiation of hate, searching for dialogue with other peoples and cultures, in the edification of what Senghor called the civilization of the universal. This aspect seems to be achieved by the third component of Césaire's definition of Negritude: *solidarity.* ... The question is to contribute to the building of a new society, where all mortals can find their place."[90]

Collective identity consciousness makes possible the building of solidarity with other peoples, just as self-esteem integrated with centered identity constitutes an individual's solid base for collaboration with others.

Recent research in Brazilian psychology comes to similar conclusions. In his dialogic relationship with João, Ricardo Franklin Ferreira sees an "African centered identity in articulation with other groups" as one founded on the consciousness and positive elaboration of a person's African origin, a base from which to articulate positive, productive, and dynamic relations with others.[91] The possibility for such an end result is an idea not easily assimilated in Brazil. The idea that permeates the reaction of Brazilians, even those most sensitive to the race issue, is that African-descendant self-esteem inevitably will be transformed into a closed exclusiveness or resentful separatism. Such reasoning usually leads directly to the idea that there is danger of reverse racism.

Césaire addresses such a concern when he states: "To insist on identity is not to turn our backs to the world or to separate ourselves from the world or to sink into community solipsism and resentment. Our commitment has no meaning unless it means not only a re-rooting but also a blooming, an overcoming and the conquest of a new and broader fraternity."[92]

Locating the values of African culture on the plane of "universal civiliza-tion," Senghor notes that in 1889, with his "Essay on Immediate Notions of Consciousness," French philosopher Henri Bergson "gives sensibility—intu-itive reason if the reader would prefer—its rightful place in humanity, that is, first place."[93] In the same year, Paul Claudel produced his play *Tête d'or*, demanding "accompaniment by drums or tom-toms." These events heralded the critical reaction in European philosophy and arts against Descartes' rigid rationalism, which as a paradigm of scientific positivism had made what Léon Daudet called the "nineteenth century of stupidity" with its racist theories and its rationalist reductionism.[94] This expression recalls another, precise and stunning, from the pen of TEN's friend and collaborator Nelson Rodrigues. Muniz Sodré recalls that Rodrigues gave "the unwary cultivators of the purity of the object" an epithet that is "picturesque, but epistemologically revealing: the 'idiots of objectivity.'"[95]

From the time of the publication of Bergson's essay, European postmod-ern literary and artistic movements like cubism, surrealism, and dadaism were built out of the shapes and attributes of African cultures.[96] However, the European tendency to appropriate the aesthetic production of "primitive" peoples obscured this influence and the world of so-called universal civiliza-tion ignored it for a long time. Senghor recalls a critic's observation about an exhibition of Senegalese art in Washington, DC, in the 1970s: "The French say that Senegalese artists imitated those of the Paris School. We must not reverse the roles, because as we know, the French artists are the ones who imi-tated black art."[97] Negritude articulated and identified the African values that postmodernism appropriated and left anonymous, and so contributed to assuring those who produced such values their rightful place in the historical cast of builders.

In a similar way, TEN articulated and identified on stage the rich and powerful dimensions of African presence in Brazilian culture and history that had long been hidden, unnamed, and unidentified. For black people to see this experience and identify with this history would be a tool for building self-esteem and an inspiration for resistance. Like their African and Caribbean colleagues, TEN's intellectuals worked to deflagrate the process of awakening consciousness that would lead African Brazilians in a common fight to improve their destiny. They were responsible for a profound con-nection between Brazilian Negritude and the anticolonialist movement of the French-language poets led by Césaire, Damas, and Senghor. TEN's artis-tic and intellectual production highlighted the broad scope and universality of African cultural values. Its work on the theme of Negritude in Brazil expressed deep similarities of African experience in South America, the Antilles, and Africa, and also involved black Brazilians in the worldwide fight for African independence and sovereignty.

SOCIOLOGY IN PRAXIS

TEN's offstage activities aimed to make it what Abdias Nascimento called a "field of psychological polarization," in which blacks and whites would have an opportunity to critically thresh out the workings of racial ideology and their effects on individuals and society.[98] Among the tools TEN forged to this end was the National Black Institute, by means of which sociologist Guerreiro Ramos organized group therapy seminars using the techniques of psychodrama and sociodrama.[99] *Quilombo* reports that "This is the first time studies are realized in Brazil with this technique based on psychoanalysis, and with this initiative the TEN intends to train a group of technicians ... that will work on the hills, in terreiro communities, and colored people's associations, collaborating, as it has done to date, toward the valorization of blacks in Brazil."[100]

The goal of the psychodrama was twofold: to offer a form of therapy and to critically discuss social reality. Psychodrama begins with the principle that society itself is drama and convention. It proposes improvised theatrical work in groups in which the therapeutic process implies a critical analysis of social relations. The stage functions as a miniature society and there the social and psychological issues are materialized. Guerreiro Ramos writes: "The patient is offered the possibility of struggling with his fears and anxieties not only in the imaginary and verbal realm but in all dimensions. On the stage, the patient can be trained into a new role or a new behavior. His re-adaptation is achieved there and the confidence that he acquires ... can be transported to real life."[101] Today, TEN's program might be called one of empowerment workshops. The social critique contained in the double concept of psychodrama fit into the role its founder envisioned for TEN as a tool to awaken blacks to their own reality, which was obfuscated by a false image. Nascimento comments that "The status of race, manipulated by whites, prevents blacks from becoming conscious of the deceit that is called racial and color democracy in Brazil."[102]

In these workshops and in his sociological analysis, Guerreiro Ramos identified the "pathology of Brazilian 'whites'"—the imperative of virtual whiteness—which he states led to an inferiority complex of the same nature as that created by colonial domination:

Brazilians in general, and particularly lettered ones, adhere psychologically to a European aesthetic standard and see the country's ethnic accidents as well as themselves from that point of view. This is true of Brazilians of color as well as light skinned ones. This fact of our collective psychology is pathological from the point of view of social science. ... The Europeanized black person generally detests even references to his race. He tends to deny being black, and one psychoanalyst discovered in black Brazilians' dreams a strong tendency to change skin. [This author verified], on carrying out his research, the vexation with which certain people of color responded to a questionnaire about race prejudice.[103]

Such issues were the subject of psychodrama and sociodrama at the National Black Institute.

Group therapy at the Institute, as well as the other offstage pursuits of the Black Experimental Theater, fit in an unexpected way into the context of the "activist sociology" of the day, in which social scientists proposed to contribute to national progress and development.[104] Guerreiro's commitment to this idea was also expressed in his participation in the creation of the Itatiaia Group[105] and the Higher Institute of Brazilian Studies (ISEB), an important postgraduate studies center and progressive think tank that informed political proposals and social policies. ISEB was founded in the same year that Guerreiro published his *Critical Introduction to Brazilian Sociology* (1957); Abdias Nascimento received its first diploma.

ISEB brought together sociologists, economists, and political scientists who proposed to help define, guide, and participate in Brazil's development process. Intellectuals with different theoretical backgrounds—among them Roland Corbisier, Hélio Jaguaribe, Nelson Werneck Sodré, Rômulo de Almeida, Celso Furtado, Cândido Mendes, and Roberto Campos—were part of the activist tendency in the social sciences represented by ISEB, which Joel Rufino dos Santos once described as a "developmentalist salad."[106] They were among the founding members of the United Nations Economic Commission on Latin America and the Caribbean, CEPAL, which raised activist sociology to the regional level: social scientists took their place at the helm of region's development.

More than scientific theory, then, sociology should be a practical tool of social intervention. The National Black Institute's psychodrama and sociodrama program, along with the other activist roles played by TEN, are an instance of this sociological praxis. Later, Ramos would cite this experience as a founding factor in the inductive methodology of his *Sociological Reduction*

(1998). He explains: "The Black Experimental Theater allowed me to engage in the *praxis* of the 'problem' and after that I came to the theory. The same occurred with my studies on infant mortality and on the country's administrative, economic, and political problems. If you don't act, if you don't participate in the societary process, you won't comprehend society."[107]

The novel aspect of TEN's sociological praxis was its move in the direction of a multidisciplinary science by incisively integrating the psychological dimension. The development of this multidisciplinary aspect, including an incursion into Heideggerian terrain, and daring to start from blacks as a *place*—a center from which it was useful to consider a new outlook on Brazil—were innovations that the sociology of the time would have serious difficulty adopting. These features are, however, characteristic of TEN, whose intellectual mentors were instrumental in the generation of critical and postmodern thought in Brazil.

TEN AND THE OTHER SOCIOLOGISTS

Guerreiro Ramos and Abdias Nascimento were partners in TEN's sociological practices; their ideas were ahead of the sociology of their time. The First Congress of Brazilian Blacks and the UNESCO research project generated occasions in which TEN's critique of ethnological and anthropological studies of "the black problem" was the assertion of Afro-Brazilian intellectual agency. In keeping with the approach of activist sociology, this critique was aimed at the failure of such studies to address the living concerns of the people whose cultural traditions they researched. TEN contested the reduction of African cultural values to the status of folklore or exotic curiosities and rejected the approach to blacks on display. For TEN's leaders, activist sociology should focus on blacks as "the people" and therefore the protagonists of development. Guerreiro Ramos's critique of Brazilian thought in sociology[108] was daring and provocative, and is still a very current work, whose import is perhaps best summed up in Clóvis Brigagão's phrase "from sociology in rolled-up sleeves to the seamless tunic of knowledge."[109]

The Black Experimental Theater proposed to favor the repositioning of blacks from "*object enunciated*" to "*enouncing subject*"[110] not only in theater but also in social sciences. The leitmotiv of the proposition was to denounce the alienation of blacks fostered by Brazilian anthropology, which studied the black population as a static, picturesque phenomenon: the idea of blacks on display characteristic of the Afro-Brazilian Congresses of 1937 and 1938. Nascimento described such an objectifying view as an example of an "epicurist-aesthetic fruition of descriptive study, a passive and alienated posture."[111] Because of this, Guerreiro Ramos claimed that the "official" anthropologists and sociologists "were not and are not mentally prepared to understand the meaning of [TEN]."[112]

Guerreiro Ramos's statement recalls the issue raised at the end of the last chapter: the procedures by which the historical agency of African Brazilians is made and kept invisible. The "official" research sponsored by UNESCO in Rio de Janeiro offers a revealing example by contributing to the fixation of a distorted image that pursues TEN to this day.

The work of sociologist Luiz de Aguiar Costa Pinto omits and distorts important aspects of TEN's activity that were recorded in the sources he cites—particularly in its newspaper *Quilombo*—and were achieved or articulated at the time that he was closely accompanying the movement.[113] There is every indication that he witnessed these facts. There is no doubt, for example, that his close observance of the movement gave him ample opportunity to know at least a little of its history. But from Costa Pinto's text it seems as if TEN came into being in 1949, during the time he approached it, for none of its earlier achievements are mentioned. Notably, Costa Pinto writes the "history" of TEN without mentioning the National Convention of Blacks in 1945–46, its *Manifesto*, or the demands it directed to the National Constituent Assembly. The only mention of the National Convention of Blacks is made in his transcription of Guerreiro Ramos's speech, which confirms that the researcher was aware of that event, one of fundamental importance to the movement.[114]

Costa Pinto's characterization of TEN's origin is typical of the author's tendentious discourse: "The fact of, when a play demanded a black person in an important role, painting a white actor black and giving him the role— wounded the sensibility of blacks with artistic vocation and led some of them, directed by Abdias Nascimento, to create a theater group composed only of blacks."[115] Costa Pinto seems to judge that the exclusion of blacks from Brazilian theater was not racial discrimination, since he states that it merely "wounded the sensibility" of certain blacks with artistic vocations. Moreover, to describe the group as "composed only of blacks" involves a deliberate falsification, since Costa Pinto was in a privileged position to witness the widely known and documented fact of whites' participation in TEN, whose proverbial doors were open to everyone. Costa Pinto's characterization contributes, however, to building its image as a gathering of black racists, which was the author's ideological objective.

The most malicious omission, however, is that of TEN as the organizer of the First Congress of Brazilian Blacks. On six occasions, Costa Pinto refers to the congress, sometimes extensively, without ever identifying its organizers or the group responsible for its realization.[116] It appears that the event sprouted directly out of the researcher's head. He reiterates the importance to his study of the congress and the documents it issued without ever recognizing that it was TEN's leadership—specifically Abdias Nascimento and Guerreiro Ramos—who lent him those documents for use in his research.[117] The reason for this procedure is clear: Luiz de Aguiar Costa Pinto bases a great deal of his analysis on the "data" collected in the course of his "participating observation" of the congress, whose importance he emphasizes on various occasions.[118] Therefore, he avoids identifying it as the initiative and achievement of TEN's leadership, the target of his sociological demoralization campaign.

When he deals with TEN's nontheatrical activities, Costa Pinto omits the programs that women initiated—including the literacy courses, children's dance courses, and the Association of Domestic Servants—and the activities they performed in defense of their rights. He focuses solely on the "ebony beauty contests"—which he concludes were designed "above all" for men of color, since white women are relatively inaccessible to them;[119] group therapy, which he describes as "a dramatic device of *let's pretend that we are white*";[120] and the political campaign, whose pre-electoral stage, according to him, allowed TEN to "increase its reach, its proposals, its influence in the eyes of blacks, whites, and especially in its own eyes."[121] Once the 1950 elections were over, Costa Pinto decrees its death: "The troupe that became a pressure group and dreamed the candid dream of negritude—declined, withered, died."[122]

As we have had the opportunity to see, the sociologist's efforts to bury TEN were in vain. However, Costa Pinto's unscientific manner of treating TEN is well recorded. Indeed, such a tone did not fail to be dispensed to another organization, the National Union of Men of Color, to which Costa Pinto refers as "Uagacê," an alliteration of its acronym UHC—roughly, "Yewaitchssee." Commenting on the proposal of the National Union of Men of Color to "take measures to create an economic agency capable of duly financing the endeavors listed," Costa Pinto—identifying his own comments by attaching his initials—writes that it "advances no details on the *modus faciendi* of the creation of this economic agency that would finance the initiatives. In the body of its paper the only indications to be found on the subject refer to the need, in order to gather these means, to 'touch the good hearts and the constructive and humanitarian spirit (and, obviously, the full pockets—C.P.) of a few rich and powerful men (probably white—C.P.)'"[123]

As for Negritude, Costa Pinto exhibits pure ignorance about its international meaning and history. He puts together a fictitious and gaudy scene of its "annunciation" in Rio de Janeiro at a party with toasts and shouts.[124] In an effort to attribute a source to this imaginary scene, he alleges that it was recounted by Ironides Rodrigues at a session of the First Congress of Brazilian Blacks in which the participants debated Rodrigues's paper on Negritude. Guerreiro Ramos, Ironides Rodrigues, Sebastião Rodrigues Alves, Guiomar Ferreira de Mattos, and Abdias Nascimento—all of them present at that session—deny this allegation.[125] Their testimony is reinforced when we observe that the spectacle Costa Pinto invented and put on display is meaningless since the origin of TEN's reference to Negritude is documented in the pages of *Quilombo*. At any rate, the sociologist makes the following evaluation, whose scientific objectivity and neutrality will assault the eyes of the careful reader:

> The idea of Negritude, the ideological sub-product of the social situation of a small elite of Negroes, also represents *par excellence* the particular formulation that this vanguard clique has given the rationalization of its problem and which therefore retains at this larval stage of its gestation as an ideology—which it may never surpass—the very clear mark of the temperaments, the preferences, the styles, the personal variants of social position and mentality of the Negro intellectuals out of whose heads the idea has sprouted. ... More than anything else, it is the flowering in a Negro elite's mind of a seed that was planted there by the attitudes of whites. It is the inverted reflection, in the Negro's mind, of the idea that whites have entertained about him; it is the result of the consciousness (also in false terms, it should be said in passing) of the resistance of whites to the Negro's social climbing. It is, in sum, reverse racism.[126]

At the outset of his work, echoing TEN's denouncement, Costa Pinto had seen in the traditional "studies of the Negro" by anthropologists who preceded him "a deeply rooted stereotype [that] convinced them there was nothing to study with respect to the Negro *just like us*, the non-African, non-illiterate, non-slave, non-rural worker Negro, the Negro not separated from whites by the immense distance that separates the top point from the base of a rigidly stratified social pyramid."[127]

Yet he does not seem to free himself from such a "deeply rooted stereotype," since he transforms the "Negro *just like us*" into an elitist, an egotistical creature that is distant from "us" and an exploiter of his people. He portrays someone psychologically unbalanced, part clown and part tyrant, reigning in the illusory dominion of his own racist performance.

Reinforcing the image of unbalance, Costa Pinto speaks with irony of the psychological complex that he attributes exclusively to the black "elite," since the "Negro-mass"—as he calls the Afro-Brazilian worker—is supposed to be exempt from it. Repeatedly, he links this elitist psychological complex to

Guerreiro Ramos's mixed-race identity.[128] To this end, Costa Pinto cites Guerreiro Ramos's first published work, a book of poetry called *The Drama of Being Two* (1937),[129] as if it were about his mixed-race genetic heritage. The work, however, does not deal with this issue; its author describes it as "a book of poetry of Catholic inspiration on the struggle between good and evil within man, which makes absolutely no reference to ethnic issues."[130] Nevertheless, Costa Pinto unfurls the reference as a banner of the identity "dilemma" supposedly suffered by Guerreiro Ramos as a result of his being mulatto. Thus, Costa Pinto implicitly resorts to the old racial determinist stereotype of the mulatto as an inherently unstable creature—"morally disorganized, psychically unharmonious, functionally unbalanced."[131]

While he rejects anthropology's treatment of blacks on display, when he deals with TEN Costa Pinto embarks on the creation of his own sociological spectacle, which he puts on display with his invention of the story of black elites and discussion of the attributes he applies to them. To this end, he hides the origin and class position of TEN's members: they were domestic servants, low-level civil servants, and unemployed people with no defined job who often went without eating between one rehearsal and another, sticking just to coffee for lack of money.[132] Abdias Nascimento is the grandson of slaves whose mother made candy and whose father was a shoemaker. Guerreiro Ramos was the son of a Bahian washerwoman. Yet Costa Pinto characterizes TEN's leadership as being detached and distant from the "Negro-mass."

A similar criticism is sometimes made against the black press of the time. According to the criticism, "black newspapers represented much more the opinion of the black middle class than the mass," as if this fact discredited them as black press. Roger Bastide evaluates this brand of critique by observing that "the argument is not convincing, because this small middle class, formed by teachers, lawyers, journalists, proofreaders, only shortly before had left the lower class, knew its desires and miseries firsthand, learned what is still not very clear or very much felt by their brothers of lower class level, and became the echo of a whole class of color."[133]

The poet Solano Trindade, who shared the Marxist ideological position with Costa Pinto, expressed a perspective similar to Bastide's when he described TEN as "the only theatrical movement that will take the masses to social theater, because its members come in fact from proletarian groups, from the hills, the suburbs, the kitchens and the factories. One of the primordial conditions for social theater is that it be done by the proletariat; and black people, as petit bourgeois as they might want to be, are always people who have all the characteristics of workers."[134]

In Costa Pinto's view, the "Negro-mass" differs from the elite in that it does not suffer from any psychological effects as a result of prejudice, but "always confronts it face to face, in every form or circumstance in which it is expressed, and destroys and defeats it in a thousand daily battles, thinking, feeling, and acting less as *race*, more as *mass*, more and more as *class*."[135] And only one legitimate role is reserved for the Negro-mass: "It is, indeed, in this sociological framework of class ... that he finds his subjective support and objective means, his ground, his roots, his strength of Antheus, in sum, *his place*, which allows him to live and face life with the dignity of a man of the people and with the security of knowing that social evolution is in his favor."[136]

Here we have a romantic exaltation of the proletariat in its certainty of victory, but also the Negro whose dignity derives from the fact that he knows "*his place*."

Costa Pinto's eminently ideological discourse disguised as scientific research was passed down in Brazilian sociology as a decisive statement on blacks in Rio de Janeiro and is still being reproduced by analysts who embark on the paths opened up by Costa Pinto,[137] as is the case in such literature as a special issue of *Dionysos*, the journal of the Ministry of Culture's Department of Theater and Scenic Arts, on TEN. The preface reveals the volume's predominant tone at the outset, when the editor concludes that "TEN's history evokes the misery of servitude: it gyrates in circles, captive — even in revolt — of what oppresses it."[138] Two essays, those of Edélcio Mostaço[139] and Júlio César Tavares,[140] are exceptions to this general tone. Another essay, however, sets out to "follow the ambiguities and ambivalences" that mark TEN's discourse and asserts that the black elite "kept falling into the trap of the prejudiced view of blacks and ended up trying, in the end, 'to whiten them.'"[141]

The *Dionysos* volume continues the sociological legacy with its precarious formulations, or clamorous ignorance, about Negritude, which is presented in a simplistic repetition of Costa Pinto's fantasy images as the ideology of neocolonialism and reverse racism. Based on analysis of the group's discourse, these texts do not take into account the pressures of the intellectual world and the media of the day, which constantly attacked the movement as racist and segregationist. Placed on the defensive, TEN sought to demonstrate that this judgment was mistaken. Hence, the recourse to certain slogans that were the codes of nonracism. Sociologists engaging in the analysis of TEN's discourse tend to judge language that by current standards is cautious and conciliatory compared to what would prevail decades later.[142]

Often these analysts mistake Negritude's techniques of irony for subservience to dominant values. The literature of Negritude—both French-language poets and Brazilian activists—sometimes threw certain notions back at
their spokesmen in a context that demonstrated the absurdity of their prejudice. For example, when speaking of TEN's beauty contests, their organizers
invoke the "eugenic value" of black women, with the implication that the
African ancestry of these women would "improve the race," in an obvious par-
ody of whitening ideology. Another technique was to invoke racial democracy
as an appeal to its proponents' coherence. It was a challenge: "If you are really
racial democrats, come and prove it by working with us instead of calling us
racists." Unable to perceive such nuances and tactics, the analysts of discourse
interpret the words literally. Not much alternative is available when faced
with such an argument except to recall, with respect to the intellectual obstacles that prevent the sociologists from perceiving such subtleties, the maxim
that not even the gods can argue against stupidity.

The almost unisonous chorus of sociologists interrogating what they call
TEN's discursive contradictions leads to a mutilated image of the movement,
minimizing the fact that it brought to the Brazilian stage a generation of black
actors and actresses of quality who came from the most humble sectors of the
population, many of them illiterate until they joined TEN. The movement's
role in the genesis of the only antidiscrimination legislation that existed
before 1988 is entirely ignored. The "elite" discourse becomes to the sociologists a legacy of TEN more important than the fact that it broke through the
hegemony of racial exclusion in Brazilian theater, organized some of the most
important events of the black social movement, and fought racial discrimination. Little room is given to consider the production, overcoming many obstacles, of theater that put racial issue on stage and earned the praise of skeptical critics incredulous at the audacity of these Negroes who dared to trespass
on an area reserved exclusively for white society.

The insistence on searching TEN's contradictory discourse for supposed
ambiguities configures—whatever the protests to the contrary—an expectation of civic omnipotence of its leaders, from whom it is expected not only
that their discourse be politically correct according to current parameters
applied in retrospect but also the miracle of multiplying loaves. In a country
where any theater endeavor has a precarious life and difficulties with ticket
sales even without doubling as a social movement hardly accepted by general
society, the "contradictory" TEN is blamed for not sustaining itself materially
even though it is recognized that its target public did not have financial

means to go to theater. It is also implicitly demanded that they engage in an extensive program of gratuitous activities with favela and outlying populations, as well as continued national political events. Not having achieved this—and not provided with financial support in order to do so—the "black elites" are accused of betraying the masses as a result of their egotism.

Once again superior to ideological differences, Marxist poet Solano Trindade publicly supported TEN:

> The governments of democratic countries help all initiatives that come from the popular masses, because these governments depend on these masses.
>
> In the United States of America, where democracy is only partial, where there are laws against men of color, the government protects black society's cultural movements.
>
> The cultural movement of Brazil's people does not receive any help and it is also the victim of the greatest injustices, like this denial of the Phoenix Theater to the Black Experimental Theater.[143]

The *Dionysos* volume continues the sociological legacy with its precarious formulations, or clamorous ignorance, about Negritude, which is presented in a simplistic repetition of Costa Pinto's fantasy images as the ideology of neocolonialism and reverse racism.

Judging from this facile posture of a new generation of sociologists, it seems that Brazilian intellectuals are arriving late to the debate on Negritude. Africans experienced and surpassed the mea culpa phase some time ago. There was an indignant generation of African and African American intellectuals who denounced Negritude in the 1960s and 1970s with arguments identical to those still used by the aforementioned sociologists. Later, though, the African world generally made peace with Negritude, recognizing its action to recover a human dignity crushed by colonialism and its historical contribution to African and African American liberation struggles.[144] In Brazil, the fear of reverse racism is still nurtured in quite a peculiar way by an elite that touts an ostentatiously antiracist posture but is unable to assimilate the African sources of Brazilian culture into its own identity. African influences are accepted as a subordinated element in a praiseworthy mixture—syncretism or cultural miscegenation—whose terms are defined from a Western point of view.

Whatever the sociologists' conclusions about Negritude in Brazil, it remains true that, beginning with the discussion of Negritude in TEN's time, an increasingly intense deflagration of black consciousness has taken place. African Brazilians expressed it in social action as well as the assertion

of identity as a political gesture. In other words, the "movement of vast proportions" announced by Abdias Nascimento in 1949 has come to exist, exert
political pressure, and win significant victories.[145]

One frankly dishonest position of Costa Pinto has prevailed to this day.
His sociological version of the black movement omitted a historical fact witnessed by him: TEN's persistent criticism of the anthropological and folkloric
approach to the "black problem." Costa Pinto suppresses TEN's role as spon-
sor and convener of the First Congress of Brazilian Blacks and goes on to use
the language that TEN had been developing since 1945 as if it were his own
invention. Crediting himself as the herald of a "new approach" that criticizes
the blacks on display procedure, he nevertheless reduces black people's own
intellectual production to the status of "very curious statements."[146] Certain
contemporary authors tend to reproduce this discourse.[147] Thus continues the
process of pilfering the social movement's historical agency and fictitiously
transforming its intellectual production into someone else's creation.

Black intellectuals did not fail to leave their own record. Abdias
Nascimento wrote:

> The "students" of Brazilian blacks transformed us, in their books, into
> a spectacle on display, and while they entertained themselves at our
> cost,—ah! the quaint dishes of black cooking, the exquisite strangeness
> of macumbas and candomblés, the picturesque dance and exotic
> music!—they couldn't even imagine that we, blacks, were people deal-
> ing with life: we acted on it and it acted on us, in sum, we discussed
> and struggled for our survival. Journalists like Raquel de Queiróz,
> Osório Borba, R. Magalhães, Jr., Henrique Pongetti, Edmar Morel,
> collaborated with us in the formation of a new consciousness about the
> problem. In this way, parallel and simultaneously with the "official"
> studies, side by side with an innocuous academicism that was develop-
> ing in the shadow of the moral and material support of the dominant—
> and oppressor—classes, another path was being forged, a new and
> unknown trail was blazed by the effort and clearheadedness of blacks
> themselves ... [who] made their action into a new, living and practical,
> chapter of our sociology.
>
> This new view, realistic and creative, had as its catalyzing center the
> Black Experimental Theater, which held ... research meetings, debates,
> and interracial orientation programs, among them ... the First Congress
> of Brazilian Blacks, in Rio in 1950, which marked the "complete turn-
> around in this type of approach to the problem," a turnabout which Mr.
> ... Costa Pinto unduly appropriates as his own initiative.[148]

TEN'S SOCIAL ACTION

In this chapter, I hope to have documented some little known dimensions of TEN's nontheatrical activity. In conclusion, certain observations are in order.

In the first place, TEN's social action was not limited to opening up opportunities for a small elite in social spaces frequented by the bourgeoisie. Abdias Nascimento writes, "We are not demanding for all blacks a Congressman's diploma or a title of Baron. I hope my words will not be distorted and interpreted maliciously. Discrimination mostly affects those in the more humble occupations" To illustrate this, he cites a want ad for a switchboard operator "with excellent appearance, white ... please do not apply without the above requisites."[149] On another occasion, Nascimento asserts that "Brazilians of color must fight simultaneously for a double transformation: a) economic-social change in the country; b) change in race and color relations."[150]

It would be difficult to encounter a clearer expression of the fact that the TEN intellectuals did not limit their goal to gaining access for black individuals to higher places in the class hierarchy. They recognized the need for socioeconomic change. Nevertheless, the sociological characterization of the movement continues to prevail. Thus, Antonio Sérgio Alfredo Guimarães, a sociologist who demonstrates broad knowledge of the study of race in Brazil and a position of solidarity with the black movement, states that "only after 1970" does the black movement open "a new battle front, this time against racial inequality. Or in other words, beyond the incidents of racial discrimination committed individually, they go on to combat also the unjust distribution of wealth, prestige, and power between whites and blacks."[151] In the same line of reasoning, only in the 1970s did there emerge, according to Guimarães, "a new political direction of the black movement ... addressing the building of a more just and more egalitarian society."[152]

The historical record does not confirm such a statement. It may be a result of the academic effort to identify in the historical evolution of black movements a linear set of phases, a procedure that is dear to scientific method. The records indicate, however, that the tenor of TEN's activity was precisely to combat racial inequality and the unjust structure of distribution of wealth, prestige, and power between whites and blacks. Such a concern is what led TEN's leadership to the nationalist and developmentalist position associated with ISEB and CEPAL. The theses espoused by these institutions were elaborated by social scientists engaged in the search for a more just society. While the workings of a capitalist economy did not favor the results they hoped for, this fact observed in retrospect does not alter their preoccupation with income distribution and issues of equality.[153] Among leftist intellectuals today there is a tendency to portray them as populists and partisans of an endemic authoritarianism, but this tendency is more a function of the ideological position of such writers than a result of scientific research. Sometimes such intellectuals allege populism in order to discredit political adversaries by identifying them with former authoritarian regimes such as those of Getúlio Vargas in Brazil and Juan Domingo Perón in Argentina.[154]

Similarly, those who claim that TEN sought only to combat topical cases of discrimination against individuals, rather than a more just distribution of wealth, prestige, and power, implicitly identify TEN with populism and invoke its leaders' developmentalist approach to support that view. I believe that such an evaluation is the mistaken consequence of confusing TEN's goals with the results it was able to obtain, in the same way that such leftist critics confuse the goals of ISEB and CEPAL intellectuals with the failure of government policies based on their theories to achieve egalitarian income distribution and social justice. One can attribute such a failure to many factors other than the goals of the activist social scientists.

Guimarães's effort to identify phases in the evolution of the black movement recalls the ideas of black activists like João, the subject in Ricardo Franklin Ferreira's research who asserts that in the late 1970s the black movement breaks with previous phases and begins to seek broader racial and social justice.[155] This effort to define phases in a linear evolution of the movement echoes precisely the evolutionist orientation of developmentalist thought that some sociologists criticize in TEN's discourse.[156] The evolutionist dimension is partly responsible for the contradictions they point out in that discourse. But we need to approach the analysis of such contradictions with the methodological respect for difference that historian Eduardo Silva suggests—tuning in to the rhythm of the actors involved, perceiving an era as a meaningful whole.[157]

The concept of development in the 1950s meant going through stages of social, economic, and political organization in order to achieve progress, that is, industrialization and economic growth measured as production of material goods. Such a concept indeed contains an evolutionist bent, which does not, however, contradict the fact that development was seen as the means to build social justice and overcome inequalities. To achieve progress meant to eradicate miserable poverty and illiteracy; these were TEN's fundamental goals. TEN's leaders advocated black people's inclusion in the modern culture of industrialization and economic growth—progress. TEN's critique of the anthropological approach to blacks on display is precisely that such an approach made no effort to address this need.

Here, in my view, are the grounds of the ambivalence in TEN's discourse when it promotes the values of black culture, inscribed dynamically on the modern backdrop of progress, and at the same time characterizes "pre-logical" and "pre-lettered mentalities" as factors of backwardness.[158] When TEN condemns government policies that maintain minorities and colored people in "archaic forms of sociability and culture, keeping them marginalized from contemporary ecumenical conditions,"[159] it is preaching the need to free them from extreme poverty, capacitating them to exercise full citizenship in modern society and viewing the black population "as a community capable of identifying and solving its own problems, with no need to appeal to political ideologies."[160] Nascimento writes: "The founding idea of TEN was the understanding that the process of freeing the mass of black people from their state of social marginalization must be based on their education *and on the creation of social and economic conditions for the education for free life to be effective.*"[161] When TEN's leaders—on very few occasions whose importance has been exaggerated by repeated quotation—couched their reference to education for free life as "training in the style of behavior of the middle and upper classes of Brazilian society,"[162] it was always in this context. They meant that the exercise of citizenship and opportunity should be the prerogative of all, without discrimination, and education was the means to that end. This theme is directly related to the concern of TEN's intellectuals with the reduction of African values to the status of folklore excluding them from the creative process. Abdias Nascimento asserts that "in Brazil they degraded our original African culture, substituting it with the culturology of poverty and illiteracy."[163] In other words, illiteracy and poverty are what prevent the dynamic development of African cultural values in a modern context.

The adoption of evolutionist concepts like that of "archaic forms" seems largely traceable to Guerreiro Ramos's identification with the rigors of scientific method.[164] Nascimento was more concerned with valuing "our African cultural origins" and the "black institutions of great vitality and deep roots" whose cultural values would be the basis for mobilizing a "social movement of vast proportions."[165] Guerreiro Ramos agrees with this last point: he writes that "The aesthetic rebellion I have dealt with in these pages will be the preliminary step toward the total rebellion of peoples of color to become the subjects of their own destiny."[166] In any event, those who interpret the reference to archaic forms as being identified with Afro-Brazilian religions should note that *Quilombo* consistently defended the right to freedom of religious practice and the spiritual and cultural values of Candomblé.[167]

Differences between Nascimento's and Guerreiro Ramos's notions of aesthetics and Negritude may be instructive in understanding apparent contradictions in TEN's work and discourse. I suggest that Guerreiro Ramos's Negritude is an aesthetic creation involving the transposition of African values to a subjective and abstract plane, while Nascimento's version is founded in their living dynamics as expressed in their original context as well as their incorporation into the arena of "official" or "erudite" artistic culture. Guerreiro Ramos's notion of aesthetics places priority on the physical beauty of an ethnic group, that is, the body differentiated and rejected by the colonialist ideology whose aesthetic value is redeemed by Negritude.[168] He seeks to incorporate this standard of beauty into the set of aesthetic values subjectively legitimized and abstractly endorsed by society. For him, the cultural values of Africa seem to be a kind of lost treasure, part of a collective memory or an underlying identity; a sort of substratum of physical and spiritual beauty whose value would emerge in artistic activity and could be tapped and mobilized creatively in the effort to educate African Brazilians for the exercise of full citizenship.[169] He does not specifically mention the spiritual values of Afro-Brazilian religion. He gives examples of an abstract spirituality expressed in poetry, the visual arts, and theatrical interpretation, and asserts that "The forces of the black soul, so long contained, constitute today the largest reserve of vitality of our civilization."[170]

Abdias Nascimento's approach is different in that he seeks the essence of African and Afro-Brazilian cultural values experienced concretely in a living, dynamic, immediate way in the religious practice of terreiro communities. He argues against the "mummification" of these values, the process of confining them to static and rigid mechanical repetition, as if they were "something almost dead, or already stuffed as a museum piece."[171] Nascimento sees them as alive and current. He emphasizes the sophistication and depth of content of these living African values, a position reinforced by his personal option for Afro-Brazilian religion. Guerreiro Ramos, on the other hand, cultivated a lofty humanism inspired by his Catholic faith but dynamically inclusive of other values.[172]

By observing these differences, I do not pretend to identify a dichotomy or postulate an ideological debate within the Black Experimental Theater. Immersed in the action necessary to achieve TEN's aims, Guerreiro Ramos and Abdias Nascimento articulated their ideas in the dynamics of that action. The existence of tensions, and even contradictions, is part of the process of forging paths.

The best expression of TEN's theoretical content — resting on African cultural, spiritual, and epistemological values — emerges in its action. Such values structure the play *Sortilégio*, making it part of the worldwide tradition of African ritual drama. By elaborating the contemporary vitality of African cultural and aesthetic values in connection with the existential experience of African descendants, the play embodies the meaning of the Black Experimental Theater in a way that the written discourse of its leaders could not do.

SORTILÉGIO: BUILDING AN AFRO-BRAZILIAN IDENTITY ON STAGE

As part of its mission to encourage the creation of dramatic literature focusing on blacks and their culture, TEN staged several original dramatic works that were written especially for TEN with that purpose in mind. Its anthology *Dramas for Blacks and Prologue for Whites* contains seven plays.[173] Among them is Abdias Nascimento's *Sortilege (Black Mystery)*. A new version of this play, *Sortilege II: Zumbi Returns* was written after the author's stay in Nigeria as Visiting Professor at the University of Ife from 1976 to 1977.[174] He introduced new mythical and symbolic dimensions into the play, but maintained its dramatic structure. In its introduction the author states that it is "simply an updated version. Almost 30 years have gone by since I wrote the first *Sortilégio*, and I considered it necessary to reformulate some details that intensify the mystery's engagement with its African roots, and that rescue from history and bring up to date Zumbi's example in the fight for African people's freedom, human dignity, and sovereignty."[175]

Written in 1951, *Sortilégio* was banned from the stage for six years by the censors. Such an event is significant because Nascimento was a member of the committee created in 1948 by the Association of Theater Critics to protest and take judicial measures against censorship, which they saw as unconstitutional.[176] The creation of the committee was a reaction against the interdiction of two plays by Nelson Rodrigues, *Senhora dos Afogados* and *Black Angel*; the latter was written for TEN and published in its anthology.[177]

Almost a decade after the committee's creation, the institution of censorship remained in force and at long last the censors liberated *Sortilégio*. Twelve years after TEN's debut with *The Emperor Jones*, the group returned to Rio de Janeiro's Municipal Theater and opened *Sortilégio* in 1957.

In his introduction to TEN's anthology, Nascimento remarks that "the theater of people of color preceded the birth of Greek drama."[178] About a thousand years before Aeschylus a libretto was written in Egypt about the death of Horus, which is equal to Aeschylean tragedy. The dramatic form of the rites, as well as the worship of Dionysus, was imitated from black Egypt. The Greeks reproduced the theatrical atmosphere of song, dance, and poem brought together in Dionysus worship. Nascimento reports the recent discovery of the "first texts of dramatic literature," which made it possible to "restore to Egypt the honor of certain discoveries that had been attributed, presumptuously, to the Greeks."[179] In addition to establishing the anteriority of the African form originating in Egypt, Nascimento's statement also tells us what form African theater takes. The origin of theater is rite, or the representation of principles and practices that link man in social life to the cosmos and to nature. The historical analysis of drama in Nascimento's prologue[180] coincides with those of Wole Soyinka[181] and Afro-Brazilian critic Leda Maria Martins.[182] Martins points out as a common phenomenon in ritual drama the individuation of the story around a hero-god, or a deified hero. In the passions of Egypt Osiris appears as the protagonist-hero, in Syria it is Tammuz, and in Babylonia the lover/husband of the mother-goddess Ischtar.[183]

Western drama progressively separates theater from ritual and the dramatic text becomes something independent of collective life and mythical and religious communion. It is now a secular act, the author's individual production for a spectator audience. It exemplifies the concept of "art for art's sake." But in African theater, despite the influence of colonial domination, the link between theater and community, rite and myth, still prevails. Moreover, as Wole Soyinka observes, certain African gods are, "the favorites of poets and dramatists, modern and traditional," and they "appear to travel well. The African world of the Americas testifies to this both in its socio-religious reality and in the secular arts and literature."[184] This is the case of Ogun, Obatala, and Shango, who are

> represented in drama by the passage-rites of hero-gods, a projection of man's conflict with forces which challenge his efforts to harmonize with his environment, physical, social, and psychic. The drama of the hero-god is a convenient expression; gods they are unquestionably, but their symbolic roles are identified by man as the role of an intermediary quester, an explorer into territories of 'essence-ideal' around whose edges man fearfully skirts.[185]

Soyinka identifies the origin of African ritual drama as the moment in which the cosmic space, that "patient, immovable and eternal immensity that surrounds man," which is the "natural home of the unseen deities, a resting-place for the departed, and a staging-house for the unborn," solicits from human beings the need to "challenge, confront and at least initiate a rapport with the realm of infinity."[186] The stage of ritual drama is the place where the hero enacts this confrontation to benefit the community, whose presence is what creates the "magical microcosm."[187] In this space charged with energy the "chthonic inhabitants" are challenged.[188] African theater integrates human social life into the cosmic whole, in a plot that involves gods, human beings, and nature. The cosmic and the human, the social world and the natural universe, are not separated. This universe as an integrated whole belongs to the deities, the ancestors, the unborn, living human beings, and the forces of nature.

Drama as a magical microcosm brings to the stage the African concept of vital continuum maintained by the flux of *axé*, the life force and cosmic energy whose constant replacement and restitution makes possible the continuity of life, the natural and spiritual world, and the cosmos itself. This endless process of restoration is achieved in the life-death-life cycle, which is symbolically materialized in the flux of vital liquids (blood, semen, sap, milk) and exchange of cosmic elements by means of *ebó* (offering).[189]

Emmanuel, the hero of Nascimento's *Sortilégio*, explores such territories. *Sortilégio* is a mystery rooted in the African concept of the cosmic whole and in the social reality of blacks in Brazil. It is part of the re-creation of African theater in the Americas, in which the cosmic mythical-ritual dimension is viscerally linked to "another dimension, in which we hear the authentic voice of blacks as a race and as a person of color: social life. To be and to live black is not a common vicissitude in Western life. Race and color differentiate us and we make the specific sensibility developed in the century of black consciousness a new creative dimension."[190]

African descendants in Brazil share the vicissitude of being black with African descendents in other parts of the Americas. Everywhere in the Americas, building African theater involves reconstituting the identity of a social group torn at the core of its human dignity over centuries of enslavement, as well as reappropriating the African cultural heritage that was denied, crushed, ridiculed, and reduced to the status of folklore.

Such goals were present in black theater in the United States in the 1920s. It was the time of the Harlem Renaissance, the profusion of African American artistic creativity peppered by a considerable dose of dialogue with and participation of Caribbean and African writers that inspired the Negritude poets and activists.[191] The National Association for the Advancement of Colored People (NAACP) defined its position on black theater by stating that its author would have to be "a destroyer of the negative images of blacks."[192] Such a position implied creating, and associating with black people, images shaped by prevailing concepts of morality and aesthetics. This is a process similar to one protagonized by the social and recreational clubs of São Paulo in that era.[193]

In an article published in 1926, W.E.B. Du Bois proposed a new theory of black theater, which included several aims. He stated that it should be about black people, showing how black life really is; by black people, written by black authors who understand what it means to be black today; for black people, directed primarily to black audiences; and near black people, located in black communities or close to the mass of black people.[194] His goal was to avoid creating a black theater distant from its community of origin, not only in the physical sense but also in the sense of style, content, message, and social impact. For Du Bois, such distance was a latent possibility in the emphasis given to the "positive image" promoted by the NAACP's position.

While different, both North American and Brazilian concepts addressed problems posed by the existence of African descendants and their community in Western society. In the 1960s and 1970s, dramatic literature and theatrical production in the United States expressed a new stage in the evolution of black theater by surpassing these ideas. Dramatist Errol Hill, for example, proposed that beyond Du Bois's formula, black theater should also seek "a spiritual and intellectual immersion in the authentic forms of black expression."[195] His statement seems to translate the legacy of Negritude to English-speaking lands, where the essence of its content and spirit were being discussed and developed in the 1960s and 1970s under the names of Afro-American/black personality and Afro-American/black cultural nationalism. The new dimension of black theater was developed in such a context.

In Brazil before 1944 there was no black theater, only conventional theater that included black stereotypes. With TEN, black theater exploded on the scene already imbued with a profound social dimension as well as Hill's spiritual and intellectual immersion in black expression. Thus it is part of the worldwide black drama that "is built not merely out of ethnic and racial attachment, but fundamentally by the elaboration of an enunciation and a thing enounced that distinguish it, in all its variations."[196]

Here the thing enounced is the reelaboration of the African ritual drama tradition in its mythical and cosmic dimensions. Brazilian blacks arrive at the reencounter with African form, carrying a heavy baggage of oppression accumulated in their experience of Western society. The denouncement, elaboration, and resolution of the problems of this oppression constitute the object of the path-breaking hero's challenge. Cosmic forces present in the persecuted religions of the *terreiro* communities play the role of mediators, intervening in the formulation of a dramatic and vital solution to the conflicts posed and putting that solution into effect.

Sortilégio begins to operate this synthesis from the very first step, the choice of literary genre. The term "mystery," in addition to evoking the worship of ancestral divinities, takes us back to the medieval European theatrical form, the Mysteries, "in whose weaving"—as in that of *Sortilégio*—we find "the hybrid use of songs, choruses, diverse visual and sonorous resources."[197] José Paulo Moreira da Fonseca noted that "in the freer, more poetic field of the Mystery, ... reality is offered in an intense stylization, one that demands the presence of invisible beings."[198] Fonseca goes on to state , "The genre chosen is one of the most difficult; it demands that one be extremely alert so that emotion is sustained and the show does not fall into an "artificial" tone. ... The author walked on a razor's edge; in works of this type it is very hard to hit the target. Abdias Nascimento hit it many times, both as writer and as actor."[199]

Adonias Filho described *Sortilégio* as "a lyrical drama whose beauty does not compromise the living reality brought to life by the sensitivity, intelligence, and perception of a black man. ... In fact what is meshed together, in a literary combination of admirable projection, is the race issue with the poetry of Rio de Janeiro Macumba."[200]

The play puts on stage "a path of individual and collective self-assertion, a rite of passage, a moral and psychological crossing by which the protagonist acquires a metonymical dimension as an alternative cultural sign."[201]

The mystery of the hero Emmanuel, a black attorney married to a white woman, is carried out by the gods through the Filhas de Santo, initiated mediums who conduct the ritual. The play is itself metaphorically an *ebó*, an offering of replacement and restitution. The Macumba ceremony runs through the play with provocative functions and intervenes in the plot's development. The gods control Emmanuel's movements and manipulate the set. Exu, "the Orisha of multiplicity and movement, functions as the propelling axis of the character's deconstruction, re-creation, recomposition, and reconstitution."[202] His function corresponds intimately to the deity's attributes in the philosophical web of Yoruba religion. The following excerpt sets the tone of Exu's intervention in the play's plot and Emmanuel's destiny:

FILHA DE SANTO II: Can color be a destiny?

FILHA DE SANTO III (*with conviction*): Destiny is *in* color. Nobody escapes their fate.

FILHA DE SANTO II: A black man when he denies Exu ...

FILHA DE SANTO I: ... forgets the Orishas ...

FILHA DE SANTO II: ... dishonors Obatala ...

FILHA DE SANTO III (*vigorous*): Deserves to die. Disappear forever.

FILHA DE SANTO I (slowly): Hard words. Our mission is not one of hate.

FILHA III (*sadistic, perverse*): Exu was trembling with hate, foaming with rage, when he gave the order:

VOICE OF EXU (*distorted, unreal*): I want the son of a bitch here on his hands and knees, before the big hour.

FILHA I (*gaining time*): He was trembling. But not with hate. Exu has only love in his heart. Exu only does good.

FILHA III: And evil. He does evil too. Exu's rage is going to crash down on his head. Here, when ...

FILHA DE SANTO II (*finishing the sentence*): ... it strikes twelve, Exu hits the street ... looking for intersections and dead ends ...

FILHA DE SANTO III (*terrible*): It is the hour of Exu. The great hour of midnight. The hour of dreadful successes.

FILHA DE SANTO I: I feel sorry for him.

FILHA DE SANTO III (*goes on without listening*): Makes your hair stand on end. Exu is going to stop time, confuse the clock: past and present, what was before and what is happening now.[203]

In the ritual of Emmanuel's transformation, Exu confounds time and submits the hero to a series of flashbacks. Emmanuel sees and relives scenes and dialogues from his life that reveal the conflicts of racist society. Most of the incidents staged in the play, like the one in which the black attorney is beaten by the police and the commissioner orders his men to "throw the African doctor in the can,"[204] are true experiences of the author or people close to him. The episode just cited, for example, involved Aguinaldo de Oliveira Camargo, who was himself an attorney and police commissioner as well as one of TEN's most outstanding actors.

The interplay of scenes lived and relived by the hero places in relief the vicissitudes of being black in Western society, which are apparent from Emmanuel's first speech. The black attorney, who is being pursued by the police, appears climbing the bank, "eyes bulging wide, tie loose in the collar, out of breath."

EMMANUEL: This time you won't get me. I'm not the idiot student you threw in the car that time. Slapping me around. Arrested for what? The car couldn't go back to headquarters empty. Cracked my head open with billies and blows. Made me do time for crimes I never even thought about committing. I didn't kill anyone. I didn't steal. Now you will never grab me again. (*he turns back to continue to run.*) There must be a way out of here. (*the Orisha comes down from the second level to the first and disappears magically into the trunk of the gameleira tree*) Jesus! What was that? A ghost? (*he approaches the trunk of the tree, sees the offering; touches it fearfully at toepoint*) Ah, it's an offering. Black cock, even. So it's for Exu. What a lot of bullshit. (*he sees the pegi*) That's the pegi ...

(*he turns to the big tree*) ... the sacred fig tree. The terreiro must
be right around here. (*worried*) But ... how did I get to this place?
This is dangerous. Stupid to come here. The police are always
raiding terreiros ... they confiscate sacred drums, arrest everyone
they can ...

FILHA I: It's so easy to grab a nigger in the dawn!

EMMANUEL (*deeply hurt*): Not just one. Lots. Like those poor bastards
who were in the can with me.

FILHA II: What crime did they commit?

FILHA III: Is it a crime to be born black?[205]

Attorney Emmanuel is a Catholic, someone who has followed Western
models and standards. Renowned Brazilian dramatist Augusto Boal, who
directed the play, observed that

Emmanuel is, above all, a black man alienated from his own blackness.
He was educated in a "white" society and learned that he had the same
rights and prerogatives as whites. ... From the discrepancy that exists
between theoretical truth and practical truth in relations between the
races was born Emmanuel's permanent conflict. ... He tried to adapt. He
developed a psychological mechanism of self-protection. ... He put on a
mask that did not have the shape of his face. He assimilated attitudes of
"white" society. His adaptation meant denying himself.[206]

Mainstream society does not allow him to realize his real self, nor does it
allow him to get ahead. It denies him full citizenship and the possibility of
personal fulfillment, whether in his love life, profession, social life, or spiritual plane. Neither the mask nor the sacrifice of self-denial is enough to free
him from being trapped, repeatedly humiliated by the police, and absolutely
frustrated in his personal life. His relationships both with his black girlfriend,
Efigênia, and with his white wife, Margarida, are made impossible by the dic-
tates of whiteness, which operate insuperable distortions of emotion and
attachments, as we will see further on.

The flashbacks and dialogues Emmanuel has with the characters that
appear in the different images projected under Exu's direction unleash a
phantasmagoric representation on three planes of reality: social, psychological, and mythical-religious. This net thrown from the beyond catches
Emmanuel, who little by little "becomes possessed by the black gods, who
enter him through his five senses: the taste of cachaça [Brazilian rum], the
smell of incense, the sound of drums, the sight of the Orisha, and the feel of

the necklace. He slowly becomes integrated into this new environment: his own."[207]

Manipulated by the cosmic forces, Emmanuel finds himself before himself, and he comprehends the false identity that was making him his own victim and oppressor. A psychological war is waged in the hero's mind, in which the different disguises that had formed his personality are unmasked. After the long journey into the depths of his psychological, social, and cultural conflicts, Emmanuel's white mask is removed by Exu and he gives Emmanuel over to his new identity, *negritude* (blackness), as a path of redemption. Literally and symbolically, Emmanuel undresses, taking off his clothes and ornaments, including his attorney's ring, symbols of the whiteness that had entrapped him:

> EMMANUEL: (*As he speaks he takes off his shirt and pants and is left in a loincloth. He throws everything over the edge of the bank.*) Take your stuff. With this bullshit you lower the heads of blackmen. You tear away their pride. You lynch the poor bastards from the inside. And they're tamed. Castrated. Docile. Good little negroes with white souls. With me you got it wrong. No bits in my mouth. Imitating you like a trained monkey. Up till now I was pretending to respect you ... to believe in you ...[208]

As he frees himself from the injunctions of whiteness, Emmanuel takes the step that puts him on the path of liberation. Entering the pegi, he calls on the Exus, who appear one by one "like fantastic dreams among the trees":

> EMMANUEL: I conjure up the phalanges of Exu the King.
> CHORUS: (*slowly, gravely, in liturgical tone*): Saravá ...
> EMMANUEL: Pagan Exu!
> CHORUS: Saravá ...
> EMMANUEL: Exu of the Winds!
> CHORUS: Saravá ...
> EMMANUEL: Exu of Darkness!
> CHORUS: Saravá ...
> EMMANUEL: Exu Lock the Streets!
> CHORUS: Saravá ...
> EMMANUEL: Exu of the Forests!
> CHORUS: Saravá ...
> EMMANUEL: Exu of the Moon!
> CHORUS: Saravá ...

EMMANUEL: Pomba Gira!
CHORUS: Pomba Girô ôô ... [209]

By invoking the Exus, Emmanuel names himself and completes his process of liberation, reintegrating himself into the universe of Afro-Brazilian culture. He knows that the police are arriving to arrest him. He assumes his own identification, takes responsibility for his acts, and in the supreme gesture of freedom gives himself over to the lance of Ogun, brandished by the Filhas de Santo. The hero breaks through the cosmic barrier as Ogun himself did, forging a passage to reunite with the gods. The offering is made; axé is restored and replenished.

Emmanuel's mystery is the reencounter with his legitimate being, overcoming its violation by the dominant system. The construction of his identity is mediated by the cosmic forces of his original culture. The supreme act that closes the play—Emmanuel's death—symbolically recalls a foundational principle of that culture: the principle of ebó, offering.[210] The offering is the means by which axé, the life force, is replaced and replenished, restoring cosmic balance. It represents the continuous cycle of death and birth that makes life possible. Emmanuel's last gesture is the offering capable of restoring harmony and renewing life where the distortions of racism had reigned.

Nascimento has crafted in this play an example of what he and Guerreiro Ramos proposed in their theories of Negritude. Not only do the cultural values of African religion structure the play itself—it is a ritual, an ebó—but they also are the moving force in Emmanuel's transformation from a personality harnessed in the trappings of whiteness to a free man in control of his destiny. Moreover, his transformation, based on these cultural values, is a catalyst for the collective redemption of his people. This aspect of the play emerges more clearly in the second version, whose title announces from the outset the emphasis the author attributes to this dimension: *Sortilege II: Zumbi Returns*.

SORTILÉGIO AND GENDER

Sortilégio focuses on the drama of its hero Emmanuel; the female characters apparently are relegated to a secondary status. Roger Bastide laments that both Efigênia, Emmanuel's black girlfriend, and Margarida, his white wife, are "prostitutes."[211] Niyi Afolabi remarks that the secondary role of the female characters reflects the male habit of focusing on Afro-Brazilian life from a patriarchal point of view and underestimating African descendant women and their specific experience.[212] Leda Maria Martins does not comment on this aspect of the play.[213]

It is noteworthy that such evaluations refer to the two female characters from the secular realm of the play, so to speak. The analysts do not seem to take into account the three Filhas de Santo or the Iyalorixá, a character added in the second version of the play. Nascimento establishes that the Iyalorixá character can be substituted with a male Babalorixá, but the author's gender preference is clear. In any case, the Iyalorixá and the Filhas de Santo embody a singular aspect of the religious communities of African origin in Brazil: the predominance of the phenomenon that enchanted anthropologist Ruth Landes and that Sueli Carneiro and Cristiane Curi called "female power in Orisha worship."[214]

The Filhas de Santo, initiated mediums and the agents of Emmanuel's transformation, play an essential and central role in the play's structure, a fact that recalls the issue of gender in the African cultural context. According to Oyeronke Oyewumi's analysis, Yoruba cultural tradition, which is a major source of the Candomblé and Macumba religions, does not establish social hierarchy or distribute social roles and prestige according to gender. She further shows that this traditional African society does not attribute any innate difference to men and women in terms of capacity for action, performance, or intelligence.[215] Such a fact takes us back to the broader issue of the continuity of African social forms in black Diaspora communities.

The predominance of women in leadership roles or with important ceremonial functions in African religion stands in contrast to the patriarchal norm of Western-dominated ex-slave societies. In a broader way, the relevant social functions and prestige of women in African-descendant communities within ex-slave societies can be seen as a function of the continuity of African cultural and social traditions.[216] Both of these phenomena are present in *Sortilégio and Sortilégio II*, symbolically represented in the Iyalorixá and Filhas de Santo. These female characters are the movers of the action throughout. They pronounce the first words of the play as the curtain opens: the names of the ingredients of an offering they are preparing for Exu. Once it is done—"Ready: offering made, obligation fulfilled"—they also announce Emmanuel's arrival and his destiny:

FILHA DE SANTO 1 (*lyrical*): ... and he will return without memory, pure and innocent as a newborn babe, to the great illuminated night of Aruanda.

FILHA DE SANTO III (*mystical*): Where the Orixás live. It must be beautiful to live in Aruanda!

FILHA DE SANTO II (*listening to the ground*): He's coming, fleeing, running away. Pursued by many.

FILHA DE SANTO III (*happy*): No one will touch him. Only the lance of Exu.

FILHA DE SANTO II (*sad*): will wound his flesh ...

FILHA DE SANTO III (*exalting*): ... shelter his spirit ... [217]

Throughout the play, the Filhas de Santo announce and determine what will happen to Emmanuel. The Orixá is their instrument, but it is they and the Iyalorisha who conduct the ritual. And it is Filhas de Santo who close the play by announcing the fulfillment of Emmanuel's destiny—"Ready: offering made, obligation fulfilled."[218] In this way, the author places at center stage the female power—of women and of female deities—in Afro-Brazilian culture.

Efigênia and Margarida are the two female characters involved romantically with Emmanuel—Efigênia is his black former girlfriend and Margarida is his white wife. These characters are not developed with great depth as individuals, although Efigênia's personality comes through as a strong one. Their function in the play is to constitute and participate in Emmanuel's psychological, social, and emotional conflicts. Efigênia and Margarida each suffer with him. But as they perform this role, they also embody and transform the central themes of the play.

In their interaction with Emmanuel and in their individual roles, Efigênia and Margarida are the play's anchors in the social reality of racism—a construction that is coherent, if not inevitable, because gender relations both *constituted by* and *constitutive of* race relations. They are the fulcrum of the mixed-race society and vehicle of the simulation of whiteness. They are both the motive and the result of the way race operates in society. Sexuality, indeed, is at the heart of racism in any ex-slave social system, as Charles V. Hamilton[219] and Cornel West both point out with respect to the United States. West's analysis fits Brazilian historical and social experience as well. He writes: "White supremacist ideology is based first and foremost on the degradation of black bodies in order to control them. ... this white dehumanizing endeavor has left its toll in the psychic scars and personal wounds now inscribed in the souls of black folk. These scars and wounds are clearly etched on the canvas of black sexuality."[220] West poses a question that precisely expresses the dilemma set on stage by Emmanuel, Efigênia, and Margarida in *Sortilégio*: "Can genuine human relationships flourish for black people in a society that assaults black intelligence, black moral character, and black possibility?"[221]

In his identity as a simulation of whiteness, Emmanuel rejects Efigênia, his true love, in favor of Margarida, a white woman. Margarida resorts to marrying

Emmanuel in order to "cover a hole," as Filha de Santo III puts it: Her lost virginity demands that she be married—even to a black man—in order to save her honor.[222] For black women, however, such solutions are not available. Based on the law that "protects girls under eighteen," Emmanuel tries to defend Efigênia to the police as a minor seduced by a white man. "Quit the crap, whore!" is the answer from the police authority. Efigênia replies: "The eternal bitterness of color. I understood that the law is not on the side of black virginity."[223]

The clashes with the police, which symbolize the violence African descendants face in racist society, almost always turn around incidents involving sexuality or gender relations in the context of race. In this sense, the female characters are the fulcrum of the play's portrayal of race relations. Indeed, one could say that Efigênia and Margarida are the instruments of the play's impact, bringing home to the audience the extent to which racism invades the lives of black people and their families at the most unexpected moments. The author's use of flashback reinforces the arbitrary nature of such invasion, which creates a permanent tension: one is constantly on the defensive, wondering where the next attack will come from:

> EMMANUEL (*recalling*): That night I was already engaged to Margarida. We went to a ball. On the way back ... at the wee hours, we decided to take a little walk. All of a sudden a police car stopped at our side:
> AGGRESSIVE VOICE I: A coon kissing a white girl.
> AGGRESSIVE VOICE II: It's assault and robbery.
> AGGRESSIVE VOICE III: He's attacking her.
> EMMANUEL: The cops beat me. ... Cuffs, punches ... kicks. They threw me in the police truck.
> MARGARIDA (*protesting*): He wasn't assaulting me. He didn't rob me. He's my fiancé. My fiancé, don't you hear?
> EMMANUEL: Me, her fiancé! Bars again! Bars.[224]

Margarida's protests are useless. As a white woman accompanied by a black man, she deserves the contempt of white society, whose ambassadors to the black community, she soon learns, are the police. If her relationship with Emmanuel were one of love, this would be part of the price exacted by white society for her betrayal. But the fact that she is using Emmanuel for her own purposes symbolizes the rarity and difficulty of such relationships being based on solid foundations, bringing satisfaction and a sense of fulfillment to the partners; this is yet another restriction that racism imposes on human beings, white and black.

The race issue is perhaps most poignantly expressed in the difference between the ways in which Margarida and Efigênia experience their gender roles. As women, both are subject to the injunctions of patriarchal society, but each experiences those injunctions in a specific way based on her race. Indeed, even the rules themselves differ according to race.

Virginity, for example, was compulsory for women at the time of *Sortilégio*, but racism makes that norm operate in different ways for black and white women. Margarida's avenue of escape from the consequences of losing her virginity—marrying Emmanuel, a black man—confirms black men's subordinate social status as well as white women's social privilege. Indeed, statistics demonstrate that race is more important than gender in defining inequality.[225] The following dialogue between Efigênia and Margarida brings out the difference that race imposes on the way the two women experience the issue of virginity:

> MARGARIDA: ... I could never imagine that men would make such a big deal about something so unimportant ...
> EFIGÊNIA: Unimportant to you. Me, ever since the instant I lost my "importance" my path was traced: the road of perdition. I had no choice.[226]

What are the choices open to Margarida? The convent, perhaps, or exile to the home of relatives in the remote interior. Or she might live out her life as an old maid and be the target of hushed commentary and whispered speculation. Finally, her marriage to Emmanuel leaves her open to being taken as a call girl or prostitute, as are many white girls who accompany black men in public. But her chances of avoiding prostitution are certainly greater than those of Efigênia. This is a social privilege conferred by whiteness.

For Efigênia, the inevitability of prostitution is determined not only by the inferior socioeconomic status that is the probable result of her race—it is less likely that her family will be able to support her—but also by the racial discrimination that denies her job opportunities, which might be open to white women. In addition, the stereotype of black women as sensual and sexually available is no small factor. Indeed, the heritage of the *mucama* from slave society[227] still haunts black women's relationships, as Emmanuel points out to Efigênia:

> EMMANUEL (*explaining, sincere*): Have you ever noticed how white men look at you? As if they were your owners? It's branded on their conscience. They don't even bother to wonder; it's enough for

them to want a black woman and they will sleep with her. What difference does it make, one more black girl in the whorehouse?[228]

The whitening imperative is another factor reinforcing the stereotype of black women who are sexually available to white men. The summons to whitening falls almost like a civic responsibility on black women, who are called upon to whiten the race by "cleansing" their wombs. Yet they cannot escape the historical reality of concubinage as the instrument of whitening, nor can they elude the resulting stereotype:

> EMMANUEL: They say black women have no shame ... But to give themselves to whites just because they are white is stupid.
> FILHA DE SANTO III: How is it white men improve the race?
> EMMANUEL: To be deflowered and then thrown aside like bitches ...
> FILHA DE SANTO III: ... Is that cleansing the blood?[229]

Multiple social and historical factors, then, consolidate the stereotype of black women as "hot," easy, and available. But the stereotype is eminently the work of discrimination itself. Efigênia, without her "importance" and bereft of choice, attempts with Emmanuel's help to build an artistic career, but she falls quickly into this trap:

> EFIGÊNIA: I was sixteen years old and I loved you, I loved you better than I ever loved any man. But I needed to make my way. They didn't care about my talent. My body was all they wanted. I made it my weapon. ... I used my body like you would use a key. ... White men have privilege: without them, you get nowhere.[230]

Margarida, the white wife, satisfies the curiosity that originates in the stereotype of black male virility and soon tires of Emmanuel, whose loneliness grows when he discovers that Margarida has aborted their child, afraid it would be born black. Provoked also by the tricks of Efigênia, whose hatred for Margarida is due not only to jealousy but also to the racial injustice she suffers, Emmanuel ends up killing Margarida and this is why he is fleeing from the police. This is the act for which he takes responsibility, redeeming himself by his ultimate gesture. This act has created an imbalance in cosmic harmony that must be redressed by offering—by the replacement and replenishing of axé. When he understands and accepts the ritual sacrifice, determined from the beginning of the play by the cosmic forces of Afro-Brazilian religion, Emmanuel's last speech is delivered calmly and decisively: "I killed Margarida. I am a free black man."[231]

Margarida functions as a mirror of the negative stereotypes of blacks and a symbol of the simulation of identity imposed on them. Efigênia exposes and elaborates the stereotype, experienced at once as something shared with Emmanuel and as an impenetrable barrier between them, making the realization of their love impossible. The impasse that Cornel West discusses is in place, as well as his question: "Is there a way out of this Catch-22 situation ...? There indeed are ways out, but there is no one way out for all black people. Or, to put it another way, the ways out for black men differ vastly from those for black women. Yet, neither black men nor black women can make it out unless both get out, since the degradations of both are inseparable though not identical."[232]

While *Sortilégio* offers a symbolic and mythical-spiritual solution for Emmanuel, for Efigênia what is left is the destiny decreed by the dominant society, but in this play only with the consent of the cosmic forces. Efigênia is given over to Pomba-Gira, the goddess of the sexual act:

> EFIGÊNIA: Satisfying my desires, my whims—(*sarcastic*) I am conquering my space, riding my moon, as you say.... Little by little my career got left by the wayside. Elegant gowns, my body, even my name, everything lost meaning. The only thing that mattered was my desire for men. Handsome, ugly, short, tall, fat, toothless.... Red or yellow. All of them were fine! (*lyrical*) So good to satisfy the desire for men!... (*mystical*) I was following a divine order. Carrying out a liturgical act. (*vulgar*) That's why I left Copacabana. I moved to Lapa.[233]

In the Macumba of Rio de Janeiro, Pomba-Gira is the female counterpart of Exu and when the Exus are invoked at the end of the play, the last name spoken is hers. As we have seen, the invocation of the Exus is the call to Emmanuel's destiny and redemption. Thus, when Pomba-Gira is invoked, implicitly Efigênia is called forth, along with the hero, to the ritual sacrifice that configures the way out of the impasse. But in the original version of the play this scene is not staged. Efigênia disappears without assuming her part of the responsibility for Margarida's death—and therefore without redeeming herself—in the instant before Emmanuel brings about his own transformation. In the last scene between the two, Emmanuel cuffs her and calls her a murderess, a prostitute in body and soul. Efigênia, "unmoved," gestures to the police with the bloodied lily and disappears. She has signaled to the agents of his sacrifice. Emmanuel is left alone:

> EMMANUEL: It's them. They're coming up here. They took both of them. My wife and the woman I loved. They took everything.

Better. All the better this way. (*shouts, interspersed with a strong laugh of triumph, that goes on until the end of the play*) Now I am free. Forever. I am a black man free of goodness. Free of fear. Free of charity, of your compassion.[234]

Thus Efigênia, the beloved one, functions as an agent of Emmanuel's salvation, but does not take part in it. Following West's formula, both of them, black man and black woman, remain unable to overcome the impasse created by the dominion of whiteness because they have not overcome it together.

With this solution, Nascimento appears to endorse one of the classic values of Western literature: the loneliness of the individual faced with his destiny. This aspect of the play was acclaimed by the critics, who not only identified with the literary device, but also found in it the key to denying Emmanuel's story as a symbol for the whole community of African Brazilians. Those who already were alarmed at the notion of a play with a black hero, interpreted by a black actor, and produced by a group of blacks with a history of political and social agitation, seemed to envision that if the play were a successful call to action they could be faced with the prospect of black Brazilians, suddenly made aware of an imagined racial oppression, flocking down from the hills to seek revenge. Thus it was imperative for the play *not* to be a call to action, and its interpretation by the critics sounds like a massive sigh of relief. So occupied are they with the hero's loneliness that the female character has no importance at all; it is as if Efigênia did not even exist in the play's dramatic structure. One critic writes:

And like the divine poet of the Comedy, who finds Paradise when the object of his desire is extinguished, naked and clean like the first of men, it is also after the death of his desires that Emmanuel can exclaim: "I killed Margarida. I am a free black man." ... This is when a man can die, he has arrived at the goal of his existence—freedom—and no longer needs to busy himself except with his own mystery. This is Abdias Nascimento's play, whose high poetic quality resides also in the fact that it does not allow itself to be marred by sustaining any thesis, in the same way that his sentiment of true liberty cannot be confused with Greek and modern man's superstitions of freedom.[235]

In the context of the racial democracy ideology, to praise the play it was necessary to deny it the intention of "sustaining any thesis." Emmanuel's drama could only be the intimate conflict of one individual, but never that of

African descendants as a whole, for such a hypothesis would constitute the antithesis of the supposed harmony between the races. In this vein, another critic comments that "A reader of *Sortilégio* cannot discern, among characters so human in their poetic transfiguration, a thesis in defense of any position. Emmanuel is not *the* black person, he is *a* black person. While he carries all the marks of his race and is able to overcome Western culture by giving in to the beliefs of his people, he is only one black man whose personality is shaped by personal tragedy.[236]

Such an interpretation of *Sortilégio* is clearly not the author's intention, for Emmanuel functions precisely as the voice of protest and the symbolic embodiment of his group. The difficulty to understand Nascimento's intention seems to be linked to Margarida's murder, given that critics were generally unable to assimilate the symbolic device, confusing it with a call to the practice of crime as a protest against racism. Such a confusion of the play's symbolism would be dangerous if Emmanuel were considered representative of his race. Nelson Rodrigues announced this confusion early on:

> And what great and almost intolerable power of life has *Sortilégio*! In its firm and harmonious dramatic structure, in its violent poetry, in its uninterrupted dramatic power, *Sortilégio* is also a great aesthetic and vital experience for the spectator. Have no doubt: the majority of critics will not understand it. ... They are going to throw stones at *Sortilégio*. But nothing will prevent the black mystery from entering into the scarce history of Brazilian drama.[237]

Agreeing with Rodrigues about the dramatic force of the play, Roger Bastide notes *Sortilégio*'s likeness to the classic Afro-American novel *Native Son*, by Richard Wright, because in each of them there is the white woman's murder. Surprisingly, though, Bastide judges this symbol to be an implicit endorsement of crime as the expression of revolt.[238] Such is not the symbolic function of Margarida's death; disappointingly, Bastide's interpretation is almost as literal as that of the conservative press of the time.

The problem in such examples, though, is with the critical analysis and not the play. What leaves a gap in the play itself is the abandonment of Efigênia's symbolic potential and the option for the final image of the lonely hero. Had Efigênia recognized her role in Margarida's death, assuming responsibility, redeeming herself, and throwing off the bonds of whiteness along with Emmanuel, the play would form a more coherent whole. Such a solution would extend the consequences of Emmanuel's redemption to his partner and thus create hope for their extension to new generations. Moreover, since gender both constitutes and is constituted by race, only by creating a symbolic solution for the gender dilemma can the play achieve a real solution for the hero's problem of race and identity. Efigênia's disappearance mars the play's presentation of a new identity that should make it possible for black man *and* woman to overcome racism and build a new life—for if Emmanuel's redemption is a lone one, the victory ends with his death, where it should begin. Only the possibility of building new life can justify his sacrifice, for that is the principle of ebó: renewal and continuance of life.

Twenty years after the first edition was published, its second version[239] is fundamentally different from the original: The dramatic solution of Efigênia's fate is revised. In the last scene, at the moment of Emmanuel's sacrifice, Efigênia "*appears and stands behind Emmanuel; she is dressed in ritual robes of Ogun.*" The Filhas de Santo announce: "Ready: offering made, obligation fulfilled," but in the new version the play does not end there:

> *Efigênia puts the crown of Ogun on her head, and brandishes the lance in her hand. The chorus, the Filhas and the Iyalorixá salute "Ogunhiê!" and throw themselves prostrate on the ground, touching their heads on the soil in dobalê, a sign of reverence and obedience. There follow a few moments of absolute silence. Then Efigênia raises the lance in an emphatic gesture of command shouting a loud "Ogunhiê!" Ogun's song gets louder and changes into a triumphal and heroic rhythm.*[240]

The Iyalorixá salutes: "Axé to all: to the dead ... those alive ... and those unborn! Axé to the victory of our struggle!" The chorus responds by repeating "axé," and here the play ends: "While they sing and dance the curtain slowly comes down."[241]

Infused with the axé of Ogun, warrior and challenger of cosmic frontiers,[242] Efigênia is promoted from anonymous prostitute to leader of her community, which is liberated because of Emmanuel's sacrifice. The realization of the hero's symbolic destiny is joined with hers and they are reintegrated into the primordial communal origin of ritual drama, emerging in freedom from the Western convention of the lone male individual standing before his destiny. The content of the play's second version radically expands its reach and makes its symbolism explicit. It is gender as the fulcrum of race that operates such a change. The African-descendant woman now acts not only as the agent of the hero's salvation but also as protagonist and leader of the community benefited by the sacrifice and by the ritual drama itself.

CONCLUSION

The play *Sortilégio*, especially its second version, expresses the essence of TEN's work: an integrated approach to African descendants' human rights, including those of culture and identity, mediated by the symbolic language of African origin. Gender, the fulcrum of race in Brazilian society, is a necessary part of such a picture. Taken as a whole, including the diverse and several areas of its action and initiatives, TEN's critique of dominant Brazilian racial ideology from the viewpoint—the place—of blacks proposed new and innovative approaches, actions, and policies for the Afro-Brazilian population and the nation.

I believe that in this chapter we have seen that TEN's work is part of the continuum of resistance and project identities that anticipates the critical multicultural demands of later movements. The intellectuals who composed its leadership anticipated concepts like the social construction of race and proposed, long before it was articulated in sociology or social psychology, a relational approach to race relations that requires a critical focus on whiteness. With its social, artistic, and cultural action and with its theoretical production, I submit that TEN contributed to the articulation of postmodern thought and social criticism in Brazil.

The black movements whose story emerges in the pages of this book forged original paths in dealing with a camouflaged version of racism conjured up by the sorcery of color. In this process, the Black Experimental Theater introduced a new dimension by emphasizing African cultural values and building the theoretical base for their promotion as a fundamental part, not only of the resistance and project identities being developed by these movements, but also of Brazilian national culture and identity. Indeed, TEN's thought and action anticipated and contributed to building the bases for the expression of Afrocentricity and the development of critical multicultural theory in Latin America. Recent development of proposals for public policy by African descendants in the region confirms that the action and discourse of the early and mid-twentieth century black organizations heralded a movement that is transforming social reality and contributing to the articulation of postmodern thought by challenging the tenacity of the sorcery of color.

6

CONCLUDING REMARKS:
THE PRIORITY OF EDUCATION

I N THESE PAGES we have been looking for references useful to a better understanding of what African-descendant identity means in Brazil. For this, a view of race as interconnected with gender is indispensable. Beyond theoretical considerations, my aim is to help inform the creation of measures to support and stimulate positive identifications for African Brazilians. Such identifications are crucial for individual and community agency. By favoring agency, we contribute to expanding opportunity for the effective exercise of citizenship and human rights. Thus, identity takes on a political dimension; it constitutes power.

The notion of identity as a "dynamic of identifications with a sense of authorship"[1] is useful because of its reference to the agency of the subject faced with options of identification. The idea is similar to the notion of identity as project, in both the Sartrian sense used by Beauvoir[2] and in the sociological sense offered by Castells.[3]

In the globalized world, the individual is faced with ephemeral but powerful signs and symbols moving in a fluctuating universe. Identity is no longer fixed as relating to a geographical cultural context, but is composed out of values apprehended as identifications. Such identifications evolve from a person's experiences and interactions, but the person can also choose identity references and elaborate upon them. One composes identifications from references apprehended as values—the building blocks of identity as project. Social movements take on such a search as they criticize the mainstream culture and uphold their own alternative signs and symbols, which are often rooted in non-Western sources, values, traditions, and struggles repressed over centuries of colonial hegemony. These are the elements of what Castells refers to as resistance identities.

The search for references with which to build identifications produces meanings, knowledge, and reflections that have contributed to the building of postmodern thought. For example, black intellectuals and movements assumed a nonbiological idea of race in their theories and activism long before sociology articulated the concept of social construction of race. Similarly, black intellectuals in Brazil arrived at the idea of white studies in the dialectics of their action, anticipating recent trends in social psychology.

While the idea of multiculturalism as identity politics is recent, the building of resistance identities by social movements begins much earlier. There is continuity and coherence in the social activism that creates new references for identifications, and these evolve over time. The twentieth century was marked profoundly by this process; W.E.B. Du Bois announced it in his oft-quoted 1903 statement that it would be the century of the color line. Resistance to colonialism was the main mover of this trend, which spilled over into Diaspora movements like that of Marcus Garvey and UNIA, the Harlem Renaissance, and Negritude. The thought of the mid-twentieth century Afro-Brazilian activists and intellectuals that I revisited in the pages of this book, and the dialogue between Huey P. Newton and Erik Erikson, illustrate two other moments in the march of this trend, which represents a historical continuum rather than a series of sudden breaks with earlier thought and practice. I submit that the identity references built over this continuum of struggle, like those of feminism and environmentalism, are capable of building project identities in the sense proposed by Castells: they transformed society and had global effects, together with feminism, environmentalism, and the assertion of other non-Western identities. One of the effects specifically of these movements is to open new horizons of self-esteem for individuals belonging to populations targeted by racism and racial discrimination. By uncovering and elaborating references for building identifications, social movements offer supports to such individuals' building of identity with a sense of authorship that help overcome the negative effects of social stigma, stereotype, and discrimination on their lives. Problems for individuals engaged in the search for values can be dramatic. To keep the range of options open, one must resist giving in to the subtle meandering of Western ethnocentrism like the fear of "essentialism" that plagues the idea of black identity. This and the warning against reverse racism may result from the projection on the "other" of Western ethnocentrism's own fears and tendencies.

Oyeronke Oyewumi and the authors she cites bring a broad base of support to the idea that so-called essentialism has its origins in a concern with the body that is peculiar to the West and that she calls somatocentricity.[4] Essentialism is the idea of race and gender constituting biological or physiological essence, determining innate capacities like talent and intellect as well as social and psychological roles. A Manichaean division in Western philosophy alienates the body from spirit and soul; hence, the body is the object and depository of neuroses and obsessions inscribed on it like an epitaph in granite. Thus, essentialism is more a characteristic of the patriarchal West itself than of women or non-Western peoples. Yet it is their cultures, histories, and identities the West tends to reduce to racial or sexual essence. An example is the transplantation of the word *negro* to the English language, where it has no meaning relating to color and could only identify race by some biological essence beyond color. The naturalization of social inequality in Western society is the best example of essentialism. Western ethnocentrism attributed to racial and sexual essence—what was judged to be the innate inferiority of women and of non-Western peoples—the cause of the inferior social status imposed on them by racism and patriarchy.

All such considerations become more complex in the Brazilian context, characterized by the process I call the sorcery of color, which creates an aspiration to virtual whiteness embodied in de-Africanized racially mixed individuals identified with Western society. Western ethnocentrism, especially when characterized by the sorcery of color, presents a double blind spot: it denies its own racism while projecting it onto a racist "other," which is not infrequently black people themselves and their social movements. In Brazil, Western society also appropriates the cultural and historical facts that could provide the base of positive black identity, including African ancestral values, and defines them according to its own interests and criteria. Faced with African descendants' efforts to reappropriate these values and historical legacy, redefining them with reference to their own social and intellectual agency, it reacts by warning about the danger of essentialism and reverse racism.

Virtual whiteness is an identity created by the sorcery of color. Whiteness as an implicit norm is the invisible, silenced ethnic identity that reigns as a "universal" value. In the context of the sorcery of color it is the aspiration of the *moreno* or *escurinho*, the euphemistic "metarace" that will accept being anything but black and has the privilege of being considered white.

The discipline of psychology is not exempt from contributing to the sorcery of color. As a science, psychology has a history of being bound by the intellectual matrix of Western ethnocentrism and participating in the elaboration of a *competent discourse* steeped in the notions, stereotypes, and attitudes of racial determinism.

When Afro-Brazilian psychologists engaged with issues of race began producing theoretical work and engaging in clinical practice, they initiated a proposal that I call Afro-Brazilian listening, meaning essentially a practice informed by the understanding of racism as pathology and the subtle workings of the sorcery of color, and aware of therapeutic alternatives available in the terreiro communities of Afro-Brazilian religion. Such a notion, then, is not defined by skin criteria but instead by place: the Afro-Brazilian ear is one that is informed by experience of the implications and effects of racism on the psyche; such experience is a function of the location from which the therapist views and experiences theory and practice. The black therapist often brings to the clinic a life experience that optimizes his or her understanding of racism as pathology. Afro-Brazilian listening also creates a focus on the relational dimension of racism, which stems from the recognition that racism involves and affects not only the person who is discriminated against but also those who, even without discriminating, reap the privileges of whiteness. The approach to racism as relational underlines the need to name whiteness as a specific identity and to reveal the respective privileges and deficits generated by racism. The relational approach is positive for the problem of racism because it increases the possibility of identifying subjective factors that determine the exclusion of blacks in various social contexts. It also helps identify processes that are influenced by implicit and unrecognized criteria of race, which favors their being questioned and redefined.

One fundamental aspect of racism and the sorcery of color has been the denial of Afro-Brazilian historical agency, which has ideologically distorted black people and communities' actions and achievements or made them invisible. In the chapters on the black movements of São Paulo and Rio de Janeiro in the twentieth century, I suggest that the integrationist discourse of the early black movement can be seen as rejection of the negatively stereotyped identity that racism imposed on blacks. Rather than a naïve submission to white society's norms or internalization of its values, the black movement's adoption of conventional behavioral styles may reflect its efforts to prove the falsehood of the stereotype and to obtain professional training and preparedness for the population's exercise of citizenship rights. Their effort was to improve the situation of a population excluded from the labor market. The history of Brazil has largely ignored these movements, denying to African Brazilians the identification references they represent. I call this the Princess Isabel syndrome, in a reference to the habit of seeing the abolition of slavery as a generous gesture of the imperial family rather than a result of the resistance of Africans and their descendants in kilombos and the organized abolition movement. Another case of this syndrome is the so-called Afonso Arinos law, the historical record of which omits the role of black organizations. These organizations, especially the Black Experimental Theater, publicized cases of discrimination and thus made possible the approval of this bill of law in 1951 by a Congress that had rejected the proposals of the National Convention of Brazilian Blacks to the Constituent Assembly of 1946.

In the making of this historical record, certain methodological attitudes and the pretense of scientific neutrality can also create distortions. I suggest that the expectations of researchers, based on criteria applied in retrospect, have led to hurried conclusions such as the supposition that early black movements in Brazil were reactionary, elitist, or naïve. In the case of the Black Experimental Theater (TEN) sociology fixed on it an image fabricated out of frankly dishonest procedures such as the omission of historical facts observed by a researcher in close proximity to the movement. An example is the outright erasing of TEN's role as the organizer of the First Congress of Brazilian Blacks. In addition, sociology attempted to deny and appropriate to white intellectuals TEN's authorship of the critique of an approach in ethnology and anthropology that observed blacks and their culture as if they were a stage show or an exhibit, rather than living people with human needs. TEN systematically denounced this academic treatment of "blacks on display," a critical initiative whose history has been written as if black intellectuals took no part in it.

The main sociological conclusion of such methodological attitudes is to allege that the early black movements sought to benefit only an elite group, that they did not understand or address structural inequality, and that they were not concerned with a more just and egalitarian society but were content with the social climbing of a few privileged blacks within the prevailing socioeconomic norms of whiteness and authoritarianism. The value judgments contained in such appraisals, invested with the academy's approval, are shared by some participants in the contemporary black movement and are sometimes advanced by analysts whose clear-sightedness and integrity allows them an unusual independence of position on issues like affirmative action and antiracist public policy. Thus, one frequently hears that in the 1970s there was a break with the past and that the black movement took an unprecedented political stance in which it finally began to concern itself with building a more just society. I maintain that, rather than representing primitive and passé stages of collective consciousness surpassed by later generations that opened new fronts of struggle, the black movements of the period 1914 to

1970 express continuity and coherence in building the foundations of the contemporary struggle and victories of the Afro-Brazilian movement.

The historical predecessors of such demands regarding public policies to combat racism—especially affirmative action—are rarely mentioned. For example, the 1945 "Manifesto" of the National Convention of Brazilian Blacks,[5] which was presented to the 1946 National Constituent Assembly, proposed a set of public policy measures that were not instituted and that TEN continued to demand in its "Program," regularly published in its journal *Quilombo*.[6]

TEN's proposals explicate its concern about social injustice and inequality; the proposals demand that public policy diminish poverty and combat the effects of discrimination. The facts about TEN's proposals, in sum, do not support the thesis of the early black movement's insensitivity or lack of understanding of the broader social issue or the collective nature of racial inequality. Nor do they support the allegation of a radical break with the past in the 1970s. My view is that historical fact supports continuity in the development of the early black movement's positions and proposals, which led in a coherent way to the contemporary positions and expressions of the antiracist black movement.

A good example of this phenomenon is TEN's reference to "blacks as the Brazilian *people*,"[7] which does not imply a renouncement of its specific racial and ethnic identity, but instead suggests the need for Brazilian society to fully incorporate the specific identity as a national rather than a foreign one. TEN's demand is for the recognition of identity as a right of citizenship. Such an idea was central to the critical analysis of the whitening ideal as social pathology: it was alienating to exclusively endorse criteria from outside the national reality. Thus, to contrast the position of "blacks as the people" against a racialist concept supposedly adopted in the 1970s appears to be a red herring.[8] On the contrary, the positions converge in the simultaneous demand for a specific Afro-Brazilian identity and for recognition of race not as the problem of blacks but a national human rights issue.

In addition to the intimate relationship between identity and citizenship, the early black movement unanimously highlighted a singular priority: education. For them, African descendants' access to all levels of the educational system was an urgent need, the target of public policies proposed in the 1945 manifesto and in TEN's program. Education was seen as the way to make possible a redefinition of stigmatized identity, as well as preparing African descendants for the labor market and for the exercise of their citizenship rights, including the vote, which was reserved for the literate.

Education is still a very current priority, considered as urgent today as it was in the 1950s. The call for education is still part of the broader context of recovering black people's original culture and history as elements to build and value their identity. The black movement won legislation mandating the inclusion of Afro-Brazilian history and culture in school curricula, which became the subject of several local and state laws. Recently, Federal Law n. 10.639 of 2003 made this inclusion mandatory nationwide.[9] However, the principle inscribed in this legislation has yet to be implemented effectively in the schools, and teachers have yet to be prepared to teach these subjects. Actors in current social movements also work to obtain the revision of children's literature and schoolbooks to correct the distortions relating to Africa world history and culture, and to equip teachers to deal with racial issues in the classroom.

The interconnectedness of race and gender stand out in today's societal context. Gender is the fulcrum of the operation of race in a society where social relations are defined by the sorcery of color. The whitening ideal—the goal of miscegenation—underlies the hegemony of virtual whiteness embodied in the de-Africanized *moreno*. The miscegenation ideal is deeply rooted in the subordination of women. White women and black women experience this subordination in different ways according to race. White women enjoy a privileged status in relation to black men and black women, but their subordination was also crucial to the operation of the whitening ideal that was the motor of miscegenation in Brazil. The interrelation of gender and race is profoundly connected to this history and therefore has specific characteristics, but in many aspects it is shared with other Diaspora societies built on slavery, including the United States.

In education, the gender issue has merited the attention of sociologists and educators like the feminist activist Moema Toscano, who observes "the weight of formal education (meaning school) in maintaining discriminatory patterns inherited from the patriarchal regime." Her description would fit the racial analysis of education perfectly; one may simply substitute the respective terms:

> In Brazil, the first studies addressing the issue of prejudice against women in education, in the school system generally, and more particularly in secondary school, date from the end of the 1970s and beginning of the 1980s. The main target of this reflection was to denounce the existence of openly sexist practices in the schools, with the tolerance, if not the complicity, of parents and teachers. In general, despite their apparent commitment to democracy and modernity, they were not aware of

the weight of their role in reproducing traditional conservative patterns that persisted in education.[10]

One can state without exaggeration that race has been more problematic than gender with regard to practical interventions in schools. Such measures involving race encounter more resistance because of the singular operation of the sorcery of color. The racist notions imbued in language and social relations are insistently denied by educators and parents, even when they are directly faced with concrete and sometimes dramatic examples brought to them by children.

Afro-Brazilian educators and the Afro-Brazilian social movement have produced a considerable body of action and literature with varied areas of emphasis, studying the issue of racial discrimination in education from several different viewpoints. One main focus is the critical evaluation of the explicit and subjacent content of schoolbooks and texts.[11] The discussion has resulted in the publication of works that present more current and less distorted versions of isolated aspects of Afro-Brazilian history and culture.[12]

The critique points out various distortions in school texts and children's and young people's literature, starting with the almost complete exclusion of the image of African descendants as the majority of the Brazilian population. The content of such texts portrays a majority white society and population in sharp contrast to the nation's social reality, particularly that of poor children in public schools. Generally, blacks appear in school texts in only two cases: when the formation of the Brazilian people is discussed and in the study of the abolition of slavery. In the first case, there are rich and detailed references to various European cultural origins, while nothing is said about blacks except that they came from Africa as slaves. Textbooks and school curricula make no reference to highly developed ancient African civilizations. They transmit the idea that "universal" civilization is a monopoly of the West and that Africans contributed little or nothing to its construction and evolution. They generally refer to black people and to Brazilian Native Americans in the past tense, as if the groups no longer existed or were not part of the country's current reality. In the case of slavery's abolition, they replace the historical role of enslaved Africans with the paternalist generosity of whites who supposedly looked out for their liberation, portrayed as a generous gift of the ruling class represented by Princess Isabel. Educational and children's literature gives the impression that Africans never fought for their own freedom. Such a notion is often reinforced with the allegation that the Portuguese brought Africans to Brazil in answer to the need for a workforce, since the Native Americans loved liberty and failed to adapt to the slave regime. Otherwise, blacks appear in this literature individually; it seems as if they do not have families. They are portrayed in positions of lower social status than whites; as animal-like or physically stereotyped; or as protagonists of episodes in which social rules are transgressed, such as the disobedient child or the adult criminal. Finally, in a general way, the educational texts lead their readers to believe that being white is advantageous and desirable and that whites are more intelligent and better looking.

Another focus of the contemporary social movement's critique of education is the presence in schools of words and representations that perpetuate the legacy of racial determinism, the most common reference being *macaco*—monkey.[13] In the Brazilian language and social consciousness, identity of African origin is intimately linked with the ideas of slavery; manual work; intellectual inferiority; technological backwardness; lack of cultural, moral, ethical, and aesthetic development; and the absence of linguistic development, since African languages are called dialects. Perhaps the most outstanding of these representations contained in language is that of black people as slaves: in schools the word *negro* (black) is often used interchangeably with the word slave; they are synonymous. Phrases like "black list," "black market," "black sheep," and other common usages of language reinforce the negative attributions of blackness that are part of its dictionary definition.[14] The implications of such language are not lost on black children, who are also frequently the targets of epithets, nicknames, and jokes that play precisely on these negative images and are tacitly endorsed by teachers and parents. Many black children, when they take such issues to the responsible adult, hear in response that they should pay no attention, that the offenses are not important, or that the offender is just kidding. The effect of such responses from an adult authority is to confirm the stereotype contained in the epithet and to undermine the child's certainty that his self-respect is being violated. This makes the black child feel guilty and reinforces the position of the child who made the comment: He was "just kidding."[15]

This brings us to a further dimension of the race issue in school: social relations among students; among teachers; among teachers, parents, and students; and among teachers, parents, and principals or headmasters.[16] Eliane dos Santos Cavalleiro shows how the unconscious complicity of teachers and parents with racist ideas reinforces feelings of inferiority and low self-esteem of Afro-Brazilian children.[17] Nilma Lino Gomes investigates how the negative concepts about blacks make teachers—many of them black themselves—tend to offer less incentive to black children and have lower expectations of them.[18] Along these lines, Maria José Lopes da Silva shows how the language of the written code taught in schools is distinct from the daily language of poor children of African origin, making learning more difficult for them.[19]

Such various critiques of education show that teachers are not prepared to deal with incidents of discrimination and manifestations of racism among students. School principals often discourage teachers who are interested in researching or holding activities on this subject, alleging that the real problem is the "psychological complex" of the teacher proposing the initiatives—who is almost always black. In sum, social relations within the school tend to reinforce the negative image stamped on black identity in the social consciousness, forming serious obstacles to the shaping of identity with a sense of authorship. Racial discrimination has been identified as a factor detrimental to Afro-Brazilian students' learning process, contributing not only to high dropout and grade repetition rates but also to low self-esteem and attendance rates.

Such confirmations of racism in education reinforce the now traditional understanding of education as a priority area of action for social transformation. Initiatives of intervention in school curricula and in the classroom itself have been carried out through government agencies and organized civil society in projects developed by nongovernmental organizations and black movement organizations, Afro-Brazilian religious communities, and cultural groups like the Afro-Reggae Cultural Group in Rio de Janeiro[20] and the Olodum and Ilê-Aiyê Blocos in Salvador, Bahia.[21] The educational initiatives in terreiro and kilombo communities are two important dimensions of this work.[22]

One of the most outstanding recent developments in public educational policy in Brazil was the elaboration, publication, and distribution by the Ministry of Education of the National Curriculum Parameters, or PCNs.[23] In this process, cultural plurality was defined as a "transversal theme" and part of the thirteenth volume of the PCNs was dedicated to this subject. Undoubtedly this fact was the result of the black movement's interventions, its efforts to bring the issue to the discussion table of the country's educational policy, and its untiring initiatives to research and publicize the need for action against racism in schools.

While recognizing its importance as a clear advance in relation to what existed before in the literature on education officially distributed with the Ministry and Council of Education's stamps of approval, a critical evaluation of the transversal theme of cultural plurality in the PCNs reveals that its multicultural perspective is rooted in liberal tradition. Transversal themes are proposals involving all disciplines and courses, cutting through the curricular content as a whole. The theme "diversity" is presented and the African matrix is mentioned, with implicit reference to the black social movement, since the thirteenth volume has cover photos from that movement's public demonstrations. The insertion of this theme in association with the transversal theme of "ethics" emphasizes the intention to place cultural plurality in a setting of respect for different cultural values, a reference for the coexistence of social and cultural groups within society.

Yet as we have had the opportunity to witness throughout the present work, it is not enough to claim diversity and respect for "other" values. To combat racism effectively, it is necessary to criticize its foundations in Western ethnocentrism's hegemony and patriarchal colonial domination. In the case of Brazil, this means unveiling racist language and curricular content, as well as naming the aggressive attitudes contained in jokes, "kidding," nicknames, and apparently unimportant incidents. The impact of these incidents on the formation of a child's personality can be devastating. Only the educator's intervention would be enough to neutralize the weight of pejorative connotations invested in the child's psyche. The traditional silence only confirms it, and at the same time reinforces not only the aggressive relational position of the white child, but also the pejorative connotation itself, with all the weight of its historical signification, as in: "Your name is a slave's name!"[24] As Afro-Brazilian educator Jeruse Romão has observed:

> Thus, to re-install another identity it is necessary to de-install the devices of racism. African Brazilians find themselves faced, then, with the concept of "inferior race" that was assigned to them by the colonizer, the oppressor, the racist. To counter this concept one must begin to speak of black people's origins. One must speak of Africa, place Africa as nation and demonstrate its civilization values, its worldview. One must, as Frantz Fanon said, be positive and overcome the culpability of being black.[25]

I maintain that the distorted image of Africa, or its omission, in Brazilian school curricula legitimizes and raises as truths notions that were elaborated to reinforce white supremacy and racial domination. This distortion, in my view, has an impact just as devastating on African descendant identities in formation as the suppression of black resistance to slavery and the representation of Afro-Brazilian religious culture as "archaic" or as "animist and fetishist cults," when not "the work of the devil." Denial of the full human dimension of African ancestry is an essential part of this population's dehumanization. Moreover, the system of significations created by racism is based in great part on a solid foundation, still only very slightly perturbed, of belief in Africans' incapacity to create civilization.

An example of the difficulty in dealing with this matter in comparison to that of gender can be found in the discourse of a feminist educator who, while giving a seminar for teachers on discrimination in the schools, emphasized the universal nature of women's oppression. The example she chose was an African ethnic group in which women serve men and eat only the leftovers when the men are finished. In the context of increasing poverty on the African continent, she noted, women are starving as a result of this patriarchal custom.

Without contesting the dramatic impact of the example as an indictment of patriarchy, I questioned its use in front of an audience whose ignorance of Africa is almost absolute, the majority imagining the Continent as roughly equivalent to one country with a homogeneous population. The negative charge with which this "country" is invested in the Brazilian social imagination informs and supports the notions of biological inferiority and racist stereotypes daily carried into the implicit significations of language and social relations, detrimental to women and to African descendants in Brazil. I wondered whether, taking these factors into consideration, it would be possible for the use of this example to contribute to the maintenance of such notions and stereotypes. The teacher responded by saying that she had named the ethnic group, therefore had not engaged in generalizations, and said that the black movement enjoys romanticizing Africa, when Africa is not what the black movement says it is: Africa is poverty and misery itself.

This is a progressive educator engaged in the fight against discrimination in schools. Yet her sensibility to the question of race seems to be circumscribed by a Western Brazilian civilization that identifies Africa as the absolute "Other." If Africa is nothing more than poverty and misery itself, then the anti-African stereotypes that reign in the Brazilian social imagination are well founded. This kind of attitude gives no consideration to the fact that Africa's poverty is a result, in great part, of the colonialist yoke that carried and continues to carry its riches to the West. The antiracist posture of this teacher is fairly representative and has the pretense of operating a divorce between the black people of Brazil and their land of origin, as if the image of one was not reflected in the making of the imaginary ideas entertained about the other. This process takes us back to the de-Africanization of the Brazilian people, one of the characteristics of racial domination exercised by the sorcery of color. When Guerreiro Ramos identifies the Brazilian people as black—"blacks in Brazil are *the people*"—and speaks of the importance of African cultural values, he is attempting "sorcery" in the direction opposite to Brazilian racial ideology.[26]

Since the publication of the PCNs, two other landmarks were the promulgation of Federal law 10.639 of 2003, altering the Law of Bases and Directives of National Education,[27] and the creation of the Ministry of

Education's Secretariat for Continued Education, Literacy, and Diversity (SECAD). Underfunded and understaffed, this agency has nevertheless produced important literature and teaching aids. One of its publications is the Federal Education Council's resolution on the implementation of Federal Law 10.639.28 In addition to presenting guidelines for teachers on the law's implementation, this resolution extends the law's principles to higher education. Since the text of the law provides for inclusion of African and Afro-Brazilian history and culture on the elementary and middle school levels (fundamental education), initially it was interpreted to apply only to those grades. The resolution establishes the need for teachers to be trained in the subjects to be included in fundamental education, which mandates their inclusion in higher education as well.

I agree with the black movement that education is a priority for antiracist social intervention, and I hope that this book will contribute to building effective and positive pedagogical action for all Brazilian social groups and children. By correcting the distortions that exist with respect to those of African origin, who are a majority of the population, we can reduce the impact of such distortions on the relational dynamics of racism. This process includes, in my view, making available references to the historical agency of African Brazilians and their ancestors. Children need references capable of supporting positive identifications in order to build their identity and self-esteem. I offer the information gathered here in the hope that it will be useful to the professionals and lay people who want to support the building of identity with a sense of authorship.

In recent years, the issue of racial inequality has been increasingly the subject of debate and publicity in Brazilian society. The government and black movement organizations in civil society mobilized in an unprecedented way for the Third World Conference against Racism held in Durban in September 2001. In a context in which affirmative action is fast becoming a part of the government's agenda, the understanding of multiple dimensions of the race issue becomes an important aspect of the exercise of citizenship in Brazil. I hope that the considerations and information gathered in this volume will contribute to this understanding and encourage an ever more frank and open discussion among the actors on the eminently multicultural and pluri-ethnic stage of this nation.

NOTES

EPIGRAPH

1. Alberto Guerreiro Ramos, *Introdução crítica à sociologia brasileira*, 2nd ed. (Rio de Janeiro: UFRJ Press, 1995), 57.

INTRODUCTION

1. Abdias Nascimento and Elisa Larkin Nascimento, eds., *Afrodiáspora. Revista do mundo negro* [*Afrodiaspora*: *Journal of Black World Thought*], 7 vols. (Rio de Janeiro: IPEAFRO, 1983–1987); A. Nascimento, *Povo negro. A sucessão e a nova república* (Rio de Janeiro: IPEAFRO, 1984); E. L. Nascimento, *Pan-Africanismo na América do Sul* (Petrópolis: Vozes; Rio de Janeiro: IPEAFRO, 1981); E. L. Nascimento, ed., *Sankofa. Matrizes Africanas da cultura brasileira* 1 (Rio de Janeiro: Rio de Janeiro State University Press, 1996); E. L. Nascimento, ed., *Sankofa. Resgate da cultura afro-brasileira*, 2 vols. (Rio de Janeiro: SEAFRO, 1994); E. L. Nascimento, ed., *Dois negros libertários. Luis Gama e Abdias Nascimento* (Rio de Janeiro: IPEAFRO, 1985); E. L. Nascimento, ed., *Ancestralidade e cidadania. O legado vivo de Abdias Nascimento* (Rio de Janeiro: IPEAFRO, 2004); E. L. Nascimento, ed., *Abdias Nascimento 90 Years—Living Memory* (Rio de Janeiro: IPEAFRO, 2006). IPEAFRO also produced a series of four videos: *Abdias Nascimento Living Memory*, *Abdias Nascimento memória viva*, *Um afro-brasileiro no mundo*, and *Momentos políticos* (2005).

CHAPTER 1

1. Erik H. Erikson, *Identidade, juventude e crise*, trans. Álvaro Cabral (Rio de Janeiro: Zahar, 1972), 21.

2. Muniz Sodré, *Claros e escuros. Identidade, povo e mídia no Brasil* (Petrópolis, Brazil: Vozes, 1999), 34–35.

3. Ibid., 39.

4. E. H. Erikson, *Childhood and Society*, 2nd ed. (New York: W. W. Norton, 1963); E. H. Erikson, *Identidade, juventude e crise*.

5. Antônio da Costa Ciampa, *A estória do Severino e a história da Severina* (São Paulo: Brasiliense, 1987), 243.

6. Ibid., 241–43.

7. Ricardo Franklin Ferreira, *Afro-descendente. Identidade em construção* (Rio de Janeiro: Pallas; São Paulo: Educ; São Paulo: FAPESP, 2000), 47.

8. Ibid., 48.

9. E. H. Erikson, *Identidade, juventude e crise*, 310.

10. R. F. Ferreira, *Afro-descendente*, 44.

11. A. C. Ciampa cites the International Colloquium on Paradigms in Social Psychology for Latin America (1997) and the Ninth National Meeting of the Brazilian Society of Social Psychology (1997) as watersheds in this debate. During the Tenth National Meeting of the Brazilian Society of Social Psychology (São Paulo, 1999) four symposiums were held on identity as a paradigm in social psychology. A. C. Ciampa, "Identidade. Um paradigma para a psicologia social?" in *A psicologia social brasileira e o contexto Latino-Americano. Programa científico e resumos*, ed. Bader Burihan Sawaia, C. P. Alves, and O. Ardans, 8–14 (São Paulo: Brazilian Association of Social Psychology [Associação Brasileira de Psicologia Social (ABRAPSO)]; São Paulo: University of São Paulo, 1999).

12. Ibid., 10.

13. Kai T. Erikson, ed., *In Search of Common Ground: Conversations with Erik H. Erikson and Huey P. Newton* (New York: W. W. Norton, 1973).

14. Among other examples of the political persecution of social movements during the 1960s and 1970s are the cases of Medgar Evers, Martin Sostre, Marvin X, Angela Y. Davis, the Chicago Seven, Dennis Banks, the Native Americans of Wounded Knee, and the prisoners who rebelled at Attica State Penitentiary in Western New York.

15. K. T. Erikson, *Common Ground*, 28, 144.

16. Ibid., 128–29.

17. Manuel Castells, *A sociedade em rede*, 3rd ed., trans. Roneide Venancio Majer and Klauss Brandini Gerhardt (São Paulo: Paz e Terra, 2000), 23 [Originally published as *The Rise of the Network Society*, vol. 1, *The Information Age—Economy, Society, and Culture* (Cambridge, MA: Blackwell Publishers, 1997)].

18. M. Castells, *O poder da identidade*, trans. K. B. Gerhardt (São Paulo: Paz e Terra, 1999), 235 [Originally published as *The Power of Identity*, vol. 2 of the trilogy *The Information Age—Economy, Society and Culture* (Cambridge, MA: Blackwell Publishers, 1997)].

19. Ibid., 423–27.

20. K. T. Erikson, *Common Ground*, 60, 43–50, 111–16.

21. M. Castells, *O poder da identidade*, 79.

22. Léon Poliakov, *O mito ariano. Ensaio sobre as fontes do racismo e dos nacionalismos*, trans. Luiz João Gaio (São Paulo: Perspectiva; São Paulo: EdUSP, 1974), xviii [originally published as *Le mythe aryen* (Paris: Calmann-Lévy, 1971)].

23. Peter I. Berger and Thomas Luckmann, *A construção social da realidade* (Petrópolis, Brazil: Vozes, 1985); Antonio Sérgio Alfredo Guimarães, *Racismo e anti-racismo no Brasil* (São Paulo: FUSP; São Paulo: Editora 34, 1999).

24. Comparative Human Relations Initiative (CHRI), *Beyond Racism: Embracing an Interdependent Future*, 4 vols. (Atlanta: Southern Education Foundation, 2000).

25. Pigmentocracy was the name given in the Report of the Second Congress of Black Culture in the Americas (Panamá, 1980). A. S. A. Guimarães (1999) refers to the use of this term by sociologists Oboler and Lipschütz.

26. Compare, for example, authors cited by Florestan Fernandes, A integração do negro à sociedade de classes (São Paulo: FFCL; São Paulo: USP, 1964), 201, 304–614; Alberto Guerreiro Ramos, Introdução crítica à sociologia brasileira, 2nd ed. (Rio de Janeiro: UFRJ Press, 1995), 159–202.

27. E. L. Nascimento, Pan-Africanismo na América do Sul (Petrópolis: Vozes; Rio de Janeiro: IPEAFRO, 1981), 12.

28. Pierre-André Taguieff, Les fins de l'antiracisme (Paris: Michalon, 1995); P.-A. Taguieff, La force du préjugé: Essai sur le racisme et ses doubles (Paris: La Découverte, 1988).

29. Michael Banton, "Race," in Dictionary of Race and Ethnic Relations, 3rd ed., ed. Ellis Cashmore (London: Routledge, 1994), 264.

30. Thomas H. Eriksen, Ethnicity and Nationalism, Anthropological Perspectives (London: Plato Press, 1993), 5.

31. A. Nascimento, ed. O negro revoltado (Rio de Janeiro: GRD, 1968), 20–21.

32. Interview with Afonso Arinos in the major rio de Janeiro daily Ultima Hora, December 14, 1951.

33. Jean-Paul Sartre, "Orfeu negro," trans. Ironides Rodrigues, Quilombo 2, no. 5, January 1950, 6–7. Quilombo was TEN's monthly newspaper.

34. Kwame Anthony Appiah, In My Father's House: Africa in the Philosophy of Culture (New York: Oxford University Press, 1992).

35. A. S. A. Guimarães, Racismo e anti-racismo.

36. K. A. Appiah defines racialism as "the view that there are heritable characteristics, possessed by members of our species, which allow us to divide them into a small set of races, in such a way that all the members of these races share certain traits and tendencies with each other that they do not share with members of any other race." K. A. Appiah, In My Father's House, 13.

37. A. S. A. Guimarães, Racismo e anti-racismo, 64.

38. A. S. A. Guimarães, "Apresentação," in Tirando a máscara. Ensaios sobre o racismo no Brasil, ed. A. S. A. Guimarães and L. Huntley (São Paulo: Paz e Terra; São Paulo: Southern Education Foundation, 2000), 24.

39. Stanislas Adotevi, "Négritude is Dead: The Burial," in New African Literature and the Arts, 3 vols., ed. Joseph Okpaku (New York: Third Press, 1973).

40. See Horace Campbell, Pan-Africanism: Struggle against Neo-Colonialism and Imperialism Documents of the Sixth Pan-African Congress, 1974 (Toronto: Afro-Carib Publications, 1976).

41. On Pan-Africanism, see George Padmore, Pan-Africanism or Communism? 3rd ed. (New York: Doubleday, 1972); C. L. R. James, A History of Pan-African Revolt, (Washington, DC: Drum and Spear, 1969); C. L. R. James, "Towards the Seventh. The Pan-African Congress: Past, Present and Future," Ch'Indaba 1, no. 2 (July–December 1976).

42. Carlos Moore, Tanya R. Sanders, and Shawna Moore, eds., African Presence in the Americas (Trenton, NJ: Africa World Press; Trenton, NJ: The African Heritage Foundation, 1995).

43. E.g., Cheikh Anta Diop, The African Origin of Civilization: Myth or Reality, trans. Mercer Cook (Westport: Lawrence Hill, 1974) [originally published as Anteriorité des civilisations Negres: Mythe ou verité historique? (Paris: Présence Africaine, 1959)]; C. A. Diop, The Cultural Unity of Black Africa, 2nd ed., trans. Présence Africaine (Chicago: Third World Press, 1978) [originally published as L'Unité culturelle de l'Afrique Noire (Paris: Présence Africaine, 1963)]; Theophile Obenga, Pour une nouvelle histoire (Paris: Présence Africaine, 1980); T. Obenga, A Lost Tradition: African Philosophy in World History (Philadelphia: Source Editions, 1995); Molefi Kete Asante, Afrocentricity, 2nd ed. (Buffalo, NY: Amulefi Press, 1980; Trenton, NJ: Africa World Press, 1989); M. K. Asante, Kemet, Afrocentricity and

Knowledge (Trenton, NJ: Africa World Press, 1990); Janheinz Jahn, *Through African Doors* (New York: Grove Press, 1969); and J. Jahn, *Muntu: An Outline of the New African Culture* (New York: Grove Press, 1961).

44. K. A. Appiah, *In My Father's House*, 100–2.

45. C. A. Diop, *Nations, negres et culture* (Paris: Présence Africaine, 1955); C. A. Diop, *Anteriorité*; C. A. Diop, *African Origin*; C. A. Diop, *Cultural Unity*; George G. M. James, *Stolen Legacy*, 2nd ed. (Philosophical Library: 1954; San Francisco: Julian Richardson Associates, 1976). T. Obenga, *Pour une nouvelle histoire*; M. K. Asante, *Afrocentricity*; Chancellor Williams, *The Destruction of Black Civilization* (Chicago: Third World Press, 1974).

46. K. A. Appiah, *In My Father's House*, 101n24.

47. M. Castells, *O poder da identidade*, 94.

48. A. Nascimento, *O Quilombismo* (Petrópolis, Brazil: Vozes, 1980), 270, 272.

49. Simone de Beauvoir, *El segundo sexo*, vol. 2, *La experiencia vivida*, trans. Pablo Palant (Buenos Aires: Psique, 1954), 13 [originally published as *Le Deuxième Sexe*, 2 vols. Paris: Gallimard, 1949].

50. Ibid., 9, 433–67; 535–92.

51. Elena Gianini Belotti, *Educar para a submissão. O descondicionamento da mulher*, 6th ed., trans. Ephraim Ferreira Alves (Petrópolis, Brazil: Vozes, 1987) [Originally published as *Dalla parte delle bambine* (Milan: Feltrinelli, 1973)]; Moema Toscano, *Estereótipos sexuais na educação. Um manual para o educador* (Petrópolis, Brazil: Vozes, 2000).

52. Neusa dos Santos Souza, ed., *Tornar-se negro* (Rio de Janeiro: Graal, 1983); Matilde Ribeiro, "Tornar-se negra. Construção da identidade de gênero e de raça," *Revista Presença de Mulher* 7, no. 28 (1995).

53. Maria Clementina Pereira Cunha, *O espelho do mundo. Juquery, a história de um asilo*, 2nd ed. (São Paulo: Paz e Terra, 1988); Nancy L. Stepan, *The Hour of Eugenics: Race, Gender and Nation in Latin America* (Ithaca: Cornell University Press, 1991).

54. M. Sodré, *Claros e escuros*, 54.

55. Jacob Pandian, *Anthropology and the Western Tradition: Toward an Authentic Anthropology* (Prospect Heights, Illinois: Waveland, 1985), 80.

56. Maria Betânia Ávila, "Feminismo e sujeito político," *Proposta* 29, no. 84/85 (March–August 2000): 7.

57. C. A. Diop, *Cultural Unity*.

58. Linda Nicholson, "Feminismo e Marx, integrando o parentesco com o econômico," in *Feminismo como crítica da modernidade*, ed. Seyla Benhabib and Drucilla Cornell, 23–37 (Rio de Janeiro: Rosa dos Tempos, 1987) [Originally published as *Feminism as Critique: Feminist Perspectives on the Politics of Gender* (Minneapolis: University of Minnesota Press, 1987)].

59. Garth E. Pauley, "W.E.B. Du Bois on Woman Suffrage: A Critical Analysis of his *Crisis* Writings," *Journal of Black Studies* 30, no. 3 (January 2000): 383–410.

60. "Du Bois's theoretical racism was, in my view, extrinsic. Yet, in his heart, it seems to me that Du Bois's feelings were those of an intrinsic racist." K. A. Appiah, *In My Father's House*, 45.

61. Gloria Hull, Patricia Bell Scott, and Barbara Smith, eds., *All the Women Are White, All the Blacks Are Men, but Some of Us Are Brave* (Old Westbury, NY: City University; Old Westbury, NY: Feminist Press, 1982); Patricia Hill Collins, *Black Feminist Thought: Knowledge, Consciousness, and the Politics of Empowerment* (New York: Routledge, 1991).

62. Chandra Talpade Mohanty, Ann Russo, Loudes Torres, eds., *Third World Women and the Politics of Feminism* (Bloomington: Indiana University Press, 1991); P. H. Collins, *Black Feminist Thought*; Oyeronke Oyewumi, *The Invention of Women: Making an African Sense of Western Gender Discourses* (Minneapolis: University of Minnesota Press, 1997).

63. S. Benhabib and D. Cornell, eds., *Feminismo como crítica*, 20.

64. Cf. O. Oyewumi, *Invention of Women* and the various essays in Albertina de Oliveira Costa and Cristina Bruschini, eds., *Uma questão de gênero* (Rio de Janeiro: Rosa dos Tempos; Rio de Janeiro: Fundação Carlos Chagas, 1992).

65. bell hooks, *Talking Back: Thinking Feminist, Thinking Black* (Boston: South End Press, 1989).

66. Luiza Bairros, "Nossos feminismos revisitados," *Estudos Feministas* 3, no. 2 (1995): 461. See also P. H. Collins, *Black Feminist Thought*.

67. Kimberlé Williams Crenshaw, "Mapping the Margins: Intersectionality, Identity Politics, and Violence Against Women of Color," in *The Public Nature of Private Violence*, ed. Martha Albertson Fineman and Rixanne Mykitiuk, 93–118 (New York: Routledge, 1994).

68. R. F. Ferreira, *Afro-descendente*, 48.

69. Judith Butler, "Variações sobre sexo e gênero. Beauvoir, Wittig e Foucault," in *Feminismo como crítica*, ed. S. Benhabib and D. Cornell.

70. A. S. A. Guimarães, *Racismo e anti-racismo*, 58, 68.

71. W.E.B. Du Bois, *Writings: The Suppression of the African Slave-Trade / The Souls of Black Folk / Dusk of Dawn / Essays and Articles*, ed. Nathan Huggins (New York: Literary Classics; New York: Viking Press, 1986), 625–51; A. Nascimento, *O negro revoltado*, 20–21; A. Nascimento, *O Quilombismo*, 270, 272.

72. M. Ribeiro, "Tornar-se negra," 24.

73. Agnes Heller, "From Hermeneutics in Social Science toward a Hermeneutics of Social Science," *Theory and Society* 18, no. 3 (May 1989): 292.

74. In African world literature alone, for example, the authors include Ottobah Cugoano, Oloudah Equiano (Gustavus Vassa), Martin R. Delaney, J. Caseley-Hayford, Kwame Nkrumah, Nnamdi Azikiwe, Marcus Garvey, Frantz Fanon, Wole Soyinka, Kofi Awoonor, James Baldwin, Ralph Ellison, Chancellor Williams, Aimé Césaire, Théophile Obenga, Walter Rodney, Malcolm X, Chinua Achebe, Chinweizu, Maulana Karenga, Steve Biko, John Henrik Clarke, George Padmore, C. L. R. James, and Julius Nyerere.

75. W.E.B. Du Bois, *Writings*, 372.

76. A. Guerreiro Ramos, *A redução sociológica*, 3rd ed. (Rio de Janeiro: UFRJ Press, 1998).

77. A. Guerreiro Ramos, *Introdução crítica* (1995), 210.

78. A. Guerreiro Ramos, "O negro desde dentro," in *Teatro Experimental do Negro. Testemunhos*, ed. A. Nascimento (Rio de Janeiro: GRD, 1966).

79. A. Guerreiro Ramos, *Introdução crítica* (1995), 198–99.

80. Jacques D'Adesky, *Pluralismo étnico e multiculturalismo. Racismos e anti-racismos no Brasil* (Rio de Janeiro: Pallas, 2001); Kabengele Munanga, ed. *Estratégias e políticas de combate à discriminação racial* (São Paulo: EdUSP; São Paulo: Estação Ciência, 1996); K. Munanga, *Rediscutindo a mestiçagem no Brasil. Identidade nacional versus identidade negra* (Petrópolis, Brazil: Vozes, 1999); José Maria Coutinho, "Por uma educação multicultural. Uma alternativa de cidadania para o século XXI," *Revista Ensaio. Avaliação e políticas públicas em educação* 4, no. 13 (October–December 1996): 381–92.

81. Federal Republic of Brazil, Executive Branch, *Constituição da República Federativa do Brasil* (1988). Brasília: Senado Federal, Subsecretaria de Edições Técnicas, 2003, 126, art. 215.

82. Charles Taylor et al., *Multiculturalism*, ed. Amy Gutman (Princeton, NJ: Princeton University Press, 1994).

83. Ibid., 42, 68–73.

84. Ibid., 42.

85. Ibid., 42. This oft-quoted phrase has been attributed to Saul Bellow.

86. Ibid., 42.

87. Ibid., 42, my emphasis.

88. Ibid., 73.

89. O. Oyewumi, *Invention of Women*, 24. She refers to research on the so-called Hottentot Venuses, statuettes portraying African women found in Europe that date from tens of thousands of years ago. Scientists applied the techniques of comparative anthropometrics

to living African women, "current specimens" of prehistoric populations in the effort to prove or disprove the identification of prehistoric African women as models for the statuettes.

90. C. Taylor et al., *Multiculturalism*, 68–69, my emphasis.

91. Peter McLaren, *Multiculturalismo crítico*, trans. Bebel Orofino Schaefer (São Paulo: Cortez; São Paulo: Paulo Freire Institute, 1997), 10.

92. Margaret Mead, *Sesso e temperamento* (Milan: Il Saggiatore, 1967).

93. A. Guerreiro Ramos, *Introdução crítica* (1995), 159.

94. Richard Delgado and Jean Stefancic, eds., *Critical White Studies: Looking Behind the Mirror* (Philadelphia: Temple University Press, 1997); K. W. Crenshaw et al., eds., *Critical Race Theory: The Key Writings that Formed the Movement* (New York: New Press, 1995).

95. W.E.B. Du Bois, "The White World," chapter 6 of *The Dusk of Dawn* in *Writings*, 652–80; and W.E.B. Du Bois, "The Souls of White Folk," in *Writings*, 923–38.

96. Iray Carone and Maria Aparecida da Silva Bento, eds., *Psicologia social do racismo. Estudos sobre branquitude e branqueamento no Brasil* (Petrópolis, Brazil: Vozes, 2002); E. Piza, "Brancos no Brasil? Ningúem sabe, ninguém viu," in *Tirando a máscara*, ed. A. S. A. Guimarães and L. Huntley, 97–126 (São Paulo: Paz e Terra; Atlanta: SEF, 2000); M. A. S. Bento, *O legado subjetivo dos 500 anos. Narcisismo e alteridade racial* (São Paulo: Center for the Study of Labor Relations and Inequality [CEERT], 2000).

97. A. Guerreiro Ramos, *Introdução crítica* (1995), 149–50, 153.

98. Joel Rufino dos Santos, "O negro como lugar," in A. Guerreiro Ramos, *Introdução crítica* (1995), 25–28.

99. M. K. Asante, *The Afrocentric Idea*, 2nd ed. (Philadelphia: Temple University Press, 1998), xii.

100. Ibid., 11.

101. Ibid.

102. Ibid., 8.

103. Ibid., 11.

104. O. Oyewumi, *Invention of Women*, xi–xiii.

105. Ibid., xiii, emphasis in the original.

106. Samuel Johnson, *The History of the Yorùbás* (New York: Routledge & Kegan Paul, 1921), xxxvii.

107. Adeleke Adeeko, "The Language of Head-Calling: A Review Essay on Yoruba Metalanguage," *Research in African Literatures* 23, no. 1 (March–June 1992): 197–200.

108. John Pemberton, "The Oyo Empire," in *Yoruba: Nine Centuries of Art and Thought*, ed. John Henry Drewal et al. (New York: Harry N. Abrams, 1989), 162.

109. O. Oyewumi, *Invention of Women*, 116.

110. Ibid., 117–18.

111. David Brookshaw, *Race and Color in Brazilian Literature* (London: Rowman & Littlefield, 1986).

112. Doris Turner, "Symbols in Two Afro-Brazilian Literary Works: Jubiabá and Sortilégio," in *Teaching Latin American Studies: Presentations to the First National Seminar on the Teaching of Latin American Studies*, ed. Miriam Willifond and J. Doyle Casteel (Gainesville: Latin American Studies Association, 1977), 41–68.

113. Teófilo de Queiroz Júnior, *Preconceito de cor e a mulata na literatura brasileira* (São Paulo: Ática, 1975); A. Nascimento, "Resposta aos racistas da Bahia," in *Combate ao racismo* (Speeches, reports and bills of law, Chamber of Deputies [House of Representatives] 47th Legislature, 1st Legislative Session, n. 228), vol. 2, 62–68 (Brasília: Câmara dos Deputados, 1983); Eliana Guerreiro Ramos Bennett, "Gabriela Cravo e Canela: Jorge Amado and the Myth of the Sexual Mulata in Brazilian Culture," in *The African Diaspora:*

African Origins and New World Identities, ed. Isidore Okpewho, Carole Boyce Davies, Ali A. Mazrui (Bloomington: Indiana University Press, 1999).
114. O. Oyewumi, *Invention of Women*, 12.
115. Ibid., 156.

CHAPTER 2

1. Gilberto Freyre, *New World in the Tropics: The Culture of Modern Brazil* (New York: Alfred A. Knopf, 1959); G. Freyre, *O mundo que o Português criou. Aspectos das relações sociais e de cultura do Brasil com Portugal e as colônias portuguesas* (Rio de Janeiro: José Olympio, 1940).
2. Anabel Cruz, "Mercosul. Iniqüidades na integração," *Observatório da cidadania* 2 (1998), 27–28.
3. U.S. Department of Health and Human Services, Health Resources and Services Administration, Maternal and Child Health Bureau, *Child Health USA 2002* (Rockville, MD: U.S. Department of Health and Human Services, 2002), 22. Today, Brazil's infant mortality rate is about twenty-nine deaths per one thousand live births, compared to twenty-five in Paraguay, fifteen in Argentina, and twelve in Uruguay, according to the U.S. Central Intelligence Agency's *World Factbook*, Rank Order—Infant Mortality Rate (Washington, DC: Central Intelligence Agency Office of Public Affairs, 2006), https://www.cia.gov/cia/publications/factbook/rankorder/2091rank.html.
4. Guido Mantega, "Brasil. Determinantes e evolução recente das desigualdades no Brasil," *Observatório da cidadania* 2 (1998), 98.
5. Roberto Borges Martins, "Desigualdades raciais e políticas de inclusão racial. Um sumário da experiência brasileira recente," (report presented to the United Nations Economic Commission for Latin America and the Caribbean [CEPAL], August 2003), 11.
6. Giorgio Mortara, "O desenvolvimento da população preta e parda no Brasil," in *Contribuições para o estudo da demografia no Brasil*, 2nd ed., ed. Brazilian Institute of Geography and Statistics (IBGE), 200–202 (Rio de Janeiro: IBGE, 1970). In the last few years, this tendency may have diminished slightly, partly as a result of activities and consciousness raising by the Afro-Brazilian social movement such as the "Don't Let Your Color Go Blank or Pass for White" campaign that was publicized during the 2000 census. See José Luis Petrucelli, *A declaração de cor/raça no censo 2000. Um estudo comparativo* (Rio de Janeiro: IBGE, 2002).
7. United Nations Development Programme (UNDP), *Report on Human Development* (New York: UNDP, 1999).
8. Marcelo Paixão, "Desenvolvimento humano e as desigualdades étnicas no Brasil. Um retrato de final de século," *Proposta, Revista Trimestral da FASE* 29, no. 86 (September–November 2000): 44. Economist Lucila Bandeira Beato and historian Wânia Sant'Anna also played important roles in the development of this research.
9. IBGE, "Minimum National Social Indicators Set" (1999), 46, http://www.ibge.gov.br/english/estatistica/populacao/condicaodevida/indicadoresminimos/default.shtm.
10. M. Paixão, "Desenvolvimento humano," Appendix 2, 48.
11. Carlos Hasenbalg, *Discriminação e desigualdades raciais no Brasil* (Rio de Janeiro: Graal, 1979); Nelson do Valle Silva, "White-Nonwhite Income Differentials: Brazil, 1940–1960" (PhD diss., Michigan University, 1978).
12. In roughly chronological order, these studies include but are not limited to: Lúcia Oliveira, Rosa Maria Porcaro, and Teresa Cristina Costa, *O lugar do negro na força de trabalho* (Rio de Janeiro: IBGE, 1981); Peggy Lovell, *Desigualdade racial no Brasil contemporâneo* (Belo Horizonte, Brazil: CEDEPLAR; Belo Horizonte, Brazil: UFMG, 1991); N. V. Silva and C. Hasenbalg, "O preço da cor. Diferenças raciais na distribuição da renda no

Brasil," *Pesquisa e Planejamento* 10 (April 1990): 21–44; N. V. Silva and C. Hasenbalg, *Relações raciais no Brasil contemporâneo* (Rio de Janeiro: Rio Fundo; Rio de Janeiro: CEAA; Rio de Janeiro: IUPERJ; Rio de Janeiro: Ford Foundation, 1992); N. V. Silva and C. Hasenbalg, "Notes on Racial Inequality and Politics in Brasil," *Estudos Afro-Asiáticos* 25 (December 1993): 141–59; IBGE, *Mapa do mercado de trabalho* (Rio de Janeiro: IBGE, 1994); IBGE, *Pesquisa nacional por amostra de domicílios, 1996. Síntese de indicadores* (Rio de Janeiro: IBGE, 1997); vol. 2 (1998) of *Observatório da cidadania*, published by Instituto del Tercer Mundo (ITM); Inter-American Trade Union Institute for Racial Equality (INSPIR) and Inter-Trade Union Departament of Statistics and Sócio-Economic Studies (DIEESE), *Mapa da população negra no mercado de trabalho. Regiões metropolitanas de São Paulo, Salvador, Recife, Belo Horizonte, Porto Alegre e Distrito Federal—Outubro de 1999* (São Paulo: INSPIR; São Paulo: DIEESE, 1999); N. V. Silva, "Extensão e natureza das desigualdades raciais no Brasil," in *Tirando a máscara. Ensaios sobre o racismo no Brasil*, ed. A. S. A. Guimarães and L. Huntley, 33–52 (São Paulo, Paz e Terra, and Atlanta: Southern Education Foundation, 2000).

13. Atila Roque and Sonia Corrêa, "A agenda do ciclo social no Brasil. Impasses e desafios," *Observatório da cidadania* 2 (1998): 1–8.

14. R. B. Martins, "Desigualdades raciais"; R. B. Martins, "Desigualdades e discriminação" (report presented to the International Labor Organization in Brazil, April 2003).

15. N. V. Silva, "Extensão e natureza," 35–36; R. B. Martins, "Desigualdades raciais," 28, 29–48; W. Sant'Anna and M. Paixão, "Desenvolvimento humano e população afro-descendente no Brasil. Uma questão de raça," *Proposta* 26, no. 73 (June–August 1997): 25.

16. N. V. Silva, "Extensão e natureza," 36–37; INSPIR and DIEESE, *Mapa da população negra*, 38, 54, 70, 85, 100, 114; R. B. Martins, "Desigualdades raciais," 37–41.

17. IBGE, *Pesquisa nacional.*

18. Mary Garcia Castro, "Mulheres chefes de família, racismo, códigos de idade e pobreza no Brasil (Bahia e São Paulo)," in *Desigualdade racial*, ed. P. Lovell, 121–60.

19. Ibid., compare with N. V. Silva, "Extensão e natureza"; R. B. Martins, "Desigualdades e discriminação"; R. B. Martins, "Desigualdades raciais."

20. R. B. Martins, "Desigualdades raciais," 79.

21. M. Paixão, "Desenvolvimento humano," 43. In 2001, this situation had improved slightly: R. B. Martins reports thirty-nine deaths per one thousand among Afro-Brazilian children as opposed to twenty-six among white children, or about 75 percent higher.

22. Molefi K. Asante and Mark T. Mattson, *Historical and Cultural Atlas of African Americans* (New York: MacMillan, 1991), 166. This discrepancy has continued over time: "The preliminary 2000 infant mortality rate for black infants was 2.5 times that for white infants. Although the trend in infant mortality rates among blacks and whites has been on a continual decline throughout the 20th century, the proportional discrepancy between the black and white rates has remained largely unchanged." U.S. Department of Health and Human Services, Health Resources and Services Administration, Maternal and Child Health Bureau. *Child Health USA 2002* (Rockville, MD: U.S. Department of Health and Human Services, 2002), 23.

23. R. B. Martins, "Desigualdades raciais," 79.

24. W. Sant'Anna and M. Paixão, "Muito além da Senzala. Ação afirmativa no Brasil," *Observatório da cidadania* 2 (1998): 112–14.

25. Ibid.; R. B. Martins, "Desigualdades raciais," 12–23.

26. David Dijaci de Oliveira et al., eds., *A cor do medo. Homicídios e relações raciais no Brasil* (Brasília: University of Brasília Press; Brasília: University of Goiás Press; Brasília: National Human Rights Movement MNDH, 1998), 52–56.

27. Data by color were suppressed in the censuses of 1900, 1920, 1940, 1950, and 1970. They were reintroduced in the annual household sample surveys of the 1970s and returned

to the census in 1980. In hospitals and health agencies it has been difficult to reintroduce the collection of data on color. R. B. Martins, for example, gives no data on health matters aside from life expectancy and infant mortality for lack of indicators.

28. Roger Bastide and Florestan Fernandes, *Relações raciais entre negros e brancos em São Paulo* (São Paulo: Anhembi, 1955); R. Bastide and F. Fernandes, *Brancos e negros em São Paulo*, 2nd ed. (São Paulo: Companhia Editora Nacional, 1959).

29. R. Bastide and F. Fernandes, *Brancos e negros*; Thales Azevedo, *As elites de cor. Um estudo de ascensão social* (São Paulo: Companhia Editora Nacional, 1955); René Ribeiro, *Religião e relações raciais no Brasil* (Rio de Janeiro: Ministry of Education and Culture, Documentation Services, 1956); Luiz de Aguiar Costa Pinto, *O negro no rio de Janeiro* (São Paulo: Companhia Editora Nacional, 1953).

30. Anani Dzidzienyo, *The Position of Blacks in Brazilian Society* (London: Minority Rights Group, 1971). See also A. Dzidzienyo, "Conclusions," in *No Longer Invisible: Afro-Latin Americans Today*, ed. Minority Rights Group (London: MRG, 1995); A. Dzidzienyo and Lourdes Casal, *The Position of Black People in Brazilian and Cuban Society* (London: MRG, 1979).

31. Thomas E. Skidmore, *Black into White: Race and Nationality in Brazilian Thought* (London: Oxford University Press, 1974).

32. E.g., Ana Célia Silva, *A discriminação do negro no livro didático* (Salvador, Brazil: CED; Salvador, Brazil: CEAO; Salvador, Brazil: UFBA, 1995); Consuelo Dores Silva, *Negro, qual é o seu nome?* (Belo Horizonte, Brazil: Mazza, 1995); Nilma Lino Gomes, *A mulher negra que vi de perto* (Belo Horizonte, Brazil: Mazza, 1995); Narcimária Corrêa do Patrocínio Luz, ed. *Pluralidade cultural e educação* (Salvador, Brazil: Bahia State Government Education Secretariat; Salvador, Brazil: Society for the Study of Black Culture [SECNEB], 1996); Leda Maria Martins, *A cena em sombras* (São Paulo: Perspectiva, 1995); Luiza Bairros, "Nossos feminismos revisitados," *Estudos Feministas* 3, no. 2 (1995): 458–63; Júlio Braga, *Na gamela do feitiço. Repressão e resistência nos candomblés da Bahia* (Salvador, Brazil: CEAO; Salvador, Brazil: UFBA, 1995); Nei Lopes, *Dicionário Banto do Brasil* 2nd ed. (Rio de Janeiro: Pallas, 2003); Helena Theodoro, *Mito e espiritualidade—Mulheres Negras* (Rio de Janeiro: Pallas, 1996); João José Reis and Flávio dos Santos Gomes, *Liberdade por um fio. História dos Quilombos no Brasil* (São Paulo: Companhia das Letras, 1996); Kabengele Munanga, *Estratégias e políticas de combate à discriminação racial* (São Paulo: University of São Paulo Press; São Paulo: Estação Ciência, 1996); Conceição Corrêa das Chagas, *Negro. Uma identidade em construção* (Petrópolis, Brazil: Vozes, 1996); João Jorge Rodrigues, *Olodum, estrada da paixão* (Salvador, Brazil: Olodum Cultural Group; Salvador, Brazil: Casa de Jorge Amado Foundation, 1996); Nucleus of Black Studies (NEN), *Série pensamento negro em educação*, 6 vols. (Florianópolis, Brazil: NEN, 1997–1999); Petronilha Beatriz Gonçalves Silva, ed. *O pensamento negro em educação no Brasil* (São Carlos, Brazil: Federal University of São Carlos UFSCar, 1997); D. D. de Oliveira et al., eds., *A cor do medo*; Maria Aparecida Silva Bento, *Cidadania em preto e branco. Discutindo as relações raciais* (São Paulo: Ática, 1998); Jorge da Silva, *Violência e racismo no rio de Janeiro* (Niterói, Brazil: Fluminense Federal University Press [EdUFF], 1998); Eliane dos Santos Cavalleiro, *Do silêncio do lar ao silêncio escolar. Racismo, preconceito e discriminação na educação infantil* (São Paulo: Contexto; São Paulo: University of São Paulo, 2000); Carlos Caroso and Jéferson Bacelar, eds. *Brasil. Um país de negros?* (Rio de Janeiro: Pallas; Salvador, Brazil: CEAO; Salvador, Brazil: UFBA, 1999); C. Caroso and J. Bacelar *Faces da tradição afro-brasileira* (Rio de Janeiro: Pallas; Salvador, Brazil: CEAO; Salvador, Brazil: UFBA, 1999); Vanda Machado, *Ilê axé. Vivências e invenção pedagógica. As crianças do Opô Afonjá* (Salvador, Brazil: Municipal Government of Salvador; Salvador, Brazil: UFBA, 1999); Cléo Martins, and Raul Lody, *Faraimará—o caçador traz alegria. Mãe Stella, 60 anos de iniciação* (Rio de Janeiro: Pallas, 1999); AMMA and Quilombhoje, *Gostando mais de nós mesmos. Perguntas e respostas sobre auto-estima e a questão racial*, 2nd ed. (São Paulo: Gente, 1999); Jurema Werneck, Maísa Mendonça, and Evelyn C. White, *O livro da saúde das Mulheres*

Negras. Nossos passos vêm de longe (Rio de Janeiro: Pallas; Rio de Janeiro: Criola, 2000); M. Paixão, *Desenvolvimento humano e relações raciais* (Rio de Janeiro: DP&A, 2003).

33. R. B. Martins, "Desigualdades e discriminação"; R. B. Martins, "Desigualdades raciais"; Ricardo Henriques, ed., *Desigualdade e Pobreza no Brasil* (Rio de Janeiro: IPEA, 2000); Luciana Jaccoud and Nathalie Behin, *Desigualdades raciais no Brasil. Um balanço da intervenção governamental* (Brasília: Institute of Applied Economic Research IPEA, 2002). Since 2001, affirmative action and quota policies have been implemented in other public agencies and universities.

34. T. E. Skidmore, *Black into White*; Célia Maria Marinho Azevedo, *Onda negra medo branco. O negro do imaginário das elites, Século XIX* (Rio de Janeiro: Paz e Terra, 1987).

35. Raymundo Nina Rodrigues, *Os africanos no Brasil*, 3rd ed. (São Paulo: Companhia Editora Nacional, 1945), 24.

36. Ibid., 28.

37. T. E. Skidmore, *Black into White*; Abdias Nascimento, *Brazil, Mixture or Massacre: Essays in the Genocide of a Black People*, 2nd ed. (Dover, MA: Majority Press, 1989 [1979]); Lília Moritz Schwarcz, *O espetáculo das raças. Cientistas, instituições e questão racial no Brasil, 1870–1930* (São Paulo: Companhia das Letras, 1993); K. Munanga, *Rediscutindo a mestiçagem no Brasil. Identidade nacional versus identidade negra* (Petrópolis, Brazil: Vozes, 1999).

38. T. E. Skidmore, *Black into White*, 66.

39. Oliveira Vianna, *Populações meridionais do Brasil* (São Paulo: Revista do Brasil; São Paulo: Monteiro Lobato, 1920); O. Vianna, *Raça e assimilação*, 2nd ed. (São Paulo: Companhia Editora Nacional, 1934).

40. The word *mucama* derives from the kimbundu *mu'kama*. N. Lopes, *Dicionário Banto*, 53.

41. A. Nascimento, *Brazil, Mixture or Massacre*, 140, 143–46; Lélia González, "A importância da organização da mulher negra no processo de transformação social," *Raça e classe* 5, no. 2 (November–December 1988): 230; L. Bairros, "Lembrando Lélia González," in *O livro da saúde das Mulheres Negras. Nossos passos vêm de longe*, ed. J. Werneck, M. Mendonça, and E. C. White, 53–54 (Rio de Janeiro: Pallas; Rio de Janeiro: Criola, 2000).

42. G. Freyre, *Casa grande e senzala*, 13th ed., 2 vols. (Rio de Janeiro: José Olympio, 1966), 13.

43. Alberto Guerreiro Ramos, *Introdução crítica à sociologia brasileira* (Rio de Janeiro: Editorial Andes, 1957), 147–48; Manuela Carneiro da Cunha, *Negros, estrangeiros* (São Paulo: Brasiliense, 1985); Letícia Vidor de Sousa Reis, "Negro em 'terra de branco.' A reinvenção da identidade," in *Negras Imagens*, ed. L. M. Schwarcz and L. V. S. Reis (São Paulo: Estação Ciência; São Paulo: EdUSP, 1996).

44. R. Nina Rodrigues, *As raças humanas e a responsabilidade penal no Brasil* (Salvador, Brazil: Aguiar e Souza; Salvador, Brazil: Progresso, 1957), 142; Silva Jr., Hédio, ed., *Anti-racismo. Coletânea de leis brasileiras (federais, estaduais, municipais)* (São Paulo: Oliveira Mendes, 1998), 8.

45. George Reid Andrews, *Black Political Protest in São Paulo, 1888–1988* (Cambridge: Cambridge University Press, 1992).

46. G. Freyre, *New World in the Tropics*. This is a later English language version of Freyre's *O mundo que o Português criou*. See also G. Freyre, *The Portuguese and the Tropics: Suggestions Inspired by the Portuguese Methods of Integrating Autochthonous Peoples and Cultures Differing from the European in a New, or Luso-Tropical Complex of Civilization* (Lisbon: Executive Committee for the Commemoration of the Vth Centenary of the Death of Prince Henry the Navigator, 1961), 261. I am grateful to Angela Gilliam for this reference.

47. Angela Gilliam, "Globalization, Identity, and Assaults on Equality in the United States: An Initial Perspective for Brazil," *SOULS: A Critical Journal of Black Politics, Culture, and Society* 5, no. 2 (Spring 2003): 95.

48. The word "kilombo"—spelled *quilombo* in Portuguese—is derived from the Kimbundu term for villages or for communities formed by people in transition. N. Lopes, *Dicionário Banto*, 215. For a more detailed history of this etymology, see Beatriz Nascimento, "O conceito de quilombo e a resistência cultural negra," *Afrodiaspora* 3, no. 6–7 (Rio de Janeiro: IPEAFRO, 1985), 41–50.

49. Richard Price, ed., *Maroon Societies: Rebel Slave Communities in the Americas*, 3rd ed. (Baltimore: Johns Hopkins University Press, 1996).

50. Federal Republic of Brazil, *Constituição da República Federativa do Brasil*, Ato das disposições constitucionais transitórias, art. 68 (Brasília: Senado Federal, Subsecretaria de Edições Técnicas, 2003), 161.

51. Hélio Santos, *A busca de um caminho para o Brasil. A trilha do círculo vicioso* (São Paulo: National Commerce Service SENAC, 2001).

52. A. Nascimento, transcription from dialogues at symposium on the eightieth anniversary of the abolition of slavery in Brazil organized by Abdias Nascimento at the request of the editors of the journal *Cadernos Brasileiros*, Rio de Janeiro, RJ, Brazil, May 13, 1958. Published in a one-volume book entitled *80 anos de abolição* (Rio de Janeiro: Cadernos Brasileiros, 1968), 21.

53. Alonso de Sandoval, *El mundo de la esclavitud negra en América* (Bogotá: Empresa Nacional, 1956).

54. Fernando Ortiz, "José Saco y sus ideas," *Revista Bimestre Cubana* no. 2 (1929): 40–45.

55. Donald Pierson, *Negroes in Brazil—A Study of Race Contact in Bahia* (Carbondale: Southern Illinois University Press, 1967), 45, 76.

56. Darcy Ribeiro was a leader of progressive public policy in education. He helped create the University of Brasilia during João Goulart's presidency in the early 1960s, as well as the public schools called Integrated Centers for Public Education (CIEPs) when he worked with Leonel Brizola's Rio de Janeiro State Government in the 1980s and 1990s. His political work in the Democratic Labor Party (PDT) and its forerunner, the Brazilian Labor Party (PTB), was complemented by his role as a researcher and spokesman of the Brazilian indigenous peoples and their cause, particularly during his exile from the military regime from 1964 to 1979.

57. Darcy Ribeiro, "A América Latina Existe?" *Cadernos Trabalhistas* 1 (1979): 87. José Martí, "Nuestra América," *La Revista Ilustrada de Nueva York*, January, 10 1891; J. Martí, *El Partido Liberal*, January 30, 1891), available at http://www.josemarti.org/jose_marti/obras/articulos/nuestramerica/01nuestramerica.htm; Nicolás Guillén, *Songoro Cosongo. Poemas Mulatos* (Mexico City: Presencia Latinoamericana, 1981); José Vasconcellos, *La raza cósmica. 1925.* (Mexico City: Espasa Calpe, 1982); Dary Ribeiro et al., Darcy Ribeiro et al., *Mestiço é que é bom!* (Rio de Janeiro: Revan, 1996), 105.

58. Léon Poliakov, *O mito ariano. Ensaio sobre as fontes do racismo e dos nacionalismos*, trans. Luiz João Gaio (São Paulo: Perspectiva; São Paulo: EdUSP, 1974); Muniz Sodré, *Claros e escuros. Identidade, povo e mídia no Brasil* (Petrópolis, Brazil: Vozes, 1999), 58–69.

59. Helena Bocayuva, *Erotismo à brasileira. O tema do excesso sexual em Gilberto Freyre* (Rio de Janeiro: Garamond, 2001).

60. A. Gilliam, "Women's Equality and National Liberation," in *Third World Women and the Politics of Feminism*, ed. Chandra Talpade Mohanty, Ann Russo, and Lourdes Torres, 226–27 (Bloomington: Indiana University Press, 1991).

61. L. González, "A importância da organização da mulher negra," 234–36.

62. Arthur Ramos, introduction to *As collectividades anormaes*, by R. Nina Rodrigues, 12–13 (Rio de Janeiro: Civilização brasileira, 1939), 12.

63. G. Freyre, *The Portuguese and the Tropics*, 261. I am grateful to Angela Gilliam for this reference.

64. D. Ribeiro, *O povo brasileiro. A formação e o sentido do Brasil*, 2nd ed. (São Paulo: Companhia das Letras, 1995), 453.

65. O. Vianna, *Raça e assimilação*, 2nd ed. (São Paulo: Companhia Editora Nacional, 1934), 230–31.

66. A. Gilliam, "Globalization, Identity, and Assaults on Equality in the United States," 95.

67. Lourdes Martínez-Echazábal, "O Culturalismo dos anos 30 no Brasil e na América Latina. Deslocamento retórico ou mudança conceitual?" in *Raça, ciência e sociedade*, ed. Marcos Chor Maio and Ricardo Ventura Santos (Rio de Janeiro: Oswaldo Cruz Foundation; Rio de Janeiro: Bank of Brazil Cultural Center, 1998), 112.

68. José Sette Câmara, "O fim do colonialismo," in *Brasil, África e Portugal*, special issue, ed. Eduardo Portella, *Tempo brasileiro*, no. 38/39 (1974): 14.

69. Pierre Verger, "African Religion and the Valorization of the African Descendants in Brazil," in *Faculty Seminar Series*, vol. 1, ed. O. Oyelaran (Ife, Nigeria: University of Ile-Ife, 1976–1977), 228.

70. G. Freyre, *Casa Grande*, xxxiv.

71. L. Martínez-Echazábal, "Culturalismo dos anos 30," 116–17.

72. Infante Dom Pedro, *Livro da virtuosa benfeitoria*, in *Obras dos príncipes de avis*, 6 vols. (Porto: Lello and Brother.Publishers, n.d.).

73. M. Sodré, *Claros e escuros*, 70–76.

74. Marianne Hester, *Lewd Women and Wicked Witches: A Study of the Dynamics of Male Domination* (New York: Routledge, 1992).

75. A. Nascimento, *O genocídio do negro brasileiro* (Rio de Janeiro: Paz e Terra, 1978), 62; A. Nascimento, *O Quilombismo* (Petrópolis, Brazil: Vozes, 1980), 227–44; L. González, "Racismo e sexismo na cultura brasileira," in *Movimentos sociais urbanos, minorias étnicas e outros estudos*, ed. Luiz Antonio Silva et al., 224–35 (Brasília: National Social Sciences Research Association ANPOCS, 1983); L. Bairros, "Lembrando Lélia González," 52–54; A. Gilliam, "A Black Feminist Perspective on the Sexual Commodification of Women in the New Global Culture," in *Black Feminist Anthropology: Theory, Praxis, Politics and Poetics*, ed. Irma McClaurin, 173–80 (New Brunswick, NJ: Rutgers University Press, 2001).

76. R. Nina Rodrigues, *As raças humanas*, 146.

77. G. Freyre, "Aspectos da influência Africana no Brasil," *Revista Cultura* 6, no. 23 (October–December 1976): 7.

78. A. Guerreiro Ramos, *Introdução crítica* (1957), 147–48; M. C. da Cunha, *Negros, Estrangeiros*, 12; A. Nascimento, *Mixture or Massacre*, 114.

79. Édison Carneiro, *80 anos de abolição*, 58.

80. R. Nina Rodrigues, *Os africanos no Brasil*, 28.

81. A. Guerreiro Ramos, *Introdução crítica* (1957), 147–48.

82. Ramos compares the titles and topics of papers presented to the First and Second Afro-Brazilian Congresses in Recife in 1934 and Salvador in 1937 with the titles of papers published by Nazi researchers on the Jews, noting the strong similarity of topics they announce.

83. A. Nascimento, *Mixture or Massacre*, 148–49; J. Braga, *Na gamela do feitiço*, 18–33.

84. L. M. Schwarcz, *O espetáculo das raças*, 203–38; Nísia Trindade Lima and Gilberto Hochman, "Condenado pela raça, absolvido pela medicina. O Brasil descoberto pelo movimento sanitarista da Primeira República," in *Raça, ciência e sociedade*, ed. M. C. Maio and R. V. Santos, 23–40 (Rio de Janeiro: Editora Fiocruz e Centro Cultural Banco do Brasil, 1998), esp. 25–36.

85. Belisário Penna, *O saneamento do Brasil* (Rio de Janeiro: Ed. dos Tribunais, 1923), 99.

86. N. T. Lima and G. Hochman, "Condenado pela raça," 27.

87. Ibid., 28.

88. The word *"bandeirantes"* refers to members of the *Bandeira*, which means "flag" and was the name of armed expeditions that explored the rural backlands (*sertões*) in search of gold mines and served as a police force subduing kilombos and other rebellious local populations.

89. N. T. Lima and G. Hochman, "Condenado pela raça," 28.

90. José Bento Monteiro Lobato, *Urupês* (Rio de Janeiro: Civilização brasileira, 1957), 271. The collection of essays that included these articles was published in 1918; it was such

a success that several editions followed shortly thereafter. The essay in which Lobato pronounces the sentence about Jeca Tatu is "Velha Praga"; in it he blames the ignorant Jeca for burning bush to clear land. Photos of the first two covers may be seen at http://lobato.globo.com/biblioteca_Geral.asp#urupes.

91. Ibid., 292.

92. A. Guerreiro Ramos, *Introdução crítica (1957)*, 145–59, 193–99; Caetana Maria Damasceno, "Em casa de enforcado não se fala de corda. Notas sobre a construção social da 'boa' aparência no Brasil," in *Tirando a máscara*, ed. A. S. A. Guimarães and L. Huntley, 165–99 (São Paulo: Paz e Terra; Atlanta: SEF, 2000), esp. 165–66, 170–75, 185–93; Neusa dos Santos Souza, ed., *Tornar-se negro* (Rio de Janeiro: Graal, 1983), 19–32, 63–64; C. D. Silva, *Negro, qual é o seu nome?* 84–96; N. L. Gomes, *A mulher negra*, 133.

93. J. B. Monteiro Lobato, *Idéias de Jeca Tatu* (São Paulo: Revista do Brasil, 1919); L. M. Schwarcz, *O espetáculo das raças*, 248 (reproduction of the illustration). In Brazilian Portuguese, "bad hair" means curly, black hair, while "good hair" is straight.

94. A. Guerreiro Ramos, "Patologia social do 'branco' brasileiro," in *Introdução crítica* (1957), 171–92, 178–84. Antonio Sérgio Alfredo Guimarães observes that the sociologists who studied race relations in the Northeast found abundantly documented "color prejudice" and discrimination, although none would venture to identify such actions and attitudes as racism. A. S. A. Guimarães, *Racismo e anti-racismo no Brasil* (São Paulo: Fundação Universidade de São Paulo; São Paulo: Editora 34, 1999), 69–146.

95. Ibid., 183.

96. R. Ribeiro, *Religião e relações*, 125.

97. A. Guerreiro Ramos, "Patologia," 180.

98. R. Ribeiro, *Religião e relações*, 215–16.

99. Ibid., 126.

100. Ibid., 216.

101. Ibid., 119.

102. A. Guerreiro Ramos, "Patologia," 181.

103. Ibid., 181.

104. Ibid., 154.

105. A. S. A. Guimarães, "Apresentação," in Guimarães and Huntley, eds., *Tirando a Máscara*, 24.

106. A. Guerreiro Ramos, *Introdução Crítica* (1957), 157.

107. A. S. A. Guimarães, *Racismo e anti-racismo*, 61.

108. Edith Piza, "Brancos no Brasil? Ningúem sabe, ninguém viu," in *Tirando a máscara*, ed. A. S. A. Guimarães and L. Huntley, 97–126 (São Paulo: Paz e Terra; Atlanta: SEF, 2000). However, this author's work is dedicated to combating racism in Brazil.

109. A. S. A. Guimarães, *Racismo e anti-racismo*, 61–62, my emphasis.

110. Some examples are A. Nascimento, *Mixture or Massacre*, 57–175; A. Nascimento, *O negro revoltado* (Rio de Janeiro: GRD, 1968), 15–61; H. Santos, *A busca de um caminho*, 61–179; L. González and C. Hasenbalg, *Lugar de negro* (Rio de Janeiro: Marco Zero, 1982); Sueli Carneiro, "Raça, classe e identidade nacional," *Thoth*. *Pensamento dos povos afrodescendentes* 2 (May/August 1997): 221–33; Ivan Costa Lima and Jeruse Romão, *Negros e currículo*, Black Thought in Education Series 2 (Florianópolis, Brazil: NEN, 1997); D. D. de Oliveira et al., eds., *A cor do medo*, 35–111; 153–61.

111. A. S. A. Guimarães, *Racismo e anti-racismo*, 68.

112. R. Nina Rodrigues, *As raças humanas*, 98.

113. E. Piza, "Brancos no Brasil," in *Tirando a máscara*, 106–19.

114. E. Piza, "Porta de vidro. Entrada para a branquitude," in *Psicologia social do racismo. Estudos sobre branquitude e branqueamento no Brasil*, ed. Iray Carone and M. A. S. Bento, 59–64 (Petrópolis, Brazil: Vozes, 2002).

115. Guilherme Figueiredo, "Apartheid, a discriminação racial e o colonialismo na África austral," *Tempo brasileiro* 38/39 (1975): 35.

116. Brazil, Federal Constitution of 1934, article 138 (b), mandates federal, state, and local authorities to encourage eugenic education; article 121 (6) restricts immigration of black people according to previously established quotas; article 145 makes prenuptial medical examinations mandatory. Hélio Silva, *As constituições do Brasil* (Rio de Janeiro: Rede Globo, n.d.), 73–75. See also President's Office, Civilian Cabinet, Subdirectorate for Juridical Matters. *Constituição da República dos Estados Unidos do Brasil (de 16 de julho de 1934)*, http://www.planalto.gov.br/ccivil_03/Constituicao/Constitui%C3%A7ao34.htm; Fernando H. Mendes de Almeida. *Constituições do Brasil* (São Paulo, Saraiva, 1963).

117. Art. 2 *Atender-se-á, na admissão dos imigrantes, à necessidade de preservar e desenvolver, na composição étnica da população, as características mais convenientes da sua ascendência européia, assim como a defesa do trabalhador nacional*. [The admission of immigrants will serve the need to preserve and develop, in the ethnic composition of the population, the more convenient characteristics of its European ancestry, as well as the defense of the national worker.] Federal Republic of Brazil, Executive Branch. Decreto Lei 7.967 de 18/09/1945 — Dispõe sobre a Imigração e Colonização, e Dá Outras Providências. Coleção de Leis do Brasil de 31/12/45 (CLBR PUB 31/12/1945 007 000312 1) (Rio de Janeiro: Imprensa Nacional, 1945), formato text/xml, código 34.577, http://www6.senado.gov.br/sicon/ExecutaPesquisaBasica.action. Also in Annibal Martins Alonso, *Estrangeiros no Brasil. Legislação anotada e atualizada* (Rio de Janeiro: Freitas Bastos, 1960).

118. Renowned abolitionist Joaquim Nabuco, cited by Júlio José Chiavanetto, *O negro no Brasil*, 3rd ed. (São Paulo: Brasiliense, 1980), 131.

119. R. Nina Rodrigues, *As collectividades anormaes* (Rio de Janeiro: Civilização brasileira, 1939).

120. R. Nina Rodrigues, *As raças humanas*.

121. Olívia Gomes da Cunha, "1933. Um ano em que fizemos contatos," *Revista USP* 28 (December 1995–February 1996): 144.

122. Afrânio Peixoto, foreword to R. Nina Rodrigues, *As raças humanas*, 11.

123. R. Nina Rodrigues, *As raças humanas*, 170–71.

124. H. Silva Jr., "Crônica da culpa anunciada," in *A cor do medo. Homicídios e relações raciais no Brasil*, ed. David Dijaci de Oliveira et al., 71–90 (Brasília: University of Brasília Press; Brasília: University of Goiás Press; Brasília: National Human Rights Movement MNDH, 1998).

125. Ibid., 80–85; Sérgio Adorno, "Discriminação racial e justiça criminal," *Novos Estudos Cebrap* 43 (November 1995); Paulo Sérgio Pinheiro, *Escritos indignados* (São Paulo: Brasiliense, 1984).

126. A. Nascimento, *O negro revoltado*, 59.

127. João Farias, Jr., *Manual de criminologia*, 2nd ed. (Curitiba: Juruá, 1996), 74–76; H. Silva Jr., "Crônica da culpa anunciada," 86, emphasis in the original.

128. E.g., Franz Exner, *Biología criminal* (Barcelona: Bosch, 1946).

129. Roberto Lyra and João Marcello Araújo, Jr., *Criminologia*, 4th ed. (Rio de Janeiro: Forense, 1995), 130–33.

130. H. Silva Jr., "Crônica da culpa anunciada," 71.

131. Ordep Serra, "A etnopsiquiatria dos ritos afrobrasileiros," lecture given at the First Symposium on Ethnopsychiatry, UFBA, Salvador, Brazil, 2000, 3. In 1999, as a result of legal action taken by major Afro-Brazilian religious leaders, the Candomblé worship objects were moved to the City Museum.

CHAPTER 3

1. Luiz Cláudio Figueiredo, *Revisitando as psicologias* (Petrópolis, Brazil: Vozes, 1995); L. C. Figueiredo, *Matrizes do pensamento psicológico* (Petrópolis, Brazil: Vozes, 1991); L. C.

Figueiredo, *A invenção do psicológico. Quatro séculos de subjetivação (1500–1900)* (São Paulo: Escuta; São Paulo: Educ, 1992).

2. L. C. Figueiredo, *Revisitando as psicologias*, 19.

3. Ibid.

4. Ibid..

5. Ibid., 19, 23.

6. L. C. Figueiredo, *A invenção do psicológico*, 27.

7. Ivan Van Sertima, *African Presence in Early Europe* (New Brunswick: Transaction Books, 1985).

8. L. C. Figueiredo, *Revisitando as psicologias*, 29–36.

9. These two formed the famous "diabolic triumvirate" with Isaac de La Peyrère, author of *Sistema theologicum ex preadamitarum hypotese* (1655). Léon Poliakov, *O mito ariano. Ensaio sobre as fontes do racismo e dos nacionalismos*, trans. Luiz João Gaio (São Paulo: Perspectiva; São Paulo: University of São Paulo Press, 1974), 107–8.

10. *Nouvelle division de la terre, par les différentes espèces ou races d'hommes qui l'habitent* (1684).

11. L. Poliakov, *O mito ariano*, 111.

12. See Chapter 1; also Oyeronke Oyewumi, *The Invention of Women: Making an African Sense of Western Gender Discourses* (Minneapolis: University of Minnesota Press, 1997); Kabengele Munanga, *Rediscutindo a mestiçagem no Brasil. Identidade nacional versus identidade negra* (Petrópolis, Brazil: Vozes, 1999); Muniz Sodré, *Claros e escuros. Identidade, povo e mídia no Brasil* (Petrópolis, Brazil: Vozes, 1999); Angela Gilliam, "A Black Feminist Perspective on the Sexual Commodification of Women in the New Global Culture," in *Black Feminist Anthropology: Theory, Praxis, Politics and Poetics*, ed. Irma McClaurin, 150–86 (New Brunswick, NJ: Rutgers University Press, 2001).

13. L. Poliakov, *O mito ariano*, 111. He cites Rousseau's *Discours sur l'origine et les fondements de l'inégalité parmi les hommes* and Voltaire's *Essai sur les moeurs et l'esprit des nations*.

14. Genesis 9:18–27.

15. Robert Graves and Raphael Patai, *Hebrew Myths: The Book of Genesis* (New York: Doubleday, 1964), 121.

16. L. Poliakov, *O mito ariano*, 130–35, 142–46, 153; K. Munanga, *Rediscutindo a mestiçagem*, 25–27.

17. Charles White, *An Account of the Regular Gradation in Man, and in Different Animals and Vegetables* (London, 1799), 134–35.

18. Richard Blackmore, dialogue with Edward Tyson, *The Lay Monastery, Consisting of Essays, Discourses, etc.*, transcribed by Ashley Montagu, Edward Tyoson, MD, FRS (Philadelphia, 1943), 402–3.

19. Voltaire, *Oeuvres complêtes*, XII (Paris: Moland), 192, 210.

20. L. Poliakov, *O mito ariano*, 130–58.

21. Ibid., 121.

22. Cheikh Anta Diop, *The African Origin of Civilization: Myth or Reality*, trans. Mercer Cook (Westport, CT: Lawrence Hill, 1974).

23. On the theories defended by Oliveira Vianna, see Thomas E. Skidmore, *Black into White: Race and Nationality in Brazilian Thought*. London: Oxford University Press, 1974; and K. Munanga, *Rediscutindo a mestiçagem*.

24. Oliveira Vianna, *Raça e assimilação*, 2nd ed. (São Paulo: Companhia Editora Nacional, 1934), 274.

25. Ibid.

26. Ibid., 275.

27. Ibid., 276.

28. Ibid., 277–78.
29. Ibid., 278.
30. Ibid.
31. Ibid.
32. Ibid., 282.
33. Ibid., 280.
34. Ibid., 279.
35. Ibid., 281–82.
36. Ibid., 285.
37. Maria José Lopes da Silva, "Fundamentos teóricos da pedagogia multirracial," pamphlet (Rio de Janeiro: M. J. L. da Silva, 1988); Raquel de Oliveira, "Relações raciais na escola. Uma experiência de intervenção" (master's thesis, Pontifical Catholic University of São Paulo, 1992); Maria Helena Souza Patto, A produção do fracasso escolar (São Paulo: T. A. Queiroz, 1993); Nilma Lino Gomes, A mulher negra que vi de perto (Belo Horizonte, Brazil: Mazza, 1995); Consuelo Dores Silva, Negro, qual é o seu nome? (Belo Horizonte, Brazil: Mazza, 1995); Ivan Costa Lima and Jeruse Romão, Negros e currículo, Black Thought in Education Series 2 (Florianópolis, Brazil: Núcleo de Estudos Negros, 1997); Eliane dos Santos Cavalleiro, Do silêncio do lar ao silêncio escolar. Racismo, preconceito e discriminação na educação infantil (São Paulo: Contexto; São Paulo: Univeristy of São Paulo, 2000); Nucleus of Black Studies (NEN), Série Pensamento Negro em Educação, 6 vols. (Florianópolis, Brazil: NEN, 1997–1999).
38. L. C. Figueiredo, Revisitando as psicologias, 29–30n17.
39. E. S. Cavalleiro, Do silêncio do lar. See also Jussara Franco and Raquel Aguiar Freire, Racismo na escola. Linguagem do silêncio (Belo Horizonte, Brazil: João Pinheiro Foundation, 1991).
40. Ricardo Franklin Ferreira, Afro-descendente. Identidade em construção (Rio de Janeiro: Pallas; São Paulo: Educ; São Paulo: FAPESP, 2000), 55–65.
41. R. F. Ferreira, "A construção da identidade do afro-descendente: A psicologia brasileira e a questão racial," in Brasil. Um país de negros? ed. Jéferson Bacelar and Carlos Caroso, 78 (Rio de Janeiro: Pallas, 1999).
42. Ibid., 81.
43. R. F. Ferreira, Afro-descendente, 60–61.
44. Marilena Chauí, Cultura e democracia. O discurso competente e outras falas (São Paulo: Moderna, 1981).
45. Maria Clementina Pereira Cunha, O espelho do mundo. Juquery, a história de um asilo, 2nd ed. (São Paulo: Paz e Terra, 1988), 115.
46. M. H. S. Patto, Psicologia e ideologia. Uma introdução crítica à psicologia escolar (São Paulo: T. A. Queiroz, 1984).
47. Raymundo Nina Rodrigues, As raças humanas e a responsabilidade penal no Brasil (Salvador, Brazil: Aguiar e Souza; Salvador, Brazil: Progresso, 1957), 34.
48. Robert Castel, A ordem psiquiátrica (Rio de Janeiro: Graal, 1978), 259 [Originally published as L'Ordre psychiatrique. L'age d'or de l'alienisme (Paris: Les Editions de Minuit, 1977)].
49. M. C. P. Cunha, O espelho do mundo, 46.
50. Ibid., 45. M. C. P. Cunha cites Juliano Moreira, "Notícia sobre a evolução da assistência a alienados no Brasil," in Archivos brasileiros de Psychiatria, Neurologia e Sciencias affins, 52 (Rio de Janeiro: Oficina De Typographia e Hospício Nacional de Alienados, 1905).
51. R. Nina Rodrigues, As raças humanas, 50.
52. Ibid., 117.
53. Ibid., 122–25.
54. O. Vianna, Populações meridionais do Brasil (São Paulo: Revista do Brasil; São Paulo: Monteiro Lobato, 1920), 109.

55. Clóvis Moura, *As injustiças de Clio* (Belo Horizonte, Brazil: Oficina de Livros, 1990), 187.

56. O. Vianna, *Raça e assimilação*, 36.

57. Ibid.

58. Ibid., 44–45.

59. Ibid., 271.

60. Ibid., 46.

61. Francisco Franco da Rocha, *Causas da loucura. Estatísticas e apontamentos hospício de São Paulo*, 8 vols (São Paulo: Typografia do Diário Oficial, 1901), 12–14.

62. Ibid.

63. F. Franco da Rocha, *Esboço de psiquiatria forense* (São Paulo: Laemmert, 1904), 2–3.

64. Ibid., 30–31, 49.

65. Hospital record of Martha C., a thirty-eight-year-old black woman admitted to Juquery in 1902. The record was examined by M. C. P. Cunha, *O espelho do mundo*, 124.

66. Ibid.

67. Ibid.

68. Hannah Arendt, *As origens do totalitarismo. A expansão do poder* (Rio de Janeiro: Documentário, 1976), 82, 85–86. See Chapter 2.

69. Nicolau Sevcenko, *A revolta da vacina. Mentes insanas em corpos rebeldes* (São Paulo: Brasiliense, 1984); Sidney Chalhoub, *Cidade Febril. Cortiços e epidemias na corte imperial* (São Paulo: Companhia das Letras, 1996); Mayla Yara Porto, "Uma revolta popular contra a vacinação," *Ciência e Cultura* 55, no. 1 (January–March 2003): 53–54.

70. Antonio Carlos Pacheco e Silva, "Aula inaugural de clínica psiquiátrica da Faculdade de Medicina da Universidade de São Paulo," *Arquivos da Assistência Geral a Psicopatas do Estado de São Paulo* 1, no. 1 (1937): 7.

71. M. C. P. Cunha, *O espelho do mundo*, 172.

72. See Chapter 2.

73. R. Nina Rodrigues, *As raças humanas*, 11.

74. Ordep Serra, "A etnopsiquiatria dos ritos afrobrasileiros," lecture given at the First Symposium on Ethnopsychiatry, UFBA, Salvador, Brazil, 2000.

75. Arthur Ramos, *As culturas negras no novo mundo*, 2nd ed. (São Paulo: Companhia Editora Nacional, 1946), 45.

76. In addition to *As culturas negras no novo mundo*, Arthur Ramos is the author of *O folclore negro no Brasil. Demopsicologia e psicanálise* [Black Folklore in Brazil: Demipsychology and Psychoanalysis], 2nd ed. (Rio de Janeiro: Casa do Estudante do Brasil, 1954), and other works in this line of investigation.

77. A. Ramos, *As culturas negras*, 188–89.

78. Roger Bastide, "Cavalos dos santos. Esboço de uma sociologia do transe místico," in *Estudos afro-brasileiros*, ed. R. Bastide, 304 (São Paulo: Perspectiva, 1973). Originally published as "Bulletin 154," *Sociology* 1, no. 3. Roger Bastide, *Estudos afro-brasileiros*, 3rd series (São Paulo: FFCL, USP, 1953), 104.

79. A. Ramos, *As culturas negras*, 189–90.

80. R. Bastide ("Cavalos dos santos," 305) cites the article "Nouvelle contribution à l'étude de la crise de possession," *Psyche* 60 (October 1951) and comments that Dr. Louis Mars's later works brought him closer to Bastide, in the direction of a more sociological interpretation.

81. The return of African families from Brazil to Africa is documented in Pierre Verger's "Flux et reflux de la traite de nègres entre lê golfe de Benin et Bahia de todos os santos," 3rd Cycle Thesis (Paris: Mouton, 1968); and J. Michael Turner, "Lês Brésiliens: The Impact of Former Brazilian Slaves upon Dahomey" (PhD diss., Boston University, 1970).

82. George Alakija, *The Trance State in the "Candomblé"* (Brasília: Ministry of Foreign Relations, official delegation of the Brazilian Government to Festac 1977), 3–4.

83. R. Bastide, *O candomblé da Bahia (rito nagô)*, 3rd ed., trans. Maria Isaura Pereira de Queiroz (São Paulo: Companhia Editora Nacional, 1978), 11–12 [originally published as *Le candomblé de Bahia (rite nagô)* (Paris: Mouton and Company, 1958)].

84. R. Bastide, "Cavalos dos santos," 315.

85. R. Bastide, *Sociologia e psicanálise*, 2nd ed., trans. Heloysa de Lima Dantas (São Paulo: Melhoramentos; São Paulo: University of São Paulo Press, 1974), 15 [originally published as *Sociologie et psychanalyse* (Paris: Presses Universitaires de France, 1950)].

86. Ibid., 220.

87. Ibid., 200.

88. Ibid., 197.

89. Ibid., 187–201.

90. Georges Dévereux, *Essais d'ethnopsychiatrie générale* (Paris: Gallimard, 1970).

91. Ibid.

92. L. C. Figueiredo, *Revisitando as psicologias*, 29–30n17.

93. O. Serra, "A etnopsiquiatria dos ritos afrobrasileiros," 4–6.

94. Ibid., 5.

95. Ibid., 7.

96. Andrea Caprara, "Polissemia e multivocalidade da epilepsia na cultura afro-brasileira," Ruy do Carmo Póvoas, "Dentro do quarto," and Núbia Rodrigues and C. Caroso, "Exu na tradição terapêutica religiosa afro-brasileira," in *Faces da tradição afro-brasileira. Religiosidade, sincretismo, anti-sincretismo, reafricanização, práticas terapêuticas, etnobotânica e comida*, ed. C. Caroso and J. Bacelar, 257–88, 213–37, 239–55 (Rio de Janeiro: Pallas; Salvador, Brazil: CEAO; Salvador, Brazil: UFBA, 1999).

97. O. Serra, "A etnopsiquiatria dos ritos afrobrasileiros," 5, citing Claude Lévi-Strauss, *Antropologia estrutural* (Rio de Janeiro: Tempo brasileiro, 1975), 215–36. Originally published as "L'Efficacité symbolique," *Revue de l'Histoire des Religions* 135, no. 1 (1949), 5–27.

98. R. F. Ferreira, *Afro-desdendente*, 63.

99. Marilza de Souza Martins, interview with Elisa Larkin Nascimento at the clinic and office of AMMA—Psique e negritude, an organization of black female psychologists, São Paulo, July 9, 2000.

100. Roberto Borges Martins, "Desigualdades e discriminação de gênero e de raça no mercado brasileiro de trabalho do século XX" (report presented to the International Labor Organization in Brazil, April 2003); R. B. Martins, "Desigualdades raciais e políticas de inclusão racial. Um sumário da experiência brasileira recente" (report presented to the United Nations Economic Commission for Latin America and the Caribbean [CEPAL], August 2003); Instituto Sindical Interamericano Pela Igualdade Racial [Inter-American Labor Union Insitute for Racial Equality] (INSPIR), and Departamento Intersindical de Estatística e Estudos Sócio-Econômicos [Inter-Labor Union Department for Statistics and Sócio-Economic Studies] (DIEESE), *Mapa da população negra no mercado de trabalho. Regiões metropolitanas de São Paulo, Salvador, Recife, Belo Horizonte, Porto Alegre e Distrito Federal—Outubro de 1999* (São Paulo: INSPIR; São Paulo: DIEESE, 1999).

101. O. Serra, "A etnopsiquiatria dos ritos afrobrasileiros," 4.

102. A. Guerreiro Ramos, *Introdução crítica à sociologia brasileira* (Rio de Janeiro: Andes, 1957), 148–65, 171–99; A. Guerreiro Ramos, "Teoria e prática do psicodrama," *Quilombo* 2, no. 6, February 1950, 6–7; A. Guerreiro Ramos, "Teoria e prática do sociodrama," *Quilombo* 2, no. 7/8, March–April 1950, 9.

103. Neusa dos Santos Souza, *Tornar-se negro* (Rio de Janeiro: Graal, 1983), 34–44.

104. Jurandir Freire Costa, "Da cor ao corpo. A violência do racismo," in *Tornar-se negro*, N. S. Souza, 16 (Rio de Janeiro: Graal, 1983).

105. N. S. Souza, *Tornar-se negro*, 18.

106. Ibid., 70.

107. Ibid., 73.

108. Frantz Fanon, *Peau noire, masques blancs* (Paris: Seuil, 1952), 112.

109. Marianne Hester, *Lewd Women and Wicked Witches: A Study of the Dynamics of Male Domination* (New York: Routledge, 1992).

110. J. F. Costa, "Da cor ao corpo," 5–8.

111. N. S. Souza, *Tornar-se negro*, 43.

112. Ibid., 78.

113. Ibid., 77.

114. Ibid., 77–78.

115. For critical analyses of Marxist approaches to the race issue, see George Padmore, *Pan-Africanism or Communism?* 3rd ed. (New York: Doubleday, 1972); Wilson Record, *The Negro and the Communist Party* (New York: Atheneum, 1971).

116. Albert Memmi, *The Colonizer and the Colonized* (Boston: Beacon Press, 1965); F. Fanon, *Peau noire*; F. Fanon, *The Wretched of the Earth*, trans. Constance Farrington (New York: Grove, 1963).

117. R. de Oliveira, "Relações raciais na escola"; N. L. Gomes, *A mulher negra*; C. D. Silva, *Negro, qual é o seu nome?*; E. S. Cavalleiro, *Do silêncio do lar*; Nucleus of Black Studies (NEN), Black Thought in Education Series, 6 vols (Florianópolis, Brazil: NEN, 1997–1999).

118. Isildinha Baptista Nogueira, "Significações do corpo negro" (PhD diss., Institute of Psychology, University of São Paulo, 1998), 169.

119. Such proliferation of data is a result of pressure brought by the Afro-Brazilian social movement and its allies within the Brazilian Institute of Geography and Statistics (IBGE), Institute of Applied Economic Research (IPEA), Inter-Labor Union Department of Socio-Economic Studies (DIEESE), and other social science research institutions, as well as universities, in the 1970s, 1980s, and 1990s. See Chapter 2.

120. J. F. Costa, "Da cor ao corpo," 5–10.

121. I. B. Nogueira, "Significações do corpo negro." This expression is used repeatedly throughout the text.

122. Ibid., 105.

123. Jacques Lacan, *O eu na teoria de Freud e na técnica da psicanálise. O seminário, Livro II* (Rio de Janeiro: Zahar, 1985), 31.

124. Regina Neri, "O encontro entre a psicanálise e o feminino. Singularidade/diferença," in *Feminilidades*, ed. Joel Birman, 13 (Rio de Janeiro: Contra Capa; Rio de Janeiro: Espaço brasileiro de Estudos Psicanalíticos, 2002).

125. Ibid.

126. Elena Gianini Belotti, *Educar para a submissão. O descondicionamento da mulher*, 6th ed., trans. Ephraim Ferreira Alves (Petrópolis, Brazil: Vozes, 1987), 68 [originally published as *Dalla parte delle bambine* (Milan: Feltrinelli, 1973)]. E. G. Belotti cites Irenäus Eibl-Eibesfeldt, *Amore e odio. Per uma storia naturale dei comportamenti elementari* (Milan: Adelphi, 1996).

127. E. G. Belotti, *Educar para a submissão*, 70.

128. Teresa Brennan, introduction to *Para além do falo. Uma crítica a Lacan do ponto de vista da mulher*, trans. Alice Xavier (Rio de Janeiro: Record; Rio de Janeiro: Rosa dos Tempos, 1997), 12, 15 [Originally published as *Between Feminism and Psychoanalysis* (London: Routledge, 1989)].

129. Ibid., 15.

130. R. Bastide, *Sociologia e psicanálise*, 199.

131. C. A. Diop, *The Cultural Unity of Black Africa*, 2nd ed., trans. Présence Africaine (Chicago: Third World Press, 1978) [originally published as *L'Unité culturelle de l'Afrique Noire* (Paris: Présence Africaine, 1963)].

132. R. Bastide, *Sociologia e psicanálise*, 199.

133. Juana Elbein dos Santos, *Os nagô e a morte* (Petrópolis, Brazil: Vozes, 1976); Helena Theodoro, *Mito e espiritualidade—Mulheres Negras* (Rio de Janeiro: Pallas, 1996).

134. Maria Aparecida Silva Bento, interview with Elisa Larkin Nascimento at Centro de Estudos da Ética nas Relações de Trabalho (CEERT), São Paulo, July 9, 2000.

135. I. B. Nogueira, "Significações do corpo negro," 170; reference to things being engraved or inscribed on the psyche occurs throughout the text.

136. M. A. S. Bento, interview at CEERT.

137. I. B. Nogueira, "Significações do corpo negro," 170.

138. N. S. Souza, *Tornar-se negro*, 78.

139. I. B. Nogueira, "Significações do corpo negro," 169.

140. M. S. Martins, interview with Elisa Larkin Nascimento at AMMA headquarters, São Paulo, July 9, 2000.

141. Maria Lúcia da Silva, interview with Elisa Larkin Nascimento at AMMA headquarters, São Paulo, July 9, 2000.

142. AMMA—Psique e negritude, *Gostando mais de nós mesmos. Perguntas e respostas sobre auto-estima e a questão racial*, 2nd ed., ed. Ana Maria Silva and E. S. Cavalleiro (São Paulo: Gente, 1999). First edition published in São Paulo by Quilombhoje-Literatura, 1996. This excerpt is taken from the cover text of the first edition.

143. Ibid.

144. M. L. da Silva, interview at AMMA headquarters.

145. Instituto do Negro Padre Batista, Departamento Jurídico, folheto informativo, São Paulo, 2001.

146. Lorenzo Zanetti, *A prática educativa do Grupo Cultural Afro-Reggae* (Rio de Janeiro: Grupo Cultural Afro-Reggae, 2001).

147. Winnicott was a British contemporary of Sigmund Freud, Anna Freud, and Melanie Klein. A pediatrician and psychoanalyst, his work with children displaced by the Second World War led him to theoretical innovations, including the notion of the "transitional object" that we all know as the security blanket. Among his major works are *Playing and Reality* (London: Routledge, 1982), *Deprivation and Delinquency* (London: Tavistock, 1984), *Holding and Interpretation* (London: Hogarth; London: Institute of Psychoanalysis, 1987), and *The Spontaneous Gesture* (London: Harvard University Press, 1987).

148. Marco Antonio Chagas Guimarães, "É um umbigo, não é? A mãe criadeira. Um estudo sobre o processo de construção de identidade em comunidades de terreiro" (master's thesis, Pontifical Catholic University of Rio de Janeiro, 1990); M. A. C. Guimarães, "O mistério do nascer. Significados na tradição religiosa afro-brasileira," in *Reflexões sobre parto e nascimento*, ed. Sinais de Vida (Rio de Janeiro: REDEH, 1995).

149. M. A. C. Guimarães, "Rede de sustentação. Um modelo winnicottiano de intervenção em saúde coletiva" (PhD diss., Pontifical Catholic University of Rio de Janeiro, 2001).

150. Marta de Oliveira da Silva, "Algumas reflexões sobre população negra e saúde mental." Paper presented at the Round Table on Health and Black People, Brasília, Ministry of Health, April 16–17, 1996, 5.

151. M. O. da Silva, "Algumas reflexões," 7.

152. Brazil, Ministry of Health (Ministério da Saúde), *Mesa redonda sobre a saúde da população negra, relatório final* (Brasília: Ministry of Health, 1996).

153. Informative folder, Program of Psychotherapeutic Assistance to Victims of Racism, Justice Program, Núcleo de Estudos do Negro [Nucleus of Black Studies] (NEN), Florianópolis, Brazil, n.d.

154. Maria Lúcia da Silva, "Espelho, espelho meu diga-me. Quem sou eu?" *Catharsis Revista de Saúde Mental* 3, no. 11 (January–February 1997): 23.

155. Ibid., 25.

156. Ibid.

157. Ibid.

158. M. L. da Silva, interview at AMMA headquarters.

159. R. F. Ferreira, *Afro-descendente*, 25–37.

160. William E. Cross, Jr., "The Cross and Thomas Models of Psycological Nigrescence," *Journal of Black Psychology* 5, no. 1 (1978): 13–19; W. E. Cross, Jr., *Shades of Black: Diversity in African-American Identity* (Philadelphia: Temple University Press, 1991).

161. Janet E. Helms, ed., *Black and White Racial Identity: Theory, Research, and Practice* (Westport, CT: Praeger, 1993).

162. R. F. Ferreira, *Afro-descendente*, 70.

163. R. F. Ferreira, *Afro-descendente*, 70–75.

164. J. F. Costa, "Da cor ao corpo," 9–15.

165. R. F. Ferreira, *Afro-descendente*, 75–84.

166. Ibid., 83, 174–75.

167. N. S. Souza, *Tornar-se negro*, 78.

168. R. F. Ferreira, *Afro-descendente*, 83–84.

169. Ibid., 137–45.

170. Ibid., 176, 178.

171. R. F. Ferreira, e-mail communication with the author on February 25, 2000.

172. The first black female Rio de Janeiro State assemblywoman, Jurema Batista, a long-time activist, spoke of black citizenship as being a "recreational" matter: we are citizens when it is time for samba, football, and typical foods, but not when it comes to defining public policy or what is culture.

173. Labor Relations and Inequality Studies Center (CEERT), *Formação sobre relações raciais no movimento sindical* (São Paulo: Unified Trade Union Federation CUT, 1999), 1. The page numbers cited are from the typed original.

174. Ibid., 16.

175. Ruth Frankenberg, *White Women, Race Matters: The Social Construction of Whiteness* (Minneapolis: University of Minnesota Press, 1993), 1.

176. Edith Piza, "Brancos no Brasil? Ninguém sabe, ninguém viu," in *Tirando a máscara. Ensaios sobre o racismo no Brasil*, ed. A. S. A. Guimarães and L. Huntley, 97–126 (São Paulo: Paz e Terra; São Paulo: Southern Education Foundation, 2000); E. Piza, "Porta de vidro. Entrada para a branquitude," in *Psicologia social do racismo. Estudos sobre branquitude e branqueamento, no Brasil*, ed. Iray Carone and M. A. S. Bento, 59–90 (Petrópolis, Brazil: Vozes, 2002).

177. CEERT, *Formação sobre*, 2.

178. Carlos Hasenbalg, *Discriminação e desigualdades raciais no Brasil* (Rio de Janeiro: Graal, 1979), 2.

179. CEERT, *Formação Sobre*, 3.

180. Ibid., 12.

181. Ibid., 5.

182. Ibid., 7.

183. Ibid., 11–12.

184. E. Piza, "Porta de vidro," 61.

185. M. A. S. Bento, *O legado subjetivo dos 500 anos. Narcisismo e alteridade racial* (São Paulo: CEERT, 2000), 11.

186. E. Piza, "Porta de vidro. Entrada para a branquitude" (post-doctorate research paper, Institute of Psychology, University of São Paulo, 2000), 6.

187. E. Piza, "Porta de vidro."

188. See Chapter 2 for a discussion of these ideas.

189. O. Vianna, *Raça e assimilação*, 230–31. See Chapter 2.

190. The founding national myth mentioned in Chapter 2.

262 NOTES TO CHAPTER 4

191. Guerreiro Ramos recounts that, "it was a great mind from São Paulo, writer Fernando Góes, who...proposed that people of color hold a Congress on Brazilian Whites. I have found myself imagining what would be the program topics of this Congress. It would probably include topics like this: anthropometric measurements of white people, the private life of whites, religions and idols of whites, the criminality of whites, adornments and housing of whites, and so on." A. Guerreiro Ramos, "Um Herói da negritude," in *Teatro Experimental do Negro. Testemunhos*, ed. Abdias Nascimento, 106 (Rio de Janeiro: GRD, 1966).

192. A. Guerreiro Ramos, "Patologia social do 'branco' brasileiro," in *Introdução crítica* (1957), 171–92.

CHAPTER 4

1. For information on Zumbi and Palmares, see Chapter 2 and the Glossary.

2. For information on the kilombo phenomenon, see Chapter 2 and the Glossary.

3. Edmar Morel, *A revolta da chibata. Levante da esquadra pelo marinheiro João Cândido* (Rio de Janeiro: Graal, 1979); Rio de Janeiro State Culture Secretariat, Museum of the Image and Sound (MIS), ed., *João Cândido, o almirante negro* (Rio de Janeiro: MIS Foundation; Rio de Janeiro: Gryphus, 1999).

4. Florestan Fernandes, *A integração do negro à sociedade de classes* (São Paulo: University of São Paulo Faculty of Philosophy, Sciences, Letters, and Humanities FFLCH; São Paulo: USP, 1964).

5. Roger Bastide, "A imprensa negra do Estado de São Paulo," in *Estudos afro-brasileiros*, ed. R. Bastide (São Paulo: Perspectiva, 1973). Originally published as Bulletin CXXI, Sociology no. 2, R. Bastide, *Estudos afro-brasileiros*, 2nd Series (São Paulo: University of São Paulo Faculty of Philosophy, Sciences, and Letters, 1951).

6. Eduardo de Oliveira e Oliveira, ed., *A imprensa negra em São Paulo* (exhibition catalogue, São Paulo: São Paulo State Pinacoteca Museum, 1977).

7. Quilombhoje, ed., *Frente Negra Brasileira. Depoimentos* (São Paulo: Quilombhoje; São Paulo: National Culture Fund, 1998); Cuti and José Correia Leite, *E disse o velho militante* (São Paulo: São Paulo Municipal Culture Secretariat, 1992).

8. This collection was later published in a facsimile edition: Abdias Nascimento, ed., *Quilombo. Edição fac-similar do jornal dirigido por Abdias Nascimento* (São Paulo: Editora 34, 2003).

9. Kim Butler, *Freedoms Given, Freedoms Won* (New Brunswick, NJ: Rutgers University Press, 1998).

10. Thomas E. Skidmore, *Black into White: Race and Nationality in Brazilian Thought* (London: Oxford University Press, 1974).

11. Federal Republic of Brazil, Federal Constitution of 1934, article 138(b): "It is the duty of the Union, the States, and the Municipalities ... to stimulate eugenic education"; article 121 (6) restricted immigration; article 145 made pre-nuptial medical examinations mandatory. Hélio Silva, *As constituições do Brasil* (Rio de Janeiro: Rede Globo, n.d.), 73, 74, 75.

12. A. Nascimento, "A luta da raça negra no Brasil. 13 de maio—Outra mentira cívica," in *Combate ao Racismo. Discursos e Projetos* 1, by A. Nascimento, 9–22 (Brasília: Chamber of Deputies, 47th Legislature, 1st Legislative Session, Separatas de Discursos, Pareceres e Projetos no. 57, 1983).

13. F. Fernandes, *A integração do negro*, 310.

14. R. Bastide, "A imprensa negra," 150, cites the following periodicals: *Getulino*, I, 35; II, 56; *A Voz da raça*, I, 16, 18, 31, 32.

15. Quilombhoje, ed., *Frente Negra*, 42.

16. R. Bastide, "A imprensa negra," 130.

17. F. Fernandes, *A integração do negro*, 318–19. Renato Jardim Moreira, with the assistance of J. C. Leite, wrote a case study for F. Fernandes' research, entitled "Social Movements in the Black Community," which F. Fernandes cites lengthily. This passage is from an interview with J. C. Leite that was recorded in this document.

18. R. Bastide, *Estudos afro-brasileiros*, 131.

19. E. O. Oliveira, *A imprensa negra*, catalogue. The pages of this catalogue are not numbered. Citations of newspaper articles in this chapter, unless indicated otherwise, are from this catalogue.

20. Ricardo Franklin Ferreira, *Afro-descendente. Identidade em construção* (Rio de Janeiro: Pallas; São Paulo: Educ; São Paulo: FAPESP, 2000), 99.

21. F. Fernandes, *A integração do negro*, 320n11.

22. F. Fernandes, *A integração do negro*, 327. F. Fernandes transcribes a flyer written by Arlindo Veiga dos Santos, entitled "Congresso da Mocidade Negra brasileira: Mensagem aos Negros brasileiros." The text was published in *O Clarim da Alvorada* 6, no. 17, June 9, 1929, pp. 1–3.

23. F. Fernandes, *A integração do negro*, 335. Here F. Fernandes transcribes a document written in late 1936 by Raul Joviano do Amaral, entitled "Frente Negra Brasileira. Suas finalidades e obras realizadas."

24. Márcio Barbosa, introduction to *Frente Negra Brasileira*, by Quilombhoje, 11–12.

25. F. Fernandes, *A integração do negro*, 345–47.

26. R. Bastide, "A imprensa negra," 156.

27. A. Veiga dos Santos, *Manifesto to the Brazilian Black People* (São Paulo: Frente Negra brasileira, July 2, 1931), transcribed in F. Fernandes, *A integração do negro*, 327.

28. Ibid., 328, emphasis in the original.

29. Quilombhoje, ed., *Frente Negra Brasileira*, 42.

30. F. Fernandes writes that A. Veiga dos Santos estimated the Front's following as 200,000 blacks in São Paulo. F. Fernandes, *A integração do negro*, 354, 325–407; Quilombhoje, ed., *Frente Negra Brasileira*, 15–129. For more information on the Black Brazilian Front, see K. Butler, *Freedoms Given, Freedoms Won*, esp. 91–132; Michael George Hanchard, *Orpheus and Power: The Movimento Negro of Rio de Janeiro and São Paulo, Brazil, 1945–1988* (Princeton: Princeton University Press, 1994), 35, 40–41, 104–6, 122; A. Nascimento, "Memories from Exile," in *Africans in Brazil: A Pan-African Perspective*, ed. A. Nascimento and E. L. Nascimento, 14–16 (Trenton, NJ: Africa World Press, 1992).

31. Quilombhoje, ed., *Frente Negra Brasileira*, 39.

32. Ibid., 51.

33. Ibid., 37–38.

34. Quilombhoje, ed., *Frente Negra Brasileira*, 38. See also F. Fernandes, *A integração do negro*, 350.

35. Quilombhoje, ed., *Frente Negra Brasileira*, 55, 83–84.

36. Ibid., 75–79.

37. Ibid., 48, 70–75; K. Butler, *Freedoms Given*, 125–26.

38. Quilombhoje, ed., *Frente Negra Brasileira*, 91.

39. Ibid., 48. The word "patrianovista" refers to Pátria Nova, one of the principal Monarchist groups.

40. Ibid., 50.

41. Ibid., 22–24.

42. Ibid., 44.

43. Ibid., 24–26, 63–64, 79–80, 94; F. Fernandes, *A integração do negro*, 353–54.

44. The committee was composed of black poet and journalist Fernando Góes, poet Rossini Camargo Guarnieri, businessman Galdino, and black activist Abdias Nascimento. A. Nascimento, "Memories from Exile," 16; A. Nascimento, "O negro revoltado," in *O negro revoltado*, ed. A. Nascimento, 33 (Rio de Janeiro: GRD, 1968).

45. A. Nascimento, "Memories from Exile," 19–20; A. Nascimento, "O negro revoltado," 32–33.

46. Carl E. Degler, *Neither Black nor White* (New York: McMillan, 1971), 180–81. Degler cites *Phylon* 3 (1942): 284–86.

47. A. Nascimento, "Memories from Exile," 15; A. Nascimento, "Depoimento," in *Memórias do exílio*, ed. Pedro Celso Uchoa Cavalcanti and Jovelino Ramos, 23–52 (Lisbon: Arcádia, 1976), 28.

48. Quilombhoje, ed., *Frente Negra brasileira*, 46.

49. John Henrik Clarke and Amy Jacques Garvey, eds., *Marcus Garvey and the Vision of Africa* (New York: Vintage Books, 1974); Tony Martin, *Race First: The Ideological and Organizational Struggles of Marcus Garvey and the Universal Negro Improvement Association* (Dover: Majority Press, 1976); Rupert Lewis, *Marcus Garvey, Anti-Colonial Champion* (Trenton, NJ: Africa World Press, 1988).

50. R. F. Ferreira, "*Uma história de lutas e vitórias. A construção da identidade de um afro-descendente brasileiro*" (PhD diss., University of São Paulo Psychology Institute, 1999). See Chapters 1 and 3. The published version of the dissertation is R. F. Ferreira, *Afro-descendente*.

51. R. F. Ferreira, *Afro-descendente*, 70.

52. Ibid., 103.

53. Ibid., 104.

54. Eduardo Silva, *Dom Obá II D'África, o príncipe do povo. Vida, tempo e pensamento de um homem livre de cor* (São Paulo: Companhia das Letras, 1997), 18.

55. Raymundo Nina Rodrigues, *Os africanos no Brasil*, 3rd ed. (São Paulo: Companhia Editora Nacional, 1945), 28.

56. See the discussion of this development in Chapter 2.

57. R. F. Ferreira, *Afro-descendente*, 104.

58. F. Fernandes, *A integração do negro*, 376.

59. Ibid.

60. R. Bastide, "A imprensa negra," 145.

61. A. Veiga dos Santos, "Congresso da mocidade"; F. Fernandes, *A integração do negro*, 390.

62. R. Bastide, "A imprensa negra," 143.

63. Dalmir Francisco, *Negro, afirmação política e hegemonia burguesa no Brasil* (master's thesis, Federal Univeristy of Minas Gerais Faculty of Philosophy and Human Sciences, Belo Horizonte, 1992), 14.

64. R. Bastide, "A imprensa negra," 142.

65. Ibid.

66. Ibid., 144.

67. F. Fernandes, *A integração do negro*, 310.

68. R. Bastide, "A imprensa negra," 142.

69. Júlio Braga, *Na gamela do feitiço. Repressão e resistência nos candomblés da Bahia* (Salvador, Brazil: CEAO; Salvador, Brazil: UFBA, 1995); Nei Lopes, *Dicionário Banto do Brasil* (Rio de Janeiro: Centro Cultural José Bonifácio, 1996); Carlos Caroso and Jéferson Bacelar, *Brasil. Um país de negros?* (Rio de Janeiro: Pallas; Salvador, Brazil: CEAO; Salvador, Brazil: UFBA, 1999); C. Caroso and J. Bacelar, *Faces da tradição afro-brasileira* (Rio de Janeiro: Pallas; Salvador, Brazil: CEAO; Salvador, Brazil: UFBA, 1999).

70. Caetana Maria Damasceno, "Em casa de enforcado não se fala de corda. Notas sobre a construção social da 'boa' aparência no Brasil," in *Tirando a máscara*, 165–99.

71. A. Nascimento, "Memories from Exile," 29–36, 96–97; A. Nascimento, *Brazil, Mixture or Massacre: Essays in the Genocide of a Black People*, 2nd ed. (Dover, MA: Majority Press, 1989), 81. [First published 1979 by Afrodiaspora Press.].

72. Michael Mitchell, "Racial Consciousness and the Political Attitudes and Behavior of Blacks in São Paulo, Brazil" (PhD diss., Princeton University, 1977), 143; see also F. Fernandes, *A integração do negro*, 381–86.

73. The information presented in this summary list of black organizations was taken from several issues of *Quilombo*, including the following: "Estados em Revista: São Paulo — Frente Negra Trabalhista: Rio Grande do Sul — União dos Homens de Cor: Bahia — A Denúncia do Prof. Thales de Azevedo," *Quilombo* 1, no. 1, December 1948, 3; "Sociedade Recreativa Floresta Aurora," *Quilombo* 1, no. 3, June 1949, 2; "Branco de alma preta," *Quilombo* 1, no. 3, June 1949, 3. For information on black organizations of the time, see also A. Nascimento, *O negro revoltado*.

74. Interview with Solano Trindade. "O Teatro Experimental do Negro e a cultura do povo contra o despejo do conjunto de cor," "Problemas e Aspirações do negro brasileiro," *Diário Trabalhista* 1, no. 188, August 25, 1946, 4. See also A. Nascimento, *O negro revoltado*; Luiz de Aguiar Costa Pinto, *O negro no Rio de Janeiro* (São Paulo: Companhia Editora Nacional, 1953).

75. "José Bernardo, Candidato à Câmara Estadual do Rio — Uma vida dedicada ao benefício da coletividade — Atividades do Centro E. Jesus do Himalaya," *Quilombo* 2, no. 10, June–July 1950, 5.

76. "Ministros, senadores e diplomatas negros. Objetivos da 'Uagacê' do Distrito Federal na palavra do Snr. Joviano Severino de Melo," *Quilombo* 1, no. 3, June 1949, 8.

77. C. E. Degler, *Neither Black nor White*, 182.

78. E. O. Oliveira, *A imprensa negra*, catalogue; statement by Aristides Barbosa, *Frente Negra brasileira*, ed. Quilombhoje, 29–33.

79. "São Paulo — Frente Negra Trabalhista," *Quilombo* 1, no. 1, December 1948, 3.

80. E. O. Oliveira, *A imprensa negra*, catalogue.

81. A. Nascimento, ed., *Quilombo. Edição fac-similar do jornal dirigido por Abdias Nascimento* (São Paulo: Editora 34, 2003).

82. J. C. Leite, transcription from dialogues at symposium on the eightieth anniversary of the abolition of slavery in Brazil organized by Abdias Nascimento at the request of the editors of the journal *Cadernos Brasileiros*, Rio de Janeiro, RJ, Brazil, May 13, 1958. Published in a one-volume book entitled *80 anos de abolição* (Rio de Janeiro: Cadernos Brasileiros, 1968), 28.

83. Sebastião Rodrigues Alves, *80 anos de abolição*, 25.

84. A. Nascimento, "O negro revoltado," 37, 51.

85. Ibid., 24, 53–54.

86. Alice Linhares Uruguay, "Artes plásticas. Cristo negro," *Jornal do Brasil* 65, no. 147, June 26, 1955, Section 5, p. 2.

87. "Pelourinho. Discriminação nas obras sociais," *Quilombo* 1, no. 2, May 1949, 8.

88. Haroldo Costa, "Queremos estudar," *Quilombo* 1, no. 1, December 1948, 4.

89. Chapter 5 explores TEN's activity in more detail.

90. "Grupo dos novos," *Quilombo*, 1, no. 4, July 1949, 7; H. Costa, "As origens do Brasiliana," in *Dionysos*, no. 28. Special issue, *Teatro Experimental do Negro*, ed. Ricardo Gaspar Müller, 139–43 (Brasília: Ministry of Culture Scenic Arts Foundation, 1988).

91. Manuel Diégues, Jr., "A África na vida e na cultura do Brasil," in "Negro brasileiro negro." Special issue, *Revista do Patrimônio Histórico e Artístico Nacional* 25, ed. Joel Rufino dos Santos (1997): 23.

92. "Close-up: Os Solano Trindade," *Quilombo* 1, no. 4, July 1949, 2.

93. Interview with S. Trindade, 4.

94. A. Nascimento, interview with Elisa Larkin Nascimento, June 14, 1996.

95. "Close-up: Os Solano Trindade," *Quilombo* 1, no. 4, July 1949, 2.

96. A. Nascimento, "Memories from Exile," 29–30; Raimundo Souza Dantas and S. R. Alves, *80 anos de abolição*, 49–50.

97. As this book goes to press in 2006, affirmative action policies are being contested by intellectuals who use these arguments and receive substantial attention from the media and the press.

98. A. Nascimento, "Memories from Exile," 39; letter to Congressman Antonio José da Silva, President of the PTB's Regional Directorate, communicating the formation of the Black Labor Directorate, Rio de Janeiro, November 28, 1946 (original in the archives of A. Nascimento, IPEAFRO—Afro-Brazilian Studies and Research Institute, Rio de Janeiro).

99. A. Nascimento, *O negro revoltado*, 59–61.

100. Letter from the PSD dated February 10, 1946; letter from the UDN dated December 27, 1945; letter from the PCB dated December 19, 1945; ibid., 38.

101. Ibid.; A. Nascimento, "Memories from Exile," 33–35; Federal Republic of Brazil, *Anais da Assembléia Constituinte*, 3, 25th Session (March 14, 1946), 414.

102. Federal Republic of Brazil, Federal Constitution of 1934, articles 138(b), 212 (6), and 145.

103. Federal Republic of Brazil, *Anais da Assembléia Constituinte*, 3, 25th Session (March 14, 1946), 409.

104. On May 13, 1946, Congressman Claudino José da Silva made the following statement at the special session in celebration of the anniversary of the abolition of slavery: "The National Constituent Assembly could very well insert into our Carta Magna a democratic provision ... assuring to all, whites or blacks, the broadest possible participation in national life." Brazil, *Anais da Assembléia Constituinte*, 9 (May 1946), 61st Session (May 13, 1946), 32–33.

105. A. Nascimento, "Memories from Exile," 34–35.

106. Ibid., 43–45; A. Nascimento, "O negro revoltado," 25–27 and photo insert (no page numbers).

107. A. Nascimento, "Memories from Exile," 43; A. Nascimento, "O negro revoltado," 27; A. Nascimento, *O negro revoltado*, 58–59 (text of the Open Letter).

108. Federal Republic of Brazil, Lei no. 1.390 (July 3, 1951) (Brasília, DF: *Diário Oficial da União*, 10 July 1951). Available at http://www.planalto.gov.br/ccivil_03/Leis/L1390.htm.

109. Afonso Arinos, speech at the Chamber of Deputies session of August 25, 1950, in *Afonso Arinos no Congresso. Cem discursos parlamentares*, ed. Afonso Arinos Filho (Brasília: Senado Federal, Gabinete da Presidência, 1999), 144.

110. M. G. Hanchard, *Orpheus and Power: The Movimento Negro of rio de Janeiro and São Paulo, Brazil, 1945–1988* (Princeton: Princeton University Press, 1994), 181n15.

111. In 1888, when Brazil was still an Empire and Emperor Dom Pedro II was in Europe for medical treatment, his daughter Princess Isabel, as Imperial Regent, faced an untenable political situation and promulgated the so-called Golden Law, a decree providing simply that slavery was declared abolished. Brazil was the last nation in the West to abolish slavery. For information on slavery in Brazil, see Robert Edgar Conrad, *Children of God's Fire: A Documentary History of Black Slavery in Brazil* (Princeton: Princeton University Press, 1983).

112. Interview with A. Arinos in the major Rio de Janeiro daily *Ultima Hora*, December 14, 1951.

113. "Declara o deputado Gilberto Freyre. Dois racismos despontam no Brasil," *Tribuna da Imprensa* 2, no. 173, July 19, 1950, pp. 1, 3.

114. Statement by A. Barbosa, Quilombhoje, ed., *Frente Negra brasileira*, 29–33.

115. Carlos de Assumpção, *Protesto. Poemas* (São Paulo: Carlos de Assumpção, 1982), 41–49.

116. Alberto Guerreiro Ramos, *Introdução crítica à sociologia brasileira* (Rio de Janeiro: Andes, 1957), 162. Marcos Chor Maio studies the negotiation and development of the UNESCO research project in his PhD dissertation, "A história do projeto UNESCO: estudos raciais e ciências sociais no Brasil" (PhD diss., University Research Institute of the State of Rio de Janeiro, Candido Mendes University, 1997).

117. Editorial, "A Conferência Nacional do Negro," *Quilombo* 1, no. 2, May 1949, 1.

118. Donald Pierson recorded this speech in his book *Negroes in Brazil—A Study of Race Contact in Bahia* (Carbondale: Southern Illinois University Press, 1967), 228.

119. A. Nascimento, "O negro revoltado," 41–43.

120. "Conferência Nacional do Negro," *Quilombo* 2, no. 3, June 1949, 6–7.

121. Ibid.; A. Nascimento, "O negro revoltado," 41–43.

122. "Primeiro Congresso do Negro brasileiro," *Quilombo*, 2, no. 6, February 1950, 10.

123. A. Nascimento, "Primeiro Congresso do Negro brasileiro," *Quilombo* 2, no. 5, January 1950, 1.

124. "Primeiro Congresso do Negro brasileiro," *Quilombo* 2, no. 6, February 1950, 3.

125. A. Nascimento, "Inaugurando o Congresso do Negro," *Quilombo* 2, no. 10, June–July 1950, 1; A. Nascimento, "Primeiro Congresso do Negro brasileiro," *Quilombo* 2, no. 5, January 1950, 1. Emphasis added.

126. Édison Carneiro, *Negros Bantus. Notas de etnografia religiosa e de folclore* (Rio de Janeiro: Civilização brasileira, 1937). L. A. Costa Pinto had written an anthropological piece called Struggles in Families that was later placed seriously in question. A. Guerrreiro Ramos, "Foi acusado de plágio no seu livro *Lutas de família*," *O Jornal* 35, no. 10, January 17, 1954, magazine section, 1, 7.

127. Darcy Ribeiro, *Os índios e a civilização. A integração das populações indígenas no Brasil moderno* (Rio de Janeiro: Civilização Moderna, 1970); D. Ribeiro, *O processo civilizatório. Etapas da evolução sociocultural* (Rio de Janeiro: Civilização brasileira, 1975); D. Ribeiro, *Configurações histórico-culturais dos povos americanos* (Rio de Janeiro: Civilização brasileira, 1975).

128. É. Carneiro, *80 anos de abolição*, 83–84.

129. L. A. Costa Pinto, *O negro no Rio de Janeiro*, 270–78, 284, 332–33.

130. Ibid., 19–41.

131. A. Nascimento, *O negro revoltado*, 293–94.

132. A. Nascimento, *O negro revoltado*, 27.

133. Ibid., 283–93.

134. Ibid., 290–91.

135. Ibid., 291–92.

136. Ibid., 158–59.

137. R. Bastide and F. Fernandes, *Brancos e negros em São Paulo*, 2nd ed. (São Paulo: Companhia Editora Nacional, 1959); Thales Azevedo, *As elites de cor* (São Paulo: Companhia Editora Nacional, 1955); René Ribeiro, *Religião e relações raciais no Brasil* (Rio de Janeiro: Ministry of Education and Culture Documentation Services, 1956).

138. L. A. Costa Pinto, *O negro no Rio de Janeiro*, 270–78, 284, 332–33.

139. A. Nascimento, "O negro revoltado," 17–18. A. Nascimento, interview with Elisa Larkin Nascimento, June 14, 1996; S. R. Alves, interview with Elisa Larkin Nascimento, July 20, 1977.

140. A. Nascimento, *O negro revoltado*, 71–72.

141. A. Nascimento, "Nós, os negros, e a UNESCO," *Panfleto*, no. 5 (September 1953): 23; A. Nascimento, "A UNESCO e as relações de raça," *Panfleto*, no. 14 (December 1953): 8; A. Guerreiro Ramos, "Interpelação à UNESCO," *O Jornal* 35, no. 10222, January 3, 1954, 2.

142. A. Nascimento, "O negro revoltado," 16–17.

143. L. A. Costa Pinto, "Ciência social e ideologia racial (Esclarecendo intencionais obscuridades)," *O Jornal* 35, no. 10222, July 10, 1954, 2.

144. M. Barbosa, introduction to *Frente Negra Brasileira*, by Quilombhoje, 10–12.

145. A. Guerreiro Ramos, "O negro desde dentro," in *Introdução crítica (1957)*, 198–99.

146. Ricardo Gaspar Müller, "Identidade e cidadania. O Teatro Experimental do Negro," in *Dionysos*. Special issue, *Scenic Arts Foundation Journal/ Ministry of Culture* 28, *Teatro Experimental do Negro*, ed. R. G. Müller (Brasília, 1988); R. G. Müller, "Teatro, política e educação. A experiência histórica do Teatro Experimental do Negro (TEN) (1945/1968)," in *Educação Popular afro-brasileira*, Black Thought in Education Series 5, ed. Ivan Costa Lima, Jeruse Romão, and Sônia Maria Silveira, 13–31 (Florianópolis: Núcleo de Estudos Negros NEN, 1999); Maria Angelica da Motta Maués, "Negro sobre negro. A questão racial no pensamento das elites negras brasileiras" (PhD diss., IUPERJ, Candido Mendes University, 1997), 170–314; M. G. Hanchard, *Orpheus and Power: The Movimento Negro of rio de Janeiro and São Paulo, Brazil, 1945–1988* (Princeton: Princeton University Press, 1994), 106–8, cites these studies without mentioning Costa Pinto but his conclusions are couched in the terms of Costa Pinto's analysis, on which those studies are based.

147. R. G. Müller, "Identidade e cidadania," 7.

148. A. Nascimento, "O negro revoltado," 16–18; A. Nascimento, "Nós, os negros, e a UNESCO," *Panfleto*, no. 5 (September 1953): 23; A. Nascimento, "A UNESCO e as relações de raça," *Panfleto*, no. 14 (December 1953): 8; A. Guerreiro Ramos, "Interpelação à UNESCO," 2.

CHAPTER 5

1. For an overview of this cultural moment, see Carlos Guilherme Motta, *Ideologia da cultura brasileira. Pontos de partida para uma revisão histórica* (São Paulo: Ática, 1977).

2. Ibid., 110–37.

3. On TEN's theatrical production, see Abdias Nascimento, ed., *Dramas para negros e prólogo para brancos* (Rio de Janeiro: Teatro Experimental do Negro, 1961) and *Teatro Experimental do Negro. Testemunhos* (Rio de Janeiro: GRD, 1966); A. Nascimento, *Sortilege (Black Mystery)*, trans. Peter Lownds (Chicago: Third World Press, 1978); A. Nascimento, *Sortilégio (mistério negro)* (Rio de Janeiro: Teatro Experimental do Negro, 1959); A. Nascimento, "An Open Letter to the First World Festival of Negro Arts," *Presence Africaine: Cultural Review of the Negro World* 30, no. 58, English Edition, 208–18; (Second Quarterly, 1966); A. Nascimento, "Carta aberta a Dacar," *Tempo brasileiro* 4, no. 10: 15–17 (September 1966); A. Nascimento, *Sortilégio II. mistério negro de Zumbi Redivivo* (Rio de Janeiro: Paz e Terra, 1979); A. Nascimento, "Teatro Experimental do Negro. Trajetória e reflexões," in *Negro brasileiro Negro*, ed. Joel Rufino dos Santos, special issue, *Revista do Patrimônio Histórico. Artístico Nacional* 25: 71–81 (1997). Cited hereafter as "TEN. Trajetória."

4. In 1821, The African Company was organized in New York. Ira Aldridge and other black Shakespearean actors who were involved in the theatrical scene created the Astor Place Coloured Tragedy Company. In 1896, the first training school for black performers was founded. The beginning of the twentieth century witnessed the creation of the Pekin Stock Company of Chicago, as well as the Lafayette Players, the Krigwa Players, and the Harlem Experimental Theater in New York. In the 1930s and 1940s, Langston Hughes and Richard Wright were outstanding among the many black authors who created their works as black theater institutions were being developed, among them the Federal Theater Project, the Negro People's Theater, and the Rose McClendon Players. Later, in 1959, Lorraine Hansberry heralded the theater of the Civil Rights era with her prize-winning play, *A Raisin in the Sun*. In the 1960s and 1970s, with the Black Power, Black Nationalism, and Black Consciousness

movements gaining momentum, Amiri Baraka (formerly Le Roi Jones), Ed Bullins, Barbara Ann Teer, Val Ward, James Baldwin, Sonia Sanchez, and other dramatists emerged, and theatrical projects such as the Negro Ensemble, New Lafayette Theater, Black Theater Alliance, National Black Theater, and Kuumba Workshop reflected the outstanding talents in the black community.

5. Leda Maria Martins, A cena em sombras (São Paulo: Perspectiva, 1995); Flora Mancuso Edwards, "The Theater of the Black Diaspora: A Comparative Study of Black Drama in Brazil, Cuba and the United States" (PhD diss., New York University, 1975); Duro Lapido et al., Teatro Africano (Havana: Instituto Cubano del Libro; Havana: Editorial Arte e Literatura, 1975).

6. For information on this phenomenon, see Paul Carter Harrison, ed., Kuntu Drama: Plays of the African Continuum (New York: Grove Press, 1974); P. C. Harrison, The Drama of Nommo (New York: Grove Press, 1972); Scott Kennedy, In Search of African Theatre (New York: Scribner's, 1973); William B. Branch, Crosswinds: An Anthology of Black Dramatists in the Diaspora (Bloomington: Indiana University Press, 1993).

7. L. M. Martins, A cena em sombras.

8. A. Nascimento, "Sortilege II: Zumbi Returns," trans. Elisa Larkin Nascimento, in Crosswinds: An Anthology of Black Dramatists in the Diaspora, ed. W. B. Branch (Bloomington: Indiana University Press, 1993); A. Nascimento, Sortilege (Black Mystery), trans. P. Lownds (Chicago: Third World Press, 1978), repr. "African-Brazilian Literature," special issue, ed. Carolyn Richardson Durham, L. M. Martins, Phyllis Peres, and Charles H. Rowell, Callaloo: Journal of African and African-American Arts and Letters 18, no. 4 (1995): 821–62.

9. L. M. Martins, A cena em sombras, 86.

10. A. Nascimento, "TEN. Trajetória," 72.

11. Ibid.

12. Ibid.

13. Ibid., 71.

14. Ibid., 73.

15. Ibid., 73.

16. "Há preconceito de côr no teatro?" Interview with Nelson Rodrigues, Quilombo 1, no. 1, December 1948, 1, 6.

17. A. Nascimento, "TEN. Trajetória," 75–76.

18. A. Nascimento, O Quilombismo (Petrópolis, Brazil: Editora Vozes, 1980), 68.

19. This dimension has been noted by specialists from the Afro-Brazilian social movement. Ivan Costa Lima, Jeruse Romão, and Sônia Maria Silveira, eds., Educação popular afro-brasileira, Black Thought in Education Series 5 (Florianópolis, Brazil: Nucleus of Black Studies NEN, 1999).

20. Daniel Caetano, "Teatro Experimental do Negro. Origem—Nenhum Auxílio do Governo—O'Neill para os negros," interview with A. Nascimento, Diário de Notícias, December 11, 1946.

21. A. Nascimento, "Uma experiência social e estética," in Teatro Experimental do Negro, 123.

22. A. Nascimento, "TEN. Trajetória," 73.

23. Ibid., 72–73.

24. A. Nascimento, "Memories from Exile," in Africans in Brazil: A Pan-African Perspective, A. Nascimento and E. L. Nascimento (Trenton, NJ: Africa World Press, 1992), 29–31.

25. José do Patrocínio was a foremost black abolitionist; May 13th is abolition day in Brazil. Favela Hill (Morro da Favela) is the one that first received the name favela, later generalized to designate shantytown communities built on hills.

26. "O povo reage contra o analfabetismo," *Diário Trabalhista*, June 28, 1946, 4.

27. Júlio Roberio, "Instrui e valoriza o negro numa compreensiva campanha cultural," *O Jornal* 31, no. 8870, March 30, 1949, Section 2, 2.

28. Alberto Guerreiro Ramos, "Um herói da negritude," *Diário de Notícias* 22, no. 9081, April 6, 1952, 1, repr. *Teatro Experimental do Negro*, 105.

29. Iray Carone, and Maria Aparecida da Silva Bento, eds., *Psicologia social do racismo. Estudos sobre branquitude e branqueamento, no Brasil* (Petrópolis, Brazil: Vozes, 2002). See also Chapter 3.

30. A. Guerreiro Ramos, "Notícia sôbre o I Congresso do Negro brasileiro," *A Manhã* 10, no. 2817, October 1, 1950, 2. See also A. Guerreiro Ramos, "Um herói da negritude," 106. Later, this proposal would be taken up again by Abdias Nascimento at the Faculty Seminar of the University of Ife, Nigéria, and at the Colloquium of the second World Festival of Black and African Arts and Culture (Lagos, Nigeria, 1977). A. Nascimento, "The Function of Art in the Development of Afro-Brazilian Culture: The Contemporary Situation," in *Faculty Seminar Series* 1, no. 1, ed. O. Oyelaran (Ife: University of Ile-Ife, Department of African Languages and Literature, 1977), 121–22.

31. Among the examples are Ana Amélia Carneiro de Mendonça, Nelson Rodrigues, Cacilda Becker, Bibi Ferreira, Olga Navarro, Maria Della Costa, Ziembinski, Jaime Costa, Leo Jusi, Willy Keller, Santa Rosa, Mário de Murtas, Péricles Leal, Carlos Drummond de Andrade, Marques Rebelo, Henrique Pongetti, Adonias Filho, Fernando Góes, Dante Laytano, Austregésilo de Athayde, Dom Hélder Câmara, Hamilton Nogueira, Thiers Martins Moreira, Gerardo Mello Mourão, Efraín Tomás Bó, Raul Nass, José Francisco Coelho, Napoleão Lopes Filho, Ricardo Werneck de Aguiar, Luiza Barreto Leite, Rosário Fusco, Enrico Bianco, Bruno Giorgi, José Medeiros; Iberê Camargo, Volpi, Manabu Mabe, Portinari, Djanira, Inimá, Ana Letícia, Lóio Pérsio, Nelson Nóbrega, Clóvis Graciano, Quirino Campofiorito, Guerreiro Ramos, Florestan Fernandes, Roger Bastide, Alberto Latorre de Faria, Roland Corbisier, Maria Yedda Leite Castro, R. Magalhães Jr. A. Nascimento, interview with Elisa Larkin Nascimento, June 14, 1996.

32. The volume *Teatro Experimental do Negro*. Testemunhos is a collection of articles from the press on TEN's activities, mostly critiques of its theatrical presentations.

33. A. Nascimento, "Memories from Exile," 39.

34. A. Nascimento, "O T. E. N. dirige-se aos partidos políticos," *Quilombo* 2, no. 7–8, March–April 1950, 5.

35. "Manifesto político dos negros fluminenses," *Quilombo* 2, no. 7–8, March–April 1950, 5.

36. Alcides Marques de Paiva, Antônio Augusto de Azevedo, Hortêncio de Souza, Moacyr Brum, et al., "Manifesto político dos negros fluminenses," ibid.

37. "José Bernardo, "Candidato à câmara estadual do Rio—Uma vida dedicada ao benefício da coletividade—Atividades do Centro E. Jesus do Himalaya," *Quilombo* 2, no. 10, June–July 1950, 5; "Isaltino Veiga dos Santos. Um homem de cor na chapa do P. D. C.," *Quilombo* 2, no. 10, June–July 1950, 5; "Geraldo Campos de Oliveira. Candidato a deputado por São Paulo," *Quilombo* 2, no. 7–8, March–April 1950, 5; "José Alcides na chapa de vereadoes do P. S. D.," *Quilombo* 2, no. 10, June–July 1950, 5; "Candidato a deputado dos negros paulistas," *Quilombo* 2, January 5, 1950, 2.

38. "' ... Mas como a cor não pega' ... Poderíamos ter uma jovem negra no concurso da Miss Universo?" *O Radical* 18, no. 5, July 27, 1948, 1.

39. Neusa dos Santos Souza, ed., *Tornar-se negro* (Rio de Janeiro: Graal, 1983); Consuelo Dores Silva, *Negro, qual é o seu nome?* (Belo Horizonte, Brazil: Mazza, 1995); Nilma Lino Gomes, *A mulher negra que vi de perto* (Belo Horizonte, Brazil: Mazza, 1995); Conceição Corrêa das Chagas, *Negro. Uma identidade em construção* (Petrópolis, Brazil: Vozes, 1996).

40. "Catty, a 'Boneca de Pixe' de 1950," *Quilombo* 2, no. 9, May 1948, 6.

41. José Leal, "Boneca de pixe," *O Cruzeiro* 20, no. 33, June 5, 1948, 30–32.

42. A. Nascimento, interview with Elisa Larkin Nascimento, June 14, 1996.

43. L. M. Martins, *A cena em sombras*, 79.

44. Ibid., 80.

45. A. Nascimento, "Memories from Exile," 40. This essay is a translation from A. Nascimento, "Depoimento," in *Memórias do exílio*, ed. Pedro Celso Uchoa Cavalcanti and Jovelino Ramos, 42 (Lisbon: Arcádia, 1976).

46. A. Nascimento, "O negro revoltado," in *O negro revoltado*, ed. A. Nascimento, 19 (Rio de Janeiro: GRD, 1968).

47. A. Nascimento, "Afro-Brazilian Art: A Liberating Spirit," *Black Art: An International Quarterly* 1, no. 1 (Fall 1976): 55, 59.

48. A. Nascimento, "Cristo negro," in *Teatro Experimental do Negro*, 148.

49. Alice Linhares Uruguay, "Cristo negro," *Jornal do Brasil*, June 26, 1955, Section 5 (Plastic Arts), 2.

50. Quirino Campofiorito, "Cristo de côr," *O Jornal*, 36, no. 10674, June 26, 1955, 2. Reprinted in *Teatro Experimental do Negro*, 143.

51. A. Guerreiro Ramos, "Semana do negro de 1955," *Diário de Notícias* 25, no. 9890, January 30, 1955, 2, repr. *Teatro Experimental do Negro*.

52. Guiomar Ferreira de Mattos, "O preconceito nos livros infantis," in *Teatro Experimental do Negro*, ed. A. Nascimento, 136–39.

53. Among the speakers were Flexa Ribeiro, then Guanabara State Secretary of Education, and later director of Education at UNESCO; the ambassador of Senegal Henri Senghor; Édison Carneiro, Grande Otelo, Nelson Pereira dos Santos, Adonias Filho, Thiers Martins Moreira, Florestan Fernandes, Alceu Amoroso Lima (Tristão de Athayde), Raymundo Souza Dantas, José Pelegrini, Álvaro Dias, and R. Teixeira Leite. A. Nascimento, "Memories from Exile," 41–42.

54. The exhibition in Salvador was held as part of the Second World Conference of African and Diaspora Intellectuals (II CIAD), July 2006. E. L. Nascimento, ed., *Abdias Nascimento 90 Years—Living Memory* (Rio de Janeiro: IPEAFRO, 2006), 120.

55. "É preciso regulamentar o trabalho doméstico." Interview with Ruth de Souza. *A Manhã* 6, no. 1365, January 20, 1946, 3; A. Nascimento, interview with Elisa Larkin Nascimento, June 14, 1996.

56. See Chapter 4.

57. "O povo reage contra o analfabetismo," *Diário Trabalhista*, June 28, 1946, 4. See text above, and notes 24, 25, 26.

58. "Absurda a exclusão das domésticas de todas as leis trabalhistas!" *Diário Trabalhista*, July 5, 1946.

59. "É preciso regulamentar," 3.

60. "Absurda a exclusão."

61. Maria Nascimento, "O Congresso Nacional das mulheres e a regulamentação do trabalho doméstico," Coluna Fala a Mulher, *Quilombo* 1, no. 4, July 1949, 3.

62. "Precisam-se de escravas," *Quilombo* 1, no. 6, February 1950, 9.

63. "A regulamentação da profissão de doméstica," presentation by G. F. de Mattos and discussion by the plenary assembly, in A. Nascimento, *O negro revoltado*, 247–62.

64. M. Nascimento, "Crianças racistas," *Quilombo* 1, no. 1, December 9, 1948, 8.

65. M. Nascimento, "Infância agonizante," *Quilombo* 1, no. 2, May 9, 1949, 8.

66. M. Nascimento, "Instalado o Conselho Nacional das Mulheres Negras," *Quilombo* 2, no. 9, May 1950, 4.

67. M. Nascimento, "Infancia agonizante," Coluna Fala a Mulher, *Quilombo* 1, no. 2, May 9, 1949, 8.

68. "Fundado o ballet infantil do T.E.N.," *Quilombo* 2, no. 10, June–July 1950, 2.

69. "Expulsaram os negros," *Revista da Semana*, no. 36, September 7, 1946, 47–50; "Artistas do Teatro Experimental do Negro realizarão seus ensaios nas ruas da cidade, despejados do Teatro Fenix," *Diretrizes*, August 21, 1946; "Expulsos do Fênix, os artistas negros ensaiarão ao ar livre!" *Vanguarda*, August 26, 1946; "Teatro no meio da rua," *Folha Carioca*, August 20, 1946.

70. A. Nascimento, "Uma experiência social e estética," in *Teatro Experimental do Negro*, ed. A. Nascimento, 125.

71. A. Nascimento, "Memories from Exile," 31.

72. This excerpt in English is my own version based on a translation found at http://www.kirjasto.sci.fi/cesaire.htm. and on the translation to Portuguese by Lilian Pestre de Almeida, which she provided for the Abdias Nascimento 90 Years—Living Memory exhibition in 2004. English language publications of this work include Aimé Césaire, *Notebook of a Return to My Native Land.* (bilingual edition), trans. Mireille Rosello and Pritchard (Newcastle upon Tyne: Bloodaxe, 1995) and *Notebook of a Return to the Native Land*, trans. Clayton Eshleman and Annette Smith (Middletown. CN: Wesleyan University Press, 2001).

73. Among the authors whose names are associated with this movement are David Diop and Birago Diop of Senegal; Edouard Glissant of Martinique; Bernárd Dadier of the Ivory Coast; Jacques Roumain, René Depestre, Léon Laleau, and Jean-F. Biére of Haiti; Gilbert Gratiant and Etienne Loro of Martinique; Guy Tirolien and Paul Niger of Guadalupe; Jean-Joseph Rabéarivelo, Jean Rabémananjara, Flavien Ranaivo of Madagascar.

74. A. Nascimento, "An Open Letter to the First World Festival of Negro Arts," *Présence Africaine: Cultural Review of the Negro World* 30, no. 58, English Edition, (Second Quarterly, 1966): 208–18.

75. Jean-Paul Sartre, "Orfeu negro," trans. Ironides Rodrigues, *Quilombo* 2, no. 5, January 1950, 6–7.

76. Roger Bastide, "O movimento negro francês," Democracia Racial, *Quilombo* 2, no. 9, May 1950, 3.

77. Nestor R. Ortiz Oderigo, "Prólogo à antologia negra de Blaise Cendrars," trans. I. Rodrigues, *Quilombo* 2, no. 9, May 1950, 8.

78. Zilá Bernd, *A questão da negritude* (São Paulo: Brasiliense, 1984), 54.

79. A. Guerreiro Ramos, "Um herói da negritude," 128–29.

80. Definition of the words "preto" and "negro," *Novo dicionário da língua portuguesa* [New Dictionary of the Portuguese Language], 6th ed., ed. Ubiratan Rosa (São Paulo: Companhia Brasil Editora, 1954). This definition is exactly the same in the more recent and most authoritative current dictionary: Aurélio Buarque de Hollanda Ferreira, ed. *Dicionário Aurélio eletrônico*, Século XXI, CD Rom Version 3.0 (Rio de Janeiro, Nova Fronteira, November 1999).

81. Ricardo Franklin Ferreira, *Afro-descendente. Identidade em construção* (Rio de Janeiro: Pallas; São Paulo: Educ; São Paulo: FAPESP, 2000), 16–20.

82. See, for example, the editorials transcribed in this chapter and Fernando Sabino, "Semente de Ódio," *Diário Carioca*, July 16, 1949, 3.

83. A. Nascimento, *O negro revoltado*, 52.

84. Ibid., 53.

85. Ibid., 50–51.

86. A. Guerreiro Ramos, "Um herói da negritude," 130.

87. Ibid., 133–34.

88. Aimé Césaire, "What Is Negritude to Me," in *African Presence in the Americas*, ed. Carlos Moore, Tanya R. Sanders, and Shawna Moore , 16 (Trenton, NJ: Africa World Press; Trenton, NJ: The African Heritage Foundation, 1995).

89. Kabengele Munanga, *Negritude. Usos e sentidos*, 47.

90. Ibid., 49.

91. R. F. Ferreira, *Afro-descendente*, 83–84.

92. A. Césaire, "What Is Negritude to Me," 19.

93. Léopold Sédar Senghor, "Negritude and the Civilization of the Universal," in *African Presence in the Americas*, 29.

94. Léon Daudet cited in L. S. Senghor, "Negritude and the Civilization," 29–30.

95. Muniz Sodré, *Claros e escuros. Identidade, povo e mídia no Brasil* (Petrópolis, Brazil: Vozes, 1999), 169.

96. Anne Baldassari, ed., *Le miroir noir, Picasso, sources photographiques, 1900–1928* (Paris: Musée Picasso, 1997).

97. L. S. Senghor, "Negritude and the Civilization," 31.

98. A. Nascimento, "Espírito e fisionomia do Teatro Experimental do Negro," in *Teatro Experimental do Negro*, ed. A. Nascimento, 79.

99. A. Guerreiro Ramos, *Introdução crítica à sociologia brasileira* (Rio de Janeiro: Editorial Andes, 1957), 148–65; 171–99; A. Guerreiro Ramos, "Teoria e Prática do Psicodrama," *Quilombo* 2, no. 6, February 1950, 6–7; A. Guerreiro Ramos, "Teoria e Prática do Sociodrama," *Quilombo* 2, no. 7/8, March–April 1950, 9.

100. "Instituto Nacional do Negro," *Quilombo* 1, no. 3, June 1949, 11.

101. A. Guerreiro Ramos, "Teoria e prática do psicodrama," 6.

102. A. Nascimento, transcription from dialogues at symposium on the eightieth anniversary of the abolition of slavery in Brazil organized by Abdias Nascimento at the request of the journal *Cadernos Brasileiros*, Rio de Janeiro, RJ, Brazil, May 13, 1950. Published as a one-volume book entitled *80 anos de abolição* (Rio de Janeiro: Cadernos Brasileiros, 1968), 21.

103. A. Guerreiro Ramos, *Introdução crítica* (1957), 153.

104. Part Three of his book is entitled "Documents of an Activist Sociology." A. Guerreiro Ramos, "Documentos de uma sociologia militante," in *Introdução crítica* (1957), 213–54. See J. R. dos Santos, "O negro como lugar," in A. Guerreiro Ramos, *Introdução crítica à sociologia brasileira*, 2nd ed., 19–30 (Rio de Janeiro: Federal University of Rio de Janeiro Press, 1995), 21; Lúcia Lippi Oliveira, "A sociologia como saber de salvação," Chapter 2 in, *A sociologia do Guerreiro* (Rio de Janeiro: UFRJ, 1995), 39–57.

105. Guerreiro Ramos and Hélio Jaguaribe were the outstanding leaders of the Itatiaia Group, composed of intellectuals who were mostly public servants from the Getúlio Vargas administration and who made it their mission to "think Brazil," engaging in the study, research, and planning of Brazilian national development issues. See J. R. dos Santos, "O negro como lugar," 20–23.

106. J. R. dos Santos, "O negro como lugar," 21.

107. A. Guerreiro Ramos, *Introdução crítica (1957)*, 210.

108. Ibid., 17–71; 123–65.

109. Clóvis Brigagão, "Da sociologia em mangas de camisa à túnica inconsútil do saber," in A. Guerreiro Ramos, *Introdução crítica* (1995).

110. L. M. Martins, *Cena em sombras*, 81.

111. A. Nascimento, *O negro revoltado*, 44.

112. A. Guerreiro Ramos, *Introdução crítica (1957)*, 163.

113. Luiz de Aguiar Costa Pinto, *O negro no rio de Janeiro* (São Paulo: Companhia Editora Nacional,1953). A second edition was published in 1998 by the Federal University of Rio de Janeiro Press, but the following references are to the first edition.

114. Ibid., 278.

115. Ibid., 277.

116. Ibid., 37, 39, 221, 225, 227, 299.

117. Ibid., 37, 39, 337.

118. Ibid., 37, 39, 225.

119. Ibid., 286.

120. Ibid., 291, emphasis in the original.

121. Ibid., 283.

122. Ibid., 284.

123. Ibid., 303.

124. Ibid., 295–96.

125. A. Guerreiro Ramos, "Interpelação à UNESCO," *O Jornal* 35, no. 10222, January 3, 1954, 2; Ironides Rodrigues, interview with Elisa Larkin Nascimento, 1977; Sebastião Rodrigues Alves, excerpt from lecture given at Brazilian Press Association 1953, in A. Nascimento, "O negro revoltado," 17; A. Nascimento, interview with Elisa Larkin Nascimento, 1983; G. F. de Mattos, interview with Elisa Larkin Nascimento, 1983; A. Nascimento, "O negro revoltado," 15–18; A. Nascimento, "Nós, os negros, e a UNESCO," *Panfleto*, no. 5, September 1953, 23; A. Nascimento, "A UNESCO e as relações de raça," *Panfleto*, no. 14, December 1953, 8; A. Nascimento, interview with Elisa Larkin Nascimento, June 14, 1996.

126. L. A. Costa Pinto, *O negro no rio de Janeiro*, 292, 333.

127. Ibid., 26, emphasis in the original.

128. Ibid., 268, 337.

129. A. Guerreiro Ramos, *O drama de ser dois* (Salvador: A. Guerreiro Ramos, 1937). It is instructive to compare Costa Pinto's reference to this book of poetry with that of sociologist Lúcia Lippi Oliveira of the Federal University of Rio de Janeiro, who devoted her graduate studies to Guerreiro Ramos's life and work. She asserts that in the 1930s, when he wrote *The Drama of Being Two*, Guerreiro Ramos was preoccupied with the dichotomy between a "personalist and communitarian revolution à la Mounier" and "the materialist revolution configured by fascism as well as communism," which he examines in his 1939 book *Introduction to Culture*. This dichotomy involves the oppositions of "culture versus civilization; person versus individual; organic versus mechanical; the tragic sentiment of life versus the bourgeois sentiment of existence; suffering versus resentment." Lippi Oliveira describes his book of poetry, *The Drama of Being Two*, as expressing "this same division of man between a natural and a supernatural being , between man and angel." Guerreiro Ramos writes: "Every man is an angel, in exile. ... [M]an finds himself between two worlds: the exterior world and the interior world." For this passage, she gives the following citation: A. Guerreiro Ramos, "O Problema do Humanismo," *Revista Norte* (1938): 1; L. L. Oliveira, *A sociologia do Guerreiro* (Rio de Janeiro: Federal University of Rio de Janeiro Press, 1995), 29–30, 35.

130. A. Guerreiro Ramos, "Interpelação à UNESCO," 2.

131. Oliveira Vianna, *Populações meridionais do Brasil* (São Paulo: Revista do Brasil; São Paulo: Monteiro Lobato, 1920), 109; Raymundo Nina Rodrigues, *As raças humanas e a responsabilidade penal no Brasil* (Salvador, Brazil: Aguiar e Souza; Salvador, Brazil: Progresso, 1957), 117. See Chapter 3nn52–54.

132. A. Nascimento, "Memories from Exile," 31–32; interview with Elisa Larkin Nascimento, June 14, 1996.

133. R. Bastide, "A imprensa negra do Estado de São Paulo," in R. Bastide, *Estudos afro-brasileiros*, 129–56 (São Paulo: Perspectiva, 1973), 130.

134. Interview with Solano Trindade, *Diário Trabalhista* 1, no. 188, August 25, 1946, 4.

135. L. A. Costa Pinto, *O negro no rio de Janeiro*, 337–38.

136. Ibid., 338, emphasis in the original.

137. Writing in English, Michael George Hanchard cites studies based on Costa Pinto's work and endorses their conclusions about the supposedly elitist and contradictory nature of TEN. M. G. Hanchard, *Orpheus and Power: The Movimento Negro of rio de Janeiro and São Paulo, Brazil, 1945–1988* (Princeton: Princeton University Press, 1994), 106–8.

138. Ricardo Gaspar Müller, "Nota introdutória," in *Teatro Experimental do Negro*, special issue, ed. R. G. Müller, *Dionysos. Revista da Fundacen/MinC* [Journal of the Scenic Arts Foundation, Ministry of Culture] 28, no. 7–8 (1988): 7.

139. Edélcio Mostaço, "O legado de Set," in *Teatro Experimental do Negro*, special issue, *Dionysos*, 53–64.

140. Júlio César Tavares, "Teatro Experimental do Negro. Contexto, estrutura e ação," in *Teatro Experimental do Negro*, special issue, *Dionysos*, 79–88.

141. Maria Angélica da Motta Maués, "Entre o branqueamento e a negritude. O TEN e o debate da questão racial," in *Teatro Experimental do Negro*, special issue, *Dionysos*, 92.

142. In her zeal to portray the elitist egotism of TEN's leadership, M. A. M. Maués goes further and describes Abdias Nascimento's "Open Letter to the Police Commissioner" as a move for personal promotion. She claims that this was the only case of discrimination denounced in the pages of *Quilombo*, which is a flagrant misrepresentation, given that every issue carried such denunciations. M. A. M. Maués, "Negro sobre negro. A questão racial no pensamento das elites negras brasileiras" (PhD diss., IUPERJ, Candido Mendes University, 1997), 187. For the text of the letter to the police commissioner, see A. Nascimento, *O negro revoltado*, 27, 58–59. See Chapter 4.

143. Interview with Solano Trindade, "Problemas e Aspirações do Negro Brasileiro," *Diário Trabalhista* 1, no. 188, August 25, 1946, 4.

144. C. Moore, T. R. Sanders, and S. Moore, eds. *African Presence in the Americas*; K. Munanga, *Negritude. Usos e sentidos* (São Paulo: Ática, 1986). See Chapter 1.

145. "The Black Experimental Theater ... is a field of psychological polarization in which there is being formed a social movement of vast proportions," A. Nascimento, "Espírito e fisionomia do TEN," lecture given at the Brazilian Press Association at the opening session of the National Conference of Blacks in May 1949, *Quilombo* 1, no. 3, June 1949, 11, reprinted in *Teatro Experimental do Negro*, 79. On the political pressure and the victories won by the black movement, see Antonio Sérgio Alfredo Guimarães and Lynn Huntley, eds., *Tirando a máscara. Ensaios sobre o racismo no Brasil* (São Paulo: Paz e Terra; Atlanta: Southern Education Foundation, 2000), 66–73, 203–36, 359–84; Luciana Jaccoud and Nathalie Beghin, *Desigualdades raciais no Brasil. Um balanço da intervenção governamental* (Brasília: IPEA, 2002), 55–64. The creation of the Special Secretariat of Policies for the Promotion of Racial Equality as part of the Presidential Cabinet in 2003, the institution of quota policies in over thirteen federal universities and of affirmative action policies in several public and private universities as well as government ministries, are among the other recent victories of this movement.

146. L. A. Costa Pinto, *O negro no rio de Janeiro*, 269.

147. Marcos Chor Maio, "Costa Pinto e a crítica ao 'Negro como espetáculo,'" foreword to L. A. Costa Pinto, *O negro no rio de Janeiro*, 2nd ed., 18–50 (Rio de Janeiro: Federal University of Rio de Janeiro Press, 1998).

148. A. Nascimento, "Nós, os negros, e a UNESCO," *Panfleto*, no. 5, September 1953, 23.

149. A. Nascimento, "O negro revoltado," 24.

150. A. Nascimento, *80 anos de abolição*, 22.

151. Antonio Sérgio Alfredo Guimarães, *Racismo e anti-racismo no Brasil* (São Paulo: University of São Paulo Foundation (FUSP); São Paulo: Editora 34, 1999), 212.

152. Ibid., 89.

153. One of CEPAL's main points of emphasis is "Equity and its relationship with the global process of development, both in the way productive structures and property condition the distribution of the fruits of development and how the latter affects economic structure and dynamics." "Acerca de la CEPAL / Historia de la CEPAL," CEPAL Web site http://www.eclac.org/cgi-bin/getprod.asp?xml=/noticias/paginas/0/21670/P21670.xml&xsl=/tpl/p18f-st.xsl&base=/tpl/top-bottom_acerca.xsl.

154. This allegation has been made, for example, against Governor Leonel Brizola of the Democratic Labor Party (PDT) by members of the Workers' Party (PT), who classify as a populist measure the creation of Integrated Centers for Public Education (CIEPs) by Brizola and his secretary Darcy Ribeiro in Rio de Janeiro State in 1983–1986 and 1991–1994. Yet the urgent need for improvement of access to quality full-day education, particularly for the mainly Afro-Brazilian poor, was evident and still persists.

155. João identifies TEN with a phase in which the movement denounced discrimination without seeking to develop ways to effectively overcome inequality, a goal that according to him was introduced in 1978 with the founding of the Unified Black Movement. R. F. Ferreira, *Afro-descendente*, 126–27, 131. See also Chapter 4.

156. M. A. M. Mauês, "Negro sobre negro," 171–83; M. A. M. Mauês, "Entre o branqueamento e a negritude"; R. G. Müller, "Identidade e cidadania," 13–15, 39–51.

157. Eduardo Silva, *Dom Obá II D'África, o príncipe do povo. Vida, tempo e pensamento de um homem livre de cor* (São Paulo: Companhia das Letras, 1997), 18. See Chapter 4.

158. A. Nascimento, "Espírito e fisionomia do TEN," 79–80.

159. A. Guerreiro Ramos, *Introdução crítica* (1957), 200–202.

160. A. Guerreiro Ramos, "Mulatos, negros e brancos reunidos," *Vanguarda* 28, no. 13.213, September 13, 1949, 3.

161. A. Nascimento, "Uma experiência social e estética," 123, my emphasis.

162. A. Nascimento, "Espírito e fisionomia do TEN," 79.

163. A. Nascimento, "O negro revoltado," 53.

164. Ironically, and almost certainly due to this self-identification as scientist, Guerreiro Ramos supported the second Declaration presented by the scientists at the closing session of the First Congress of Brazilian Blacks. A. Nascimento, *O negro revoltado*, 283–94. See Chapter 4.

165. A. Nascimento, "Espirito e fisionomia do TEN," 79.

166. A. Guerreiro Ramos, "O negro desde dentro," in *Teatro Experimental do Negro*, 134.

167. Édison Carneiro, "Como se desenrola uma festa de candomblé—Em Recife é Xangô e no Rio, Macumba," *Quilombo* 1, no. 1, December 1948, 4–5; É. Carneiro, "Liberdade de culto," *Quilombo* 2, no. 5, January 1950, 2, 7; É. Carneiro, "'Xangô' de Vicente Lima," *Quilombo* 2, no. 6, February 1950, 2; É. Carneiro, "O problema da liberdade de culto," *Quilombo* 2, no. 10, June–July 1950, 4, 11; Katherine Dunham, "O Estado dos cultos entre os povos deserdados," *Quilombo*, 2, no. 10, June–July 1950, 6–7, 10.

168. A. Guerreiro Ramos, "O negro desde dentro," 130–34.

169. A. Guerreiro Ramos, "O negro no Brasil e um exame de consciência," in *Teatro Experimental do Negro*, 83–89.

170. Ibid., 87.

171. A. Nascimento, "O Primeiro Congresso do Negro brasileiro," *Quilombo* 2, no. 5, January 1950, 1.

172. A. Guerreiro Ramos, "Nascimento's Artistic Faith," catalogue of Abdias Nascimento's exhibition of paintings at the Inner City Cultural Center, Los Angeles, February 1975, 2–4.

173. A. Nascimento, *Dramas para negros*, containing the following plays: *O filho pródigo* by Lúcio Cardoso; *O castigo de Oxalá* by Romeu Crusoé; *Auto da noiva* by Rosário Fusco; *Sortilégio (mistério negro)* by A. Nascimento; *Além do rio (Medea)* by Agostinho Olavo; *Filhos de santo* by José de Morais Pinho; *Aruanda* by Joaquim Ribeiro; *Anjo negro* by N. Rodrigues; *O emparedado* by Tasso da Silveira. In addition to these, Abdias Nascimento refers in his prologue to other plays also written for TEN or following in its path: *Orfeu da Conceição*, by Vinícius de Morais; *Um caso de Kelê*, by Fernando Campos; *O cavalo e o santo* by Augusto Boal; *Yansã, mulher de Xangô* by Zora Seljan; *Os irmãos negros* by Klaynér P. Velloso; *O processo do cristo negro* by Ariano Suassuna; *Caim e Abel* by Eva Ban; *Plantas Rasteiras* by José Renato; *Orfeu negro* by I. Rodrigues; *Pedro Mico* by Antônio Callado; *Gimba* by Gianfrancesco Guarnieri; *Chico-Rei* by Walmir Ayala.

174. A. Nascimento, *Sortilégio II. mistério negro de Zumbi redivivo* (Rio de Janeiro: Paz e Terra, 1979). The English language version is "Sortilege II: Zumbi Returns," trans. E. L. Nascimento, in *Crosswinds: An Anthology of Black Dramatists in the Diaspora*, ed. W. B. Branch (Bloomington: Indiana University Press, 1993).

175. A. Nascimento," Prefácio," in *Sortilégio II. mistério negro de Zumbi redivivo*, 11–16 (Rio de Janeiro: Paz e Terra, 1979); ibid., 14.

176. "Ilegal a proibição de peças teatrais pela censura policial," *Diario Carioca*, February 6, 1948.

177. N. Rodrigues, *Senhora dos afogados. Tragédia em três atos e seis quadros* (1955), in N. Rodrigues, Teatro, vol. 2, 429–96 (Rio de Janeiro: Serviço Nacional do Teatro, 1960); N. Rodrigues, *Anjo negro. Tragédia em três atos e quatro quadros* (1946), in N. Rodrigues, Teatro, vol. 1, 195–261 (Rio de Janeiro: Serviço Nacional do Teatro, 1960); N. Rodrigues, *Anjo negro. Peça em três atos*, in *Dramas para negros*, ed. A. Nascimento, 309–74.

178. A. Nascimento, "Prólogo para brancos," in *Dramas para negros*, ed. A. Nascimento, 11.

179. He cites Gaston Baty and René Chavance, *El arte teatral* (Mexico City, Mexico: Fondo de Cultura Económica, 1951), 18.

180. A. Nascimento, "Prólogo para brancos," in *Dramas para negros*, ed. A. Nascimento.

181. Wole Soyinka, *Myth, Literature and the African World*. London: Cambridge University Press, 1976.

182. L. M. Martins, *A cena em sombras*.

183. Ibid., 95.

184. W. Soyinka, *Myth, Literature*, 1.

185. Ibid.

186. Ibid., 2–3.

187. Ibid.

188. Ibid., 3.

189. Juana Elbein dos Santos, *Os nagô e a morte* (Petrópolis, Brazil: Vozes, 1977).

190. A. Nascimento, "Prólogo para brancos," 9–10.

191. A. Césaire, "What Is Negritude to Me," 17.

192. L. M. Martins, *A cena em sombras*, 70. L. M. Martins cites W.E.B. Du Bois, "Krigwa Players Little Negro Theater," *The Crisis* (July 1926): 134.

193. See Chapter 4.

194. W.E.B. Du Bois, "Krigwa Players," 134.

195. Errol Hill, "Black Black Theatre in Form and Style," *The Black Scholar* 10, no. 10 (1979).

196. L. M. Martins, *A cena em sombras*, 86.

197. Ibid., 104.

198. José Paulo Moreira da Fonseca, "Nota sôbre *Sortilégio* e alguns dos problemas que envolveu," in *Teatro Experimental do Negro*, 159.

199. Ibid., 159, 160.

200. Adonias Filho, "A peça *Sortilégio*," in *Teatro Experimental do Negro*, 163.

201. L. M. Martins, *A cena em sombras*, 104.

202. Ibid., 107.

203. A. Nascimento, *Sortilégio* (1959), 14–16. Translation of excerpts by E. L. Nascimento.

204. A. Nascimento, *Sortilégio* (1959), 45.

205. A. Nascimento, *Sortilégio* (1959), 18–19.

206. Augusto Boal, "Notas de um diretor de *Sortilégio*," in *Teatro Experimental do Negro*, 150–51.

207. A. Boal, "Notas de um diretor," 152.

208. A. Nascimento, *Sortilégio* (1959), 74–76.

209. Ibid., 77–79.

210. I am in no way referring to the idea of human sacrifice—Emmanuel's death is a symbolic representation, just as Margarida's death, far from being an endorsement of murder, symbolically represents Emmanuel's act of freeing himself from the imposture of whiteness.

211. R. Bastide, "Introduction" (typed manuscript) written in 1972 for the English language version of TEN's anthology. Excerpts cited in A. Nascimento, "Prefácio," *Sortilégio II*, 13–14.

212. Niyi Afolabi, "A visão mítico-trágica na dramaturgia Abdiasiana," *Hispania* 81 (September 1998): 530–40.

213. L. M. Martins, *A cena em sombras*.

214. Ruth Landes, *Cidade das mulheres* (Rio de Janeiro: Civilização brasileira, 1967); Sueli Carneiro and Cristiane Curi, "O poder feminino no culto aos Orixás," paper presented at the 3rd Congress of Black Culture in the Americas, São Paulo, 1982. Helena Theodoro, *Mito e espiritualidade—Mulheres Negras* (Rio de Janeiro: Pallas, 1996); and the film *Iyá Mi Agbá*, by J. E. dos Santos, Society of Black Culture Studies in Brazil (1976).

215. Oyeronke Oyewumi, *The Invention of Women: Making an African Sense of Western Gender Discourses* (Minneapolis: University of Minnesota Press, 1997).

216. Niara Sudarkasa, *The Strength of our Mothers* (Trenton, NJ: Africa World Press, 1996); H. Theodoro, *Mito e espiritualidade*.

217. A. Nascimento, *Sortilégio* (1959), 17–18.

218. Ibid., 81.

219. Charles V. Hamilton, "Not Yet 'E Pluribus Unum': Racism, America's Achilles' Heel," in *Beyond Racism: Race and Inequality in Brazil, South Africa, and the United States*, ed. C. V. Hamilton et al. (Boulder, CO: Lynne Reiner Publishers, 2001).

220. Cornel West, *Race Matters* (New York: Random House; New York: Vintage Books, 1994), 122–23.

221. Ibid., 123.

222. A. Nascimento, *Sortilégio* (1959), 65–67.

223. Ibid., 44–45.

224. Ibid., 41–42.

225. See Chapter 2.

226. A. Nascimento, *Sortilégio* (1959), 64.

227. See Chapter 2 for discussion of the mucama.

228. A. Nascimento, *Sortilégio* (1959), 33–34.

229. Ibid., 39.

230. Ibid., 48, 49, 62.

231. Ibid., 79.

232. West, *Race Matters*, 27.

233. A. Nascimento, *Sortilégio* (1959), 47, 49–50.

234. Ibid., 74.

235. Gerardo Mello Mourão, "Sortilégio," in *Teatro Experimental do Negro*, 155–56.

236. Adonias Filho, "A peça *Sortilégio*," 164.

237. N. Rodrigues, "Abdias. O negro autêntico," in *Teatro Experimental do Negro*, 157–58.

238. R. Bastide, "Introduction" (typed manuscript) written in 1972 for the English language version of TEN's anthology, 6.

239. A. Nascimento, *Sortilégio II*; A. Nascimento, "*Sortilege II: Zumbi Returns*."

240. A. Nascimento, *Sortilégio II*, 139–40; A. Nascimento, "*Sortilege II: Zumbi Returns*," 244–45.

241. Ibid., 140, 245.
242. W. Soyinka, *Myth, Literature*, 2–3.

CHAPTER 6

1. Ricardo Franklin Ferreira, *Afro-descendente. Identidade em construção* (Rio de Janeiro: Pallas; São Paulo: Pontifical Catholic University of São Paulo Press Educ; São Paulo: São Paulo State Research Support Foundation FAPESP, 2000), 48.

2. Simone de Beauvoir, *El segundo sexo*, 2 vols. Vol. 2, "La experiencia vivida," trans. Pablo Palant (Buenos Aires: Psique, 1954), 9, 13, 433–67, 535–92. Originally published as *Le deuxième sexe*, 2 vols. (Paris: Gallimard, 1949).

3. Manuel Castells, *O poder da identidade*. Vol. 2, *A Era da informação. Economia, sociedade e cultura*, trans.K. B. Gerhardt (São Paulo: Paz e Terra, 1999), 22–28. Originally published as *The Power of Identity*. Vol. 2 of the trilogy *The Information Age. Economy, Society, and Culture* (Cambridge, MA: Blackwell Publishers, 1997).

4. Oyeronke Oyewumi, *The Invention of Women: Making an African Sense of Western Gender Discourses* (Minneapolis: University of Minnesota Press, 1997), 1–30.

5. "Manifesto à Nação brasileira," in *O negro revoltado*, ed. Abdias Nascimento, 59–61 (Rio de Janeiro: GRD, 1968).

6. "Nosso programa," in *Quilombo. Edição fac-similar do jornal dirigido por Abdias Nascimento*, ed. A. Nascimento (São Paulo: Editora 34, 2003), nos. 1–5 (December 1948–January 1950), 3.

7. Alberto Guerreiro Ramos, *Introdução crítica à sociologia brasileira* (Rio de Janeiro: Andes, 1957), 157, emphasis in the original.

8. "Starting in the 1970s, the [Brazilian] black movement radically changes the basis of its policy, adopting a racialist posture." Antonio Sérgio Alfredo Guimarães, "Apresentaçao," in *Tirando a máscara. Ensaios sobre o racismo no Brasil*, ed. A. S. A. Guimarães and L. Huntley (São Paulo: Paz e Terra; São Paulo: Southern Education Foundation, 2000), 24. Guimarães bases his characterization of racialism on the adoption of the statistical criterion of adding together the *preto* and *pardo* populations in one group called *negros* or Afro-Brazilians. Such a conclusion is simply the application of value judgment to a criterion that has been adopted by the majority of social science researchers that specialize in this area. Roberto Borges Martins, "Desigualdades raciais e políticas de inclusão racial. Um sumário da experiência brasileira recente" (Report presented to the Economic Committe for Latin America and the Caribbean [CEPAL], Santiago, August 2003), 11.

9. Hédio Silva Jr., ed., *Anti-racismo. Coletânea de leis brasileiras (federais, estaduais, municipais)* (São Paulo: Oliveira Mendes, 1998); Federal Republic of Brazil, Legislative Branch, Lei 10.639 de 09/01/2003 — Lei Ordinária (Brasília, Brazil: Imprensa Nacional/ *Diário Oficial da União*, January 10, 2003), 000001, 1 (Lei de Diretrizes e Bases da Educação Nacional). Available at http://www6.senado.gov.br/sicon/ExecutaPesquisaAvancada.action#.

10. Moema Toscano, *Estereótipos sexuais na educação. Um manual para o educador* (Petrópolis, Brazil: Vozes, 2000), 21–22.

11. E.g., Maria de Lourdes Chagas Deiró Nosella, *As belas mentiras. As ideologias subjacentes aos textos didáticos* (São Paulo: Moraes, 1981); Fúlvia Rosemberg, *Literatura infantil e ideologia* (São Paulo: Global Editora, 1984); Esmeralda V. Negrão, "Preconceitos e discriminações raciais em livros didáticos infanto-juvenis," *Cadernos de Pesquisa Fundação Carlos Chagas* 65 (May 1989): 52–65; Maria José Lopes da Silva, "Fundamentos teóricos da pedagogia multirracial," pamphlet (Rio de Janeiro: M. J. L. da Silva, 1988); Ana Célia Silva, *A discriminação do negro no livro didático* (Salvador, Brazil: Editorial and Didactic Center; Salvador, Brazil: Afro-Oriental Studies Center; Salvador, Brazil: Federal University of Bahia,

1995); Petronilha Beatriz Gonçalves Silva, *O pensamento negro em educação no Brasil. Expressões do movimento negro* (São Carlos, Brazil: Federal University of São Carlos UFSCar, 1997).

12. E.g., Inaldete Pinheiro Andrade, *Pai Adão era Nagô* (Recife, Brazil: Luiz Freire Cultural Center, 1989); Rogério Barbosa, *Sundjata. O príncipe leão* (Rio de Janeiro: Agir, 1995); Alfredo Boulos, Jr., *20 de Novembro. A consciência nasceu na luta* (São Paulo: FTD, 1992); Júlio Emílio Braz, *Liberteiros. A luta abolicionista no Ceará* (São Paulo: FTD, 1993); Geni Guimarães, *A cor da ternura* (São Paulo: FTD, 1989); Joel Rufino dos Santos, *História/ histórias*, 5ª a 8ª Séries (São Paulo: FTD, 1992); J. R. dos Santos, *Zumbi* (São Paulo: Editora Moderna, 1986); Luiz Galdino, *Palmares* (São Paulo: Ática, 1993).

13. E.g., Célia Maria Marinho Azevedo, *Onda negra medo branco. O negro do imaginário das elites, Século XIX* (Rio de Janeiro: Paz e Terra, 1987); Nucleus of Black Studies (NEN), *Série pensamento negro em educação*, 6 vols. (Florianópolis, Brazil: NEN, 1997–1999); Nilma Lino Gomes, *A mulher negra que vi de perto* (Belo Horizonte, Brazil: Mazza, 1995); Consuelo Dores Silva, *Negro, qual é o seu nome?* (Belo Horizonte, Brazil: Mazza, 1995); P. B. G. Silva, *O pensamento negro*; Kabengele Munanga, *Superando o racismo na escola* (Brasília: Ministério de Estado da Educação, 1999); Eliane dos Santos Cavalleiro, *Do silêncio do lar ao silêncio escola. Racismo, preconceito e discriminação na educação infantil* (São Paulo: Contexto; São Paulo: University of São Paulo, 2000).

14. See the discussion on negritude in Chapter 6.

15. C. D. Silva, *Negro, qual é o seu nome?*; E. S. Cavalleiro, *Do silêncio do lar*.

16. E.g., Manoel de Almeida Cruz, *Alternativas para combater o racismo segundo a pedagogia interétnica* (Salvador, Brazil: Afro-Brazilian Cultural Nucleus, 1989); M. J. L. da Silva, *"Fundamentos teóricos"*; São Paulo State Education Secretariat, Working Group for Afro-Brazilian Matters (GTAAB), *Escola—Espaço de luta contra a discriminação* (São Paulo: State Education Secretariat, 1988); NEN, *Série pensamento negro*; K. Munanga, *Superando o racismo*; J. R. dos Santos, *A questão do negro na sala de aula* (São Paulo: Ática, 1990).

17. E. S. Cavalleiro, *Do silêncio do lar*.

18. N. L. Gomes, *A mulher negra*.

19. M. J. L. da Silva, "Fundamentos teóricos."

20. Lorenzo Zanetti, *A prática educativa do Grupo Cultural Afro-Reggae* (Rio de Janeiro: Grupo Cultural Afro-Reggae, 2001).

21. João Jorge Rodrigues, *Olodum, estrada da paixão* (Salvador, Brazil: Olodum Cultural Group; Salvador, Brazil: Casa de Jorge Amado Foundation, 1996); Ilê-Aiyê, *Cadernos de educação*, 6 vols. (Salvador, Brazil: Bloco Carnavalesco Ilê-Aiyê, 1995–1998).

22. E.g., M. A. Cruz, *Alternativas para combater*; Narcimária Corrêa do Patrocínio Luz, ed., *Pluralidade cultural e educação* (Salvador, Brazil: Bahia State Education Secretariat and Black Culture Studies Society of Bahia SECNEB, 1996); Raquel de Oliveira, "Relações raciais na escola. Uma experiência de intervenção" (master's thesis, Pontifical Catholic University of São Paulo, 1992); Ivan Costa Lima, Jeruse Romão, Sônia Maria Silveira, eds., *Educação popular afro-brasileira*, Black Thought in Education Series 5 (Florianópolis: Nucleus of Black Studies NEN, 1999); Vanda Machado, *Ilê Axé. Vivências e invenção pedagógica. As crianças do Opô Afonjá* (Salvador, Brazil: Salvador Municipal Government and UFBA, 1999); Maria da Glória da Veiga Moura, "Ritmo e ancestralidade na força dos tambores negros" (São Paulo, PhD Diss. University of São Paulo, 1997).

23. Federal Republic of Brazil, Executive Branch, Basic Education Secretariat, *Parâmetros curriculares nacionais*, 9 vols. (Brasília: Ministry of Education and Sports, 1997).

24. C. D. Silva, *Negro, qual é o seu nome?*

25. J. Romão, "Há o tema do negro e há a vida do negro. Educação pública, popular e afro-brasileira," in *Educação popular afro-brasileira*, ed. J. Romão, I. C. Lima, S. M. Silveira, Black Thought in Education Series 5 (Florianópolis: Núcleo de Estudos Negros, 1999), 41.

26. A. Guerreiro Ramos, *Introdução crítica (1957)*, 157; A. Guerreiro Ramos, "O negro desde dentro," in *Introdução crítica (1957)*, 193–99.

27. Federal Republic of Brazil, Legislative Branch. Lei 10.639 de 09/01/2003—Lei Ordinária (Brasília, Brazil: Imprensa Nacional/ *Diário Oficial da União*, January 10, 2003), 000001, 1 (Lei de Diretrizes e Bases da Educação Nacional). Available at http://www6.senado.gov.br/sicon/ExecutaPesquisaAvancada.action#.

28. Federal Republic of Brazil, Executive Branch., National Council of Education, *Diretrizes curriculares nacionais para a educação das relações étnico-raciais e para o ensino de história e cultura afro-brasileira e africana* (Brasília, Brazil: Special Secretariat of Policies for the Promotion of Racial Equality and Ministry of Education, 2004). Multi-lingual edition (Portuguese, English, French, Spanish): Federal Republic of Brazil, Executive Branch., National Council of Education, *National Curricular Guidelines to the Education of Ethnic-Racial Relations and to the Teaching of Afro-Brazilian and African History and Culture* (Brasília, Brazil: Ministry of Education, UNESCO and Inter-American Development Bank, n.d.).

LIST OF ABBREVIATIONS

ANB	Association of Brazilian Blacks [Associação do Negro Brasileiro]
ANPOCS	National Social Sciences Graduate Studies and Research Association [Associação Nacional de Pós-graduação e Pesquisa em Ciências Sociais]
CCBB	Bank of Brazil Cultural Center [Centro Cultural Banco do Brasil]
CEAA	Afro-Asian Studies Center [Centro de Estudos Afro-Asiáticos]
CEAO	Afro-Oriental Studies Center [Centro de Estudos Afro-Orientais]
CED	Editorial and Didactic Center [Centro Editorial e Didático]
CEDEPLAR	Regional Planning and Development Center [Centro de Desenvolvimento e Planejamento Regional]
CEERT	Labor Relations and Inequality Studies Center, Center for the Study of Inequality in Labor Relations, or Center for the Study of Ethics in Labor Relations [Centro de Estudos da Desigualdade nas Relações de Trabalho, Centro de Estudos da Ética nas Relações de Trabalho]
CEPAL	United Nations Economic and Political Commission on Latin America and the Caribbean [Comissão Econômica e Política para a América Latina e o Caribe das Nações Unidas]

CHRI	Comparative Human Relations Initiative
CUT	Unified Trade Union Federation [Central Única dos Trabalhadores]
DIEESE	Inter-Trade Union Department of Statistics and Socio-Economic Studies [Departamento Inter-Sindical de Estatísticas e Estudos Sócio-Econômicos]
EDUC	Pontifical Catholic University of São Paulo Press [Editora da PUC-SP]
EDUSP	São Paulo University Press [Editora da Universidade de São Paulo]
FAPESP	São Paulo State Research Support Foundation [Fundação de Amparo à Pesquisa do Estado de São Paulo]
FASE	Federation of Social Work and Educational Institutions [Federação de Entidades de Assistência Social e Educação]
FFCL	Faculty of Philosophy, Sciences, and Letters, University of São Paulo (former name) [Faculdade de Filosofia, Ciências, e Letras, nome antigo]
FFLCH	Faculty of Philosophy, Sciences, Letters, and Humanities, University of São Paulo (current name) [Faculdade de Filosofia, Letras e Ciências Humanas, nome atual]
FIOCRUZ	Oswaldo Cruz Foundation [Fundação Oswaldo Cruz]
FUSP	University of São Paulo Foundation [Fundação Universidade de São Paulo]
IBGE	Brazilian Institute of Geography and Statistics [Instituto Brasileiro de Geografia e Estatística]
INSPIR	Inter-American Trade Union Institute for Racial Equality, AFL-CIO Solidarity Center [Instituto Interamericano de Solidariedade e Pela Igualdade Racial]
IPEA	Institute of Applied Economic Research [Instituto de Pesquisas Econômicas Aplicadas]
IPEAFRO	Afro-Brazilian Studies and Research Institute [Instituto de Pesquisas e Estudos Afro-Brasileiros]
ISEB	Higher Institute of Brazilian Studies [Instituto Superior de Estudos Brasileiros]
ITM	Third World Institute [Instituto del Tercer Mundo], Montevideo, Uruguay
IUPERJ	University Research Institute of the State of Rio de Janeiro [Instituto Universitário de Pesquisas do Estado do Rio de Janeiro]
MINC	Ministry of Culture [Ministério da Cultura]
MNDH	National Human Rights Movement [Movimento Nacional de Direitos Humanos]

NEN	Nucleus of Black Studies [Núcleo de Estudos Negros]
PCB	Brazilian Communist Party [Partido Comunista Brasileiro]
PNAD	National Household Sample Survey [Pesquisa Nacional por Amostragem de Domicílios]
PUC	Pontifical Catholic University [Pontifícia Universidade Católica]
REDEH	Human Development Network [Rede de Desenvolvimento Humano]
SEAFRO	Special Secretariat for the Defense and Promotion of Afro-Brazilian Populations, Rio de Janeiro State Government [Secretaria Extraordinária de Defesa e Promoção das Populações Afro-Brasileira, Governo do Estado do Rio de Janeiro]
SECNEB	Society for the Study of Black Culture in Bahia and Brazil [Sociedade de Estudos da Cultura Negra do Estado da Bahia e do Brasil]
SEF	Southern Education Foundation
SENAC	National Commerce Service [Serviço Nacional do Comércio]
TEN	Black Experimental Theater [Teatro Experimental do Negro]
UCAM	Candido Mendes University [Universidade Candido Mendes]
UERJ	Rio de Janeiro State University [Universidade do Estado do Rio de Janeiro]
UFBA	Federal University of Bahia [Universidade Federal da Bahia]
UFMG	Federal University of Minas Gerais [Universidade Federal de Minas Gerais]
UFRJ	Federal University of Rio de Janeiro [Universidade Federal do Rio de Janeiro]
UNDP	United Nations Development Program
UNE	National Student Union [União Nacional de Estudantes]
UNESCO	United Nations Organization for Education, Science and Culture
UNIA	United Negro Improvement Association
USP	University of São Paulo [Universidade de São Paulo]1

GLOSSARY OF BRAZILIAN WORDS

Auto: Mystery play
Búzios: Cowrie shells
Caboclo: A person of mixed African and Native Brazilian heritage; dark-skinned resident of the rural backlands of Brazil
Cachaça: Brazilian rum
Caipira: Humble country farmer, hillbilly
Candomblé: Afro-Brazilian religious practice and tradition
Capoeira: Afro-Brazilian martial art
Chibata: Whip
Cortiço: Urban slum dwelling; a building with many small rooms
Dobalê: Gesture of reverence made by lying prostrate and touching the forehead to the ground
Ebó: Offering
Egun: Brazilian version of the Yoruba word for the illustrious ancestor
Egungun: Yoruba for the illustrious ancestor
Eléèkó: Female order of power and ancestor worship in Yoruba society
Escurinho: Literally "little dark one"; euphemism for black
Exu: Elegba; trickster; orixá of contradiction and dynamics; carrier of axé, the life force
Exus: Elegba appears in many forms; according to tradition each person has his or her Exu
Favela: Brazilian slum or shantytown
Filhas de Santo: Initiates in Afro-Brazilian religious tradition

Folguedos: Folk festivals

Géledés: Female order of ancestor worship in Yoruba tradition; name of black women's organization based in São Paulo, Brazil

Iaô or Iyawô: Initiate in the Afro-Brazilian religious tradition

Iemanjá or Yemanjá: Deity of the sea (Mammy-Water); mother of all the Orixás

Integralist: Member of the nationalist movement led by Plínio Salgado in the 1930s and 1940s

Itamarati or Itamaraty: Brazilian Ministry of Foreign Relations

Iyabá: Female deities in Yoruba and Afro-Brazilian religious tradition

Iyami: Female initiates and authorities in Afro-Brazilian religious tradition

Iyalorixá: Priestess of Afro-Brazilian religious tradition

Iyawô or Iaô: Initiate in the Yoruba or Afro-Brazilian religious tradition

Kilombos: Communities of Africans who refused slavery, which existed all over the Americas and all over Brazil throughout its history. Some were very large; it is estimated that Palmares had 30,000 inhabitants, an enormous population for the seventeenth century. Thousands of these communities have been identified in contemporary Brazil.

Luso-Tropicalism: Gilberto Freyre's theory of Portuguese colonialism as nonracist and socially harmonious as a result of an alleged Portuguese penchant for miscegenation

Macumba: Afro-Brazilian religion in Rio de Janeiro

Malês: Islamicized Africans in Brazil

May 13th: Date of the Brazilian Abolition Proclamation in 1888

Mestizo: Mixed race individual

Metarace: Gilberto Freyre's expression for the mixed race population resulting from miscegenation in Brazil

Morenidade: Identity based on the rejection of blackness and exaltation of light-skinned mixed race

Moreno: The preferred Brazilian term for mixed race person, generally implying a light skin color but often used to refer to dark-skinned individuals without using the offensive term *negro* (black); a euphemism for black

Mucama: Servant woman working in the intimate world of domestic life; often but not always a concubine

Obatala: Orixá of peace and patience; identified with Jesus Christ in Umbanda

Ogun: Orixá of war and vindictive justice; identified with Saint George in Umbanda

Orixá or Orisha: Deities who are the forces of nature

Oxalá or Oshala: Obatala

Oxum or Oshun: Goddess of love, creativity, and fertility

Palmares: Republic of united kilombos who resisted Portuguese, Dutch, and Brazilian repression from 1595 to 1695

Pegi: Small chapel dedicated to one or more orixás in a terreiro

Pomba-Gira: Female counterpart of Exu; goddess of the sexual act

Quilombo: Kilombo

Revolt of the Cowrie Shells: Another name for the Revolt of the Tailors, referring to the conspirators' use of a cowrie shell in necklace or bracelet as code of identification

Revolt of the Farroupilhas: Independence movement in Rio Grande do Sul that demanded abolition of slavery

Revolt of the Tailors: Late eighteenth-century independence movement in Salvador, Bahia, led by Afro-Brazilian intellectuals

Revolt of the Vaccine: Rio de Janeiro population's reaction to the government's violent imposition of sanitary and public health measures

Revolts of the Malês: A series of rebellions led by Islamic Africans in Bahia in the early nineteenth century

Senzala: Collective slave quarters

Sertanejo: Inhabitant of the rural backlands

Sertão: Rural backlands of Brazil, often referring to the drought-ridden areas of the Northeast

Sertões: Plural of sertão, another way of referring to the rural backlands

Shango: Yoruba king of Oyo, deity of justice, lightning, thunder, and war

Syncretism: Sharing of references, beliefs, and practices from different religions in one religious practice, as exemplified in Umbanda

Tailors' Revolt: Revolt of the Tailors

Terreiro: Place of worship of African religion; literally backyard; front yard; any plot of cleared land but usually one around a house

Terreiro community: The community of people who worship in a terreiro

Umbanda: A popular religion in Brazil that mixes references, beliefs, and practices from African religion, Christianity, Kardecist Spiritism, and other origins

Xangô: Shango

Yemanjá: Deity of the sea (Mammy-Water); mother of all the Orixás

Zumbi of Palmares: Last king of Palmares, leader of its resistance

BIBLIOGRAPHICAL NOTE TO
THE ENGLISH EDITION

T HIS BOOK was originally published in Brazil as *O Sortilegio da Cor—Identidade, Raça e Gênero no Brasil* (2003). It was written in the effort to record and reflect upon aspects of Afro-Brazilian experience and contribute to the incorporation of African and Afro-Brazilian history and culture into the country's school curricula. The English edition has the further objective of enriching the dialogue among researchers on various aspects of Afro-Brazilian experience. To further this goal, I offer here a brief overview of English-language sources on issues discussed in this book.

The first reference in such an overview is Ghanaian political scientist Anani Dzidzienyo, whose groundbreaking book *The Position of Blacks in Brazilian Society* (1971) rejected the traditional view of Brazilian race relations presented in works such as those by Donald Pierson (1967) and Carl E. Degler (1971). These writers emphasize the plurality of racial classification in Brazil, in keeping with the traditional contention that in Brazil such plurality indicates the existence of relatively little racism and racial discrimination. This idea is summed up in the expression "racial democracy," which has come under increasing criticism, particularly since the 1970s. In addition to firm scholarship, Dzidzienyo brought to the issue an African viewpoint, which liberated his critical appraisal of the Brazilian "etiquette of race relations" from standardized precepts that had deterred other analysts from perceiving how this etiquette is grounded on the same assumptions about blacks and whites that under gird overtly segregationist or explicitly discriminatory social patterns.

Thomas E. Skidmore's 1974 work, *Black into White: Race and Nationality in Brazilian Thought*, engages in a classic study of "whitening" as a national ideal and the articulated goal of Brazilian public policy. Skidmore challenges Degler's "mulatto escape hatch" theory by questioning the extent to which persons of mixed blood have reaped real benefits from the racial democracy ideology.

During the time he was in exile in Nigeria, Abdias Nascimento published *"Racial Democracy" in Brazil: Myth or Reality?* (1977). The book is an indictment of Brazilian racism that was written for the Colloquium of the Second World Festival of Black and African Arts and Culture. This contribution was suppressed as a result of actions by Brazil's military government, which mobilized its diplomatic corps in Lagos to prevent the paper from being presented at the Colloquium. Nevertheless, Nascimento registered as an observer to the event and the contribution was published in expanded form by Ibadan's Sketch Publishers.

Nelson do Valle Silva's empirical study, *Black-White Income Differentials: Brazil, 1940–1960* (1978), dispenses with the mulatto category entirely. The author groups mixed-blooded people with blacks and shows that income differentials between whites and nonwhites in Brazil cannot be fully explained by factors other than discrimination. His work complements that of Carlos Hasenbalg (1979), *Racial Discrimination and Inequality in Brazil*: both give substance to the Afro-Brazilian social movement's position that racial discrimination has existed consistently in Brazil since the abolition of slavery. All of these works point out the need for policy measures to overcome institutional racism.

Meanwhile, in the same vein, Abdias Nascimento also published the book *Mixture or Massacre? Essays in the Genocide of a Black People* (1989 [1979]). He edited, along with the present author, a special issue of the *Journal of Black Studies* (1980), featuring translations of articles by African Brazilians that introduce the English-speaking public to the Afro-Brazilian social movement.

George Reid Andrews's 1991 book, *Blacks and Whites in São Paulo, 1888–1988*, studies black movements in São Paulo and describes income disparities between blacks and whites as the result of government and property owners' interventions in the postabolition labor market. Andrews writes that these interventions benefited European immigrants.

The authors listed above contest the conclusions of Brazilian sociologist Florestan Fernandes, whose classic work on black movements in São Paulo— published in English as *The Negro in Brazilian Society* (1969)—attributes the existence of racial inequality and prejudice to the legacy of slavery. His text is an extensive and documented study of black activism in São Paulo in the first half of the twentieth century.

In 1991, the story of black resistance in Brazil was told for the first time from the viewpoint of African-descended Brazilians in *Africans in Brazil: A Pan-African Perspective*, a collection of texts by Abdias Nascimento that were co-authored, translated and edited by this author. The work makes reference to movements such as Negritude and Pan-Africanism, as well as the broader social context of Africans in Brazil and the Americas.

Howard Winant's 1994 book, *Racial Conditions: Theories, Politics and Comparisons*, underscores the insufficiency of structural analysis and the need to identify power relations embedded in the cultural, political, and economic fabric of Brazilian social relations. Such a contention echoes the earlier assertions of African and Afro-Brazilian intellectuals such as Anani Dzidzienyo and Abdias Nascimento.

Published in the same year, Michael G. Hanchard's work, *Orpheus and Power*, studies black movements in Rio de Janeiro and São Paulo between 1944 and 1988. This is a valuable in-depth look at recent Afro-Brazilian movements. Hanchard characterizes earlier organizations, including the Black Experimental Theater, as elitist groups whose ideology contradicted their professed goals. This idea is seriously questioned in *The Sorcery of Color*. Ultimately, such a notion derives from conclusions reached by a white Marxist Brazilian sociologist, Luiz de Aguiar Costa Pinto, whose work, motives, and methodology I examine in Chapters 5 and 6 of this book.

The Minority Rights Group of London, which published Anani Dzidzienyo's pioneering work in 1971, edited an anthology in 1995 entitled *Afro-Latin Americans Today: No Longer Invisible*. The book includes essays on fifteen countries and a conclusion written by Dzidzienyo himself. Another anthology, *Black Brazil*, edited by Larry Crook and Randal Johnson and published in 1999, brings together essays by mostly African and Afro-Brazilian activists, politicians, and intellectuals.

In her pioneering book, *Freedoms Granted, Freedoms Won* (1998), Kim Butler examines twentieth-century black movements in the cities of São Paulo and Salvador. She places these movements in the context of the African Diaspora and characterizes their activities as varied, evolving forms of self-determination.

In his book *Making Race and Nation* (1998), Anthony Marx carries out a comparative study of race and nationality, in which he deals with issues critical to the evolution of ideas about race and the experience of race relations in Brazil, South Africa, and the United States. A similar approach was taken, involving social actors who participated in such an evolution of ideas, in a collective research publication sponsored by the Southern Education Foundation of Atlanta (SEF). Lynn Walker Huntley coordinated the Comparative Human Relations Initiative as part of the preparatory work for the Third World Conference against Racism (Durban 2001). The Initiative brought together researchers, intellectuals, activists, and representatives of social movements in meetings that were held in the three countries mentioned above, culminating in a forum at the Durban Conference itself. The papers and proceedings have been published on the Internet at http://www.beyondracism.org and in two anthologies, *Beyond Racism: Embracing an Interdependent Future* (Comparative Human Relations Initiative, 2000), and *Beyond Racism: Race and Inequality in Brazil, South Africa, and the United States* (Huntley et al. 2001).

In another comparative study, *Race in Another America: The Significance of Skin Color in Brazil*, Edward Telles seeks to establish parameters for understanding race in Brazil by reviewing key moments in the evolution of racial policy, the black movement, and thought about race in Brazil. However, his brief account of the early black movement makes no mention of the National Convention of Brazilian Blacks and its proposals to the National Constituent Assembly of 1946, nor does Telles deal with the black movement's role the in the genesis of the 1951 Afonso Arinos Law.

In 2004, I edited a special issue of the *Journal of Black Studies* on African descendants in Brazil. The issue brought together essays by Afro-Brazilian authors and researchers on subjects such as racial inequality, human rights violations, *kilombo* communities, African religions in Brazil, public policy, and affirmative action.

This bibliographical note is by no means exhaustive, but I hope it will be useful as a reference point for those interested in further reading in English. In the present work, two dimensions are included that have not been significantly addressed in any of the literature to date: the role of psychology as a discipline in the evolution of thought on race in Brazil and an in depth look at the TEN—Black Experimental Theater—as a major Afro-Brazilian social and artistic movement of the mid-twentieth century.

SELECTED BIBLIOGRAPHY

80 anos de abolição. Rio de Janeiro: Cadernos Brasileiros, 1968. Transcription of dialogues at symposium on the eightieth anniversary of the abolition of slavery in Brazil organized by Abdias Nascimento at the request of the editors of the journal *Cadernos Brasileiros*, Rio de Janeiro, RJ, Brazil, May 13, 1958.

"Absurda a Exclusão das Domésticas de Todas as Leis Trabalhistas!" *Diário Trabalhista* 1, no. 144, July 5, 1946, 5.

Adeeko, Adeleke. "The Language of Head-Calling: A Review Essay on Yoruba Metalanguage." *Research in African Literatures* 23, no. 1 (March–June 1992): 197–200.

Adonias Filho. "A peça *Sortilégio*." *Diário de Notícias*, October 10, 1958. Reprinted in *Teatro Experimental do Negro. Testemunhos*, edited by Abdias Nascimento, 163–64. Rio de Janeiro: GRD, 1966.

Adorno, Sérgio. "Discriminação racial e justiça criminal." *Novos Estudos Cebrap* 43 (November 1995).

Adotevi, Stanislas. "Negritude is Dead: The Burial." In *New African Literature and the Arts*. Edited by Joseph Okpaku. 3 vols. New York: Third Press, 1973.

Afolabi, Niyi. "A visão mítico-trágica na dramaturgia Abdiasiana." *Hispania* 81 (September 1998): 530–40.

Alakija, George. *The Trance State in the "Candomblé."* Brasília: Ministry of Foreign Relations, official delegation of the Brazilian Government to the Second World Festival of Black and African Arts and Culture, 1977.

Almeida, Fernando H. Mendes de. *Constituições do Brasil*. São Paulo: Saraiva, 1963.

Alonso, Annibal Martins. *Estrangeiros no Brasil. Legislação anotada e atualizada*. Rio de Janeiro: Freitas Bastos, 1960.

Amaral, Raul Joviano do. "Frente Negra Brasileira. Suas finalidades e obras realizadas." São Paulo, 1936. Prepared for Fernandes, Florestan. *A integração do negro à sociedade de classes*. São Paulo: FFLCH, USP, 1964.

AMMA—Psique e Negritude. *Gostando mais de nós mesmos. Perguntas e respostas sobre auto-estima e a questão racial.* 2nd rev. ed. Edited by Ana Maria Silva and Eliane dos Santos Cavalleiro. São Paulo: Gente, 1999. First published, São Paulo: Quilombhoje Literatura, 1996.

Andrade, Inaldete Pinheiro. *Pai adão era nagô.* Recife, Brazil: Centro de Cultura Luiz Freire, 1989.

Andrews, George Reid. *Black Political Protest in São Paulo, 1888–1988.* Cambridge: Cambridge University Press, 1992.

——. *Blacks and Whites in São Paulo, 1888–1988.* Madison: University of Wisconsin Press, 1991.

Appiah, Anthony Kwame. *In My Father's House: Africa in the Philosophy of Culture.* New York: Oxford University Press, 1992.

Arendt, Hanna. *As origens do totalitarismo. A expansão do poder.* Rio de Janeiro: Documentário, 1976.

Arinos, Afonso. Interview in *Última Hora,* December 14, 1951.

Arinos Filho, Afonso, ed. *Afonso Arinos no Congresso: Cem discursos parlamentares.* Brasília: Senado Federal, Gabinete da Presidência, 1999.

"Artistas do Teatro Experimental do Negro realizarão seus ensaios nas ruas da cidade, despejados do Teatro Fenix," *Diretrizes,* August 21, 1946.

Asante, Molefi K. *The Afrocentric Idea.* 2nd ed. Philadelphia: Temple University Press, 1998.

——. *Afrocentricity.* 2nd rev. ed. Trenton, NJ: Africa World Press, 1989. First published, Buffalo, NY: Amulefi Press, 1980.

——. *Kemet, Afrocentricity and Knowledge.* Trenton, NJ: Africa World Press, 1990.

Asante, Molefi K., and Mark T. Mattson. *The Historical and Cultural Atlas of African Americans.* New York: MacMillan, 1991.

Assumpção, Carlos de. *Protesto. Poemas.* São Paulo: Carlos de Assumpção, 1982.

Ávila, Maria Betânia. "Feminismo e sujeito político." *Proposta* 29, no. 84/85 (March–August 2000).

Azevedo, Célia Maria Marinho. *Onda negra medo branco. O negro do imaginário das elites, Século XIX.* Rio de Janeiro: Paz e Terra, 1987.

Azevedo, Thales. *As elites de cor. Um estudo de ascensão social.* São Paulo: Companhia Editora Nacional, 1955.

Bairros, Luiza. "Lembrando Lélia González." In *O livro da saúde das Mulheres Negras. Nossos passos vêm de longe,* edited by Jurema Werneck, Maísa Mendonça, and Evelyn C. White, 42–61. Rio de Janeiro: Pallas; Rio de Janeiro: Criola, 2000.

——. "Nossos feminismos revisitados." In "Dossiê Mulheres Negras." Special issue, *Estudos Feministas* 3, no. 2 (1995): 458–63.

Baldassari, Anne, ed. *Le miroir noir, Picasso, sources photographiques, 1900–1928.* Paris: Musée Picasso, 1997.

Banton, Michael. "Race." In *Dictionary of Race and Ethnic Relations.* 3rd ed. Edited by Ellis Cashmore. London: Routledge, 1994.

Barbosa, Márcio. "Introdução." In *Frente Negra Brasileira. Depoimentos,* edited by Quilombhoje, 9–12. São Paulo: Quilombhoje; São Paulo: National Culture Fund, 1998.

Barbosa, Rogério. *Sundjata. O príncipe leão.* Rio de Janeiro: Agir, 1995.

Bastide, Roger. *O candomblé da Bahia (Rito nagô).* 3rd ed. Translated by Maria Isaura and Pereira de Queiroz. São Paulo: Companhia Editora Nacional, 1978. Originally published as *Le candomblé de Bahia (Rite nagô).* Paris: Mouton and Company, 1958.

——. "Cavalos dos santos. Esboço de uma sociologia do transe místico." In *Estudos afro-brasileiros,* edited by Roger Bastide, 293–323. São Paulo: Perspectiva, 1973. Originally published as "Bulletin 154." *Sociology* 1, no. 3. Roger Bastide, *Estudos afro-brasileiros*, 3rd series. São Paulo: FFCL, USP, 1953.

——, ed. *Estudos afro-brasileiros*. São Paulo: Perspectiva, 1973.

——. "A imprensa negra do Estado de São Paulo." In *Estudos afro-brasileiros*, edited by Roger Bastide, 129–56. São Paulo: Perspectiva, 1973. Originally published as "Bulletin CXXI." *Sociology*, no. 2. Roger Bastide, *Estudos afro-brasileiros*, 2nd series. São Paulo: FFCL, USP, 1951.

——. "Introduction." In *Dramas for Blacks and Prologue for Whites*, edited by Abdias Nascimento, translated by Elisa Larkin Nascimento. Unpublished manuscript, 1972. English language version of *Dramas para negros e prólogo para brancos*, edited by Abdias Nascimento. Rio de Janeiro: TEN, 1961.

——. *Sociologia e psicanálise*. 2nd ed. Translated by Heloysa de Lima Dantas. São Paulo: Melhoramentos; São Paulo: EdUSP, 1974. Originally published as *Sociologie et psychanalyse*. Paris: Presses Universitaires de France, 1950.

Bastide, Roger, and Florestan Fernandes. *Brancos e negros em São Paulo*. 2nd ed. São Paulo: Companhia Editora Nacional, 1959.

——. *Relações raciais entre negros e brancos em São Paulo*. São Paulo: Anhembi, 1955.

Baty, Gaston, and René Chavance. *El arte teatral*. Mexico City: Fondo de Cultura Económica, 1951.

Beauvoir, Simone de. *La experiencia vivida*. Vol. 2, *El segundo sexo*. Translated by Pablo Palant. Buenos Aires: Psique, 1954. Originally published as *Le deuxième sexe*. 2 vols. Paris: Gallimard, 1949.

Belotti, Elena Gianini. *Educar para a submissão. O descondicionamento da mulher*. 6th ed. Translated by Ephraim Ferreira Alves. Petrópolis, Brazil: Vozes, 1987. Originally published as *Dalla parte delle bambine*. Milan: Feltrinelli, 1973.

Benhabib, Seyla, and Drucilla Cornell, eds. *Feminismo como crítica da modernidade*. Translated by Nathanael da Costa Caixeiro. Rio de Janeiro: Rosa dos Tempos, 1987. Originally published as *Feminism as Critique*. Oxford: Basil Blackwell, 1987.

Ben-Jochannan, Yusef, and George F. Simmons. *Cultural Genocide in the Black and African Studies Curriculum*. New York: Alkebu-lan, 1972.

Bennett, Eliana Guerreiro Ramos. "Gabriela Cravo e Canela: Jorge Amado and the Myth of the Sexual Mulata in Brazilian Culture." In *The African Diaspora: African Origins and New World Identities*, edited by Isidore Okpewho, et al., 227–33. Bloomington: Indiana University Press, 1999.

Bentes, Raimunda Nilma de Melo. *Negritando*. Belém, Brazil: Graphitte, 1993.

Bento, Maria Aparecida Silva. *Branqueamento. Um dilema a ser resolvido*. São Paulo: CEERT, 1995.

——. *Cidadania em preto e branco. Discutindo as relações raciais*. São Paulo: Ática, 1998.

——. *O legado subjetivo dos 500 anos. Narcisismo e alteridade racial*. São Paulo: CEERT, 2000.

——. "Resgatando a minha bisavó. Discriminação racial e resistência nas vozes de trabalhadores negros." Master's thesis, PUC of São Paulo, 1992.

Berger, Peter I., and Thomas Luckmann. *A construção social da realidade. Tratado de sociologia do conhecimento*. Petrópolis, Brazil: Vozes, 1985.

Bernal, Martin. *Black Athena: The Afroasiatic Roots of Classical Civilization*. 3 vols. New Brunswick, NJ: Rutgers University Press, 1987.

Bernd, Zilá. *A questão da negritude*. São Paulo: Brasiliense, 1984.

Black Experimental Theater [Teatro Experimental do Negro] (TEN). "Nosso Programa." In *Quilombo. Edição fac-similar do jornal dirigido por Abdias Nascimento*, edited by Abdias Nascimento. São Paulo: Editora 34, 2003. First published, 1948.

Boal, Augusto. "Notas de um diretor de Sortilégio." In Teatro Experimental do Negro. Testemunhos, edited by Abdias Nascimento, 150–54. Rio de Janeiro: GRD, 1966.

Bocayuva, Helena. Erotismo à Brasileira. O tema do excesso sexual em Gilberto Freyre. Rio de Janeiro: Garamond, 2001.

Boulos, Alfredo, Jr. 20 de Novembro—A consciência nasceu na luta. São Paulo: FTD, 1992.

Braga, Júlio. Na gamela do feitiço. Repressão e resistência nos candomblés da Bahia. Salvador, Brazil: CEAO, UFBA, 1995.

Branch, William B., ed. Crosswinds: An Anthology of Black Dramatists in the Diaspora. Bloomington: Indiana University Press, 1993.

Braz, Júlio Emílio. Liberteiros—A luta abolicionista no Ceará. São Paulo: FTD, 1993.

Brazil, Federal Republic of. Executive Branch. Basic Education Secretariat, Parâmetros curriculares nacionais. 9 vols. Brasília: Ministry of Education and Sports, 1997.

———. Constituição da República Federativa do Brasil (1988). Brasília: Senado Federal, Subsecretaria de Edições Técnicas, 2003.

———. "Law Decree 7.967 de 18/09/1945—Provisions on Immigration and Colonization, and other Matters." Collection of Laws of Brazil. PUB 31/12/1945 007 000312 1. Rio de Janeiro: Imprensa Nacional, 1945, formato text/xml, código 34.577. Available at http://www6.senado.gov.br/sicon/ExecutaPesquisaBasica.action.

———. Law no. 1.390, July 3, 1951. Brasília, DF: Diário Oficial da União, July 10, 1951. Available at http://www.planalto.gov.br/ccivil_03/Leis/L1390.htm.

———. Ministry of Health. Mesa redonda sobre a saúde da população negra, relatório final. Brasília: Ministry of Health, 1996.

———. National Council of Education. Diretrizes curriculares nacionais para a educação das relações étnico-raciais e para o ensino de história e cultura afro-brasileira e africana. Brasília: Special Secretariat of Policies for the Promotion of Racial Equality and Ministry of Education, 2004.

———. National Council of Education. National Curricular Guidelines to the Education of Ethnic-Racial Relations and to the teaching of Afro-Braizlian and African History and Culture. Brasília: Ministry of Education; Brasília: UNESCO; Brasília: Inter-American Development Bank, n.d.

———. President's Office, Civilian Cabinet, Subdirectorate for Juridical Matters. Constituição da República dos Estados Unidos do Brasil (de 16 de julho de 1934). Brasília, DF. Available at https://www.planalto.gov.br/ccivil_03/Constituicao/Constitui%C3%A7ao34.htm.

Brazil, Federal Republic of. Legislative Branch. Anais da Assembléia Constituinte, 3, 25th Session, beginning February 1946.

———. Lei 10.639 de 09/01/2003—Lei Ordinária (Brasília, Brazil: Imprensa Nacional/ Diário Oficial da União, January 10, 2003), 000001, 1 (Lei de Diretrizes e Bases da Educação Nacional). Available at http://www6.senado.gov.br/sicon/ExecutaPesquisaAvancada.action#.

Brennan, Teresa. "Introdução." In Para além do falo. Uma crítica a lacan do ponto de vista da mulher, edited by Teresa Brennan and translated by Alice Xavier. Rio de Janeiro: Record; Rio de Janeiro: Rosa dos Tempos, 1997. Originally published as Between Feminism and Psychoanalysis. London: Routledge, 1989.

Brigagão, Clóvis. "Da sociologia em mangas de camisa à túnica inconsútil do saber." In Introdução crítica à sociologia brasileira, 2nd ed., by Alberto Guerreiro Ramos, 9–18. Rio de Janeiro: UFRJ Press, 1995.

Brookshaw, David. Race and Color in Brazilian Literature. London: Rowman and Littlefield, 1986.

Butler, Judith. "Variações sobre sexo e gênero. Beauvoir, Wittig e Foucault." In Feminismo como crítica da modernidade, edited by Seyla Benhabib and Drucilla Cornell, 139–54. Rio de Janeiro: Rosa dos Tempos, 1987.

Butler, Kim. *Freedoms Given, Freedoms Won*. New Brunswick, NJ: Rutgers University Press, 1998.

Caetano, Daniel. "Teatro Experimental do Negro. Origem—Nenhum auxílio do governo—O'Neill para os negros." Interview with Abdias Nascimento. *Diário de Notícias*, December 11, 1946.

Câmara, José Sette. "O fim do colonialismo." In "Brasil, África e Portugal." Special issue, edited by Eduardo Portella, *Tempo Brasileiro*, no. 38/39 (1974): 3–23.

Campbell, Horace. *Pan-Africanism: Struggle against Neo-Colonialism and Imperialism. Documents of the Sixth Pan-African Congress, 1974*. Toronto: Afro-Carib Publications, 1976.

Campofiorito, Quirino. "Cristo de côr." *O Jornal* 36, no. 10674, June 26, 1955, 2. Reprinted in *Teatro Experimental do Negro. Testemunhos*, edited by Abdias Nascimento, 143–45. Rio de Janeiro: GRD, 1966.

Caprara, Andrea. "Polissemia e multivocalidade da epilepsia na cultura afro-brasileira." In *Faces da tradição Afro-Brasileira*, edited by Carlos Caroso and Jéferson Bacelar, 257–88. Rio de Janeiro: Pallas; Salvador, Brazil: CEAO, UFBA, 1999.

Carlos Chagas Foundation [Fundação Carlos Chagas]. "Diagnóstico sobre a situação de negros (Pretos e pardos) no Estado de São Paulo." Special issue, edited by Fúlvia Rosemberg, *Cadernos de Pesquisa da Fundação Carlos Chagas* 63 (November 1986): 412.

Carneiro, Édison. "Como se desenrola uma festa de candomblé—Em Recife é Xangô e no Rio, Macumba." *Quilombo* 1, no. 1, December 1948, 4–5.

——. *Ladinos e crioulos*. Rio de Janeiro: Civilização Brasileira, 1964.

——. "Liberdade de culto." *Quilombo* 2, no. 5, January 1950, 2, 7.

——. *Negros bantus—Notas de etnografia religiosa e de folclore*. Rio de Janeiro: Civilização Brasileira, 1937.

——. *A sabedoria popular*. Rio de Janeiro: Instituto Nacional do Livro, 1957.

Carneiro, Sueli. "Raça, Classe e Identidade Nacional." *Thoth. Pensamento dos povos afro-descendentes* 2 (May/August 1997): 221–33.

Carneiro, Sueli, and Cristiane Curi. "O poder feminino no culto aos Orixás." Paper presented at the Third Congress of Black Culture in the Americas. São Paulo: PUC of São Paulo, 1982.

Carone, Iray, and Maria Aparecida Silva Bento, eds. *Psicologia social do racismo. Estudos sobre branquitude e branqueamento, no Brasil*. Petrópolis, Brazil: Vozes, 2002.

Caroso, Carlos, and Jéferson Bacelar, eds. *Brasil. Um país de negros?* Rio de Janeiro: Pallas; Salvador, Brazil: CEAO, UFBA, 1999.

——. *Faces da tradição Afro-Brasileira*. Rio de Janeiro: Pallas; Salvador, Brazil: CEAO, UFBA, 1999.

Castel, Robert. *A ordem psiquiátrica*. Rio de Janeiro: Graal, 1978. Originally published as *L'Ordre psychiatrique. L'age d'or de l'alienisme*. Paris: Les Editions de Minuit, 1977.

Castells, Manuel. *O poder da identidade*. Vol. 2, *A era da informação—Economia, sociedade e cultura*. Translated by Klauss Brandini Gerhardt. São Paulo: Paz e Terra, 1999. Originally published as *The Power of Identity*. Vol. 2, *The Information Age—Economy, Society, and Culture*. Cambridge, MA: Blackwell Publishers, 1997.

——. *A sociedade em rede*. Vol. 1, *A era da informação—Economia, sociedade e cultura*. 3rd ed. Translated by Roneide Venancio Majer and Klauss Brandini Gerhardt. São Paulo: Paz e Terra, 2000. Originally published as *The Rise of the Network Society*. Vol. 1, *The Information Age—Economy, Society, and Culture*. Cambridge, MA: Blackwell Publishers, 1997.

Castro, Mary Garcia. "Mulheres chefes de família. Racismo, códigos de idade e pobreza no Brasil (Bahia e São Paulo)." In *Desigualdade racial no Brasil contemporâneo*, edited by Peggy Lovell, 121–60. Belo Horizonte, Brazil: CEDEPLAR, UFMG, 1991.

"Catty, a 'Boneca de pixe' de 1950." *Quilombo* 2, no. 9, May 1948, 6.

Cavalleiro, Eliane dos Santos. *Do silêncio do lar ao silêncio escolar. Racismo, preconceito e discriminação na educação infantil.* São Paulo: Contexto; São Paulo: USP, 2000.

Césaire, Aimé. *Discours sur le colonialisme.* Paris: Présence Africaine, 1955.

——. *Notebook of a Return to my Native Land.* Bilingual edition. Translated by Mireille Rosello and Pritchard. Newcastle upon Tyne, UK: Bloodaxe, 1995.

——. *Notebook of a Return to the Native Land.* Translated by Clayton Eshleman and Annette Smith. Middletown, CN: Wesleyan University Press, 2001.

——. *The Tragedy of King Christophe.* New York: Grove Press, 1969.

——. "What Is Negritude to Me." In *African Presence in the Americas,* edited by Carlos Moore, Tanya R. Sanders, and Shawna Moore, 13–20. Trenton, NJ: Africa World Press; Trenton, NJ: The African Heritage Foundation, 1995.

Chagas, Conceição Corrêa das. *Negro. Uma identidade em construção.* Petrópolis, Brazil: Vozes, 1996.

Chalhoub, Sidney. *Cidade febril. Cortiços e epidemias na corte imperial.* São Paulo: Companhia das Letras, 1996.

Chauí, Marilena. *Cultura e democracia. O discurso competente e outras falas.* São Paulo: Moderna, 1981.

Chiavanetto, Júlio José. *O negro no Brasil.* 3rd ed. São Paulo: Brasiliense, 1980.

Ciampa, Antônio da Costa. *A estória do severino e a história da severina.* São Paulo: Brasiliense, 1987.

——. "Identidade. Um paradigma para a psicologia social?" In *A psicologia social Brasileira e o contexto Latino-Americano. Programa científico e resumos,* edited by Bader Burihan Sawaia, C. P. Alves, and O. Ardans: 8–14. São Paulo: Brazilian Association of Social Psychology [Associação Brasileira de Psicologia Social (ABRAPSO)]; São Paulo: USP, 1999.

Clarke, John Henrik, and Amy Jacques Garvey, eds. *Marcus Garvey and the Vision of Africa.* New York: Vintage Books, 1974.

Collins, Patricia Hill. *Black Feminist Thought: Knowledge, Consciousness, and the Politics of Empowerment.* New York: Routledge, 1991.

Comparative Human Relations Initiative (CHRI). *Beyond Racism: Embracing an Interdependent Future.* 4 vols. Atlanta: SEF, 2000.

Conrad, Robert Edgar. *Children of God's Fire: A Documentary History of Black Slavery in Brazil.* Princeton: Princeton University Press, 1983.

Convenção Nacional do Negro Brasileiro [National Convention of Brazilian Blacks]. "Manifesto à Nação Brasileira." In *O negro revoltado,* edited by Abdias Nascimento. Rio de Janeiro: GRD, 1968.

Costa, Haroldo. "As origens do Brasiliana." In "Teatro Experimental do Negro." Special issue, edited by Ricardo Gaspar Müller, *Dionysos. Revista da Fundacen/MinC* 28 (1988): 139–43.

Costa, Jurandir Freire. "Da cor ao corpo. A violência do racismo." In *Tornar-se negro,* by Neusa dos Santos Souza, 1–16. Rio de Janeiro: Graal, 1983.

Costa Pinto, Luiz de Aguiar. "Ciência social e ideologia racial. Esclarecendo intencionais obscuridades." *O Jornal* 35, no. 10, July 10, 1954, 2.

——. *O negro no Rio de Janeiro.* São Paulo: Companhia Editora Nacional, 1953.

——. *O negro no Rio de Janeiro.* 2nd ed. Rio de Janeiro: UFRJ Press, 1998.

Coutinho, José Maria. "Por uma educação multicultural. Uma alternativa de cidadania para o Século XXI." *Revista Ensaio. Avaliação e Políticas Públicas em Educação* 4, no. 13 (October/December 1996): 381–92.

Crenshaw, Kimberlé Williams, ed. *Critical Race Theory: The Key Writings that Formed the Movement.* New York: New Press, 1995.

——. "Mapping the Margins—Intersectionality, Identity Politics, and Violence against Women of Color." In *The Public Nature of Private Violence*, edited by Martha Albertson Fineman and Rixanne Mykitiuk, 93–118. New York: Routledge, 1994.

Crook, Larry, and Randal Johnson. *Black Brazil: Culture, Identity, and Social Mobilization.* Los Angeles: UCLA Press, 1999.

Cross, William E., Jr. "The Cross and Thomas Models of Psychological Nigrescence." *Journal of Black Psychology* 5, no. 1 (1978): 13–19.

——. *Shades of Black: Diversity in African-American Identity.* Philadelphia: Temple University Press, 1991.

Cruz, Anabel. "Mercosul. Iniqüidades na integração." *Observatório da cidadania* 2 (1998): 27–30.

Cruz, Manoel de Almeida. *Alternativas para combater o racismo segundo a pedagogia interétnica.* Salvador, Brazil: Afro-Brazilian Cultural Nucleus, 1989.

Cunha, Euclides da. *Os sertões (Campanha de Canudos).* Rio de Janeiro: Laemmert, 1902.

Cunha, Manuela Carneiro da. *Negros, estrangeiros.* São Paulo: Brasiliense, 1985.

Cunha, Maria Clementina Pereira. *O espelho do mundo. Juquery, a história de um asilo.* 2nd ed. São Paulo: Paz e Terra, 1988.

Cunha, Olívia Gomes da. "1933. Um ano em que fizemos contatos." *Revista USP* 28 (December 1995–February 1996): 142–63.

Cuti, and José Correia Leite. *E disse o velho militante.* São Paulo: São Paulo Municipal Culture Secretariat, 1992.

D'Adesky, Jacques. *Pluralismo étnico e multiculturalismo. Racismos e anti-racismos no Brasil.* Rio de Janeiro: Pallas, 2001.

Du Bois, W.E.B. *As almas da gente negra.* Translated by Heloísa Toller Gomes. Rio de Janeiro: Nova Aguilar, 1999. Originally published as *The Souls of Black Folk.* New York: New American Library, 1903.

——. "Krigwa Players Little Negro Theater." *The Crisis,* July 1926.

——. *Writings: The Suppression of the African Slave-Trade / The Souls of Black Folk / Dusk of Dawn / Essays and Articles.* Edited by Nathan Huggins. New York: Literary Classics/Viking Press, 1986.

Damasceno, Caetana Maria. "Em casa de enforcado não se fala de corda. Notas sobre a construção social da 'boa aparência' no Brasil." In *Tirando a máscara. Ensaios sobre o racismo no Brasil,* edited by Antonio Sérgio Alfredo Guimarães and Lynn Huntley, 165–99. São Paulo: Paz e Terra; Atlanta: SEF, 2000.

Degler, Carl E. *Neither Black nor White: Slavery and Race Relations in the United States and Brazil.* New York: MacMillan, 1971.

Delgado, Richard, ed. *Critical Race Theory.* Philadelphia: Temple University Press, 1997.

Delgado, Richard, and Jean Stefancic, eds. *Critical White Studies: Looking behind the Mirror.* Philadelphia: Temple University Press, 1997.

Dévereux, Georges. *Essais d'ethnopsychiatrie générale.* Paris: Gallimard, 1970.

Diegues, Manuel, Jr. "A África na vida e na cultura do Brasil." In "Negro Brasileiro Negro." Special issue, edited by Joel Rufino dos Santos, *Revista do Patrimônio Histórico e Artístico Nacional* 25 (1997): 11–27.

——. "Teatro Experimental do Negro." Special issue, edited by Ricardo Gaspar Müller, *Dionysos. Revista da Fundacen/MinC* [Journal of the Ministry of Culture National Scenic Arts Foundation] 28 (1988): 285.

Diop, Cheikh Anta. *The African Origin of Civilization: Myth or Reality.* Translated by Mercer Cook. Westport: Lawrence Hill, 1974. Originally published as *Anteriorité des civilisations negres: Mythe ou verité historique?* Paris: Présence Africaine, 1959.

———. *The Cultural Unity of Black Africa*. 2nd ed. Translated by Présence Africaine. Chicago: Third World Press, 1978. Originally published as *L'unité culturelle de l'Afrique Noire*. Paris: Présence Africaine, 1962.

———. *Nations negres et culture*. Paris: Présence Africaine, 1955.

Dunham, Katherine. "O Estado dos cultos entre os povos deserdados." *Quilombo* 2, no. 10, June–July 1950, 6–7, 10.

Durham, Carolyn Richardson, Leda Maria Martins, Phyllis Peres, and Charles H. Rowell, eds. "African-Brazilian Literature." Special Issue, *Callaloo: Journal of African and African-American Arts and Letters* 18, no. 4 (1995).

Dzidzienyo, Anani. "Conclusions." In *No Longer Invisible: Afro-Latin Americans*, edited by Minority Rights Group, 345–58. London: Minority Rights Group, 1995.

———. *The Position of Blacks in Brazilian Society*. London: Minority Rights Group, 1971.

Dzidzienyo, Anani, and Lourdes Casal. *The Position of Black People in Brazilian and Cuban Society*. London: Minority Rights Group, 1979.

"É preciso regulamentar o trabalho doméstico." Interview with Ruth de Souza. *A Manhã* 6, no. 1365, January 20, 1946, 3. Edwards, Flora Mancuso. "The Theater of the Black Diaspora: A Comparative Study of Black Drama in Brazil, Cuba and the United States." PhD diss., New York University, 1975.

Eriksen, Thomas H. *Ethnicity and Nationalism, Anthropological Perspectives*. London: Plato Press, 1993.

Erikson, Erik H. *Childhood and Society*. 2nd ed. New York: W. W. Norton, 1963.

———. *Identidade, juventude e crise*. Translated by Álvaro Cabral. Rio de Janeiro: Zahar, 1972. Originally published as *Identity: Youth and Crisis*. New York: W. W. Norton, 1968.

Erikson, Kai T., ed. *In Search of Common Ground: Conversations with Erik H. Erikson and Huey P. Newton*. New York: W. W. Norton, 1973.

Exner, Franz. *Biología criminal*. Barcelona: Bosch, 1946.

"Expulsaram os negros." *Revista da Semana* 47, no. 36, September 7, 1946, 47–50.

"Expulsos do Fênix, os artistas negros ensaiarão ao ar livre!" *Vanguarda*, August 26, 1946.

Fanon, Frantz. *Os condenados da terra*. 2nd ed. Rio de Janeiro: Editora Civilização Brasileira, 1979. Originally published as *Les damnés de la terre*. Paris, 1961. Reprinted in 2002 by La Découverte.

———. *Pele negra, máscara branca*. Salvador, Brazil: Fator, 1983. Originally published as *Peau noire, masques blancs*. Paris: Seuil, 1952.

Farias, João, Jr. *Manual de criminologia*. 2nd ed. Curitiba: Juruá, 1996.

Fernandes, Florestan. *A integração do negro à sociedade de classes*. São Paulo: FFLCH, USP, 1964.

———. *The Negro in Brazilian Society*. New York: Columbia University Press, 1969. Reprinted in 1971 by Atheneum.

———. *O negro no mundo dos brancos*. São Paulo: Difusão Européia do Livro, 1972.

Ferreira, Ricardo Franklin. *Afro-descendente. Identidade em construção*. Rio de Janeiro: Pallas; São Paulo: Educ; São Paulo: FAPESP, 2000.

———. "A construção da identidade dos afro-descendentes. A psicologia brasileira e a questão racial." In *Brasil. Um país de negros?* edited by Jéferson Bacelar and Carlos Caroso, 71–86. Rio de Janeiro: Pallas, 1999.

———. "*Uma história de lutas e vitórias. A construção da identidade de um afro-descendente brasileiro*." PhD diss., Psychology Institute, USP, 1999.

Figueiredo, Guilherme. "Apartheid, a discriminação racial e o colonialismo na África austral." In *Brasil, África e Portugal*. Special issue, edited by Eduardo Portella, *Tempo Brasileiro* 38/39 (1975): 33–58.

Figueiredo, Luiz Cláudio M. *A invenção do psicológico. Quatro séculos de subjetivação (1500–1900)*. São Paulo: Escuta; São Paulo: Educ, 1992.

———. *Matrizes do pensamento psicológico*. Petrópolis, Brazil: Vozes, 1991.
———. *Revisitando as psicologias*. Petrópolis, Brazil: Vozes, 1995.
Fonseca, José Paulo Moreira da. "Nota sôbre *Sortilégio* e alguns dos problemas que envolveu." In *Teatro Experimental do Negro. Testemunhos*, edited by Abdias Nascimento, 159–62. Rio de Janeiro: GRD, 1966.
Franco da Rocha, Francisco. *Causas da loucura. Estatísticas e apontamentos, hospício de São Paulo*. 8 vols. São Paulo: Typografia do Diário Oficial, 1901.
———. "Contribution a l'étude de la folie dans la race noire." *Annales Médico-Psychologique* 9, book XIV, year 69 (1911).
———. *Esboço de psiquiatria forense*. São Paulo: Laemmert, 1904.
Frankenberg, Ruth. *White Women, Race Matters: The Social Construction of Whiteness*. Minneapolis: University of Minnesota Press, 1993.
Freyre, Gilberto. "The Afro-Brazilian Experiment." *The UNESCO Courier* 5 (August–September 1977): 10–11.
———. "Aspectos da influência Africana no Brasil." *Revista Cultura* 6, no. 23 (October–December 1976): 6–14.
———. *Casa grande e senzala*. 13ᵗʰ ed. 2 vols. Rio de Janeiro: José Olympio, 1966. First published, 1933.
———. "Declara o deputado Gilberto Freyre. Dois racismos despontam no Brasil." *Tribuna da Imprensa* 2, no. 173, July 19, 1950, 1, 3.
———. *The Mansions and the Shanties: The Making of Modern Brazil*. Translated by Harriet de Onís. New York: Alfred A. Knopf, 1963. Originally published as *Sobrados e mocambos: Decadência do patriarcado rural e desenvolvimento do urbano*. São Paulo: Companhia Editora Nacional, 1936.
———. *The Masters and the Slaves: A Study in the Development of Brazilian Civilization*. Translated by Samuel Putnam. New York: Alfred A. Knopf, 1946. Originally published as *Casa Grande e Senzala*.
———. *O mundo que o português criou. Aspectos das relações sociais e de cultura do Brasil com Portugal e as colônias portuguesas*. Rio de Janeiro: José Olympio, 1940.
———. *New World in the Tropics: The Culture of Modern Brazil*. New York: Alfred A. Knopf, 1959.
———. *The Portuguese and the Tropics—Suggestions Inspired by the Portuguese Methods of Integrating Autochthonous Peoples and Cultures Differing from the European in a New, or Luso-Tropical Complex of Civilization*. Lisbon: Executive Committee for the Commemoration of the Vth Centenary of the Death of Prince Henry the Navigator, 1961.
Gilliam, Angela. "A Black Feminist Perspective on the Sexual Commodification of Women in the New Global Culture." *Black Feminist Anthropology: Theory, Praxis, Politics and Poetics*, edited by Irma McClaurin, 150–86. New Brunswick, NJ: Rutgers University Press, 2001.
———. "Globalization, Identity, and Assaults on Equality in the United States: An Initial Perspective for Brazil." *SOULS: A Critical Journal of Black Politics, Culture, and Society* 5, no. 2 (Spring 2003): 81–106.
———. "Reclaiming Honor, Resurrecting Struggle: Black Women, Patronage, and the Global Heritage of Afrophobia." Paper presented at the Fourth World Congress of Archaeology at Capetown University in January 1999.
———. "Women's Equality and National Liberation." In *Third World Women and the Politics of Feminism*, edited by Chandra Talpade Mohanty, Ann Russo, and Lourdes Torres, 215–36. Bloomington: Indiana University Press, 1991.
Gomes, Nilma Lino. *A mulher negra que vi de perto*. Belo Horizonte, Brazil: Mazza, 1995.
González, Lélia. "Griot e Guerreiro." In *Axés do sangue e da esperança*, by Abdias Nascimento, v-ix. Rio de Janeiro: Achiamé, 1983.
———. "A importância da organização da mulher negra no processo de transformação social." *Raça e Classe* 5, no. 2 (November–December 1988): 223–44.

———. "Mulher negra." *Afrodiáspora. Revista do Mundo Negro* 3, no. 6–7 (1986): 94–106.

———. "Racismo e sexismo na cultura brasileira." In *Movimentos sociais urbanos, minorias étnicas e outros estudos,* edited by Luiz Antonio Silva et al., 224–35. Brasília: ANPOCS, 1983.

González, Lélia, and Carlos Hasenbalg. *Lugar de negro.* Rio de Janeiro: Marco Zero, 1982.

Graves, Robert and Raphael Patai. *Hebrew Myths: The Book of Genesis.* New York: Doubleday, 1964.

Guimarães, Antonio Sérgio Alfredo. "The Misadventures of Nonracialism in Brazil." In *Beyond Racism: Race and Inequality in Brazil, South Africa, and the United States,* edited by Lynn Huntley et al., 157–85. Boulder, CO: Lynne Reinner, 2001.

———. *Racismo e anti-racismo no Brasil.* São Paulo: USP Foundation; São Paulo: Editora 34, 1999.

Guimarães, Antonio Sérgio Alfredo, and Lynn Huntley, eds. *Tirando a máscara. Ensaios sobre o racismo no Brasil.* São Paulo: Paz e Terra; Atlanta: SEF, 2000.

Guimarães, Geni. *A cor da ternura.* São Paulo: FTD, 1989.

Guimarães, Marco Antonio Chagas. "É um umbigo, não é? A mãe criadeira. Um estudo sobre o processo de construção de identidade em comunidades de terreiro." Master's thesis, PUC of Rio de Janeiro, 1990.

———. "O mistério do nascer. Significados na tradição religiosa afro-brasileira." In *Sinais de vida, reflexões sobre parto e nascimento,* edited by Solange Dacach, 4–11. Rio de Janeiro: REDEH, 1995.

———. "Rede de sustentação. Um modelo winnicottiano de intervenção em saúde coletiva." PhD diss., PUC of Rio de Janeiro, 2001.

Hamilton, Charles V. "Not Yet 'E Pluribus Unum': Racism, America's Achilles' Heel." In *Beyond Racism: Race and Inequality in Brazil, South Africa, and the United States,* edited by Charles V. Hamilton et al., 187–230. Boulder, CO: Lynne Reiner Publishers, 2001.

Hanchard, Michael George. *Orpheus and Power: The Movimento Negro of Rio de Janeiro and São Paulo, Brazil, 1945–1988.* Princeton: Princeton University Press, 1994.

Harrison, Faye V., ed. *Decolonizing Anthropology: Moving Further toward an Anthropology for Liberation.* 2nd ed. Washington, DC: Association of Black Anthropologists, 1997.

Harrison, Paul Carter. *The Drama of Nommo.* New York: Grove Press, 1972.

———, ed. *Kuntu Drama: Plays of the African Continuum.* New York: Grove Press, 1974.

Hasenbalg, Carlos. *Discriminação e desigualdades raciais no Brasil.* Rio de Janeiro: Graal, 1979.

———. *Raça, classe e mobilidade.* Rio de Janeiro: Marco Zero, 1982.

Heller, Agnes. "From Hermeneutics in Social Science toward a Hermeneutics of Social Science." *Theory and Society* 18, no. 3 (May 1989).

———. *Para mudar a vida—Felicidade, liberdade e democracia.* São Paulo: Brasiliense, 1982.

Helms, Janet. E., ed. *Black and White Racial Identity: Theory, Research, and Practice.* Westport, CT: Praeger, 1993.

Henriques, Ricardo, ed. *Desigualdade e pobreza no Brasil.* Rio de Janeiro: IPEA, 2000.

Hester, Marianne. *Lewd Women and Wicked Witches: A Study of the Dynamics of Male Domination.* New York: Routledge, 1992.

Hill, Errol. "Black Black Theatre in Form and Style." *The Black Scholar* 10, no. 10 (1979).

Hollanda Ferreira, Aurélio Buarque de, ed. *Dicionário Aurélio eletrônico, Século XXI,* Version 3.0. Rio de Janeiro: Nova Fronteira, 1999.

hooks, bell. *Talking Back: Thinking Feminist, Thinking Black.* Boston: South End Press, 1989.

Hull, Gloria, Patricia Bell Scott, and Barbara Smith, eds. *All the Women Are White, All the Blacks Are Men, but Some of Us Are Brave.* Old Westbury, NY: City University of New York and Feminist Press, 1982.

Huntley, Lynn et al., eds. *Beyond Racism: Race and Inequality in Brazil, South Africa, and the United States.* Boulder, CO: Lynne Reinner, 2001.

Ilê-Aiyê. *Cadernos de educação.* 6 vols. Salvador: Bloco Carnavalesco Ilê-Aiyê, 1995–1998.

"Ilegal a Proibição de Peças Teatrais pela Censura Policial." *Diario Carioca,* February 6, 1948.

Instituto Brasileiro de Geografia e Estatísticas (IBGE). *Mapa do mercado de trabalho.* Rio de Janeiro: IBGE, 1994.

——. "Minimum National Social Indicators Set." Available at http://www.ibge.gov.br/. Accessed 1999.

——. *Pesquisa nacional por amostra de domicílios, 1996. Síntese de indicadores.* Rio de Janeiro: IBGE, 1997.

"Instituto Nacional do Negro." *Quilombo* 1, no. 3, June 1949, 11.

Inter-American Trade Union Institute for Racial Equality (INSPIR) and Inter-Trade Union Department for Statistics and Socio-Economic Studies (DIEESE). *Mapa da população negra no mercado de trabalho. Regiões metropolitanas de São Paulo, Salvador, Recife, Belo Horizonte, Porto Alegre e Distrito Federal—Outubro de 1999.* São Paulo: INSPIR/DIEESE, 1999.

Jaccoud, Luciana, and Nathalie Beghin. *Desigualdades raciais no Brasil. Um balanço da intervenção governamental.* Brasília: IPEA, 2002.

Jahn, Janheinz. *Muntu: An Outline of the New African Culture.* New York: Grove Press, 1961.

——. *Through African Doors.* New York: Grove Press, 1969.

James, C. L. R. *A History of Pan-African Revolt.* Washington, DC: Drum and Spear, 1969.

——. "Towards the Seventh. The Pan-African Congress: Past, Present and Future." *Ch'Indaba* 1, no. 2 (July–December 1976).

James, George G. M. *Stolen Legacy.* 2nd ed. San Francisco, CA: Julian Richardson Associates, 1976. First published, New York: Philosophical Library, 1954.

Johnson, Samuel. *The History of the Yorùbás.* New York: Routledge and Kegan Paul, 1921.

Kennedy, Scott. *In Search of African Theatre.* New York: Scribner's, 1973.

Labor Relations and Inequality Studies Center (CEERT). *Formação sobre relações raciais no movimento sindical.* São Paulo: CUT, 1999.

Lacan, Jacques. *O eu na teoria de Freud e na técnica da psicanálise. O Seminário, Livro II.* Rio de Janeiro: Zahar, 1985.

Landes, Ruth. *Cidade das mulheres.* Rio de Janeiro: Civilização Brasileira, 1967.

Lapido, Duro et al. *Teatro Africano.* Havana: Instituto Cubano del Libro and Editorial Arte e Literatura, 1975.

Leal, José. "Boneca de pixe." *O Cruzeiro* 20, no. 33, June 5, 1948, 30–32.

Lewis, Rupert. *Marcus Garvey, Anti-Colonial Champion.* Trenton, NJ: Africa World Press, 1988.

Lima, Ivan Costa, and Jeruse Romão, eds. *Negros e currículo.* Black Thought in Education Series 2. Florianópolis, Brazil: NEN, 1997.

Lima, Ivan Costa, Jeruse Romão, and Sônia Maria Silveira, eds. *Educação popular afro-brasileira.* Black Thought in Education Series 5. Florianópolis, Brazil: NEN, 1999.

Lima, Nísia Trindade, and Gilberto Hochman. "Condenado pela raça, absolvido pela medicina. O Brasil descoberto pelo movimento sanitarista da primeira república." In *Raça, ciência e sociedade,* edited by Marcos Chor Maio and Ricardo Ventura Santos, 23–40. Rio de Janeiro: FIOCRUZ; Rio de Janeiro: CCBB, 1998.

Lopes, Nei. *Novo dicionário Banto do Brasil.* 2nd ed. Rio de Janeiro: Pallas Editora, 2003. First published, Rio de Janeiro: Rio de Janeiro Municipal Government, José Bonifácio Cultural Center, 1996.

Lovell, Peggy, ed. *Desigualdade racial no Brasil contemporâneo.* Belo Horizonte, Brazil: CEDEPLAR, UFMG, 1991.

Luz, Marco Aurélio. *Agadá. Dinâmica da civilização africano-brasileira.* Salvador, Brazil: SECNEB; Salvador, Brazil: UFBA, 1995.

——. *Cultura negra e ideologia do recalque*. Petrópolis, Brazil: Vozes, 1979.

——, ed. *Identidade negra e educação*. Salvador, Brazil: Ianamá, 1989.

Luz, Narcimária Corrêa do Patrocínio, ed. *Pluralidade cultural e educação*. Salvador, Brazil: Bahia State Government Secretariat of Education; Salvador, Brazil: SECNEB, 1996.

Lyra, Roberto, and João Marcello Araújo, Jr. *Criminologia*. 4th ed. Rio de Janeiro: Forense, 1995.

Machado, Vanda. *Ilê Axé. Vivências e invenção pedagógica. As crianças do Opô Afonjá*. Salvador, Brazil: Salvador Municipal Government; Salvador, Brazil: UFBA, 1999.

Maio, Marcos Chor. "Costa Pinto e a crítica ao 'Negro como Espetáculo.'" In *O negro no Rio de Janeiro*, 2nd ed., by Luiz de Aguiar Costa Pinto, 17–50. Rio de Janeiro: UFRJ Press, 1998.

——. "A história do projeto UNESCO. Estudos raciais e ciências sociais no Brasil." PhD diss., IUPERJ, UCAM, 1997.

——. "A questão racial no pensamento de Guerreiro Ramos." In *Raça, Ciência e Sociedade*, edited by Marcos Chor Maio and Ricardo Ventura Santos, 179–93. Rio de Janeiro: FIOCRUZ; Rio de Janeiro: CCBB, 1998.

Maio, Marcos Chor, and Ricardo Ventura Santos, eds. *Raça, ciência e sociedade*. Rio de Janeiro: FIOCRUZ; Rio de Janeiro: CCBB, 1998.

Mantega, Guido. "Brasil. Determinantes e evolução recente das desigualdades no Brasil." *Observatório da cidadania* 2 (1998): 95–101.

Martin, Tony. *Race First: The Ideological and Organizational Struggles of Marcus Garvey and the Universal Negro Improvement Association*. Dover, MA: Majority Press, 1976.

Martínez-Echazábal, Lourdes. "O culturalismo dos anos 30 no Brasil e na América Latina. Deslocamento retórico ou mudança conceitual?" In *Raça, ciência e sociedade*, edited by Marcos Chor Maio and Ricardo Ventura Santos, 107–24. Rio de Janeiro: FIOCRUZ; Rio de Janeiro: CCBB, 1998.

Martins, Cléo, and Raul Lody, eds. *Faraimará—O caçador traz alegria. Mãe Stella, 60 anos de iniciação*. Rio de Janeiro: Pallas, 1999.

Martins, Leda Maria. *A cena em sombras*. São Paulo: Perspectiva, 1995.

Martins, Marilza de Souza. Interview by Elisa Larkin Nascimento at AMMA headquarters, São Paulo, on July 9, 2000.

Martins, Roberto Borges. "Desigualdades e discriminação de gênero e de raça no mercado brasileiro de trabalho do Século XX." Report presented to the International Labor Organization in Brazil, Brasília, Brazil, April 2003.

——. "Desigualdades raciais e políticas de inclusão racial. Um sumário da experiência Brasileira recente." Report presented to the United Nations Economic Commission on Latin America and the Caribbean (CEPAL), Santiago, Chile, August 2003.

Marx, Anthony. *Making Race and Nation: A Comparison of the United States, South Africa, and Brazil*. Cambridge: Cambridge University Press, 1998.

"'... Mas como a cor não pega' ... Poderíamos ter uma jovem negra no concurso da Miss Universo?" *O Radical* 18, no. 5, July 27, 1948, 1.

Mattos, Guiomar Ferreira de. "O preconceito nos livros infantis." In *Teatro Experimental do Negro. Testemunhos*, edited by Abdias Nascimento, 136–39. Rio de Janeiro: GRD, 1966.

Maués, Maria Angelica da Motta. "Negro sobre negro. A questão racial no pensamento das elites negras brasileiras." PhD diss., IUPERJ, UCAM, 1997.

McLaren, Peter. *Multiculturalismo crítico*. Translated by Bebel Orofino Schaefer. São Paulo: Cortez and Paulo Freire Institute, 1997.

Medeiros, Carlos Alberto. *Na lei e na raça. Legislação e relações raciais, Brasil-Estados Unidos*. Rio de Janeiro: State University of Rio de Janeiro Public Policy Library, 2004.

Mello Mourão, Gerardo. "Sortilégio." In *Teatro Experimental do Negro. Testemunhos*, edited by Abdias Nascimento, 155–56. Rio de Janeiro: GRD, 1966.

Memmi, Albert. *The Colonizer and the Colonized*. Boston: Beacon Press, 1965.

"Ministros, senadores e diplomatas negros. Objetivos da 'Uagacê' do Distrito Federal na palavra do Snr. Joviano Severino de Melo." *Quilombo* 1, no. 3, June 1949, 8.

Minority Rights Group (MRG). *No Longer Invisible: Afro-Latin Americans Today.* London: MRG, 1995.

Mitchell, Michael. "Racial Consciousness and the Political Attitudes and Behavior of Blacks in São Paulo, Brazil." PhD diss., Princeton University, 1977.

Mohanty, Chandra Talpade, Ann Russo, and Lourdes Torres, eds. *Third World Women and the Politics of Feminism.* Bloomington: Indiana University Press, 1991.

Monteiro Lobato, José Bento. *Idéias de Jeca Tatu.* São Paulo: Revista do Brasil, 1919.

——. *Urupês.* Rio de Janeiro: Civilização Brasileira, 1957. First published, São Paulo: Monteiro Lobato, 1918.

Moore, Carlos. "Abdias do Nascimento e o surgimento de um pan-africanismo contemporâneo global." In *O Brasil na mira do Pan-Africanismo,* by Abdias Nascimento, 17–32. Salvador, Brazil: CEAO, UFBA, 2002.

Moore, Carlos, Tanya R. Sanders, and Shawna Moore, eds. *African Presence in the Americas.* Trenton, NJ: Africa World Press; Trenton, NJ: The African Heritage Foundation, 1995.

Moreira, Juliano. "Notícia sobre a evolução da assistência a alienados no Brasil." *Archivos Brasileiros de psychiatria, neurologia e sciencias affins.* Rio de Janeiro: Oficina De Typographia e Hospício Nacional de Alienados, 1905.

Moreira, Renato Jardim, and José Correira Leite. "Movimentos sociais no meio negro." In *A Integração do negro à sociedade de classes,* by Florestan Fernandes. São Paulo: FFLCH, USP, 1964.

Morel, Edmar. *A revolta da chibata. Levante da esquadra pelo marinheiro João Cândido.* Rio de Janeiro: Graal, 1979.

Mortara, Giorgio. "O desenvolvimento da população preta e parda no Brasil." In *Contribuições para o estudo da demografia do Brasil,* 2nd ed., edited by IBGE, 198–206. Rio de Janeiro: IBGE, 1970.

Mostaço, Edélcio. "O legado de Set." In "Teatro Experimental do Negro." Special issue, edited by Ricardo Gaspar Mûller, *Dionysos, Revista da Fundacen/MinC* [Journal of the Scenic Arts Foundation, Ministry of Culture] 28 (1988): 53–63.

Moura, Clóvis. *As injustiças de Clio.* Belo Horizonte: Oficina de Livros, 1990.

Moura, Maria da Glória da Veiga. "Ritmo e ancestralidade na força dos tambores negros." PhD diss., USP, 1997.

Müller, Ricardo Gaspar. "Identidade e cidadania. O Teatro Experimental do Negro." In "Teatro Experimental do Negro." Special issue, edited by Ricardo Gaspar Müller, *Dionysos. Revista da Fundacen/MinC* 28 (1988): 11–52.

——. "Nota introdutória." In "Teatro Experimental do Negro." Special issue, edited by Ricardo Gaspar Müller, *Dionysos, Revista da Fundacen/MinC* 28 (1988): 7–8.

——. "Teatro Experimental do Negro." Special issue, edited by Ricardo Gaspar Müller, *Dionysos. Revista da Fundacen/MinC* 28 (1988).

——. "Teatro, política e educação. A experiência histórica do Teatro Experimental do Negro (TEN)—(1945/1968)." In *Educação popular afro-brasileira,* edited by Ivan Costa Lima, Jeruse Romão, and Sônia Maria Silveira, 13–31. Black Thought in Education Series 5. Florianópolis, Brazil: NEN, 1999.

Munanga, Kabengele, ed. *Estratégias e políticas de combate à discriminação racial.* São Paulo: Estação Ciência; São Paulo: EdUSP, 1996.

——. *Negritude. Usos e Sentidos.* São Paulo: Ática, 1986.

——. *Rediscutindo a mestiçagem no Brasil. Identidade nacional versus identidade negra.* Petrópolis, Brazil: Vozes, 1999.

——. "A resistência histórica dos povos negros." *Revista da Cultura Vozes* 93, no. 4 (1999): 42–73.

———, ed. *Superando o racismo na escola*. Brasília: Ministério de Estado da Educação, 1999.

Nascimento, Abdias. "Afro-Brazilian Art: A Liberating Spirit." *Black Art: An International Quarterly* 1, no. 1 (Fall 1976): 54–62. Translated by Elizabeth A. Larkin (Elisa Larkin Nascimento).

———. *Axés do sangue e da esperança. Orikis*. Rio de Janeiro: Achiamé, 1983.

———. *O Brasil na mira do Pan-Africanismo*. Salvador, Brazil: CEAO, UFBA, 2002.

———. *Brazil, Mixture or Massacre: Essays in the Genocide of a Black People*. 2nd ed. Translated by Elisa Larkin Nascimento. Dover, MA: Majority Press, 1989. First published, Buffalo, NY: Afrodiaspora Press, 1979.

———. "Carta aberta a Dacar." *Tempo Brasileiro* 4, no. 9/10 (1966): 15–17.

———. *Combate ao racismo. Discursos e projetos*. Vol. 1. Brasília: Chamber of Deputies, 47th Legislature, 1st Legislative Session, Separatas de Discursos, Pareceres e Projetos, no. 57, 1983.

———. *Combate ao racismo. Discursos e projetos*. Vols. 1–6. Brasília: Chamber of Deputies, Separatas de Discursos, Pareceres e Projetos. 47th Legislature, 1st Legislative Session, nos. 57 and 228; 2nd Legislative Session, nos. 47 and 186; 3rd Legislative Session, nos. 57 and 149, 1983–1986.

———. "Cristo negro." In *Teatro Experimental do Negro. Testemunhos*, edited by Abdias Nascimento, 146–49. Rio de Janeiro: GRD, 1966.

———. "Depoimento." In *Memórias do exílio*, edited by Nelson Werneck de Aguiar, Pedro Celso Uchoa Cavalcanti, and Jovelino Ramos, 23–52. Lisbon: Arcádia, 1976.

———, ed. *Dramas para negros e prólogo para brancos*. Rio de Janeiro: Teatro Experimental do Negro, 1961.

———. "Espirito e fisionomia do Teatro Experimental do Negro." *Quilombo* 1, no. 3, June 1949, 11. Reprinted in *Teatro Experimental do Negro. Testemunhos*, edited by Abdias Nascimento, 78–81. Rio de Janeiro: GRD, 1966.

———. "Uma experiência social e estética." In *Teatro Experimental do Negro. Testemunhos*, edited by Abdias Nascimento, 122–25. Rio de Janeiro: GRD, 1966.

———. "The Function of Art in the Development of Afro-Brazilian Culture: The Contemporary Situation." In *Faculty Seminar Series*, vol. 2, edited by Olasope Oyelaran, 64–186. Ife, Nigeria: University of Ile-Ife, 1977.

———. *O genocídio do negro brasileiro*. Rio de Janeiro: Paz e Terra, 1978.

———. "A luta da raça negra no Brasil. 13 de maio—Outra mentira cívica." In *Combate ao racismo. Discursos e projetos*, vol. 1, by Abdias Nascimento, 9–22. Brasília: Chamber of Deputies, 47th Legislature, 1st Legislative Session, Separatas de Discursos, Pareceres e Projetos no. 57, 1983.

———. "Memories from Exile." In *Africans in Brazil: A Pan-African Perspective*, by Abdias Nascimento and Elisa Larkin Nascimento, 3–69. Trenton, NJ: Africa World Press, 1992.

———. "O negro revoltado." In *O negro revoltado*, edited by Abdias Nascimento, 15–63. Rio de Janeiro: GRD, 1968.

———, ed. *O negro revoltado*. Rio de Janeiro: GRD, 1968.

———, ed. *O negro revoltado*. 2nd ed. Rio de Janeiro: Nova Fronteira, 1982.

———. "Nós, os Negros, e a UNESCO." *Panfleto*, no. 5 (September 1953): 23.

———. "An Open Letter to the First World Festival of Negro Arts." *Présence Africaine: Cultural Review of the Negro World* 30, no. 58, English Edition (Second Quarterly, 1966): 208–18.

———. "O. T. E. N. Dirige-se aos partidos políticos." *Quilombo* 2, no. 7–8, March–April 1950, 5.

———. *Povo negro. A sucessão e a nova república*. Rio de Janeiro: IPEAFRO, 1984.

———. "Prefácio." In *Sortilégio II. Mistério negro de Zumbi redivivo*, by Abdias Nascimento, 11–16. Rio de Janeiro: Paz e Terra, 1979.

———. "Prólogo para brancos." In *Dramas para negros e prólogo para branco*, edited by Abdias Nascimento, 7–27. Rio de Janeiro: Teatro Experimental do Negro, 1961. Reprinted in *Sortilégio II. Mistério negro de Zumbi redivivo*, by Abdias Nascimento. Rio de Janeiro: Paz e Terra, 1979.

———. "*Racial Democracy" in Brazil: Myth or Reality?* Ibadan, Nigeria: Sketch Publishers, 1977.

———. "Resposta aos racistas da Bahia." In *Combate ao racismo*, vol. 2, by Abdias Nascimento, 62–68. Brasília: Câmara dos Deputados, 1983.

———. *O Quilombismo*. Petrópolis, Brazil: Vozes, 1980.

———. *O Quilombismo*. 2nd ed. Brasília: Palmares Cultural Foundation; Rio de Janeiro: OR, 2002.

———. *Quilombo. Edição Fac-similar do jornal dirigido por Abdias Nascimento*. São Paulo: Editora 34, 2003.

———. *Sortilege (Black Mystery)*. Translated by Peter Lownds. Chicago: Third World Press, 1978. Reprinted in "African-Brazilian Literature." Special issue, edited by Carolyn Richardson Durham, Leda Maria Martins, Phyllis Peres, and Charles H. Rowell, *Callaloo: Journal of African and African-American Arts and Letters* 18, no. 4 (1995): 821–62.

———. *Sortilege II: Zumbi Returns*. Translated by Elisa Larkin Nascimento. In *Crosswinds: An Anthology of Black Dramatists in the Diaspora*, edited by William B. Branch, 203–49. Bloomington: Indiana University Press, 1993.

———. *Sortilégio (Mistério negro)*. Rio de Janeiro: Teatro Experimental do Negro, 1959.

———. *Sortilégio II. Mistério negro de Zumbi redivivo*. Rio de Janeiro: Paz e Terra, 1979.

———, ed. *Teatro Experimental do Negro. Testemunhos*. Rio de Janeiro: GRD, 1966.

———. "Teatro Experimental do Negro. Trajetória e reflexões." In "Negro Brasileiro Negro." Special issue, edited by Joel Rufino dos Santos, *Revista do Patrimônio Histórico e Artístico Nacional* 25 (1997): 71–81.

———. "A UNESCO e as relações de raça." *Panfleto*, no. 14 (December 1953): 8.

Nascimento, Abdias, and Elisa Larkin Nascimento. *Africans in Brazil: A Pan-African Perspective*. Trenton, NJ: Africa World Press, 1991.

———, eds. *Afrodiáspora. Revista do mundo negro/ Afrodiaspora. Journal of black world thought*. 7 vols. Rio de Janeiro: IPEAFRO, 1983–1987.

———, eds. *Journal of Black Studies* 11, no. 2 (1980).

Nascimento, Beatriz. "O conceito de quilombo e a resistência cultural negra." *Afrodiaspora* 3, no. 6–7 (1985): 41–50.

Nascimento, Elisa Larkin, ed. *Abdias Nascimento 90 Years—Living Memory*. Rio de Janeiro: IPEAFRO, 2006.

———, ed. "African Descendants in Brazil." Special issue, *Journal of Black Studies* 34, no. 6 (July 2004).

———, ed. *Dois negros libertários. Luis Gama e Abdias Nascimento*. Rio de Janeiro: IPEAFRO, 1985.

———. *Pan-Africanism and South America: Emergence of a Black Rebellion*. Buffalo, NY: Afrodiaspora, 1980.

———. *Pan-Africanismo na América do Sul*. Petrópolis, Brazil: Vozes; Rio de Janeiro: IPEAFRO, 1981.

———, ed. *Sankofa. Matrizes africanas da cultura brasileira*. Vol. 1. Rio de Janeiro: UERJ Press, 1996.

———, ed. *Sankofa. Resgate da cultura afro-brasileira*. 2 vols. Rio de Janeiro: SEAFRO, 1994.

———. *O sortilégio da cor. Identidade, raça e gênero no Brasil*. São Paulo: Summus, Selo Negro, 2003.

National Convention of Brazilian Blacks. "Manifesto à nação brasileira." In *O negro revoltado*, edited by Abdias Nascimento, 59–61. Rio de Janeiro: GRD, 1968.

Negrão, Esmeralda V. "Preconceitos e discriminações raciais em livros didáticos infanto-juvenis." In *Diagnóstico sobre a situação de negros (Pretos e pardos) no Estado de São Paulo.* Special issue, edited by Fúlvia Rosemberg. *Cadernos de Pesquisa da Fundação Carlos Chagas* 63 (1986): 52–65.

Neri, Regina. "O encontro entre a psicanálise e o feminino. Singularidade/ diferença." In *Feminilidades*, edited by Joel Birman, 13–34. Rio de Janeiro: Contra Capa; Rio de Janeiro: Espaço Brasileiro de Estudos Psicanalíticos, 2002.

Nicholson, Linda. "Feminismo e Marx, integrando o parentesco com o econômico." In *Feminismo como crítica da modernidade*, edited by Seyla Benhabib and Drucilla Cornell, 23–37. Rio de Janeiro: Rosa dos Tempos, 1987. Originally published as *Feminism as Critique: Feminist Perspectives on the Politics of Gender.* Minneapolis: University of Minnesota Press, 1987.

Nina Rodrigues, Raymundo. *Os Africanos no Brasil.* 3rd ed. São Paulo: Companhia Editora Nacional, 1945.

——. *Os Africanos no Brasil.* 5th ed. São Paulo: Companhia Editora Nacional, 1977.

——. *As collectividades anormaes.* Rio de Janeiro: Civilização Brasileira, 1939.

——. *As raças humanas e a responsabilidade penal no Brasil.* Salvador, Brazil: Aguiar e Souza; Salvador, Brazil: Progresso, 1957. First published, Rio de Janeiro: Editora Guanabara, 1894.

Nogueira, Isildinha Baptista. "Significações do corpo negro." PhD diss., Institute of Psychology, USP, 1998.

Nosella, Maria de Lourdes Chagas Deiró. *As belas mentiras. As ideologias subjacentes aos textos didáticos.* São Paulo: Moraes, 1981.

Nucleus of Black Studies (NEN). Black Thought in Education Series. 6 vols. Florianópolis, Brazil: NEN, 1997–1999.

"O Povo Reage Contra o Analfabetismo." *Diário Trabalhista*, June 1946, 4.

"O Problema da Liberdade de Culto." *Quilombo* 2, no. 10, June–July 1950, 4, 11.

"O Teatro Experimental do Negro e a cultura do povo contra o despejo do conjunto de cor." Interview with Solano Trindade. "Problemas e Aspirações do Negro Brasileiro." *Diário Trabalhista* 1, no. 188, August 25, 1946, 4.

Obenga, Theophile. *A Lost Tradition: African Philosophy in World History.* Philadelphia: Source Editions, 1995.

——. *Pour une nouvelle histoire.* Paris: Présence Africaine, 1980.

Oliveira, David Dijaci de et al., eds. *A cor do medo. Homicídios e relações raciais no Brasil.* Brasília: University of Brasília Press; Brasília: University of Goiás Press; Brasília: National Human Rights Movement MNDH, 1998

Oliveira, Ivone Martins de. *Preconceito e autoconceito. Identidade e interação na sala de aula.* São Paulo: Papirus, n.d.

Oliveira, Lúcia, Rosa Maria Porcaro, and Teresa Cristina Costa. *O lugar do negro na força de trabalho.* Rio de Janeiro: IBGE, 1981.

Oliveira, Lúcia Lippi. *A sociologia do Guerreiro.* Rio de Janeiro: UFRJ Press, 1995.

Oliveira, Raquel de. "Relações raciais na escola. Uma experiência de intervenção." Master's thesis, PUC of São Paulo, 1992.

Oliveira, Eduardo de Oliveira e, ed. *A imprensa negra em São Paulo.* Exhibition Catalogue. São Paulo: São Paulo State Pinacoteca Museum, 1977.

Omotoso, Kole. *Season of Migration to the South—Africa's Crises Reconsidered.* Capetown: Tafelburg, 1994.

Ortiz, Fernando. "José Saco y sus ideas." *Revista Bimestre Cubana*, no. 2 (1929): 39–54.

Oyewumi, Oyeronke. *The Invention of Women: Making an African Sense of Western Gender Discourses.* Minneapolis: University of Minnesota Press, 1997.

Padmore, George. *Pan-Africanism or Communism?* 3rd ed. New York: Doubleday, 1972.

Paiva, Alcides Marques de, Antônio Augusto de Azevedo, Hortêncio de Souza, Moacyr Brum, et al. "Manifesto político dos negros fluminenses." *Quilombo* 2, no. 7–8, March–April 1950, 5.

Paixão, Marcelo. "Desenvolvimento humano e as desigualdades étnicas no Brasil. Um retrato de final de século." *Proposta, Revista Trimestral da FASE* 29, no. 86 (September–Novembro 2000): 30–51.

———. *Desenvolvimento humano e relações raciais.* Rio de Janeiro: DP&A, 2003.

Pandian, Jacob. *Anthropology and the Western Tradition: Toward an Authentic Anthropology.* Prospect Heights, IL: Waveland, 1985.

Patto, Maria Helena Souza. *A produção do fracasso escolar.* São Paulo: Teóphilo A. Queiroz, 1993.

———. *Psicologia e ideologia. Uma introdução crítica à psicologia escolar.* São Paulo, Teóphilo A. Queiroz, 1984.

Pauley, Garth E. "W.E.B. Du Bois on Woman Suffrage: A Critical Analysis of His *Crisis* Writings." *Journal of Black Studies* 30, no. 3 (January 2000): 383–410.

Pemberton, John. "The Oyo Empire." In *Yoruba: Nine Centuries of Art and Thought*, edited by Henry John Drewal, John Pemberton III, Rowland Abiodun, and Allen Wardwell. New York: Harry N. Abrams, 1990.

Penna, Belisário. *O saneamento do Brasil.* Rio de Janeiro: Editorial dos Tribunais, 1923.

Petrucelli, José Luis. *A declaração de cor/raça no censo 2000. Um estudo comparativo.* Rio de Janeiro: IBGE, 2002.

Pierson, Donald. *Negroes in Brazil—A Study of Race Contact in Bahia.* Carbondale: Southern Illinois University Press, 1967.

Pinheiro, Paulo Sérgio. *Escritos indignados.* São Paulo: Brasiliense, 1984.

Piza, Edith. "Brancos no Brasil? Ninguém sabe, ninguém viu." In *Tirando a máscara. Ensaios sobre o racismo no Brasil*, edited by Antonio Sérgio Alfredo Guimarães and Lynn Huntley, 97–126. São Paulo: Paz e Terra; Atlanta: SEF, 2000.

———. "Porta de vidro. Entrada para a branquitude." Post-doctorate research paper, Institute of Psychology, USP, 2000.

———. "Porta de vidro. Entrada para a branquitude." In *Psicologia social do racismo. Estudos sobre branquitude e branqueamento no Brasil*, edited by Iray Carone and Maria Aparecida da Silva Bento, 59–90. Petrópolis, Brazil: Vozes, 2002.

Poliakov, Léon. *O mito ariano. Ensaio sobre as fontes do racismo e dos nacionalismos.* Translated by Luiz João Gaio. São Paulo: Perspectiva; São Paulo: EdUSP, 1974. Originally published as *Le mythe Aryan.* Paris: Lévy, 1971.

Porto, Mayla Yara. "Uma revolta popular conta a vacinação." *Ciência e Cultura* 55, no. 1 (January–March 2003): 53–54.

Póvoas, Ruy do Carmo. "Dentro do quarto." In *Faces da tradição afro-brasileira*, edited by Carlos Caroso and Jéferson Bacelar, 213–37. Rio de Janeiro: Pallas; Salvador, Brazil: CEAO, UFBA, 1999.

Price, Richard, ed. *Maroon Societies: Rebel Slave Communities in the Americas.* 3rd ed. Baltimore: Johns Hopkins University Press, 1996.

Quilombhoje, ed. *Frente Negra Brasileira. Depoimentos.* São Paulo: Quilombhoje; São Paulo: National Culture Fund, 1998.

Ramos, Alberto Guerreiro. *O drama de ser dois.* Salvador: Alberto Guerreiro Ramos, 1937.

———. "Foi acusado de plágio no seu livro *Lutas de família.*" *O Jornal* 35, no. 10, January 17, 1954, 1, 7.

——. "Um herói da negritude." *Diário de Notícias* 22, no. 9081, April 6, 1952, 1. Reprinted in *Teatro Experimental do Negro. Testemunhos*, edited by Abdias Nascimento, 104–6. Rio de Janeiro: GRD, 1966.

——. "Interpelação à UNESCO." *O Jornal* 35, no. 10222, January 3, 1954, 2.

——. *Introdução à cultura*. Salvador: Cruzada da Boa Imprensa, 1939.

——. *Introdução crítica à sociologia brasileira*. Rio de Janeiro: Andes, 1957.

——. *Introdução crítica à sociologia brasileira*. 2nd ed. Rio de Janeiro: UFRJ Press, 1995.

——. "Mulatos, negros e brancos reunidos." *Vanguarda* 28, no. 13.213, September 13, 1949, 3.

——. "O negro desde dentro." *Forma. Arquitetura, artes plásticas, dança, teatro*, no. 3, October 1954. Reprinted in Alberto Guerreiro Ramos, *Introdução crítica à sociologia Brasileira*, 193–99. Rio de Janeiro: Andes, 1957. Reprinted in *Teatro Experimental do Negro. Testemunhos*, edited by Abdias Nascimento, 128–35. Rio de Janeiro: GRD, 1966.

——. "O negro no Brasil e um exame de consciência." In *Teatro Experimental do Negro. Testemunhos*, edited by Abdias Nascimento, 82–92. Rio de Janeiro: GRD, 1966.

——. "Notícia sobre o Primeiro Congresso do Negro Brasileiro." *A Manhã* 10, no. 2817, October 1, 1950, 2.

——. "Patologia social do 'branco' brasileiro." In *Introdução crítica à sociologia brasileira*, by Alberto Guerreiro Ramos, 171–92. Rio de Janeiro: Andes, 1957.

——. *A redução sociológica*. 3rd ed. Rio de Janeiro: UFRJ Press, 1998.

——. "Semana do Negro de 1955." *Diário de Notícias*, 25, no. 9890, January 30, 1955, 2. Reprinted in *Teatro Experimental do Negro. Testemunhos*, edited by Abdias Nascimento, 140–42. Rio de Janeiro: GRD, 1966.

Ramos, Arthur. *As culturas negras no novo mundo*. 2nd ed. São Paulo: Companhia Editora Nacional, 1946.

——. "Introdução." In *As collectividades anormaes*, by Nina Rodrigues, 12–13. Rio de Janeiro: Civilização Brasileira, 1939.

Record, Wilson. *The Negro and the Communist Party*. New York: Atheneum, 1971.

Reis, João José, and Flávio dos Santos Gomes. *Liberdade por um fio. História dos quilombos no Brasil*. São Paulo: Companhia das Letras, 1996.

Reis, Letícia Vidor de Sousa. "Negro em 'Terra de branco.' A reinvenção da identidade." In *Negras imagens*, edited by Lília Moritz Schwarcz and Letícia Vidor de Sousa Reis, 31–54. São Paulo: Estação Ciência; São Paulo: EdUSP, 1996.

Ribeiro, Darcy. "A América Latina existe?" *Cadernos Trabalhistas* 1 (1979).

——. *As Américas e a civilização. Processo de formação e causas do desenvolvimento desigual dos povos americanos*. 3rd ed. Petrópolis, Brazil: Vozes, 1979.

——. *Configurações histórico-culturais dos povos americanos*. Rio de Janeiro: Civilização Brasileira, 1975.

——. *Os Índios e a civilização. A integração das populações indígenas no Brasil moderno*. Rio de Janeiro: Civilização Moderna, 1970.

——. *O povo brasileiro. A formação e o sentido do Brasil*. 2nd ed. São Paulo: Companhia das Letras, 1995.

——. *O processo civilizatório. Etapas da evolução sociocultural*. Rio de Janeiro: Civilização Brasileira, 1975.

Ribeiro, Darcy et al. *Mestiço é que é bom! Quem é Darcy Ribeiro*. Rio de Janeiro: Revan, 1996.

Ribeiro, Matilde. "Tornar-se negra. Construção da identidade de gênero e de raça." *Revista Presença de Mulher* 7, no. 28 (1995).

Ribeiro, René. *Religião e relações raciais no Brasil*. Rio de Janeiro: Ministry of Education and Culture Documentation Services, 1956.

Ribeiro, Ronilda Iyakemi. *Alma africana no Brasil. Os iorubás*. São Paulo: Oduduwa, 1996.

Rio de Janeiro State Culture Secretariat, Museum of the Image and Sound (MIS), ed. *João Cândido, o almirante negro*. Rio de Janeiro: Gryphus; Rio de Janeiro: The Museum of the Image and Sound Foundation, 1999.

Roberio, Júlio. "Instrui e valoriza o negro numa compreensiva campanha cultural." *O Jornal* 31, no. 8870, March 30, 1949, Section 2, 2.

Rodrigues, João Jorge. *Olodum, estrada da paixão*. Salvador, Brazil: Olodum Cultural Group; Salvador, Brazil: Casa de Jorge Amado Foundation, 1996.

Rodrigues, Nelson. "Abdias. O negro autêntico." In *Teatro Experimental do Negro. Testemunhos*, edited by Abdias Nascimento, 157–58. Rio de Janeiro: GRD, 1966.

———. "Há preconceito de côr no teatro?" *Quilombo* 1, no. 1, December 9, 1948, 1, 6.

Rodrigues, Núbia, and Carlos Caroso. "Exu na tradição terapêutica religiosa Afro-Brasileira." In *Faces da tradição Afro-Brasileira*, edited by Carlos Caroso and Jéferson Bacelar, 239–55. Rio de Janeiro: Pallas; Salvador, Brazil: CEAO, UFBA, 1999.

Romão, Jeruse. "Há o tema do negro e há a vida do negro. Educação pública, popular e afro-brasileira." In *Educação popular afro-brasileira*, edited by Ivan Costa Lima, Jeruse Romão, and Sônia Maria Silveira. Black Thought in Education Series 5. Florianópolis: Núcleo de Estudos Negros, 1999.

Roque, Atila, and Sonia Corrêa. "A agenda do ciclo social no Brasil. Impasses e desafios." *Observatório da cidadania* 2 (1998): 1–8.

Rosemberg, Fúlvia, ed. "Diagnóstico sobre a Situação de Negros (Pretos e Pardos) no Estado de São Paulo." Special issue, *Cadernos de Pesquisa da Fundação Carlos Chagas* 2, no. 63: 412.

———. *Literatura infantil e ideologia*. São Paulo: Global, 1984.

Sabino, Fernando. "Semente de Ódio." *Diário Carioca* 22, no. 6458, July 16, 1949, 3.

Said, Edward W. *Orientalismo. O Oriente como invenção do Ocidente*. São Paulo: Companhia das Letras, 1990.

Sandoval, Alonso de. *El mundo de la esclavitud negra en América*. Bogotá: Empresa Nacional, 1956.

Sant'Anna, Wânia, and Marcelo Paixão. "Desenvolvimento humano e população afro-descendente no Brasil. Uma questão de raça." *Proposta* 26, no. 73 (June–August 1997): 20–37.

———. "Muito Além da Senzala. Ação afirmativa no Brasil." *Observatório da cidadania* 2 (1998): 111–20.

Santos, Hélio. *A busca de um baminho para o Brasil. A trilha do círculo vicioso*. São Paulo: SENAC, 2001.

Santos, Joel Rufino dos. *História/histórias*, 5ª a 8ª Séries. São Paulo: FTD, 1992.

———. "O negro como lugar." In *Introdução crítica à sociologia Brasileira*, 2nd ed., by Alberto Guerreiro Ramos, 19–29. Rio de Janeiro: UFRJ Press, 1995.

———. *A questão do negro na sala de aula*. São Paulo: Ática, 1990.

Santos, Juana Elbein dos. *Iya mi agba*. Documentary film. Salvador, Brazil: SECNEB, 1976.

———. *Os nagô e a morte*. Petrópolis, Brazil: Vozes, 1977.

São Paulo State Education Secretariat, Working Group for Afro-Brazilian Matters (GTAAB). *Escola. Espaço de luta contra a discriminação*. São Paulo: State Education Secretariat, 1988.

Sartre, Jean-Paul. "Orfeu negro." In *Reflexões sobre o racismo*, 3rd ed., by Jean-Paul Sartre. São Paulo: Difusão Européia do Livro, 1963. Originally published as "Orphée noir." Preface to *Anthologie de la nouvelle poésie nègre et malgache de langue française*, by Léopold Sédar Senghor. Paris: Presses Universitaires de France, 1948.

———. "Orfeu negro." Translated by Ironides Rodrigues. *Quilombo* 2, no. 5, January 1950, 6–7.

Schwarcz, Lília Moritz. *O espetáculo das raças. Cientistas, instituições e questão racial no Brasil, 1870–1930*. São Paulo: Companhia das Letras, 1993.

Schwarcz, Lília Moritz, and Letícia Vidor de Sousa Reis, eds. *Negras imagens*. São Paulo: Estação Ciência; São Paulo: EdUSP, 1996.

Senghor, Léopold Sédar. "Negritude and the Civilization of the Universal." In *African Presence in the Americas*, edited by Carlos Moore, Tanya R. Sanders, and Shawna Moore, 21–32. Trenton, NJ: Africa World Press; Trenton, NJ: The African Heritage Foundation, 1995.

Serra, Ordep. "A Etnopsiquiatria dos ritos afrobrasileiros." Lecture given at the First Symposium on Ethnopsychiatry, UFBA, Salvador, Brazil, 2000.

Sevenco, Nicolau. *A revolta da vacina. Mentes insanas em corpos rebeldes*. São Paulo: Brasiliense, 1984.

Silva, Ana Célia. *A discriminação do negro no livro didático*. Salvador, Brazil: CED; Salvador, Brazil: CEAO, UFBA, 1995.

Silva, Antonio Carlos Pacheco e. "Aula inaugural de clínica psiquiátrica da Faculdade de Medicina da Universidade de São Paulo." *Arquivos da Assistência Geral a Psicopatas do Estado de São Paulo* 1, no. 1 (1937).

Silva, Consuelo Dores. *Negro, qual é o seu nome?* Belo Horizonte, Brazil: Mazza, 1995.

Silva, Eduardo. *Dom Obá II D'África, o príncipe do povo. Vida, tempo e pensamento de um homem livre de cor*. São Paulo: Companhia das Letras, 1997.

Silva Jr., Hédio, ed. *Anti-racismo. Coletânea de leis brasileiras (federais, estaduais, municipais)*. São Paulo: Oliveira Mendes, 1998.

———. "Crônica da culpa anunciada." In *A cor do medo. Homicídios e relações raciais no Brasil*, edited by David Dijaci de Oliveira et al., 71–90. Brasília: University of Brasília Press; Brasília: University of Goiás Press; Brasília: National Human Rights Movement MNDH, 1998.

Silva, Hélio. *As constituições do Brasil*. Rio de Janeiro: Rede Globo, n.d.

Silva, Jorge da. *Violência e racismo no Rio de Janeiro*. Niterói, Brazil: Fluminense Federal University Press (EdUFF), 1998.

Silva, Maria José Lopes da. "Fundamentos teóricos da pedagogia multirracial." Pamphlet. Rio de Janeiro: Maria José Lopes da Silva, 1988.

Silva, Maria Lúcia da. "Espelho, espelho meu diga-me. Quem sou eu?" *Catharsis Revista de Saúde Mental* 3, no. 11 (January–February 1997): 22–26.

Silva, Marta de Oliveira da. "Algumas reflexões sobre população negra e saúde mental." Paper presented at the Round Table on Health and Black People, Brasília, Ministry of Health, April 16–17, 1996.

Silva, Nelson do Valle. "Extensão e natureza das desigualdades raciais no Brasil." In *Tirando a máscara. Ensaios sobre o racismo no Brasil*, edited by Antonio Sérgio Alfredo Guimarães and Lynn Huntley, 33–52. São Paulo: Paz e Terra; Atlanta: SEF, 2000.

———. "White-Nonwhite Income Differentials: Brazil, 1940–1960." PhD diss., Michigan University, 1978.

Silva, Nelson do Valle, and Carlos Hasenbalg. "Notas sobre desigualdade racial e política no Brasil." *Estudos Afro-Asiáticos* 25 (December 1993): 141–59. Rio de Janeiro: CEAA, IUPERJ, UCAM; Rio de Janeiro: Ford Foundation.

———. "O preço da cor. Diferenças raciais na distribuição da renda no Brasil." *Pesquisa e Planejamento* 10 (April 1990): 21–44.

———. *Relações raciais no Brasil contemporâneo*. Rio de Janeiro: Rio Fundo; Rio de Janeiro: Afro-Asian Studies Center (CEAA); Rio de Janeiro: University Research Center of the State of Rio de Janeiro (IUPERJ); Rio de Janeiro: UCAM; Rio de Janeiro: Ford Foundation, 1992.

Silva, Petronilha Beatriz Gonçalves. *O pensamento negro em educação no Brasil. Expressões do movimento negro*. São Carlos, Brazil: UFSCar, 1997.

Skidmore, Thomas E. *Black into White: Race and Nationality in Brazilian Thought*. London: Oxford University Press, 1974.

———. *Preto no Branco. Raça e nacionalidade no pensamento brasileiro*. Rio de Janeiro: Paz e Terra, 1976.

Sodré, Muniz. *Claros e escuros. Identidade, povo e mídia no Brasil*. Petrópolis, Brazil: Vozes, 1999.

Souza, Neusa dos Santos, ed. *Tornar-se negro*. Rio de Janeiro: Graal, 1983.

Soyinka, Wole. *Myth, Literature and the African World*. London: Cambridge University Press, 1976.

Stepan, Nancy L. *The Hour of Eugenics: Race, Gender and Nation in Latin America*. Ithaca, NY: Cornell University Press, 1991.

Sudarkasa, Niara. *The Strength of Our Mothers*. Trenton, NJ: Africa World Press, 1996.

Taguieff, Pierre-André. *Les fins de l'antiracisme*. Paris: Michalon, 1995.

———. *La force du préjugé. Essai sur le racisme et ses doubles*. Paris: La Découverte, 1988.

Tavares, Júlio César. "Teatro Experimental do Negro. Contexto, estrutura e ação." In "Teatro Experimental do Negro." Special issue, edited by Ricaro Gaspar Müller, *DIONYSOS. Revista da FundacenMinC* 28 [Journal of the Ministry of Culture Scenic Arts Foundation] (1988): 79–87.

Taylor, Charles et al. *Multiculturalism*. Edited and introduced by Amy Gutman. Princeton: Princeton University Press, 1994.

"Teatro no Meio da Rua." *Folha Carioca*, August 20, 1946.

Telles, Edward. *Race in Another America: The Significance of Skin Color in Brazil*. Princeton: Princeton University Press, 2004.

———. *Racismo à Brasileira. Uma nova perspectiva sociológica*. Translated by Ana Arruda Callado, Nadjeda Rodrigues Marques, and Camila Olsen. Rio de Janeiro: Relume Dumará; Rio de Janeiro: Ford Foundation, 2003.

Theodoro, Helena. *Mito e espiritualidade—Mulheres Negras*. Rio de Janeiro: Pallas, 1996.

Toscano, Moema. *Estereótipos sexuais na educação. Um manual para o educador*. Petrópolis, Brazil: Vozes, 2000.

———. *Introdução à sociologia educacional*. 7th ed. Petrópolis, Brazil: Vozes, 1991.

Trindade, Solano. "O Teatro Experimental do Negro e a cultura do povo contra o despejo do conjunto de cor." In "Problemas e Aspirações do Negro brasileiro," *Diário Trabalhista* 1, no. 188, August 25, 1946, 4.

Turner, Doris J. "The Black Protagonist in Abdias Nascimento's Sortilegio and Eugene ONeill's Emperor Jones." *Diaspora* 2, no. 2 (1993): 166–75.

———. "Symbols in Two Afro-Brazilian Literary Works: Jubiabá and Sortilégio." In *Teaching Latin American Studies: Presentations Made at the First National Seminar on the Teaching of Latin American Studies*, edited by Miriam Willifond and J. Doyle Casteel, 41–68. Gainesville, FL: Latin American Studies Association, 1977.

Turner, J. Michael. "Lês Brésiliens: The Impact of Former Brazilian Slaves upon Dahomey." PhD diss., Boston University, 1970.

United Nations Development Program (UNDP). *Report on Human Development*. New York: United Nations, 1999.

Uruguay, Alice Linhares. "Cristo negro." In "Coluna artes plásticas," *Jornal do Brasil* 65, no. 147, June 26, 1955, Section 5, 2.

Van Sertima, Ivan, ed. *African Presence in Early Europe*. New Brunswick: Transaction Books, 1985.

———. *Black Women in Antiquity*. New Brunswick: Transaction Books, 1984.

———. *They Came Before Columbus: African Presence in Ancient America*. New York: Random House, 1976.

Veiga dos Santos, Arlindo. "Congresso da mocidade negra Brasileira. Mensagem aos negros Brasileiros." *O Clarim da Alvorada* 6, no. 17, June 9, 1929, 1–3.

——. *Manifesto aos Negros Brasileiros*. São Paulo: Frente Negra Brasileira, July 2, 1931.

Verger, Pierre. "African religion and the valorization of the Brazilians of African descent." In *Faculty Seminar Series* 1, Part 1, edited by Olasope Oyelaran, 217–41. Ife, Nigeria: University of Ile-Ife, 1977.

——. *Flux et Reflux de la traite de nègres entre lê golfe de Benin et Bahia de Todos os Santos*. Paris: Mouton, 1968.

Vianna, Oliveira. *Populações meridionais do Brasil*. São Paulo: Revista do Brasil; São Paulo: Monteiro Lobato, 1920.

——. *Raça e assimilação*. 2nd ed. São Paulo: Companhia Editora Nacional, 1934.

Werneck, Jurema, Maísa Mendonça, and Evelyn C. White, eds. *O livro da saúde das Mulheres Negras. Nossos passos vêm de longe*. Rio de Janeiro: Pallas; Rio de Janeiro: Criola, 2000.

West, Cornel. *Race Matters*. New York: Random House; New York: Vintage Books, 1994.

Williams, Chancellor. *The Destruction of Black Civilization*. Chicago: Third World Press, 1974.

Winant, Howard. *Racial Conditions: Theories, Politics and Comparisons*. Minneapolis: University of Minnesota Press, 1994.

Winnicott, Donald Woods. *Deprivation and Delinquency*. London: Tavistock, 1984.

——. *Holding and Interpretation*. London: Hogarth and the Institute of Psychoanalysis, 1987.

——. *Playing and Reality*. London: Routledge, 1982.

——. *The Spontaneous Gesture*. London: Harvard Univeristy Press, 1987.

World Conference for Action Against Apartheid. *Report of the World Conference for Action Against Apartheid, Lagos, August 22–26, 1977*. 2 vols. United Nations A/CONF.91/9. New York: United Nations, 1977.

"'Xangô' de Vicente Lima." *Quilombo* 2, no. 6, February 1950, 2.

Zanetti, Lorenzo. *A prática educativa do Grupo Cultural Afro-Reggae*. Rio de Janeiro: Grupo Cultural Afro-Reggae, 2001.

Ziegler, Jean. *Os vivos e a morte*. Rio de Janeiro: Zahar, 1977.

INDEX

Note: brackets surrounding a page locator indicate the page on which an endnote number appears in the text; the term itself is actually referred to in the corresponding endnote. Thus, e.g., endnote number 74 appears on page 30, but the text of the endnote appears on page 249.